MENDOTA AND THE RESTIVE RIVERS OF THE INDIAN AND CIVIL WARS 1861–'65

D1640643

DANE PIZZUTI KROGMAN

**MENDOTA AND THE RESTIVE RIVERS OF THE
INDIAN AND CIVIL WARS 1861–'65**
Copyright © 2023 by Dane Pizzuti Krogman

ISBN:

Paperback: 978-1639456574

Hardcover: 978-1639456581

e-book: 978-1639456598

Writers' Branding
1-877-608-6550
www.writersbranding.com
media@writersbranding.com

Contents

Introduction v

Where the Waters Meet 1

Drums and Bugles 8

Bull Run 27

Going to War 39

The Mills Springs Campaign 44

On to Shiloh 57

Little Crow 90

The Uprising 97

Endless Marching and a Skirmish.......................104

Antietam Creek 111

Do No Harm...120

Armory Hospital 133

War at Home and in the West...............................138

A New Year 148

The Late Great Thirty-Eight 159

The Long Days Dying..184

The Young Cut Hair 207

The Punitive Expeditions......................................214

Veterans at Last 219

Corralled at Chickamauga....................................227

Over the Top at Mission Ridge 245

Veteranized..254

Belle Isle 267

Another Kind of Prison Camp 273

Halfway to Paradise 277

The Road to Hell...301

Come, See Paradise...308

Never Forever 327

Sultana...357

The Homecoming...387

Acknowledgments..414

About the Author..416

INTRODUCTION

Reexamine all that you have been told... Dismiss that which insults your soul.

—Walt Whitman

The past is never dead. It is not even past.

—William Faulkner

As I had grown up in the mid-twentieth century nearly equal distance between the two cities of Saint Paul and Minneapolis, Minnesota, near the village of Mendota, it was old Fort Snelling and the heights around the junction of the Minnesota and Mississippi Rivers that would become the place where history made its first mark on my journey and love of the place I called home for most of my life. In the 1950s and '60s, Mendota was a small village of little consequence— and today probably still is—but for a boy at that time, it was a fascinating place of exploration and play. I attended Henry Sibley High School, and the mascot of the school was an Indian warrior. Most of us kids could not understand the connection. Why would a White Civil War-era general have a school named in his honor and an Indian as a mascot? This, in itself, was worth explorating. Who was this man, and why were we honoring him as a namesake that could be referenced to the Indian Wars that started in 1862 and lasted up until the end of the nineteenth century?

Fort Snelling was undergoing a complete renovation when I was coming of age. Mendota itself had the Sibley House as the only historical place of importance. Further downriver was the levee at Saint Paul, and crossing the Mendota bridge would take one directly to Minneapolis with the first point of interest at Fort Snelling. It was all so much ancient history, but intuitively I found it important to seek out what had taken place at these locations.

When I was in elementary school, we celebrated the one hundredth anniversary of statehood in 1958. Artifacts were shown from the Dakota and Chippewa Natives that had once been the sole occupants of this land. Military items from the Civil and Indian Wars were displayed, and we were told stories of the great deeds White men had done to settle the land and "civilize" the Indians. Most of these stories carried a sense of falsehood. My curiosity grew over the years; and I could not help but want to find some truth and meaning as to why, how, and what transpired. It was no longer enough to seek the riverbanks and location of the old concentration camp for arrowheads. As I grew into my teens and adult years, I spent more and more time asking questions and scouring the library and historical society for information on these people who made up the history of my home.

Yes, all the great men had been written about, but who were the common folks who made the sacrifices that were led by these so-called great leaders? They could have been me at another time or any of my friends and relatives. They could have been the Native Americans that I came to know while working odd jobs or the Native friends I made while taking Native American history courses in college.

Throughout my childhood and even my adult years, Mendota and its one-sided history remained buried in the back of my mind. Events that took place there lacked human details and human dimensions. It was difficult to find the line between myth and history. While still in grade school, I searched the school library and local public libraries to see what I could learn about the great Sioux Uprising, the concentration camps, and the men who went off to fight in the war of "Southern arrogance." Nothing much ever turned up that rang true.

If the events that took place at the fort were truly as disturbing as I imagined, then why hadn't this disgraceful part of the state's history been fully revealed from all sides involved? It would take a few more decades for me to begin the research that would convince me to make this attempt at telling the story from the viewpoint of historical fact and family fiction combined.

I moved to South Carolina in the early '90s to further my exploration of the great American Civil War. It was there at an antique store that I came across a first edition printing of the book *Minnesota in the Civil and Indian Wars, 1861–1865* published and printed in 1890. I purchased it for ten dollars. Soon after, I found in a flea market in Savannah, Georgia, a copy of the book *A Civil War Drummer Boy: The Diary of William Bircher, 1861–65*. I purchased it for seven dollars. William had been a drummer with the Second Minnesota Volunteer Regiment.

I spent the better part of twenty years exploring Civil War history traveling through South Carolina, Georgia, Virginia, Pennsylvania, Maryland, and other states. The battlefields, prison camps, forts, museums, and park rangers became paramount in my accumulation of detailed knowledge.

I finally settled in North Carolina and found myself interested in the infamous Cherokee Indian Trail of Tears. It was in 1998 when I finally decided someone had to tell the tale of Minnesota's own Trail of Tears.

I've had always wanted to tell this story from the perspective of those who lived it; so the story evolved into a fictional narrative of one family who settled in the river village of Mendota, Minnesota, and lived through the period in the state's history that, to this *day*, has not been surpassed.

The Simmons family is entirely fictitious. They never existed but could have. Their experiences are based partially on my imagination and partially on the diary of William Bircher as well as many people I have met over the years who have passed on their own stories of their families' experiences during that trying time. The bulk of this book, though, comes from the historical documentation of *Minnesota in the Civil and Indian Wars* book, which was published in 1890 and encompasses all of the historical recollections and documentation of the regiments and main players in this human drama.

> *We were told that they wished merely to pass through our country…to seek for gold in the far west… Yet before the ashes of the council are cold, the Great Father is building his forts among us… His presence here is…an insult to the spirits of our ancestors. Are we then to give up their sacred graves to be allowed for corn?*

> —Red Cloud

WHERE THE WATERS MEET

Supporting Native American ties to Minnesota, archaeologists have documented human activity to at least nine thousand to twelve thousand years ago. Historically the Minnesota region was strategically important to Native American peoples for thousands of years as they used the waterways for transportation and food and to develop an extensive trade relationship with other Native peoples; trade items from this and other regions have been found along the entire Mississippi River. By the 1600s, there were two main groups of people living in present-day Minnesota— the Dakota and the Ojibwe.

With the spring thaw, the rivers rose and, with their waters, would flow the highways of war.

At the junction of the Minnesota and Mississippi Rivers, high upon the river bluffs sat old Fort Snelling. The location for this Western fort originally named Fort Saint Anthony was established in 1819 by the army engineer and explorer Zebulon Pike. In 1805, Lieutenant Zebulon Pike acquired Pike's purchase from the Sioux Nation for the United States, comprising one hundred thousand acres of land in the area. A significant European-American settlement began in the 1810s. Following the war of 1812, the United States Department of War built a chain of forts and installed Indian agents at them between Lake Michigan and the Missouri River. These forts primarily protected the

1

Northwestern territories from Canadian and British encroachment. The army founded Fort Saint Anthony (later Fort Snelling) in 1819.

Across the rivers from the fort was the small village of Mendota. In 1858, Minnesota became the thirty-second state admitted to the Union; and in 1861, it was the youngest state to participate in the Civil War. Mendota was one of the first permanent settlements in the new state. In 1861, it had a population of only a few families and less than fifty people. One of those people was Henry Hastings Sibley. He was the first territorial governor of Minnesota. Living in Mendota, he had personal and business connections with Fort Snelling. After moving from Mackinac, Michigan, where he was a partner in the American Fur Trading Company, he ran the sutler's store (1836–1839) at Fort Snelling and contracted for mail delivery (1837–1839). He also maintained close ties with the Protestant missionaries who arrived in 1835.

An ardent outdoorsman and hunter, Sibley established ties with the Dakota who lived nearby. He had a relationship with a young Dakota woman, who bore him a daughter, Helen, in August 1841. Sibley acknowledged the child and provided for her support and education. In 1843, however, he married Sarah Jane Steele. She was the sister of Franklin Steele, the new Fort Snelling sutler. On the high bluff across the river from Fort Snelling, he built a beautiful Victorian-style stone house. The Sibley House, considered the oldest private residence in Minnesota, was built between 1835 and 1836 by a team of over one hundred White and Dakota laborers, directed by John Mueller. It was made of limestone blocks cut from a nearby quarry.

Down the hill from his house was the proper village of Mendota. The Simmons family built a log house just a bit uphill from the base of the river. Their humble prairie-style cottage made of split wood and sod was hardly big enough to hold Dan Simmons; his wife, Louise; daughter, Sara; and two boys, William and John. Dan was a fur trapper, tinsmith, and lumberman. He had been a laborer for most of his life, and surviving the harsh climate of the North made him look much older than his thirty-five years.

On April 12–13, 1861, the bombardment of Fort Sumter near Charleston, South Carolina, by the Confederate States Army and the return of gunfire and subsequent surrender by the United States Army started the American Civil War. The newly elected president Lincoln did not have the power to declare war on the Southern states, but he did have the power to declare a state of insurrection and therefore decided to call up troops to put down the rebellion. To the general population, this was as good as declaring war, and war fever ran all through the land. Even in the new state of Minnesota, most men were anxious to join up for the "cause." This included Dan Simmons and his two sons.

Having been the governor of Minnesota, Henry Sibley was prepared to go to war as well and was waiting for orders from the new state governor, Alexander Ramsey, when the war broke out. Fort Snelling would now become the staging area for Minnesota men to enlist and train for departure east and south to fight in the rebellion. The Simmons family of Mendota agreed that it was their patriotic duty to fight for the preservation of the Union. Dan Simmons, the father of this prairie family of five, made the impulsive decision to cross the river to Fort Snelling and enlist in the First Minnesota Volunteer Infantry Regiment. His two sons, John and William, decided they were going to join up with him but, both being underage, were forced to stay home. Dan, against his wife's pleading, signed on to First Minnesota as a teamster to drive a supply wagon. Being a family man over the age of thirty, he accepted the position as he thought it would keep him, for the most part, out of direct combat, which was a comfort to his wife.

As the sun set over Fort Snelling and the village of Mendota on a crisp April evening in 1861, the few residents of the village mingled on the single dirt street that cut through it. There was a new excitement in the air as folks chattered on about the coming war. The Simmons brothers, William and John, chased each other with broken tree limbs, which to them represented rifles. They pretended they were in combat. Their mother, Louise, stepped out of the door of the family cabin and yelled at the boys.

"John! William! Stop that foolishness and get in here right now!

Your father needs to talk to you two, now!"

The boys ignored their mother and continued playing.

Dan then stepped up next to his wife and called out, "She said, *now!*"

The boys dropped their fake weapons and rushed to the door. Out of breath and panting, they ran into the house and sat at the rough-cut wood dinner table. Their younger sister, Sara, thin with deep-black eyes and a matching head of long black hair, teased them. She was small for a twelve-year-old but not at all shy about expressing her views.

"Pa's going to get the lickin' stick and give it to you."

William was a short, stout boy of just fifteen. He responded, "No, he won't."

John was the tallest member of the family at five feet nine, which, in 1861, was well above average for a sixteen-year-old male. He supported his brother with "We got in just in time."

Sara pestered them again, "Will too."

The bantering went on between the siblings.

"Will not."

"Will too."

"No, he won't. We got in just in time."

"Finished all our chores too."

Sara brought it to an end with

"He's plenty mad." John then replied, "About what?"

"He and Ma been going at it again about the war."

Dan and Louise took seats at the table.

Dan responded to his children, "Nobody is gettin' a lickin', but I do have something important to say."

Before he could start, John interrupted him, "Well, if you signed up, we're goin' too!"

Dan showed an angry face to his sons, but Louise reached out to stop him from lashing out. Louise was the quintessential hardened prairie wife of the era and region but always had a kind word for everyone. She was just twenty-nine years old when the war broke out. She now

spoke calmly to her family, "He ain't signed up yet, and he ain't goin'
to, and that's the end of that!"

John snapped back, "Ah…but, Ma! He's got to."

William agreed, "Yeah, all the men in the state have signed on.
We ain't no cowards in this family. He must do his part. We can't let
no stinking hillbilly rebels push us around."

Dan looked at his wife. "The boys are right, Louise. I'm going
whether you like it or not, and that's final."

John settled back and responded to his father's remark, "You
better hurry up, Pa. I heard today that the First Regiment of Minnesota
Volunteers was already full up."

Dan continued, "That's just the first one thousand regulars. They
still need teamsters, and if they'll take me like that, I figure your ma here
won't have to worry so much as I won't be too close to the shootin' war."

With a sigh, Louise replied, "At least promise me that."

William then shouted out, "I'm going too. I know how to drive
a team!"

Dan laid down the law, "No, you're not! You are both staying here!
You're both too young."

William was upset now. "But why? If we must wait until we are
eighteen, the war will have passed us by."

Louise wrung her hands in frustration. "Yes, with any luck, it will
pass us all by very soon."

Dan tried again, "You'll both stay here and protect your mother
and sister."

William wasn't having it. "But who'll take care of you?"

Dan gave him a stern look. "I can take care of myself."

John joined in, "No, sir! We are going with you. Ma! He needs
us to take care of him."

William interrupted, "Ma! What if he gets sick or wounded?
He's so old."

Dan barked back, "They have regimental hospitals and surgeons
for that."

John was now fuming. "If they are anything like what we've seen over at Fort Snelling, then that's all the more reason you'll need us."

Louise hung her head and began to weep.

Sara moved in to comfort her. She looked at her brothers with anger. "Look what you two have done now! Pa's right. You must stay with us. I can't take care of Ma alone nor handle the livestock and do all the other chores by myself."

Dan settled back to enjoy his dinner. "All right, that settles it. I'm off tomorrow morning. John, you're the oldest, so you'll take charge here. I expect you to protect the family while I'm gone. William, you'll see to it that Sara gets her schooling, and I want both of you to—"

"What?"

Dan eyed his sons. "Keep a special lookout for Injun trouble," John spoke again.

"Why? They never bother anybody."

Dan snapped back, "Chief Little Crow is just across the river with his Santee Sioux."

William protested, "Yeah? So what? He's been tamed and signed a peace treaty, and he dresses White and acts White as anybody. I even heard his people don't listen to him anymore. They think he's weak."

Dan shook a finger at his son. "Once a savage, always a savage."

John joined in agreement with his brother, "The Dakota have sworn to uphold the peace, and their word has always been good."

Dan tried to reason with his boys again, "Ever since Lincoln called up troops, we have been hearing that drum from their camp every night."

Sara was now most curious. "What does it mean?"

Dan looked at her. "It means they know us Whites are going to war against each other, and that opens the door for them to revolt."

William continued the debate, "Ha! Do you think Little Crow is that stupid to attack us? They live right under the walls of the fort!"

John now took sides with his father, "Sure, but soon that fort will be empty."

William made his case, "Won't they just fill it back up with US regulars like in the past?"

Dan continued, "If this war lasts more than a few months, no. All the regular army troops are already on their way to Washington, and old Colonel Sibley here with a few farmer militiamen will be hardly a match against a murderous hoard of redskins."

John replied, "And I bet Little Crow will find a way to get the Chippewa aligned with him to join in against the Whites."

William countered with "I don't think so. They're natural enemies."

Dan tried to end the discussion, "That's smart thinking. So, you see, there just might be a good reason for you to fight here instead of in some Southern swamp."

Sara set bowls around the table. "You guys are all so stupid. War, war, war…"

William winked at her. "We fight to save the honor of our womenfolk."

Dan ended the discussion, "Okay! Now that that's settled, Louise, how about we get some of that stew in our bellies?"

Louise and Sara then came forth with the evening meal.

DRUMS AND BUGLES

Aroused and angry,
I thought to beat the alarm,
and urge relentless war;
But soon my fingers failed me, my face
drooped, and I resigned myself,
To sit by the wounded and soothe
them, or silently watch the dead.

—Walt Whitman, "Drum Taps"

Dan was standing in his yard chopping logs as Louise exited the cabin and walked up to her husband. A fresh spring breeze rustled through the trees as Dan chopped and stacked the wood. Louise took in a deep breath of the piney smell of the river village and paused a moment to take in a new life sprouting up around the landscape.

Dan stopped for a moment and looked lovingly at his wife. "Beautiful, isn't it?" Dan leaned his axe up against his log stack and took Louise's hand.

"Yes, I love this time of year." She took another long, deep breath. "So?"

Dan took up his axe again. "So what?"

"Did they take you?" she asked.

He split a log in two. "Sure enough, they did."

She put a hand out to stop him. "Did you get that teamster job?"

8

Dan set another log on the tree stump. "Yep. I'm one of the last to get in."

Louise responded, "I guess that's a good thing then."

Dan swung the axe. The log split in one single motion.

"If it keeps you from worrying."

"It does a little but not much," she replied.

Dan set another log. "It's only a three-month enlistment. Congress thinks this whole thing will blow over before Christmas." He split the log as Louise spoke.

"When was Congress ever right on anything?"

Dan answered, "Never."

Louise sighed. "My point exactly."

Dan stopped for the moment. "Listen. I'll be home in three months, one way or another. If it lasts longer, which it won't, we have all been promised a thirty-day furlough after our three months are up."

"Stop this and come into the house."

Dan paused for a moment but set another log anyway. "Not until I've got you three months of wood cut up."

Louise was beginning to get emotional. "Leave it for the boys. We've got plenty from the looks of that pile."

Dan stopped long enough to lean his axe once again. "Right. If I did that, I can maybe promise you three hours' worth of wood or, at best, three weeks. No, I'll finish up and then come in."

Louise returned to the cabin.

It was late into the night. Sara snuggled up next to her mother as she tried to prepare dinner. John and William lay next to each other in a rough straw mattress bed on another side of the cabin, reading from their school primer. Smoke and warmth from the hearth filled the cabin with a comforting feeling. From outside, the rhythm of the continual wood splitting echoed through the house.

Sara winced at every hack. "Is he ever going to finish?"

Louise sat next to her and put some vegetables and meat in a boiling pot of water that hung above the fire. "He will when he reaches his goal."

Sara shuddered as the axe hit wood again. "When? That noise is driving me crazy!"

John and William responded in unison, "After three months' worth."

Outside Dan set one final log on top of the chopping stump, lifted his axe, and sliced the log into two pieces.

He stacked the last two pieces of wood onto the pile, then took the axe and gave it one heavy blow into the stump, sinking the blade deep into the stump. Pleased with himself, he headed into the cabin.

On May 10, 1861, the First Regiment of Minnesota Volunteers had its status changed from a three-month unit to a full three years regiment. On this same night, as the Simmons family was trying to sleep, the cadence of the Native drumming from the lower riverbanks of Fort Snelling interrupted any peace the family was hoping for.

Sara crawled in between her mother and father to seek some comfort. "Gosh, how many more nights of this? That drumming and wailing are driving me insane."

Dan got up out of bed and rousted out his sons. They left the cabin.

Standing on the ridge of his land that overlooked the fort, he turned to John. "This is what I was talking about."

"Do you think they'll attack us?" asked William.

Dan continued, "Well, all I know is several companies of the First are being sent upstate to Fort Ripley, Ridgely, and Fort Abercrombie as a precaution."

"Are you in one of those companies?" asked John.

Dan answered, "No, I'm staying at the fort until we get orders to go east."

"When do you think that will be?" asked John.

Dan shrugged. "Take a good look. Those Injuns are pretty angry. Now let's head back in and try to get some rest."

Walking back to the cabin, William paused to catch the spring breeze against his face. "Ah, I love this time of year."

Back in the cabin, Louise and Sara had moved to the comfort of the hearth.

High atop the bluff of the village of Mendota, Henry Hastings Sibley, the territorial governor of Minnesota, puffed on a cigar as he looked out of one of the well-crafted windows of his elegant stone house that sat high on the bluff across the river from the fort and the Lower Sioux Indian village. He looked out across the river to take in the drumming, chanting, and dancing of the powwow. He then turned to his wife, Jane, as she entered the room to join him.

"Well, my dear. Nothing more to see here. I'm going to bed."

Jane placed a hand on his shoulder. "As you should. You have a big day tomorrow. What time do the companies of the First leave for the outlying forts?"

"At 7:00 a.m."

"I'm glad you're not going." She took his hand and pulled him close. "Those savages have been making a ruckus the past couple of months."

"Yes, they have," he replied as he led her out of the sitting room and up to a staircase to their bedroom.

At the river's edge, Chief Little Crow was holding council with his son, Wowinapa, in a tepee. Little Crow was a weathered man of about fifty. His son was nearing thirty. The bonfire from outside gave an eerie hue to the interior of the tepee. This was a rare opportunity that they found themselves alone. As the drumming vibrated, the tepee and the exterior firelight flickered against its walls.

Little Crow made a statement to his son, "There has been much movement in the fort these days. What have you heard?"

Wowinapa answered, "The two great tribes of Whites are preparing for war."

"What are these tribes called?"

"They have many names, but I think they will be known as the Blues and the Grays," replied Wowinapa.

"But all of the men in the fort seem to be wearing red and black," said Little Crow.

"I've heard they are waiting on their government supplies," Wowinapa responded.

Little Crow thought for a moment and then asked, "Do you think there is some truth to the fact that we, too, are not getting our promised annuities?"

Wowinapa shrugged it off and turned to look out of the tepee. "Now would be our time to react, and I think everyone is anxious to take back what is ours. You never should have signed that last treaty. Many still hate you for it."

"Do you hate me for it?"

"We should prepare for war too, is all I am saying."

The drumming, dancing, and Native singing continued into the night.

Spring had passed, and summer had come on, bringing a stifling heat and humidity that covered the two rivers at the Fort Snelling junction. The mosquitoes were so thick along the rivers and communities that one could hardly breathe without inhaling a mouthful of the annoying pests. It was June 21, 1861, and the First Minnesota Regiment was finally reunited at Fort Snelling. The companies that had been sent to the outlying forts had not seen any action other than being overcome with boredom. They had not encountered any trouble from the Natives, and their service was better needed in the war down south. They were now under orders to proceed to Washington, DC. They would first travel by steamboat to Lacrosse, Wisconsin, where they would be put on a train, and then on to DC by rail. The regiment was preparing to move out on the morning of the twenty-second. Henry Sibley would make a personal visit to the fort landing to see the men off.

The morning of the twenty-second arrived hot and steamy. With the darkness of night still upon them, Sibley and his wife, Jane, finished a breakfast of ham, eggs, coffee, and fried potatoes. As they sat in their modern kitchen dining area, the soldiers on the other side of the river were choking down raw carrots, raw potatoes, and chunks of moldy hardtack soaked in coffee.

Jane cleared the table. "What time do the steamers leave?" "At 6:00 a.m., in one hour."

"You'd better hurry then. I hope you have a good speech prepared."

Sibley told her he did, then gathered his things and headed for the door. He gave Jane a quick kiss before leaving.

"How many men from Mendota are in the regiment?" she asked.

Sibley paused to think a moment. "Only Dan Simmons, I believe."

"Will you say something special to him?" she replied.

"No, he's no more special than the others," said Sibley. Henry then headed out the door. "I'll be back soon, and don't worry about Dan Simmons and his family. We'll take care of them."

The soldiers of the First Regiment cleaned their mess plates and squared up their gear. The entire regiment was called into formation and stood by ready at attention, awaiting orders to move out. They were dressed in an odd, unconventional uniform made up of black wool trousers, red flannel overshirts, and black slouch hats. Their accouterments and weapons appeared to be outdated Mexican-American War issue. They were given the order to march by companies in columns of four abreast as they filed out of the main gate of the fort and down the road that led to the riverboats waiting at the embarkation point. Passing the Dakota Indian settlement, they lined up and waited to board the *Northern Belle* and *War Eagle*, which both were lying at the fort's wharf and had steam up and were ready to embark the boys.

Chaplain E. D. Neill cut his service short as the men were most anxious to leave. He finished with a quick prayer as Sibley approached the dock just in time to see the soldiers begin to file on board. Sibley shook the hands of the men as they passed him one by one and filed onto the river steamers. Dan Simmons then stepped up in place and steadied himself under the weight of his equipment and backpack. His family was at his side. Sara tried to comfort her mother as she fought to hold back her tears. The attention of William and John was more directed to the men boarding.

Sibley put out his hand. "Dan, take care of yourself. Jane and I will be looking in on your family from time to time. You need not worry about anything."

Dan shook Sibley's hand and began to board. Louise stopped him and took his hand. She pressed something into his grasp. Dan looked down at the small token. It was a tintype photo of his wife and children.

Louise cried as she choked out a few final words. "Write to us often and pray this damned rebellion is over with soon."

Sara butted in, "Yeah, like next week!"

Dan gave his wife and daughter a quick hug and kissed them, then put out his hand to the boys. "I don't want to hear about any mischief from you two. You're men now, and you have to keep this family together and protect your mother and sister."

John spoke for the two of them as he nudged his younger brother, "You'll have no trouble from us."

William couldn't hold his tongue. "But, Pa! They just announced that a second regiment will be filling ranks starting today. Please! Can we follow you in?"

Dan lashed out as Louise and Sara broke down, "Enough of that talk! You're upsetting your mother. *No more*! You're too young and—"

William cut him off, "And with your permission, they'll take us. We already asked, and the colonel said it was okay if you or Ma signed."

Dan threw Sibley a harsh look. "Is this your doing?"

Sibley sheepishly responded, "Those are the rules. Musicians and drummers are needed, but I did not encourage your boys, Dan."

John stood up for Sibley, "We found out on our own."

Dan then patted both his sons on the shoulder and turned to board the steamer. Louise and Sara broke down and wept. Dan disappeared into the crowd of soldiers on the deck. He turned and gave a weak emotion-filled wave to his family. The steamers cast off their lines, and so the First Regiment of Minnesota Volunteers was headed off to war.

A few nights later, the Simmons family sans Dan nestled around the cabin fire. Sara poked at the coals.

John paged through the family Bible and stopped to look at an illustration of glorious war. He showed it to William. "Boy, o', boy, now that's for us! Remember what Reverend Neill said to the First Regiment at their send-off?"

John took the Bible out of the hands of his brother and perused the picture again. "Yeah, I sure do. Any man who fails to do his duty and fight for his God and country will not receive a place in heaven. Ma, we must go. We men, ain't we? Pa said we were men now."

Louise, spinning yarn with Sara's help, responded somewhat angrily, "So he did, but I'm not signing you boys over to your death."

William persisted, "Please, Ma! You heard the reverend too. It's for God and country!"

"And a sure place in heaven," added John.

Sara joined in on the debate, "It's going to take more than that for you two to get into heaven."

Louise wanted to end this. "I agree with Sara. No! No war for you two, and that's my final word!"

John wouldn't let it go. "They said they'd teach me to play the bugle and William will learn to drum. Those are important jobs and safe too. We'll be musicians."

"That's right," added William. "Even if there is a fight, the musicians become litter bearers. We won't be in the actual fighting. It will be just like going camping."

Louise shook her head and tended to her yarn.

John forced the issue again. "Please, Ma! Just think about it. Please? This could be the best and only good thing that ever happens in our lives."

"I doubt that," said Louise.

William joined in to support his brother, "Besides, Colonel Sibley may take over the Second Minnesota Regiment, and so we'll be under his command and care. Otherwise, we can just lie about our age, and then they'll give us a gun and put us in the line. Do you prefer that?"

Sara fanned the ashes in the fireplace. "Musicians? That's a joke. You both only know two songs, and you can barely sing those. Ha!"

John, now about to give up, continued, "Aw, Ma! We're going to go anyway. You can't stop us. I'm going to follow Dad. You know he needs us."

Louise gave in with a long sigh. "I'll talk to Mr. Sibley in the morning and get his opinion. But no promises! This restlessness with the Indians may just be a calm before the storm, and then what are Sara and I to do?"

A day or two passed before Louise had her meeting with Sibley. The smell of fresh brewing coffee filtered through the Sibley house as Louise took a seat across the desk from Sibley. Jane brought in cups, saucers, coffee pot, and pastries, setting them up on the desk in Henry's office. Sibley poured coffee for the two and offered up sugar and cream to Louise.

She refused the cream and sugar with a polite "No, thank you. You know why I'm here. I just want some peace from my boys and this enlistment stuff."

Sibley settled back into his chair. "I don't know what your boys have told you, but honestly I don't know what the governor has in store for me. Though, in my opinion, boys are indeed needed for the regiments, their principal job is to communicate messages on the field. When under fire, drums and bugles are the only things that the troops can hear."

Louise was listening intently, then responded, "Can you promise me they won't be sent into battle?"

"No, I can't promise, but I truly doubt the Second Regiment will even be called into action."

"Then what is the plan for them?"

Sibley lifted his coffee cup and turned to glance out his window toward the fort. "I assume they will be left at Fort Snelling as a home guard. So imagine this. Your boys come home every night after drill and practice. They spend their days at the fort. It's a winning solution. The boys get to serve their country, and you get to keep them close to your bosom. And, don't forget, twenty-six dollars a month pay combined for the two. That will go a long way."

"Why do I feel like I'm being conned?" She took a long thoughtful pause, then continued, "If I do sign away my boys today, will you personally take them over the river and get them settled into the ranks?"

Sibley smiled and reached for his quill and ink bottle. "Not only that, but I'll also bring them home to you that very evening for supper."

Louise let out a long, forlorn sigh but not one of relief. "Very well then. I've got the muster papers right here. I don't know how those boys got them, but they did."

Louise pulled the papers from her bag, and Sibley dipped a quill into the inkpot and handed it to her.

He showed her where to sign. "Right here and here."

Louise signed the papers and prepared to leave. "I'm not at all happy about this."

"Trust me, they'll be fine. But keep in mind they still have to pass a physical exam."

Louise shook off her anxiety. "That won't be a problem. They're good, strong, healthy boys." Louise handed the pen and muster papers over to Sibley.

Sibley got up to show Louise to the door. "Have them ready for me at 6:00 a.m. tomorrow. I'll take them over, and I assure you no harm will come to them." Sibley walked Louise to the door and politely showed her out. He took her arm and led the way. "I'll show you out."

As Louise exited, she turned to thank him. "Thank you so much for setting my mind at ease." She then left and walked a lonely path back down the hill to her cabin.

The last night for the boys in their family cabin was one of anxiety for all. As Sara prepared to serve dinner, the boys excitedly stuffed a couple of homemade canvas duffel bags with their belongings. Louise sat near the fire, wringing her hands in worry. The sound of the Native drums echoed through the cabin.

Sara was upset and began to verbally assault her brothers, "You're both so stupid!"

Louise snapped at her, "Don't call your brothers stupid."

"But it's just dumb boy stuff. You and I shouldn't be left alone, even if it is just during the daytime," Sara snapped back at her mother. Louise set a calming voice. "Don't be scared, and don't worry.

Colonel Sibley promised me they would remain safe."

Sara watched her brothers collect their belongings. "I'm not scared and certainly not worried. It's those Injuns on the other side of the river that concern me. Remember that time those two Chippewa boys just walked right in and helped themselves to all the sugar in the pantry?"

"I sure do," replied her mother.

As William and John fought over who would take the family Bible, Sara summed it up, "But Pa was nearby, so nothing happened."

Louise turned her attention to her sons as they squabbled over the book.

John shouted at William, "I'm the oldest! It's mine to care for!"

William lashed back, "I take better care of things. You'll just lose it."

Louise broke them up, "Stop it, both of you! The book stays here where it belongs! Don't worry, Sara. The boys will be back every night. There is nothing to fear."

"Except the day," replied Sara.

John threw a look of discontent at his sister. "Quit being such a baby. Pa taught you how to use his old shotgun, didn't he?"

Sara moved to a separate corner. "Sure, but unlike you, I'm in no hurry to try it on anyone. You know, you two can still get out of this. They ain't taken you yet."

William stepped up to her. "We ain't no cowards."

Louise took sides with Sara, "Nobody will think the less of you for staying home and protecting your loved ones."

John stopped the discussion, "Nope, we're going."

Louise returned to her chair, defeated. "Then finish up and get to bed. The colonel will be here before dawn."

The boys cinched up their duffel bags and set them next to the door.

Henry Sibley knew everyone in Mendota, and the entire community looked up to him as one who was true to his word and one to be trusted. On the morning that he was to escort the Simmons boys across the river for their induction into the Second Minnesota Regiment, he left home long before sunrise and had a little trouble finding his way in the dark to the Simmons cabin. It was a short walk downhill from his house, yet there was no smooth path. He had to push his way through the underbrush and a tangle of roots from the large oak, elm, and pine trees that were common in the region.

As he made his way onto the Simmons property, he paused for a moment to observe the stack of wood that Dan had prepared for the coming months. Birds and insects were already awake and making plenty of noise. Chickens cackled, pecked, and scratched at the dry earth along the walk to the cabin entrance. As he stepped up to the door of the cabin, he lingered to inhale the smell of freshly fried bacon. He then reached for his pistol secured in his army-issue holster, took the weapon out, and, with the butt of the pistol, knocked on the door. Inside the cabin, Sara made a rush for the door with her mother close behind. They opened the door to Sibley's greeting.

Before Sibley could speak, Sara yelled out, "He's here!" Sibley politely removed his hat and handed it to Louise. She turned to her boys. "Come on, boys."

Sibley holstered his gun and replied, "Are my troops ready?"

John and William ran to the door with their duffle bags slung over their shoulders. "We sure are!" they said in unison.

Sara and Louise gave the boys a quick hug and sent them all off into the darkness.

Sibley led the way. "Come along, boys. We must catch the ferry across the river before light."

Now they stumbled along a path that led them directly down a steep ravine toward the river's edge. As they approached the river, they heard the rush and gurgle of the water before they broke into a hollow filled with the early-morning fog.

The ferry that was docked at the river's edge was barely visible. They were greeted by a weathered old Native. His name was Bob Thunder. Bob was asleep leaning up against the railing of the ferry as the three passengers jumped on board and startled him to wake.

He greeted them with "That will be three cents for the three of you."

William couldn't believe the outrageous price. "But we are just crossing over to the fort."

Bob gave him an evil stare. "Don't matter. Saint Paul levee or the fort, still one cent per person unless, of course, you're a baby or a woman. You ain't babies, are ya?"

John was anxious to set him straight. "We going to join up for the cause."

"So you're a couple of warriors then?" countered Bob. "We will be soon," added William.

Sibley put three pennies into Bob's hand.

As the boat cast off, John inquired, "Tell me, Mr. Thunder. I heard you were once a great Chippewa brave. Is that right? You ever kill any of those Sioux?"

Old man Thunder began to glide the ferry across the river. "Sure, we had a couple of scrapes in my time, but those days are long gone. We don't fight each other anymore."

"Why is that?" asked William.

Thunder smiled back at him. "Once you get done fighting your people, you'll figure it out. Besides, we got a bigger enemy now."

John asked, "Who's that?"

Thunder didn't answer. He just concentrated on getting the ferry lined up for docking at the fort pier.

As Sibley and the boys were about to step off the ferry after Thunder docked and secured a line, he finally spoke, "You say you are going to fight for the cause? What cause is it this time?"

"Freedom," said William.

"Oh, they use that word a lot. Don't believe it," replied Thunder as they all stepped off onto the pier.

Sibley paused to shake Bob's hand. "Thanks for the ride, old Thunder."

Bob responded, "Take care of those babies, old man."

John turned around anxiously. "We'll be catching a ride back with you around sunset."

Bob shook his head. "A lot of you boys have been saying that lately, but somehow you all just disappear." Bob threw Sibley a wink and a nod.

Sibley and the two boys walked past a fully loaded ox cart and its owner as it waited to load onto the ferry for the return trip across the river to Mendota. They began the long hike up the road that led to the fort's main gate. Sibley led them through the gate. The guards saluted Sibley and let them pass without any interference. The boys followed Sibley across the damp parade ground to the office of the mustering captain. The three entered the office and stood before the desk of Captain Osman. Sibley presented the muster papers to Osman.

The captain scanned over the papers, then spoke, "Okay, a drummer and a bugler. Which one is which?"

"Bugle for me," said John. "Drum," said William.

Osman set the papers aside for the moment. "I assume you both already know how to play those instruments?"

The boys replied in unison, "Nope."

Osman shook his head. This was all too common for him. "Okay then, after your physical, you'll report to the sergeant of musicians for your first lessons. But right now, go to the infirmary and see the surgeon. Do you know where that is?"

Sibley spoke up, "I'll take them, Captain."

Osman looked to Sibley and saw that the colonel had taken responsibility for the boys. "Okay, you can leave, and if the surgeon accepts you for service, come back here and sign your muster sheet for enlistment into Company A, Second Minnesota Volunteers."

Both John and William gave an excited reply, "Yes, sir! Thank you, sir!"

The boys rushed out of the office ahead of Sibley, who followed behind until he caught up to them and pointed them in the direction of the fort infirmary. As the boys stepped into the infirmary, a surgical assistant told them to strip down to their underwear. The boys did and then hung their clothes onto a wooden peg.

The fort surgeon gestured for them to stand before him. "Stand on one foot. Now the other."

They did as they were told and moved on to the next part of the exam.

"Follow my finger with your eyes only." They passed this test as well.

"Now open your mouths and show me your teeth and bite down hard." The surgeon inspected the inside of their mouths. "Good, good. Okay, you both passed. Now go back and sign your muster sheets. You do know how to write your names?"

The boys nodded, dressed, then left the infirmary and returned to Captain Osman's office.

Captain Osman looked over his recruits. "Very well. Now go find yourselves the quartermaster and get your uniforms and accouterments. Do you think you can do that on your own?"

The boys nodded and walked out. Sibley walked out as well, and then after he took the boys back to the quartermaster and saw to it that they were secure and safe, he then departed and headed out of the fort without as much as a goodbye.

The late June morning found the sun breaking over the eastern wall of the fort. The morning dew had recently burned off, and William and John swaggered across the parade ground dressed in their new blue wool uniforms. William spotted a row of benches in front of the long barracks. He headed in that direction.

John followed him.

"How about we rest here for a moment and see if anybody notices us?" William took a seat on a bench.

"That's a swell idea." John slapped William on his shoulder. "Well, we're in!"

William then noticed a young sergeant marching toward them. "We sure are! Exciting, ain't it?"

The sergeant stopped in front of them and eyed them up and down. The sergeant, Moffett, spoke, "So you two are my new musicians?"

"That's us," said John.

"Good. Follow me. I'm Sergeant Major Moffett, and from now on, you'll only answer to me. You're both fresh fishes, right?"

John grinned and nudged his brother, finding humor in the words. "How's that?"

Moffett turned and headed off, gesturing for the boys to follow him. "You don't know anything about music or your instruments?"

William was the first off the bench. "Right. Nothing at all."

Moffett, carrying a riding crop, cracked it against his hip as the boys walked behind him. "Not to worry. You will soon enough. By the time we get our marching orders, you'll know all you need to know. Today and tonight, you will learn all the basic word commands. Tomorrow we'll start on the music and issue you some equipment."

John was shocked. "Tonight?"

Moffett ignored the exclamation. "Except for meals, washing, and church, musicians practice and drill twelve to sixteen hours a day every day."

William couldn't believe what was happening. "But we were told we were to go home every night."

John added, "Our mother is expecting us for dinner."

Moffett halted and turned to the boys. "Who told you that? Sibley?"

John stared him in the face. "Yes, the colonel of the regiment." Moffett had a good laugh. "He's not the colonel of this regiment, at least not yet, so until that time, you take orders only from me! Got it?"

William stuttered a bit in response, "Sure, but…"

Moffett began to walk on toward the horse stables. "But what? You mustered in, right?"

John spoke, trying to defend their argument, "As musicians, yes."

Moffett halted one more time to drive home his point. "And that's what you will become but only after I say so. Until then, grab your packs and fall in with those other sorry-looking slobs lined up in front of the short barracks over there. They'll find a place for you in the horse stables."

John and William couldn't believe what they have just heard. "Horse stables?"

Moffett pointed to the company of musicians. John and William saw a nervous-looking line of young soldiers.

"Yes, the stables. That will be your new home from now on. The corporal on the end of the line, the short one that looks like a weasel, he'll help you get squared away."

The boys walked off in the direction of the music company and fell in line.

Louise and Sara climbed the rough path up the hill to the Sibley house. It was way past sunset, and the climb was made more difficult in the dark. Louise reached the door of the splendid stone house. She knocked, and Sibley opened the door to invite her in. He led her into his office and offered her and Sara a place to sit on a beautiful Victorian couch.

"Louise, Sara? Please rest yourselves and tell me what's on your mind."

Louise's voice came off as an attack. "Henry, where are my boys? It's way past dark, and you promised!"

Sibley lit a cigar and leaned back. "I'm so sorry, Louise. My commission for the Second Regiment has been held up. They are under strict army regulations now. Can I get you two anything to eat or drink?"

Sara butted in, "No, thank you! How long have you known you weren't getting your commission?"

Louise stifled Sara, "What are you going to do about this?"

Sibley puffed on his cigar as he gave Sara a sly smile. "I found out this morning, and there's nothing much I can do now. But if I am given command of the Third Regiment, I can get them transferred into my ranks. Until then, we must just wait. I'm truly sorry."

"You're a liar! That's what you are, Mr. Sibley," Sara said in return.

Louise grabbed Sara by her arm and pulled her close. "Henry! I trusted you, and you flat out lied to me!"

Sibley continued, "That's not true. Things change suddenly as they often do in the army. I'm sorry, but I promise you again. I'll get this straightened out."

Louise shook her head in anger. "When will I see them again?"

Sibley set his cigar aside and leaned across the desk. "Sundays are set aside for family visits. You can see them then, but be forewarned.

Musicians hardly get a break. When they are not practicing, they must do officer laundry and care for livestock, as well as help the cooks."

Sara stood up and pulled at her mother's arm. "Come on, Momma. Let's get out of here."

Louise got up in a huff, and they left. They slipped and slid on their walk down the path back to their cabin. A drizzle had turned into heavy rain.

At Fort Snelling, the Simmons brothers had resigned themselves to their fate and, after a couple of weeks of hard duty, had gained a bit of acceptance among the other musicians as well as other soldiers in the regiment. The summer had turned into a wet one of constant rain on and off. It was nearly July, and all the soldiers were beginning to get upset with the conditions of army life. They were all anxious for a change from the constant drilling and other routines that could affect the mind and body of a soldier. As on any other day, the musicians formed up early on the parade ground. Heavy rain drenched the company of musicians. William, one of the shortest members, stood at the end of the front rank. He had covered himself with his rubber poncho. Moffett, about to inspect his company, stopped in front of him.

"Did I tell you the poncho was for you?" "No, Sergeant Major!"

"Then take it off and cover that drumhead with it. You get that head wet, and that drum is useless, am I right, soldier?"

"Yes, Sergeant Major," William barked back. He pulled off his poncho and hurriedly covered the drum with it.

Moffett gave him a stern look and put him to the test. "Okay, do you think you can roll out a decent breakfast call for the regiment today?"

Sheepishly William replied, "I'll try."

"Don't try it! Just do it!" commanded Moffett.

William did his best, but the wet drumhead had lost its tension. The drumroll went flat.

Moffett had heard enough and scolded William, "Enough! Stop! Fall out, get inside, and dry out that head. Reset your snares, and let's see if you can get decent lunch and dinner call today. Everyone, pay attention! Private Simmons here thinks he is more important than his instrument. If you cannot take care of your equipment, you are useless to us on the battlefield! Your drums and bugles are of utmost importance to the field officers. I'll repeat this again and again. Every bugle call or drumroll is a field command that officers need to form ranks and conduct maneuvers on the field. Therefore, because Private

Simmons cannot communicate when it is time for breakfast, none of you will eat this morning."

After a brief pause, Moffett relieved his charges, "Okay, fall out! You've got two hours before the drill call. That's two hours of practice you can get in. So! Get to it!"

The entire company let out a groan with much mumbling and complaining as they broke ranks and headed for the shelter of their stable. The drummers and buglers headed in separate directions to practice on their own. Finally the thunderstorm had passed, and the sun had broken through. The parade ground was beginning to dry out, but regular infantry soldiers slogged through mud and grass as they practiced their marching and maneuvering. William and the other drummers had found a dry spot to sit on the ground in front of a wooden plank bench. In precise unison, they tapped out the various beats and rhythms. From a distance, the sound of buglers practicing spilled over the parade ground.

BULL RUN

The hardships of forced marches are often more painful than the dangers of battle.

—General Thomas Stonewall Jackson

Then, sir, we will give them the bayonet!

—Stonewall Jackson's reply
to Colonel B. E. Bee when he
reported that the enemy was
beating them back at the first
battle of Bull Run, July 1861

The road to Centreville was clogged with retreating Union troops as well as wealthy spectators who had come out in the morning to watch the battle and were expecting a huge Union victory. But unfortunately the tide of battle had turned to the rebels' hands, and the Union Army was running in panic back to Washington, DC. The First Minnesota Volunteer Regiment was one of the few units that were retreating in some military order. The road was littered with supplies from the Union troops who had run and thrown away their weapons and gear in the panicked retreat. Dan sat atop his supply wagon, which had now been pressed into service as an ambulance, and maneuvered it around the discarded equipment and wounded or exhausted soldiers. Confederate shells passed overhead and exploded randomly among the retreating troops. A hansom cab rushed past Dan's wagon. Its occupants were part of the DC elite, and they were still sipping wine and eating from picnic baskets as a shell exploded nearby.

The shock rocked Dan's wagon, but he managed to regain control over his mules. Sergeant Binns, an older soldier of about thirty years old, ran up to Dan. His left hand was wrapped in a blood-soaked bandage that had been made from his undershirt. Binns, a Scottish native, spoke with an accent. He noticed Dan's wagon stopped on the road and jogged up to Dan's side. Wincing in pain, he climbed up and took a seat next to Dan.

"Hold up there, Dan! How about a ride? My hand pains me so much I just can't bear it any longer."

Dan saw the man was in great pain and suffering. "Sure, but climb in the back. Hop up! I got some room though you may have to push some of those others out of the way. If any of them have expired, just roll them out the back. The gravediggers and vultures can have them."

Binns crawled back into the wagon and positioned himself behind Dan. "Looks like you've got yourself a proper ambulance now, eh?"

Dan slapped the reigns onto the backs of his mules to try to get them to move. He turned his head back to continue his conversation with Binns. "Sure do. What happened to you guys out there? I missed the whole show."

Binns told the tale of their first battle. "You should be happy you did. Well, we were called in at the last moment to protect Rickett's battery but got overrun anyway. Put up a hell of a fight, though. We didn't go down easy. I think old secesh will remember the First from now on."

Binns showed off his hand to Dan. Blood dripped from the ragged bandage onto the wooden plank seat of the wagon.

Dan did a quick double take. "That doesn't look good."

"Took a ball right between the fingers when I was reloading, and the darn thing passed up to my wrist. I can't move my hand or fingers. I guess I'm out of this war for a while, and that's okay by me. Damn it all! Sure does hurt like hell, though. Guess I'll have to doctor for this one."

Dan shook his head in disbelief. "I'm taking all the wounded to Centreville. They've set up a hospital there."

Suddenly the high-pitched squeal of an incoming shell caused Dan to instinctively flinch. Another shell came screaming in and landed within yards of the wagon. The explosion rolled the wagon over. All the wounded who were capable got up and ran. Dan and Binns helped each other up and carried on by foot. Dan checked on his mules. One of them was severely wounded and screeching in pain. Dan unholstered his pistol and shot the animal. He then held his head and collapsed.

Binns knelt to him. "You okay, old man?"

Dan came to and slowly got to his feet. "Don't know. Just shook up, I think."

"Can you walk?"

He took Dan by his arm to help him regain his footing. Dan got to his feet and took a few steps with Binns's help. They leaned on each other.

Binns removed Dan's cap and looked at his head. "Looks like you got hit by something. Just an awful bruise. No blood."

Dan shook it off. "I've been hurt worse shoeing my horse. I'm okay, but look at this mess we left. That wagon is going to hold up the entire retreat."

"Leave it to the pioneers," Binns said as he shrugged it off. Dan started walking along the road. "Looks like we're walking." Binns stepped up to his side. "We got far to go?"

"On foot, I reckon, for about two hours. How are you holding up?"

Binns groaned in pain and held his arm tight to his side. "Okay, but every step just sends an awful stabbing sensation through my whole body. You may have to use your pistol to put me out of my misery unless you got some medicine in that wagon."

The two men had walked about a quarter mile when a couple of Washington elites, a tipsy congressman and his much younger woman, passed by on foot. The gentleman took a flask from his frock coat and pointed it to Binns as a salute. The elderly politician then pulled from the flask before handing it to Binns.

"Take this, my man, and thank you for your gallant service today. That should take the edge off."

Binns chugged down the entire flask of whiskey.

The congressman turned to his lady. "Darling, I'm afraid that man is about to lose his hand for sure. Make a note that the surgeons of the army get ample supplies of this fine Kentucky brew for our boys in blue."

The lady gave him a puzzled look. "But these boys are wearing red. How do we know they are not secesh?"

"Because, my dear, they are running away. The secesh have won the day."

Binns returned the empty flask to the man. "Maybe, but they have not won the war," said Binns as he and Dan continued their hike toward the hospital, away from the Manassas battlefield.

Back at Fort Snelling, it was another boring day of practice and drill for the Simmons brothers. John had made a friend with one of the other young buglers. His name was Lars; and he was sixteen years old, a tall, lanky Norwegian boy. It was the end of June, and the news of the battle of Bull Run had all the Second Regiment full of questions and had left them anxious for their turn to do battle. The two buglers strolled along the river road and chatted among themselves mostly about their future and when things might change so they could experience something different from the usual routine.

John waved his bugle in front of himself in frustration. "What are we doing here anyway? We haven't had a day's rest in weeks. All we do is march and practice these darn things. Have you heard any news?"

"I have heard something from that stupid-looking first sergeant in K Company," said Lars.

"The one who looks like a goat left out in the rain? Boyd? What did he say?"

Lars halted for a moment to look at the catfish swimming in a shallow pool at the river's edge. "Yeah, that's his name. Well, he said that his captain said that the Second Regiment was about to move out."

John looked on in anticipation. "Where? When? Why?"

Lars ignored the fish and moved on. "Well, I guess the old First took a hell of a beating at Bull Run, but they made a good showing of it and have been assigned to stay in the Army of the Potomac around Washington, and we are to fill in someplace in the western army."

John was puzzled. "They made a good showing of taking a beating? That doesn't seem to wash. Any idea where we would go exactly? Did he say?"

Lars picked up a small flat stone and skipped it across the river. "Boyd heard him say Kentucky."

John skipped a stone as well. "Ha! Mine went farther. I wouldn't mind seeing Kentucky. Did he say when?"

Lars shrugged off John's remark and continued the stroll. "Soon, I think. Maybe within the month or whenever the colonel thinks we are ready for a fight."

John caught up to him. "Well, Kentucky or wherever, I'm ready to leave this place. Are they doing any fighting in Kentucky?"

Lars nodded and replied, "Little bit, I suspect. Mostly skirmishing and such, so I heard. But, you know, Kentucky is a border state, so there are a lot of Union folks there that aren't taking to the rebel cause. So it might mean just police work protection of the people who sympathize with us."

John nodded in agreement. "Anything is better than sitting here day in and day out."

Lars turned around and started to head back up the road to the fort. "Yeah, I've had enough of it too. I can't take much more of this. Honestly I think those darkies got it better than us."

"Do you believe we are fighting this war for them?"

Lars gave his opinion of the situation of the slaves. "I'm sure not. I mean, I never saw a darky, and I ain't got no idea how they get treated, but I heard mules got it better than them, and that ain't right, but I ain't gonna put my life on the line to save no darky. I joined up to save the Union."

"Yeah, whatever that means."

The boys reached the long, inclined road leading up to the fort.

They passed the shallow pool of catfish.

Lars pointed to it. "Well, we ain't darkies, but we sure are treated like mules, and I would fight to save your mule ass."

John smiled. "Thanks, I'd do the same for you. Are you thinking about dinner again?"

"Yeah, I sure would like some fried catfish like Ma used to make," said Lars.

The boys continued their walk up to the fort.

With the first major land battle of the war behind them, the Union Army was regrouping around Washington, DC. Dan had been resupplied with a new wagon, and his duties would include following the marching army up the peninsula on its way to Richmond, Virginia, where the new general of the army, McClellan, had taken over and reshaped the army into the strong fighting unit it would become. In the meantime, Colonel Sibley was still without permanent orders and spent most of his time writing letters to Governor Ramsey in hope that he would soon be given his command. The Simmons brothers were still spending the remainder of the summer of 1861 being bored with their usual routine of musical practice, marching, and maneuvering, as well as an occasional moment when they were given rifle practice so, in case they might be needed in a fighting role, they would at least be familiar with the weapons.

Louise Simmons had sent a message up the hill to the Sibley house, requesting that Colonel Sibley come to visit her and explain the situation of her boys. She and Sara had been living in fear the entire summer as the Natives had been so unnerving that they hoped to have John and William released from service and sent back home to protect the homestead. Three companies of the Second Minnesota Regiment had already been sent to minor forts in other parts of the state to defend against an Indian attack if one was to come, but the music company was not one of them. This was a relief to Louise, but she still wanted answers from Sibley. After Sibley received the note from Sara, he reluctantly left his house and made the walk down the hill to the Simmons cabin. Once he was invited inside Sara, Louise and he relaxed around the cabin table.

Louise opened the conversation as politely as possible, "Rumors are spreading that you have some news about the Indians and the Second Regiment. Is it good or bad? Autumn is upon us, and I'm worried."

"Little bit of both, I guess," he said. "What is it? Please tell us."

Sibley lit one of his cigars and took a slow drag. "The Second will be moving out in two weeks to a month. They are expected to join the western brigades by October."

Anger rose in Louise's voice. "But you said they would be here until their enlistments were up."

Sibley turned away sheepishly and ashamed. "I got a letter from Governor Ramsey two days ago. I had requested my regiment again and planned to transfer your sons into it, but it appears Congress isn't happy with the way things are going in the war. The North has taken too many whippings, and all regiments ready for combat are to be called into action."

The shock came over the faces of Louise and Sara. "Action? Where are they sending my boys?" Sibley replied gently, "Kentucky for now."

Louise responded bitterly, "Henry! I don't know what to say. Dan barely made it out alive in that mess at Manassas. Losing him would have been tragic enough, but losing either one of my boys is something I am just not willing to do. You must find a way to get them out of their enlistments."

Sibley waved her off. "I told you many times already. When I'm given my regiment, I'll get them transferred into it."

"And do you think that will happen before the regiment is ordered onto the boats?"

Sibley responded, now obviously anxious to leave, "Right. Not very likely, but we'll hope and pray. The good news is the entire regiment is getting one week's leave before moving out, starting the end of this month. Your boys will be home by October 1 or earlier for their leave. I'll send word to you when I get exact dates."

Louise hung her head to cry. "If that's the best I'm getting, I'll suppose I'll have to take it."

Sara leaned in to comfort her mother. She gave Sibley a mean-spirited look. "Oh, Mama, it's one week anyway." Then she looked directly at Sibley. "You're a mean, terrible man."

Louise hugged her daughter. "No, Sara, it's all my fault. I only have myself to blame. I never should have signed away my boys."

The Army of the Potomac, now ruled by General McClellan, was moving down a long plank road on the peninsula of eastern Virginia.

Dan sat atop his supply wagon and drove his mule team on the plank road that ran parallel to the Potomac River. He slapped the reigns on the backs of his two mules.

"Hem, Sally! Haw, Betsy!"

The mules strained against their yokes. The wagon stalled in the mud as it slipped off the wet planks and nearly slid into a ditch. Dan reached for his whip. The captain of his company, Hans, a young German immigrant of about twenty-five years of age, reached up and stopped Dan from pulling out his whip.

He spoke calmly in his thick German accent, "No, no, Corporal. Don't beat those animals. Kind words will get you through. Now let's get this wagon rolling. We need the regiment supplied by nightfall."

Dan was having none of it. He reached for his whip again. "Do you think kind words are going to win this war?"

Hans held him back. "Let me try."

Hans walked to the front of the wagon and faced the mules. He took their bridles in hand and gently talked to them, "Now, now. Easy does it, girls."

He moved their heads from left to right and back again. The mules twisted and bucked, but the wagon began to move forward.

"Okay, Dan! Give them the word, and let's get this wagon train back on the road. We should be reaching our bivouac in about five miles."

Dan slapped the reins, and the wagon jerked. "Any idea where this is all going?"

Hans looked back up at Dan. "Not a clue. We are just part of what McClellan is calling the Peninsula Campaign. On to Richmond!"

Dan spanked the mules again. "Hem, Betsy! Haw, Sally!"

The mules obeyed the command for left and right and managed to shift the wagon back onto the plank road. The wagon moved on, followed by a long line of other supply wagons, which were followed by a long line of marching, dust, and mud-covered Union troops.

The cold winds of October had brought more heavy, cold rain and the usual feeling of winter's wrath about to set upon the people of Minnesota. John and William had been given their leave before the regiment departed for the war. Home at last even for this short time had brought contentment back to the cabin. Henry Sibley and his wife, Jane, were invited to the Simmons cabin to visit with the boys; and they all sat around the dinner table.

As young Sara Simmons stoked the coals in the fire, she opened a conversation with Sibley's wife. "Mrs. Sibley, is it true your first name is Sara too?"

Jane Sibley gave a nod and a wink to young Sara. "Indeed, it is. My middle name is Jane, but unlike you, I spell my Sara with an *h*."

"So then you prefer to be called by your middle name?"

"Yes, I do. I'm quite used to it. Besides, this town is only big enough for one Sara, and it may as well be you."

Sara grinned, then directed her attention to Henry. "Mr. Sibley?" "Yes?"

"John has been telling us about your visits to the fort."

Sibley got up to warm himself by the fire. "Is that so? And what has he been telling you?"

"Soldiers were saying that you met Jane at your sutler's store that you owned at the fort. And the rumor is that you actually like the Indians and that you once had a Dakota girlfriend."

Sibley glanced at his wife as Louise gave Sara a stern look. "Enough!" said Louise.

"That's true. We met when my father bought out Henry and took over the business," Jane responded gently to disarm any conflict that may arise between mother and daughter. "Sara? Do you think this rumor is true?"

Sara nodded against her mother holding her mouth shut. Louise released her.

Jane continued, "How old are you now? Twelve? Is that right?" Sara nodded.

"Then I think you are old enough to hear the truth so we can put an end to this rumor."

Louise butted in, "Jane, that's not necessary."

Jane continued, "When Henry first came here, well, that was over twenty years ago, and there weren't any White women in this territory at all."

All ears were now turned toward Jane and her story, but it was Sibley himself who spoke up.

"I was hardly into my twenties when the American Fur Company sent me here to set up a store at Fort Snelling and build a trading relationship with the Indians living here. Yes, I became close friends with many of them, and I was introduced to a young woman."

Jane capped it off, "Whom he loved." Sara was shocked. "No kidding?" Sibley nodded in affirmation.

Sara continued her questioning, "William said that you had a half-breed daughter too!"

Sibley responded, "I do. Her name is Helen." "When did you last see her?"

"Well, it's been several years. You see, after I half raised her, she passed on and is no longer with us. She was the daughter of the Dakota chief Mdewakanton. Her name is translated to Red Blanket Woman, but of course, as she was my only child, I gave her the Christian name of Helen. One year after her death, I met Jane, and then we got married."

William now spoke out of turn, "Colonel, we know you are very knowledgeable about the Dakota, and since you were a de facto member of the tribe, do you have any idea what they are all worked up about? Are they going to attack Mendota or any other place? Will there be an uprising?"

Sibley took his time in answering. "Well, there has been some recent trouble with the Indian agent."

Sara now jumped in, "You mean that slimy skink Tom Galbraith? What has he done now?"

Sibley answered, "It's what he hasn't done that has caused all the trouble."

Everyone listened intently.

"He hasn't been paying out the government annuities as promised to the Indians in their treaty."

Sara asked again, "So what does that mean?"

Jane answered this time, "It means they can't eat. How would you like it if your mother had no food to feed you?"

Sara looked down. "I guess I'd be pretty upset too." Then Sibley asked Sara, "Upset enough to go to war?" Sara nodded. "Maybe. Do you think they'll start a war?" "I don't think so, but we must be prepared."

Jane followed up with "Which is why the new governor has made Henry the commander in charge of all new Minnesota regiments being formed and trained for the rebellion with the South."

Now Louise was curious for more information. "Is that right, Henry?"

Sibley answered her directly, "Yes, and if this war continues much longer and the Dakota do take up arms against anyone, all Minnesota units that can be expended will return to the state to fight the Indian war."

Louise continued, "What do you think the likelihood of an Indian revolt will be?"

"Well, we are headed into late autumn now, and I think they'll settle in for the winter, and if Galbraith meets their demands and honors the treaty, we'll have no disturbance."

John looked up. "And if he doesn't?"

"Then I'm guessing they'll wait for better weather to start any kind of fight," Sibley added.

With the visit complete, the attention now turned to the Native powwow that had started up on the other side of the river.

William got up and headed for the cabin door. "Let's go have a look-see."

They all rose and walked out of the cabin. From their view on top of the Mendota bluff, they could see the huge bonfire and the Dakota dancing and chanting.

GOING TO WAR

We are never prepared for so many to die. So you understand? No one is. We expect some chosen few. We expect an occasional empty chair, a toast to the dear departed comrades. Victory celebrations for most of us, a hallowed death for a few. But the war goes on. And men die. The price gets even higher. Some officers can pay no longer. We are prepared to lose some of us but never all of us. But that is the trap. You can hold nothing back when you attack. You must commit yourself totally. And yet if they all die, a man must ask himself, Will it have been worth it?

—Michael Shaara, *The Killer Angels*

On October 14, 1861, the consolidated regiment of the Second Minnesota departed Fort Snelling at the Mendota wharf. Their send-off was nearly as spectacular as the First Regiment's; and certainly, for Louise and Sara, it was just as sad a departure as when Dan had left. Sibley would stay behind in his comfortable house high atop the Mendota bluff and work on organizing the newer regiments into one Indian-fighting division as now it was feared across the state that the Dakota were most certainly going to revolt. Governor Ramsey had put him in command, and even though he had promised Louise he could now transfer her sons into a regiment that would most likely see only duty on the prairie, Louise decided to let her boys go with the regiment they had become accustomed to. All in all, she felt it was safer for her boys to be surrounded by newfound friends and officers that they were now very close to.

The regiment loaded onto the riverboat steamers early in the morning. Their first stop would be downriver a few miles at Saint Paul. The city was decked out in red, white, and blue bunting and so wrought up with excitement to see the regiment off that any work for the day was given up in celebration. The regiment was made to march through the streets of the city and was greeted by young boys wearing red, white, and blue neckties; girls carrying bouquets that they waved at them; old men who waved walking sticks; and all who collectively cheered the regiment on. They were handed pastries and flower notes and given all kinds of good wishes. This parade soon ended as they caught up to their boats, which were now waiting for them at the Saint Paul levee dockage. Their journey would now take them to La Crosse, Wisconsin. At La Crosse, the regiment was transferred to the railroad and arrived, without noteworthy adventure, at Chicago on the morning of the sixteenth and then marched to and quartered in the Wigwam, the large temporary building where Abraham Lincoln had been nominated for the presidency at the National Republican Convention the year before.

They spent the night there and marched the next day to the Pittsburgh and Fort Wayne Railroad depot and boarded a train for Pittsburgh, where they arrived in the afternoon of the eighteenth. Here they were most hospitably received and conducted to a public hall, where a bountiful hot supper was served by an association of loyal and generous ladies who personally attended the tables, to which the soldiers did ample justice. This kind of reception and others like it were not lost upon the soldiers. They remembered and talked of them wherever they went, and many a campfire was brightened by the memory of the kind words and gracious and sympathetic attention of women, to whom all Union soldiers were as sons and brothers.

Here the regiment's orders were changed from Washington, DC, to Kentucky; and on the nineteenth, they embarked on three small steamers and, after a delightful voyage down the Ohio River, arrived at Louisville on the twenty-second, where Colonel Van Cleve of the Second Minnesota reported the arrival of the regiment to General W. T. Sherman, then commanding the Department of the Cumberland, and received orders to proceed by rail that evening to Lebanon Junction, thirty miles south on the Louisville and Nashville Railroad. They were loaded on a train of open flatcars and spent the night in a cold rainstorm, making the trip at about six miles per hour, stopping awhile at every sidetrack until, about 4:00 a.m., they disembarked and stacked arms in a field near the junction. This was to be their new camp and home until new orders were given.

Sometime in the next day, October 23, their baggage and tents arrived on another train, which had started with the regiment but, in some inexplicable manner, had run slower than they had. The camp was set in regulation style, in a field just within the angle formed by the main and Lebanon branch tracks, and at a retreat camp, the regimental guard was mounted. To John and William, as far as they were concerned, the war had now started. The boys remained here for several weeks. The only break from the routine of drilling was when detachments to guard the railroad bridges were sent out. Guard and picket duty and instruction made up their days and nights. Reveille was sounded an hour before daylight. This was a chore that John did not relish, but it was his duty. He did abide by it without complaint, at least not to Moffett.

After reveille, the companies were called into formation and had to stand to arms until sunrise to guard against a surprise by the enemy. The campground was damp and unhealthy, and in these tedious morning hours, the fog settled over the soldiers like a cold, wet blanket. The regimental sick list increased considerably until the ground was drained by deep ditches between the rows of tents, and the practice was adopted of serving every man. At early roll call, a cup of hot coffee was supplied along with hardtack, which kept the soldiers warm and cheerful until breakfast time.

On the thirty-first of October, the paymaster called upon the regiment and squared up all accounts to the first of November, and this relieved some of the tension of boring camp life. John and William spent as much time together as possible, but they also had made friends among their company as well as the regiment as a whole.

Most of the officers knew them and respected them as hardworking, disciplined young lads. When they had free time, which wasn't often, they were often ordered to find a fresh spring and bring back to camp full canteens and barrels of fresh water for the cooks and messmates of all companies, including their own.

Colonel Van Cleve took a liking to William's innocence, and it was not unusual to see the old man inquiring as to William's health and that of the other men. One would think that William was soon to be promoted to aid to the colonel. John, on the other hand, was closer to Moffett. Indeed, by the time their first month in Kentucky had passed, the two brothers had found a new and meaningful family.

Thanksgiving and Christmas were soon approaching; and on the fifteenth of November, General D. C. Buell assumed the command at Louisville and, on the second of December, organized the troops in Kentucky into the army of Ohio. General George

H. Thomas assumed command on the sixth of the First Division, comprised of the First, Second, and Third Brigades, the Second Minnesota Regiment being assigned to the Third, which was composed as follows: Third Brigade, Colonel R. L. McCook commanding; Eighteenth Regiment, United States Infantry, Colonel H. B. Carrington; Second Regiment, Minnesota Volunteers, Colonel H. P. Van Cleve; Thirty-Fifth Regiment, Ohio Volunteers, Colonel F. Van Derveer; and Ninth Regiment, Ohio Volunteers, Lieutenant Colonel

G. Kanimerling.

A letter from home addressed to John sent from Louise explained that the Third Regiment of Minnesota Volunteers would be joining them soon in Kentucky and that Sibley was once again ordered to stay in Minnesota and wait for further orders in case a Dakota uprising was to take place. According to Louise, the situation at home was still unpredictable and unstable.

On the eighth of December, the Third Minnesota Regiment arrived to relieve the Second Minnesota Regiment at Lebanon Junction; and the next day, the Second Regiment went by rail thirty-seven miles to Lebanon, where General Thomas had established his headquarters. Now, for the first time, they were brigaded with other troops and had an opportunity to compare themselves with other regiments. The Ninth Ohio, whose colonel (Robert L. McCook) was their brigade commander, was composed entirely of Germans, few of whom could speak English. The Thirty-Fifth Ohio was their senior regiment by several months of service, mostly in Kentucky. Both these regiments were brigaded with the Second Minnesota from this time until their muster out, at the expiration of their three years of service, and this would give the men time and opportunity for close acquaintance and comradeship, which developed almost immediately.

John and William had little spare time to meet with members of the Third Minnesota. A rumor spread among the camp of an impending revolt of the Dakota and Minnesota regiments now forming at Fort Snelling. The newly formed regiments were being held back from entering the war and were being held in the state until things calmed down with the Sioux.

Sibley was to be put in command of all remaining troops in the home state. Shifting of regiments into an army corps seemed to be the new novelty for the end of 1861. The Eighteenth United States Regular Infantry was one of the newly organized regiments of three battalions of eight companies each. They held themselves somewhat apart from the volunteers; and before the volunteer regiments had got fairly on the same plane with them as soldiers, they were placed with other regular regiments in a brigade by themselves, the Eighty-Seventh Indiana taking their place in the brigade alongside the Second Minnesota. Here they came into the immediate presence of George H. Thomas, then a new brigadier general of volunteers, under whom—as their division, corps, or army commander—they would serve for quite some time.

THE MILLS SPRINGS CAMPAIGN

*Some of us volunteered to fight for Union. Some came
in mainly because we were bored at home and this
looked like it might be fun. Some came because we
were ashamed not to. Many of us came...because it
was the right thing to do. All of us have seen men die.
Most of us never saw a Black man back home. We
think on that too. But freedom...is not just a word.*

—Jeff Shaara, *The Killer Angels*

On the morning of the first of January 1862, the brigade folded their
tents, loaded the baggage train, and, with bands playing and colors
displayed, marched out on the Columbia Pike. Thirteen wagons were
allotted for the tents and baggage of each regiment, and they were
loaded to their roofs. Each man, except the musicians, was expected
to carry his musket and accouterments, with forty rounds of ball
cartridges, knapsack with all his personal property, overcoat, blanket,
canteen, and haversack with three days' rations in it—in all, forty to
forty-five pounds.

They marched that day fourteen miles and, the next twelve
miles, encamped near Campbellsville. There they found that most of
the men were tired, sore footed, and hungry; and many of them had
tossed off their overcoats, blankets, or some other part of their loads

on the way. The roads were, however, hard and smooth. The wagons had come up in good time, so comfortable camps were made very quickly. The brigade remained there four days while the wagon trains went back to Lebanon and returned with more rations and supplies and, on the seventh, marched again with somewhat-better preparation than before, the men carrying more rations and less unnecessary stuff in their knapsacks.

On the eighth, they passed through Columbia; and there, leaving the pike, they turned eastward on the dirt road. It immediately began to rain, and before night, the road was almost impassable. The next ten days were spent alternately in short but tedious marches in the mud, slush, and rain and in waiting for the wagon trains to come up; so about half the nights and days, the troops, without shelter, were lying in the woods or fields along the roadside.

This, in midwinter, was a very discouraging experience to William and John on their first campaign. Yet they learned speedily to make themselves as comfortable as circumstances permitted; and things were never so bad that some fun could not be had though, as John noted to William, it was not at all just like the camping at home. It was bound to be another dreary, cold, wet night; and General Buell had issued an order that no private property should be appropriated without proper authority. Thus far, the fuel had been furnished by the quartermaster; but this one evening, the regiment encamped in some open fields where there was no cut wood or forest accessible. The fields were, however, well fenced with dry rails; and after some exasperating delay, authority was obtained to use, in this emergency, only the top rail of the fence along the color line.

Cheery campfires were soon blazing, and the men had plenty of fuel all night. Next morning, the fence was gone. The company commanders were called to account for its disappearance but were unable to find any man who took any but the top rail. As the brigade passed through the country, they found usually only old men, women, and children at home, most of the able-bodied citizens having joined some regiment on one side or the other. In some cases, the brothers had enlisted in opposing regiments. Generally the people at home were not seriously foraged upon or molested, but occasionally pigs and geese did come into the camp and were duly "mustered into the army."

On the seventeenth of January, the head of the column arrived at Logan's Crossroads, nine miles north of Zollicoffer's entrenched rebel camp at Beech Grove and seven miles west of Somerset, where the First Brigade, commanded by General Schoepf, was posted. Beech Grove was a naturally good position, on the north bank of the Cumberland and on the east side of Oak Creek at its junction with the river. Mill Springs, by which name the campaign and battle would later be known, was on the south bank of the Cumberland, opposite Beech Grove, and had no relation to the battle as far as is known; neither had Fishing Creek, from which the Confederates named the affair that took place on the nineteenth at Logan's Crossroads. There the Union Army halted for the closing up of the column and to await Schoepf's brigade, which was ordered to join them.

The First and Second East Tennessee (Union) Infantry Regiments, under Brigadier General Carter, was temporarily attached to the division at this time, also a battalion of the Michigan engineer troops. On the eighteenth, of the forces present, Second Minnesota, Ninth Ohio, and Twelfth Kentucky, with the engineer battalion, were encamped around Thomas Headquarters on the Columbia-Somerset Road, three-quarters of a mile west of Logan's house. At and near Logan's house were the Fourth Kentucky, Tenth Indiana, First and Second East Tennessee, the battalion of Wolford's cavalry, and two Ohio batteries, Kenny's and Standart's. Schoepf—with Wetmore's Kentucky Battery, the Thirty-Third Indiana, and Seventeenth and Thirty-Eighth Ohio—were at Somerset; and Tenth Kentucky and Fourteenth Ohio were on the road, some miles back toward Columbia. All these forces joined the brigade the afternoon and evening after the battle, as did the Thirty-Fifth Ohio. The Eighteenth Regulars were still farther away and did not arrive until several days afterward. So the Union Army had, present and available for the battle, seven regiments, two battalions, and two batteries. Only four regiments and one battalion were, however, engaged seriously enough to have any casualties.

On the opposing side, General Crittenden, the Confederate commander, in his report giving the order of march, named in his column of attack eight regiments, three battalions, and two batteries. All his regiments were engaged in the battle and lost heavily on the field, according to his official report and casualty list. Between Thomas Headquarters and Logan's farm, the Columbia-Somerset Road ran nearly east and west. Another road led from Logan's farm southward to Beech Grove and Mill Springs and is called the Mill Springs Road in the reports. The battlefield of the nineteenth was on both sides of this road, from half a mile to a mile south from the crossroads or junction at Logan's house. The ground was undulating and mostly covered with thick woods and brush, with some small open fields enclosed by the usual rail fence of the country.

The night of the eighteenth, Company A was on the picket line. William and John were not posted with them as Colonel Van Cleve kept all the musicians back in camp with the remainder of the regiment. They would be held in reserve, as was customary, to act as stretcher bearers if that need arose. It was the darkest night with the coldest and most pitiless and persistent rain the boys ever knew. It was with great difficulty that the sentinels could be visited or relieved at all during the night; and the cooking of supper or even of coffee was, in the absence of shelter, out of the question. Nothing happened to break the tedious monotony of the night; but it had occurred to William and John and the rest of the regiment on picket duty or in the camp that, if they had known that Crittenden's forces had, at midnight, turned out of their comfortable tents and dry blankets and, all those six weary hours, were sloshing along in the mud and storm and darkness, they could have much enjoyed the contemplation of their physical and spiritual condition.

John remarked to his brother, "It is of some comfort to us soldiers on such a night as this to think that his enemy over there was at least as wet and cold and wretched as he is himself."

William could not answer because he was shivering so hard from the misery of being cold and wet but nodded in agreement.

At daybreak, the enemy's advance struck the picket line of Tenth Indiana. First a musket shot, another, and then five or six more in quick succession rang out with startling distinctness over on the Mill Springs Road, a mile or more to the left and front of the general Union Army camp. This was the first rebel shot the Simmons boys had ever heard. Every man was keenly awake and alive with expectation; then again, on the Mill Springs Road, firing broke out nearer than before, scattering at first, then thicker and faster as the enemy's advance encountered the picket reserve of which Company A of Second Minnesota was part.

Within moments, Sergeant Moffett ordered his drummers for each company to form up with their respective companies but held William back to beat out the long roll, which was the signal for the entire regiment to form up for battle. Within moments, the entire brigade made haste to move out. The Second Minnesota—with her companion regiment, the Ninth Ohio—moved off together toward Logan's Farm. Then the firing broke out again as the enemy came up to the Tenth Indiana and later to the Fourth Kentucky, those regiments having hastily got into position in the woods about half a mile in front of their camps.

There the enemy was held for some time and were compelled to bring up and deploy their two brigades for an attack in full force. In the meantime, Second Minnesota and Ninth Ohio arrived (nine companies of each) and, in good order, were put into the field under General Thomas's direction, the Second taking the line first occupied successively by the Tenth and Fourth (which regiments had retired to replenish their ammunition) and Ninth Ohio forming on the right; the Mill Springs Road divided the two newly arrived regiments. The new line was immediately advanced some distance through the woods, guiding on the road. The rain had now ceased, but the air was loaded with mist and smoke. The underbrush in their part of the field was so thick that a man was hardly visible a musket's length away.

Suddenly the Second's lines came against a rail fence with an open field in front, and a line of the enemy's troops was dimly seen through the mist some twenty or thirty yards distant in the field. The firing commenced immediately, and in a few minutes, the enemy's line just mentioned had disappeared. It was, in fact, his second line, the first being literally under the guns and noses of the Second Regiment, only the fence intervening. The sudden arrival of the Second at this fence was a surprise to the rebel Twentieth Tennessee, which was already just arrived there; and it was a surprise to the Union boys to discover, in the heat of the engagement, that the opposite side of the fence was lined with recumbent rebels.

Here, as Colonel R. L. McCook wrote later in his official report, "the contest was at first almost hand to hand. The enemy and Second Minnesota were poking their guns through the same fence." This condition of affairs could not and did not last long after the boys of the Second discovered and got up, jumped the fence, and were after them; many of the enemies were killed and wounded there but more of them after they got up and were trying to run away. Some remained and surrendered.

William would write home to his sister about the battle.

> The sudden arrival of the Second at this fence was a surprise to the rebel Twentieth Tennessee, which had already just arrived there, and it was a surprise to the Minnesota boys to discover, in the heat of the engagement, that the opposite side of the fence was lined with rebels lying on their bellies ready to shoot at us. Here, the contest was at first almost hand to hand. The enemy and Second Minnesota were poking their guns through the same fence. This condition of affairs could not and did not last long after the boys in blue discovered and got after them; many of the enemies were killed and wounded there

but more of them as they tried to make a hasty retreat. Soon after this struggle at the fence line, the captain ran up to John and tapped him on the shoulder, giving him the signal to sound the alarm. John blasted out the call to charge the enemy. The Second Minnesota rose, jumped the fence rails, and chased after the Confederates, who were running away in defeat. As the boys made good in their charge, an officer from Company K ordered John and me to help with the other musicians in policing the field for dead, wounded, and any supplies we could make use of from the dead. Within a few moments, the men gathered up the prisoners and marched them off. John and I walked side by side across the battlefield and did the duty which we were ordered.

As they approached the fighting ground, they noticed the trees flecked with bullets and the underbrush appeared to be cut away as with a scythe. The dead and wounded lay along the fence, on one side the blue and on the other the gray; further on, the dead and wounded were everywhere scattered across the open field and lay in a windrow along a ridge where the second line of battle had stood. The boys halted for a moment to look at where the body of Confederate General Zollicoffer was laid out beside a wagon track. His face was splattered with mud from passing horses and men. Sporadic shots rang out as the battle ended. The two boys stopped for a moment to gaze out at the dead and wounded lying in the field as prisoners passed by them to the rear.

The boys moved on, William still filled with adrenaline and shivering from the fear and cold as he turned to his brother.

"So this is the hero stuff we've been so anxious to see?"

John patted him on his shoulder and replied, "I've seen enough of it, I think."

William, now catching his breath, sighed. "Maybe Pa was right.

We should have stayed home. Were you as scared as me?"

John looked at a corpse, then answered, "You were scared?" "You couldn't hear by my drumming how bad my hands were shaking?"

"My lips were so dry from fear I could hardly get a note out." The boys smiled at one another, trying to laugh off their panic, and continued to police the field.

On the tenth of February, the soldiers of Second Minnesota and the entire brigade folded their tents again and began the return march to Louisville. In the afternoon, they stopped to encamp a mile north of Somerset, where they remained the next day and said goodbye to their comrades in the hospitals, many of who were too sick or too badly wounded to be moved. It rained and snowed alternately as it did nearly every day of the march to the Ohio River. The roads were almost impassable, and the companies were ordered each to march with its wagon to help it along as it often became necessary to do. On the fourteenth they arrived at Crab Orchard, where they struck the I pike, as macadamized roads were called in that country; and thenceforward the marching was less tedious though the weather did not much improve.

On the fifteenth, they passed through Stanford and, on the sixteenth, arrived at Danville, where they rested one day while it rained. On the eighteenth, they made a long march, passing through Perryville, and encamped within two or three miles of Lebanon. On the nineteenth, they marched all day in a drenching rainstorm and encamped on the farm of Dr. Jackson, a brother of the man who killed Colonel Ellsworth at Alexandria, Virginia, in the summer of 1861. The doctor was absent under military arrest; but his hospitality was freely drawn upon by the tired and hungry men, who left nothing there next morning that could be drunk, eaten, or carried away.

On the twenty-fourth, they passed through Bardstown and, on the twenty-fifth, arrived at Louisville about 3:00 p.m. and were received with a most enthusiastic welcome. The sidewalks were full of loyal men, and flags were waved to them from windows and porches as they gaily marched the principal streets toward the river. At the National Hotel, the regiment was halted and faced to the front while a deputation of the Loyal Ladies of Louisville came out and presented the beautiful silk banner to replace their battle-scarred original national flag.

In a letter home to Louise, John wrote:

> The main street of Louisville was crowded with men, women, and children who had all turned out to see the victors of the battle parade through town. At the head of the column was our Second Minnesota Regiment. The regimental band was playing "When Johnny Comes Marching Home Again." The citizens sang along with the band until the color guard of the regiment halted and turned to face a group of lovely ladies posted in front of the National Hotel. The color sergeant dipped the battle-and weather-torn regimental flag to the ladies, and one of the women stepped forward to remove the flag from the staff. It was here that I'm afraid your youngest son was smitten with the love of a Southern belle. Her name is Mary, and she appears to be of good health and the same age as William. Like most of the people here, she is a Unionist, and you should not have to worry in that regard.

As the flag was being presented, Mary stepped up to help one of the elder women who was presenting the flag. They both seemed to be having a hard time removing the old flag when William, now the drummer posted to the color guard, without orders, stepped out of line to lend a hand. With his help, the flag was removed. The young lady blushed as William's hand moved along the top of hers as they fastened the new banner to the pole.

"Sorry, miss," William said as he blushed.

Mary stepped back and shyly replied, "Please, call me Mary."

William, not at all comfortable speaking to a pretty young girl, choked out a response, "Is that your name? *Oh!* Stupid me. Of course, it is."

Mary held out a gloved hand and curtsied to him. "And you are?"

William, not sure how to react, stiffened to attention. "Private William Simmons, Second Minnesota Regiment."

At this moment, the other woman who had helped with the flag intervened, "Well then, Private Simmons, where do you hail from?"

"Mendota, Minnesota, ma'am" was William's shy response. "And you've come all this way to help save our state and the Union?" the older woman asked.

"We're doing our best, ma'am."

Colonel Van Cleve pushed his way into the ceremony. "Ma'am, is this boy bothering you?"

"No, sir, my niece and I were just impressed how handsome and fine-looking a body of you Midwesterners are and are glad we have you in our city," replied the aunt of the young girl.

Van Cleve now nudged William along. "Private, you may return to your post. I'll take it from here."

William saluted and turned to step back into line but not before giving Mary a smile and nod. "Yes, sir!"

Van Cleve unrolled the flag as the color sergeant raised the flag high and let the wind catch it. It fully opened in the wind. Gold letters inscribed on the red stripes of the American flag read "Mill Springs. January 19, 1862, Second Regiment Minnesota Volunteer Infantry. Presented on Behalf of the Loyal Ladies of Louisville."

Van Cleve then called out loudly to the regiment, "Three cheers for the ladies of Louisville!"

Three rousing hurrahs rose from the collective throats of the men of the Second Minnesota. Then the color guard fell back into line, and the regimental band struck up another song.

The parade moved on down the street.

As William was marching and drumming along with the band, Mary rushed up to him and shyly handed him a small bouquet and a note. "Please be careful, William, and do write to me once in a while, will you?"

William was stunned and hardly knew how to respond. "Yes, yes, of course. Thank you."

Mary gently touched him on his shoulder as the regiment moved off. The sidewalks were full of loyal Union men, women, and children. Federal flags were waved to the regiment from windows and porches as the regiment proudly marched the principal street toward the river, where a steamboat awaited them.

After a brief stop at the pier and a response by Colonel Van Cleve, the march was resumed, and the regiment went on board the large steamer *Jacob Strader* at the levee. Meantime, on the sixth, Fort Henry and, the sixteenth, Fort Donelson had been captured; and the way was now open to Nashville by the Ohio and Cumberland Rivers. On the twenty-sixth, the baggage, mules, and wagons were taken aboard at Portland, just below the falls and three miles from Louisville levee.

John and William leaned on the steamboat's railing and looked out at the passing town of Louisville.

As John dropped his haversack and other equipment, he commented to his brother, "It sure is nice to be sailing again."

William sat on the deck and removed his worn-out boots. "I'm so footsore from marching I've about worn through my brogans."

John removed his boots as well and put on a fresh pair of socks. "I guess that resupply came just in the nick of time, but I still think you should have taken a pair off one of those dead guys back at Mills Spring. You would have made a better impression on your new girl-friend. Now she may never see you with a decent pair of shoes." John adjusted his new brogans.

"And I told you it's bad luck to wear a dead man's shoes."

John settled back to sleep. "You may be right, but if we have to wait another six months for resupply and those sutlers keep on skinning folks alive for a new pair of shoes, I'll take my chance with a dead man's boots."

William pulled his drumsticks from his haversack and tapped out a long roll on the deck of the boat.

John looked out over the river, interrupting William. "You heard what the captain said, right?"

William paused for a moment. "You mean about Grant?"

John continued, "Yeah, he took Fort Henry on the sixth and Donelson on the sixteenth."

William did not seem to care. "Um, hurrah for Grant."

John looked at his brother with concern. "You don't seem so pleased. What's wrong with you? You comin' down with the trots?"

William shook his head and continued to tap out the long roll. John continued, "Good, Moffett said the regiment has lost 15 percent total to sickness since we left the state. We're starting to thin out, and so are you."

William looked at his brother. "Livin' off hardtack and salt pork isn't going to put on any weight now, is it?"

John agreed, "I suppose not, and top that with a ten-mile hike every day."

William stopped his drumming and gave his brother a hard, solemn look.

John seemed more concerned now. "What? You okay?" William grinned. "Her name is Mary."

John broke into a long laugh. "So that's it! You are sick! Hey, everyone! Gather around! Our little drummer boy is lovesick!"

Some of the men moved in to get in on the joke.

William was not pleased with the heckling he was getting. "Yeah? Maybe I am lovesick. So what? She gave me her address and asked me to write."

Sergeant Major Moffett stepped into the group. "Don't let these sad sacks tease you. If you have a sweetheart to write to, that's a good thing. Let's see those flowers she gave you."

William reached into the breast pocket of his tunic and pulled out the squashed small bouquet.

Moffett took a close look and sniffed the flowers. "Ah! Forget-me-nots. Nice." He handed them back to William.

William got up and headed to the railing of the boat and leaned over. He dropped the flowers into the river stem by stem.

ON TO SHILOH

Oh! What a terrible scene does Shiloh's field present this morning. It is a scene of death; its victims lay everywhere. The blood of about thirteen thousand warriors has been shed here in the last two days. My God! What a sacrifice, what a flow of blood. But liberty has claimed it for an emancipated mind, and may it water well the great tree of universal freedom and cause it to extend its branches fosteringly over a struggling people. In these two days of battle, the Seventh sustained a heavy loss.

—Diary of Private Daniel L. Ambrose
Tuesday, April 8, 1862

John stepped to his brother's side and put his arm around his shoulder. "Lovesick, I can handle, but just don't get sick on me. I don't want to have to leave you in a hospital as all those others we left behind in Louisville. Sergeant Moffett? What was the final tally at the Mills Springs fight?"

Moffett answered, "Thirteen killed. Thirty-three wounded. No missing. Another fifteen disabled by sickness. But hopefully they'll soon catch up to us."

"Where will that be?"

"We're on our way to Nashville, boys! And what's in Nashville, you ask?"

The boys nodded.

"Grant and Sherman. I suspect something big is about to happen. At the least, we are to gain control of all the rivers."

John turned to ask Moffett another question. "How many days of this easy sailing do you think we'll get?"

"Depending on what stops we have to make, I'd put us in Nashville by the fourth of March. So get some rest now while you can because you can expect we'll be marching a long way to catch up with the rest of the army."

William nudged his brother. "I'll take that week of easy livin'." William and John and some of the others dropped their knapsacks and bedrolls, then laid them out on the deck and proceeded to drift off into slumber.

On the twenty-eighth, the regiment arrived at Smithland and entered the Cumberland and passed Fort Donelson on the first of March and Clarksville on the second, arriving at Nashville the next day. On the fourth, they disembarked and encamped about three miles out of the city on the Granny White Pike. Here they had a pleasant and healthy camp and fine spring weather. Ample supplies of clothing, rations, and ammunition were issued and accumulated; and a good many of the sick and slightly wounded, who had been left behind, now joined the regiment for duty. Meantime, arrangements had been made for a junction of Buell's and Halleck's forces to be affected near the great bend of the Tennessee River, Savannah, on the east bank, being finally designated by General Halleck as the point.

On the sixteenth of March, McCook's division of Buell's army commenced the march toward the appointed rendezvous, followed in order, one day apart, by those of Nelson, Crittenden, Wood, and Thomas. The division which included the Minnesota boys, having had a battle already, was, in this new campaign, assigned to the rear of the column and marched on the twentieth, passing through the city and out on the Franklin Pike some eight or ten miles. On the twenty-first, they passed through Franklin and camped a few miles south of the village, remaining there on the twenty-second.

On the 23d, their division moved up two or three miles to Spring Hill, and here they found the road in front of them occupied by the camps and trains of the preceding divisions. The bridge over Duck River at Columbia had been destroyed. The river was at flood height. No pontoons or other bridge material was available, and the divisions all waited six days for the water to subside. On the twenty-ninth, a bridge was improvised. A ford, deep and rapid but practicable with care, was found; and the crossing commenced. It was slow and tedious work, and it was not until the second of April that the rear division (including the Second Minnesota) had a clear way to proceed.

On the fourth, the road in front of them was so obstructed with the trains of the other divisions that they remained in camp; it was raining heavily all day and night. On this day, General Grant telegraphed, in reply to Nelson's message of the third, that he could be in Savannah with his division on the fifth and that he, Nelson, need not hasten his march as transports to convey him to Pittsburgh Landing would not be ready before the eighth. The rain ceased on the fifth, and the regiment marched about twelve miles, keeping close up to the column leading them.

The next day, the sixth, the troops ahead of them seemed to be showing more speed; and they began to pass the wagon trains as they overtook them instead of keeping behind them as they typically had been doing. So notwithstanding the bad condition of the roads and the frequent detours to pass around the stalled trains, they marched twenty-two miles before dark. During the afternoon, whenever they halted for rest, they could hear the rumbling of the cannonade in the distant west; and they knew that a great battle was in progress. About sunset, it began to rain again and grew so dark that a man in the column could scarcely see his file leader within arm's reach. Still they tramped on—tired, cold, wet, and hungry—until about eleven o'clock, when the brigade was turned into a soft-plowed cotton field to spend the rest of the night. The situation here would have been utterly forlorn had it not been enlivened by the order at midnight "to cook three days' rations and be ready to march at 4:00 a.m." The cooking was omitted, but they were ready to march at daybreak.

Heavy rain fell on the federal column of soldiers as it marched at a quick step. The wagon train ahead of them has slowed to a stop at a pontoon bridge.

Colonel Van Cleve, sitting high in the saddle, urged his men of the Second Minnesota forward. "Come on, boys! Let's pass this train! How about we beat the supply wagons for once?"

The Simmons brothers huffed and puffed as they sprinted forward to catch up with their colonel.

Van Cleve saw William running up and called out to him, "Drummer! You there! Boy! Hold up."

William stopped next to Van Cleve's horse.

Van Cleve pointed to William and called out an order, "Give me a double quickstep."

William was quick to respond, saluted, and pulled his drumsticks from his sling. "Yes, sir!"

As William beat out a double-quick cadence, John moved in next to his brother. He looked up at Van Cleave, who was about to move on. "What's the big rush, sir?"

Van Cleve steadied his horse. "Word has it Grant and Sherman are about to move on Johnston's army at Pittsburgh Landing. If we hurry, we can get in on this one."

"How much further?" "Couple of more days at least."

John was a bit puzzled. "At this pace?"

Van Cleve smiled and turned in his saddle. "You don't want to miss the big show, do you?"

John was now a bit excited at the prospect of a big battle and also that the colonel was speaking to him. "Is this going to be a big one?"

Van Cleve urged his horse to walk on to cross the river. He looked down at the boys as he left. "The rebs have got two full army corps down there up against our eight full divisions. If we get there in time, yes, we can end the war right here and now."

John turned to William. "Come on, Will! The first one across gets a kiss from Mary!"

William was not humored. "Not on your life! She's all mine!"

The boys raced for the river as William sped up the tempo of his drumbeat. Van Cleve waved his men forward, and there was a rush to ford the overflowing river.

"That's the tempo, boys! Let's go get 'em!"

The first company of soldiers came to a quick stop as they saw the hold up at the river's edge. A battery of cannon was stuck in the mud, its caisson wheels buried up to the axle. The horses couldn't budge as they were stuck up to their fetlocks. The rushing water of the river was about to wash away the temporary log bridge the pioneers had set in place earlier in the day. The gun crew worked to lift the cannon up and out of the mud while teamsters struggled to urge the horses on. William slung his drum, put his sticks in his sling, and joined in to help the men. John followed.

The gun crew sergeant hollered at the boys, "You boys, git! Git out of here before that bridge goes!"

Van Cleve rode up. "You heard him! Go on! Lead the regiment across! And, drummer, keep that tempo going."

"Yes, sir, Colonel!" said William as he reached for his sticks again.

The brothers dashed across the bridge moments before it was washed away. The rest of the regiment followed, but most had to wade or swim across in the onrush of water.

The halts on the seventh were few and short, but their progress in the wretched condition of the road was slow and tedious though they marched toward the sound of the guns all day. The regiment arrived at Savannah in the afternoon of the eighth to spend another night in the rain without shelter, but the men had the time before dark to select a grass field and get fuel for their bivouac. The rain had stopped, and the moon shone brightly over the wide-open cotton field. The regiment settled in for the night. John, William, and a few of the other musicians sat around a campfire in front of their huge Sibley tent. Sergeant Major Moffett joined his boys.

61

As Moffett made himself welcome, John asked of him, "What's the order, Sergeant?"

Moffett poked at the fire. "Prepare three days' rations. Cook if you have time, but be prepared to march at 4:00 a.m."

William couldn't believe what he has just heard. "That's just over four hours from now!"

Moffett silenced him with firm words, "You wanted the order? Well, that's it. Also… I've been told the road ahead is as bad as what it was today, if not worse. We've got about seventy-five miles ahead of us. There will be a lot of stopping and running as there was today."

Thunder rumbled in the distance, and all turned their heads in the direction of the sound.

William asked of Moffett, "Is that a thunderstorm headed our way? I don't know if we can take much more rain."

"No…that's the sound of cannon fire." "It's that loud from that far away?"

Moffett rose and prepared to move on. "Yep, and we just keep marching toward that sound until it's so loud you can't think."

John elbowed William. "Oh, boy! This really could be the big one! Sergeant Major?"

"What is it, Simmons 1?"

"There's a rumor going around that all musicians will be issued rifles and falling in with the ranks. Is that true?"

William replied with a smile, "I sure hope so."

Moffett began to move away from his charges. "That's partially true, yes. All those who can't carry a tune will take up arms, but it seems the colonel has taken a fondness for both Simmons 1 and Simmons 2, which means you two will stay as you are."

The other musicians jeered and mocked the brothers. Moffett started to walk off.

John asked as he left, "But why us?"

Moffett halted a moment to answer him. "Beats me, but don't worry. You'll see the elephant soon enough of it, just doing your regular battlefield duties."

John punched his brother in the shoulder out of disappointment. "Ah, shucks, Will…"

John did not sleep at all as he knew he must blow reveille an hour before the regiment moved out. The regiment formed up without any breakfast. Men pulled whatever hardtack was left in their haversacks or any other foodstuff, maybe a potato or carrot, and munched as they marched.

The progress in these wretched conditions of the road was slow and tedious though they continued their march toward the sound of the guns. The march was long, and well after dark, they straggled into another open field. This one was wet and somewhat gravelly, which would mean another sleepless or restless night. The regiment was preparing to bivouac in a large open grass field. The soldiers milled about looking for fuel for fires to spend another night in the rain with little or no shelter.

Moffett once again gathered around his small company of musicians.

"Gather round, boys, and listen up. We are only here for the night. In the morning, steamers will take us upriver to Pittsburg Landing. There was a hell of a battle the last two days at a place called Shiloh just above the river. Yes, we missed the battle. But the good news is Sherman and Grant took the day and have held the field."

A disgruntled William spoke up, "Late to the dance once again. So what are they doing with us if it's all over?"

"Grant is chasing what's left of Johnston's army into Mississippi, and we'll catch him there, but first rest as best you can because tomorrow we head to the battlefield and bury our dead."

John moaned, "This is not what I signed up for."

"It is what you signed up for. Okay now, enough grousing. Get as much rest as you can. Those steamers will be waiting at sunrise. Stack your arms and cover your instruments! That's all."

Before Moffett departed, John once again spoke up, "Any news on when our wagons, tents, and supplies will arrive?"

"We've outmarched the entire train. It may be several days before they catch up. Do the best you can with what you have."

And so the regiment turned in. Most were just relieved the march was over for the day, and they rested contentedly having missed the battle. Still some mumbled among themselves in the disappointment of having been denied being part of the big fight.

The next morning, April 9, steamers came to Savannah; and embarking, they were taken up to Pittsburgh Landing, where at noon they stacked arms and rested on the Shiloh battlefield. The weather had cleared up, and though their wagons and tents did not arrive for several days, they were comfortable enough without them. The burial of the dead and collection of the wounded would now fully occupy a large portion of the men for two or three days. The musicians would be getting the brunt of the dirty work.

The regiment was marched to the river's edge, and they boarded two steamers at Pittsburg Landing. Two navy gunboats with siege mortars were docked nearby, and they lobbed their large ordinance over the bluffs and toward the Shiloh battlefield. John and William mingled with the others on deck in search of a spot to lie down. They found an open space and slid down next to a couple of other soldiers. John nodded off, and William nudged him awake.

"What good is all that shelling going to do if this is just a mop-up operation?"

John opened his eyes. "I think they are just trying to make sure no rebs come back to reclaim the field."

The noise did not seem to bother John. William, on the other hand, was quite unsettled by it.

"That makes sense, but they sure are loud about it. How's a guy supposed to get any sleep in this army?"

John rolled on his side to confront his brother. "Just put it out of your mind. Tell me. What was it that Mary said in that letter to you? That should calm you down."

William reached into his breast pocket and removed the letter. He read from it, "I hope you and your brother are well and you finish up with your hero business soon. And when you finish your business, wherever you are, maybe you two could come back to Louisville and find some business here."

John smiled slyly at his brother. "There! Do you see? She said 'you two,' not just you. That means she likes me too."

William playfully slapped the letter across John's face. "Oh yeah? Well, who is she addressing her letter to?"

John rolled back over to continue his nap. "All right, well, maybe you could ask if she has a friend. But I prefer she has a nice figure just like Mary. I don't want any big-arsed German women."

William nodded and replied, "Sure, I'll ask. Are you taking a fancy to these bony Southern gals?"

John mumbled, then fell fast asleep. "I guess, if that's all there is to look at, one can get used to it."

William was finally able to shake off the noise of the shelling; and he, too, fell off to sleep. The short trip upriver was soon over; and the regiment was woken not from the shelling, which had now ended, but by the yelling of the sailors who were now bringing the boats into their dockage. The regiment rose from its collective slumber. They picked up their equipment and weapons and fell in line to disembark. Still half asleep, they marched off the boats in good order, drummers tapping out a simple, relaxing route-step beat.

The regiment marched in columns of four onto a clearing of the battlefield. All heads were rubbernecking to get a glimpse of what was in store for them. They were given the order to stack arms, which they did, then they were ordered to fall out and rest. Some of the men were anxious to see the sights and the remains of the battle. John and William were among them, and while others prepared the tents and camp, they walked off across the torn landscape. They were followed by a younger drummer from a different company of the regiment. His name was Vandyke.

He was fourteen years old, tall and lanky, and didn't look as young as he was.

John looked over his shoulder at him. "Who is that guy following us?"

William paused to look back and then responded, "Oh, that's Vandyke. He transferred into the regiment from a company of the Ninth Ohio after the Mill Springs battle."

John was now puzzled. "Why? Was that company surrendered?" Vandyke overheard them and rushed forward to join in. "We were on provost guard duty during the battle, and after the battle, they sent all the musicians home, but I wanted to stay. I prefer not to go back to my home. So they said, if I could find a regiment that would take me, I could transfer, so I did."

William introduced Vandyke to John, "This is my brother, John." Vandyke extended his hand. "Nice to meet you, John."

John shook his hand and then turned to his brother. "How long have you known this guy?"

"We've had stockade guard duty together the past two weeks."

Vandyke stepped off to the side, not wanting to impose on the brothers. "Sorry if I'm a bother. I can leave you guys alone if you like."

John opened to him nicely. "No, that's okay. You can tag along. We're just going to forage some wood and try to make lunch. Join us and help if you like. By the way, how old are you?"

The three walked off together.

Vandyke answered, "Sure, I'd like to help. I can build a fire. I'm fourteen."

John gave him a curious look. "Um, fourteen? Are you old enough to drink coffee?"

Vandyke seemed happy to have made another acquaintance. "Ma won't let me, and Pa give me a lickin' if I do, but since I've been in… yeah, I drink it as often as anybody. Don't much like the taste, though. Would rather have chocolate with it."

William joined the conversation, "I don't think we are going to find any chocolate out here."

"Well, we'll have plenty of time tomorrow, I hear, for rummaging through haversacks."

"What did you hear?"

Vandyke was quick to respond, "The entire regiment is on burial detail starting tomorrow. So I reckon we can make better use of anything we find than those poor dead boys can."

The boys then had to cross a small creek. With a couple of quick jumps, they cleared it easily, but they turned and halted on the other side. Dead men were lying in the mud on the edge of the creek. Their bodies were mixed up with sacks of grain and government stores. Some were lying in the water and others trampled entirely out of sight in the deep mud. This was where the great stampede over the Union camp occurred, and the boys were left speechless as they stood in awe at the horrible sight before them. The boys soon shook off the ugly sight and carried on with their walk across the battlefield. The rumbling of the gunboats could be heard in the distance, and the shells fell far ahead of them out of their immediate danger. The boys continued up a hill to Shiloh church, took a quick look around at the carnage, and then headed back to their bivouac area.

John spoke first, "Well…that was something to see."

William shook his head in disgust. "I've seen enough for today."

Vandyke changed the subject, "When are those transports supposed to arrive with our backpacks and other gear?"

"I suspect it's going to be a few days," said John.

William added, "We should start making shelter like the others are doing. I'm sick of all this rain and sleeping in these wet clothes." Vandyke contributed, "Without our tents, shelter halves, or rubber blankets, what do we do? You can see it's going to be another rain-filled night."

The boys made their way to a tree line and, like the other men were doing, started to strip bark from the trees and began laying it on the ground for a simple ground cover. With boughs from pine trees, they built themselves a lean-to shelter. Vandyke started a fire while John and William finished up with the shelter. Vandyke was having a difficult time getting the fire started.

"Willy? You got any dry pine cones?" William nodded. "Yeah, right here."

William tossed his haversack to Vandyke. It was full of cones. Vandyke tore into them and pulled them apart to find the dried wool on the fibers of the cones. He packed the fibers into a small roll of tinder and then struck steel to flint to make a spark. Soon he had a fire going. The three comrades now settled in for the evening under the comfort of their new shelter.

At 4:00 a.m., John, standing in the center of the field, sounded reveille. The camp slowly came to life. Campfires were being restoked; and a breakfast of lard, hardtack, and coffee was being prepared by the small huddles of men about the camp. The rain had stopped, and the sun began to heat the men. As the men walked about in the morning sun, steam rose from their wet wool uniforms. The men all knew what the day would bring, and they traded their instruments and rifles for shovels.

As soon as the men had eaten, they wandered out onto the battlefield. The three companion musicians made their way across the Shiloh battlefield. They carried picks and shovels as did most of the other members of the regiment. They made their way over broken-down fences and fallen timber to look over the field. As they wove their way through the dead troops lying in the front of the fence line, they saw scattered groups of men discussing the battle and its results, relating exciting incidents and adventures of the fray. Here was one fellow pointing out bullet holes in his coat or cap. In the distance, the dead were laid out in every direction and every stage of decomposition. There were squads of men scattered all over the field digging trenches and rolling the dead into them.

The boys came upon a tree on the side of the field where the Confederates made their last stand. The tree was riddled with shot, and its bark and leaves were shattered. Carved into the tree was the name of the Confederate general Johnston. At the base of the tree was a lump of earth that covered his body.

William pointed to the grave. "So this is where the great general fell."

John nodded and replied, "At least he got a somewhat-proper burial."

Vandyke was not convinced. He pointed to where animals had been digging at the grave. "Three inches of dirt over a body is a proper burial? The birds and hogs will be picking at his bones in no time."

John responded, "He'll keep long enough until they can get him shipped off to his home."

Vandyke kicked at the fresh dirt over the body. "I don't know about that. Have you seen the wild hogs around these parts?"

William lit up. "Yeah, and maybe we should think about getting us one for dinner."

The boys moved off to join the others. As they walked on, they saw more of the destruction left from the battle. The battlefield was strewn with the wreck and carnage of war. Caissons, dismounted cannon, and dead artillery horses and their dead riders were piled up in heaps; and the warm sun caused an unbearable stench. The boys removed cloths from their haversacks and covered their faces from the stink. Here they saw where a wounded soldier had been pinned to the ground by a fallen limb of a tree, and the shells set fire to the dry leaves. The poor fellow had been burned alive to a crisp. Here again another fellow pointed out a great tear in the sleeve of his blouse made by a flying piece of shell; there a man was laughing as he held up his crushed canteen and showed off his tobacco box with a hole in the lid and a bullet among his fine cut. Yonder knots of men were frying pork and cooking coffee about their fires, making ready for lunch.

The boys passed beyond what was the front and evidence of the terrible carnage before them. On all sides were hastily dug graves with crude headboards telling a poor fellow's name and regiment; yonder was a tree on whose smooth bark the names of two other Confederate generals who fell here in the gallant charge had been carved by some thoughtful fellow. The trees around about were chipped by the bullets and stripped almost bare by the leaden hail while a log house nearby in the clearing had been so riddled with shot and shell that scarcely a whole shingle was left to its roof.

But the sights became more fearful as they stepped out beyond the front line. Here they picked their way carefully among the fallen timber and down the slope to the scene of that fearful Confederate charge. The ground was soaked with recent rain and was now mixed with blood and mud. The heavy noon mist, which hung like a pall over the field, forced the boys to squint at rendered objects indistinctly visible and all the ghastlier. As their eyes panned over so much of the field as the shrouding mist allowed them to see, they beheld a scene of destruction, terrible indeed, if there ever was one in this world of 1862. Dismounted gun carriages, shattered caissons, knapsacks, haversacks, muskets, bayonets, and accouterments were scattered over the field in the wildest confusion—horses, poor creatures, dead and dying, and, most awful of all, dead men by the hundreds.

Most of the Union soldiers had been buried already, and pioneers yonder in the mist were busily digging trenches for the poor fellows in gray. As they passed along, they stopped to observe. Bodies, mostly Confederate, were thickly lying here and there like grass before a scythe in the summertime. Some were dead in the position they died still looking defiant and grasping their guns. Others were so calm in their last solemn sleep.

William was sickened at the dreadful sight of a headless Confederate drummer. He kneeled to vomit and then begged his comrades to come away. "Come away, boys. I can't bear it anymore."

Vandyke knelt to comfort William. "Let's join that group of pioneers over there."

Vandyke pointed to a squad of Union pioneers who were rolling dead Confederates into a mass grave. He walked off in that direction. John took a knee next to his brother and urged him to follow. "Come on. The sooner we get those fellows underground, the sooner we can get some rest without the stink."

William rose, and the brothers jogged to catch up to Vandyke.

John said to his brother, "How can that boy stand it? He must have an iron gut."

William stopped to vomit again. "His father is a butcher." "I still don't see how that helps," answered John.

The boys toiled together under the sun for the remainder of the day.

As the sun began to set, Sergeant Major Moffett walked up to his charges and dismissed them. "Okay, boys, that's enough for tonight. Get back to camp, get some food in your bellies, and prepare for tomorrow."

"What's tomorrow?" asked John.

"Same as today, and I suspect the same the day after that or until we have this field cleaned up and all the dead covered."

The exhausted boys straggled back to their shelters and gathered their accouterments for making dinner.

John asked of his two partners, "What are we having tonight?" William replied first, "I dug some wild sweet potatoes and carrots. Got us two squares each of hardtack."

Then Vandyke answered, "And I got some bacon off a dead reb and still have some coffee beans to crush."

John seemed pleased enough. "So that gives us two square meals each for the day? Let's hurry it up. Moffett will be calling on me soon to blow taps, and I want to get some grub in me before then."

The boys finished their meals, and they wrapped themselves up in their damp wool blankets and turned in for another restless night of sleep. Before John could join his two bunkmates, he walked to the center of the camp and blew on his bugle taps. Campfires flickered out as the regiment rolled into their crude sleeping nests.

William rolled over to face Vandyke's back. "I sure hope those wagons get here soon. Mud is starting to seep up from under this bark, and I think I'm coming down with the trots."

John soon entered the shelter, and he pulled all three blankets over the boys. They snuggled together to gain as much body heat as they could off each other.

"This will all pass," he whispered.

The next couple of days would be a repeat of the work that had to be done to complete the mopping up of the battlefield. All that remained of the scars of war would be the lumps of dirt that marked shallow graves, shell holes, and the ripped-up fence lines and torn trees. In a few years, Mother Nature would cure all signs of there ever having been such a struggle of human insanity.

Before the regiment started its march toward Corinth, there would be promotions and discharges to deal with. The army leadership was constantly in a state of flux, and it seemed it would remain that way until the generals had a decisive plan. Here Colonel Van Cleve was promoted to brigadier general and mustered out of the regiment. Lieutenant Colonel George was promoted to colonel, Major Wilkin to lieutenant colonel, and Captain Bishop to major. All their commissions dated March 21, 1862.

As General Thomas had been assigned to command a corps, Brigadier General W. T. Sherman assumed command, with Thomas, of the division; and Lieutenant Colonel Wilkin was detailed as inspector general at his headquarters. He was on detached service thereafter most of the time until he was mustered out of the regiment on August 26, 1862, to become colonel of the Ninth Minnesota Volunteers. At this camp, the regimental band was mustered out on the twenty-fourth of April by the order of General Buell, and the men went home, leaving most of their instruments there in the woods. William and John were not mustered out, however, as the new colonel decided he still needed good buglers and drummers for each company for battlefield communication needs. Vandyke was sent to Company K along with William and John.

The musicians who were sent back home were good but did not take kindly to actual soldiering and were no doubt quite willing to quit there. General Halleck arrived at Shiloh on the eleventh of April and, after reorganizing the two armies of Buell and Grant and reinforcing them by the army of the Mississippi under Pope and by a division from Missouri and one from Arkansas, commenced the Siege of Corinth. It was nearly May when the regiment began its march toward Corinth. When the regiment was finally fallen into marching formation, Sergeant Moffett stood before his company of musicians, which was now reduced to just his best drummers and buglers. Heavy rain was falling and soaking the men through to the bone.

Moffett called the men to attention, then gave them their orders, "Okay, we've got about a five to six miles march ahead of us today in this drenching rain. After we make camp, General Sherman wants to inspect the division, so we must look our best! The good news is our wagons have caught up with us. Not only that, the teamsters will have set up your tents, and provisions will be put out for you. But orders are there are to be no fires in camp. We will be pushing on to Corinth, Mississippi. And one more thing, we are pursuing those rebs that ran from Shiloh."

The men groaned.

"That's right. Grant wants to destroy them now before they can regroup with Bragg's army. They're dug in at Corinth. Also, just to make this march as miserable as possible, we'll be stopping every few miles to throw up works and defensive positions as we move toward Corinth."

The sight of the regiment was one of a miserable, threadbare, waterlogged group of boys who looked like they could barely stand, let alone march a few miles.

Moffett barked out the order to march, "Okay! At the route step! Forward march!"

The drummers tapped out the steady, lazy beat as the entire regiment stepped off and slogged along the mud-filled and rutted road. Vandyke, William, and John marched side by side.

John looked at his brother. "How's your gut today?"

William moaned a bit. "About as empty as can be. But I think I'll be okay."

Vandyke spoke up, "Maybe they'll have some decent grub waiting for us in camp. I heard a couple of boys in the Ohio regiment got themselves a couple of hogs last night."

John added to what Vandyke has just said, "It's true. I talked to them, and they'll make a trade."

"What have we got to trade?" asked William.

"I got me a pile of reb souvenirs, and I know those boys. They'll trade," said Vandyke.

Moffett strolled alongside his men. He spoke to the three boys, "Keep this to yourselves, you three."

William gave him a puzzled look. "What's that?"

Moffett answered, "After we get to camp, Company K, along with you three, are all going out on picket duty."

A grin came over John's face. "Picket duty?"

"That's right. You'll all be issued a rifle and forty rounds." "Why us? Why now?" asked Vandyke.

Moffett gave them the news, "Orders from Grant. He says he wants everyone in a battle line, especially those without any combat experience."

The brigade was making a general advance and entrenchment of the Union lines about once a week, with almost daily skirmishing during the intervals, bringing them by the end of May in such a position that Corinth had to be defended or evacuated. A volley of explosions and a dense cloud of smoke in the front of the brigade at daybreak on the thirtieth of May announced the final departure of the Confederate Army, which, with persistence and impudence to be admired, had held the greatly superior Union force at bay for nearly two months.

The regiment marched into the vacated and desolate streets of Corinth that day with a feeling of disgust and humiliation at the escape of the enemy that they thought they ought to have captured or, at least, to have broken up and defeated. A show of pursuit had to be made, and they continued the march after the retreating enemy for several days, passing through Danville and Rienzi. After this, they moved out from the Corinth battlefield to make camp where the trains had caught up to the army and had set up camp again in a pleasant yet rocky field with shade and spring water. They had pulled back five or six miles from Corinth, and it seemed they were now in for a rest.

Large tents and all the other comforts that could be had in the camp were waiting for the regiment. They filed into camp and then immediately broke off into their separate small mess squads to get some food. The boys fell in line with other members of the regiment to get their share of dinner that had already been prepared by the cooks. With their tin plates and cups in hand, they moved along the food line. John was at the head of the line.

William was right behind him and asked his brother about the meal, "What's the fare there, John?"

John turned back to answer. "Wild hog, bread, sweet potatoes, and coffee, it looks like."

Vandyke, behind William, gave him a nudge. "That ought to go easy on your gut."

"I hope so, but you've seen how the trots come and go, then flare up again with some of the others. How many did we leave back at that hospital in Louisville?" asked William to John.

"A third of the regiment, I heard."

Vandyke filled his plate. "Ah, you'll be okay. I overheard there is an iron-infused spring nearby that the boys before us were bathing in, and it's been a cure-all for most all their ills."

William scoffed. "Bathing in iron water? I don't see how that could be any miracle cure."

"Well, I'm going to try it anyway. I need a good bath," said Vandyke.

William scoffed again. "Are you crazy? After almost a whole month of nonstop rain and you need a bath? I'll settle for some dry clothes and a warm blanket."

John filled his plate and started to leave the line. "When are they going to let us make some fires?"

William and Vandyke caught up to him.

"I heard, after we capture those rebs, we'll get a long rest," Vandyke said to the other two.

William countered sarcastically, "Yeah, we rest when we're dead, right, John?"

"That's what Pa always used to say."

Their work at Corinth ended on May 28. General Sherman inspected the regiment as it marched by in review with the rest of the brigade. With Corinth no longer an objective, the troops not involved with the actual siege were very demoralized. They had been prepared for battle and looked forward to it very much. But the army would soon be on the move again. At least the rain had stopped for the time being, and spring was in the air. The songbirds had now replaced the scream of shells and distant explosions.

When Sherman had completed his review, the regiment was told to stand easy. Vandyke reached into his haversack and cartridge box, then started to unload ammunition, dropping the unspent cartridges onto the ground. William and John looked around and noticed the entire regiment emptying their sacks and pockets, spreading their unspent cartridges onto the ground as well. William and John started to dump their cartridges too.

William spoke up in disgust, "Three weeks, we've been dragging around over one hundred rounds each. What for? Not even a single minor skirmish."

John agreed. "What's the point? I doubt we'll ever get into a real battle."

Vandyke was not so agreeable. "After seeing Shiloh, are you sure you want to get into the fray? I'm glad they're running off. I'm no hero."

William added to the debate, "Well, I'm beginning to think General Halleck is a fool. Here he has one of the finest-trained and equipped armies of one hundred thousand strong in the Union, and he's just using us as bait or, worse yet, ditch diggers."

John scoffed. "One hundred thousand strong? More like fifty thousand strong and fifty thousand sick."

Sergeant Moffett strolled up to the gang. "Boys! Pick up those rounds and get ready to move on the works. This siege isn't over with yet. There are still rebels in there." Moffett pointed. "Look through those trees. We're only about a hundred rods from where the rebel works were. No more talk about the general! The rest of the division has had Corinth under siege for the better part of the month. They're driving the last of them out now, and we are to walk in and hold the city and rebuild the crossroads. You may get your skirmish yet."

William was not convinced. "So? Why do we need the extra weight of these rounds if all we are going to do is work as laborers? Why don't Halleck use all those darkies that have been following us for the past weeks?"

Moffett was not about to argue. "Enough! Just get ready to fall in and take those works! We move out in ten minutes."

Soon the regiment was called to duty. The Second Minnesota Company marched up to the outer works of what had been the Confederate fort at Corinth, Mississippi. The Union siege guns had done a great deal of destruction. A few dead Confederates were draped over their protective works. The regiment came to a halt behind their skirmish line. The skirmish line fired off sporadic shots at the last of the retreating rebels. With the complete rout of the Confederates, the boys were set to work once again as laborers, toiling with pick and shovel. This time, their manual labor duties involved tearing up the railroad crossroads of Corinth, Mississippi.

William started complaining once again, "Okay, tell me again why we are doing this and not off chasing the rebs back home."

Vandyke had an answer. "The Confederate secretary of war called this intersection the backbone of the Confederacy. To lose it would be a sure bet in losing the war."

John responded, "I'm okay with that, but I think it's having more impact on my backbone than theirs."

The other two nodded in agreement and carried on with the work until Vandyke interjected more.

"And General Halleck says our capture of this town renders Southern control of anything west of Tennessee meaningless, which means we have stopped all movement of arms, munitions, and other supplies to the enemy. Better yet, General Sherman says this opens the door for us to now strike Vicksburg or Chattanooga."

John paused to gape at Vandyke. "Okay, General, does that mean we are going on the offensive?"

At this point, Moffett walked up. "You boys will see some action soon enough. But for now, let's get this railhead secured. We move out again tomorrow." Moffett noticed William grimace in pain as he leaned on his shovel. "Are you okay, Simmons 2?"

Vandyke explained, "He's still sick with the trots."

Moffett was not sympathetic. "So is most of the battalion, Private. No excuse to stop. You boys will have plenty of time to rest." "Yeah, when we're dead from being worked to death," replied John sarcastically.

Moffett was a bit more encouraging now. "Just tough it out for one more day. Tomorrow we move to clean ground, and then soon we'll begin our long march back to Louisville. It may take a while to get there, but when we get close to the rivers, we'll have supply boats waiting for us with medicine and a surgeon."

The next day, they moved three miles east from Corinth, where they got several days of rest on fresh, clean ground. Some reorganization had been going on, however, in their absence; and they found General Thomas again in command of the division. Preparations were soon completed for a new campaign. Buell's army had been projected eastward with Chattanooga and East Tennessee as the apparent objectives; and the divisions of McCook, Crittenden, and Nelson were already well advanced in that direction when, on the twenty-second of June, the brigade broke camp and commenced the march along the Memphis and Charleston Railroad, repairing it as they went along and reaching Iuka Springs on the twenty-fifth.

The other two brigades of the division were several days' march in advance of the entire brigade, and as they moved eastward, troops from Grant's army followed and were stationed in detachments to guard the railroad bridges left behind them. At Iuka, they were paid off for two months, chiefly in the then-new postal currency which they had not before seen. On the twenty-seventh, the march eastward was again resumed, and the regiment arrived on the twenty-ninth at Tuscumbia, Alabama. Here they camped in an open field just at the edge of the village and near a remarkably copious spring of pure water.

General Thomas's division was assembled again; and on the Fourth of July, which was also William's sixteenth birthday, they had a national salute from the three batteries and a grand parade of the twelve regiments, after which some appropriate and patriotic addresses were made by generals Steedman and McCook and perhaps others. Governor Ramsey of Minnesota, coming from Washington, visited shortly afterward, though briefly allowing him to compare the Second Minnesota Regiment with those from other states; and he was, as he said, quite satisfied with their representation of the state.

Finding themselves located here for some considerable time, their camp was put in good order and made comfortable, and the usual course of company and battalion drill and instruction was instituted. The company musicians, who, in the presence of the band, had been quite overlooked if not forgotten, were hunted up and investigated. Those who were not, in fact, musicians were exchanged in their companies for other men who were or could become such. A principal musician was appointed. Bugles and fifes and drums were supplied to them, and the same discipline was applied to them that prevailed with the other men of the regiment. A few weeks of faithful instruction and practice made them quite proficient in martial music, and the drum and bugle corps of Second Minnesota received a good deal of attention and commendation from the other regiments and were much appreciated by their men.

On the twenty-sixth of July, their pleasant camp was broken up, and they crossed the Tennessee River to Florence. On Tuesday, the twenty-ninth of July, they marched again eastward. The weather was hot and the road dusty, but there seemed to be no urgent haste. Their progress was leisurely and comfortable. The great fields, erewhile in cotton, were now all in corn and afforded plenty of roasting ears for the soldiers and forage for the mules. The darkies came in troops from every plantation as they passed and joined the "Lincum sogers," bringing horses, mules, cattle, pigs, poultry, bedding, and everything else they could lead or carry. They had just begun to realize what the war meant to them, and they were quite ready to go out from bondage, despoiling their old masters as they went.

On the third of August, they marched through Athens, Tennessee. This was a lovely village and had been noted as the last place in the state to haul down the Union flag. On the seventh of August 1862, they arrived at Winchester, Tennessee, where they remained twelve days. About this time, Company C of the Third Minnesota Regiment was attached to the Second Regiment. This company was on detached duty when the regiment was surrendered at Murfreesboro, July 13, 1862; and pending the exchange and return of their comrades, it was sent to the Second Regiment for duty. It was a fine company of soldiers and remained with them for several weeks, leaving on the thirtieth of September for Minnesota, where they would join the remainder of the Third Regiment in putting down the Dakota rebellion which was sweeping over the state.

On the nineteenth of August, the Second Regiment moved from Winchester to Decherd and thence, by short marches and intermediate halts of one to three days, to Pelham Gap, thus consuming the time to August 31 while Bragg's forces were making their way across the mountains and around the left flank of the Union forces toward Nashville. During these days, they got news of the Indian outbreak and massacre in Minnesota, which created much apprehension and excitement as many of their men had families or friends in the threatened frontier counties. Lieutenant Colonel Alex Wilkin was, on the twenty-sixth of August, appointed colonel of the Ninth Minnesota Regiment; and Major J. W. Bishop was commissioned as lieutenant colonel and would take over command of the Second Minnesota, also Captain J. B. Davis of Company F as major of Second Minnesota from the same date. Adjutant S. P. Jennison, about the same time, was appointed lieutenant colonel of the Tenth Minnesota Regiment; and Lieutenant Charles F. Meyer took the vacated place as adjutant of the Second.

On the first of September, they marched to Manchester; and their wagon trains with tents and baggage having been sent via Murfreesboro to Nashville, they encamped for the night in the fair-ground buildings. The next day, they resumed the march toward Murfreesboro, arriving there on the fourth. Pursuing a northward march, they arrived at Nashville on the seventh and encamped at the edge of the city. Most of the army had already crossed the Cumberland, but it was given out that the brigade would remain at Nashville, which they did for a week while the divisions north of the river were watching Bragg's movements. By the fourteenth, his army was across the river at points higher up the river and farther north than Nashville. The race for Louisville began.

The Union brigade left Nashville on the fourteenth, crossed the river, and encamped just north of Edgefield. Here they received five days' rations of flour, coffee, and sugar only. No clothing or shoes, which were especially needed. In the next three days, they marched on the hard, dusty pike seventy miles to Bowling Green. Here, on the eighteenth, more rations of flour were issued; and they crossed the Barren River, in which they found the first supply of drinkable water since leaving the Cumberland. On the nineteenth of September, they marched a full twenty-five miles and, on the twentieth, overtook the other divisions and, passing through their camps, came up to the enemy's rear picket line near Cave City, where they extended their line of battle to right and left and posted a picket line, confronting the enemies' line.

This was the seventh day of the march, which was without a parallel in their experience thus far. It was the dry season of the year, and in this part of Kentucky, there was no living water except the Barren River between the Green and Cumberland Rivers. The farmers had depended on a scanty supply on the sinkholes, which were saucerlike depressions in the fields with clay subsoil bottoms, which filled with water in winter and spring but, at this season, were nearly exhausted by evaporation. Then Bragg's men were ahead of them anyway, and they made it their business to enrich the already viscid water with dead mules and camp offal of all sorts so it could not be drunk and could hardly be used to mix their "dough gods." These were made by moistening flour on a rock with water; and after pounding it into a tough dough, it was spun into a long roll about an inch in diameter, wound around a ramrod, and so baked.

These, with scanty rations of bacon, constituted a depressingly thin diet for the hard service required of the army. They had no tents or cooking utensils or baggage of any sort, except such as was carried on pack mules or the men's backs, and even these had become sadly deficient as they had not been able to get any supplies at Nashville. Occasionally they got apples or peaches off the trees along the road, but generally they were cleaned off by the troops ahead of them. On this last evening, they got orders to cook three days' rations and prepare for a battle that would probably take place the next day. The enemy, however, moved on early next morning; and the footrace began again. Their division, however, remained in camp while the others passed on and took the road ahead of them.

On the twenty-second of September, they moved camp about two miles to a place near Cave City, where, at the bottom of a natural pit about a hundred feet deep, an underground stream of pure water came to the light. A steep path and steps led down to it; and all day long, it was alive with soldiers, each laden with as many canteens as he could carry. The boys spent the day mainly filling up, like camels, with cold, fresh water in preparation.

On the twenty-third, they started again, crossing Green River about noon, and camped at Bacon's Creek after a march of about twenty miles. On the twenty-fourth, they started at daybreak and marched fast all day, making thirty miles, and halted for the night four or five miles north of Elizabethtown. The race was now telling on the footsore rebels also; and during that and the previous day, they passed their exhausted stragglers to the number of several hundred, leaving them to be gathered up as prisoners by the rear guard. Bragg's army was, however, ahead of them and within a one-or two-day march of Louisville. The next day, they left the railroad and parallel pike and went straight to the Ohio River at the mouth of the Salt River, making the twenty miles in less than seven hours and reaching the riverbank about noon a tired, hungry, footsore crowd.

"Thank God for the Ohio River and hardtack!" exclaimed the champion grumbler of the regiment. "I'll never complain again."

Here were the steamers that Moffett had promised over two months ago. The next day, they were to be embarked also but not before Moffett appeared with news for the boys.

At the junction of these two rivers, not far from Louisville, the regiment was halted and lined the banks of the river. There was a supply boat anchored out of reach of the boys sitting square in the river. William sat down on the dusty edge of the river and reached for the blood-soaked rags that were wrapped around his feet that made up an excuse for shoes. He looked down the line at other members of his company. Several other soldiers were in just as bad condition—threadbare and worn-out uniforms, shoe less, and with deep expressions of anger, confusion, exhaustion, and misery. Those still standing yelled and waved to the riverboat captain to come to shore and unload. Their hollering was met with a blast from the boat's whistle and nothing more. The boys continued to beg for him to throw off some pork and hardtack, but he refused.

The new colonel Bishop then rode up on his horse to quiet his men. "Boys! All your hollering will do no good! Go back to camp and wait. As soon as he sees you are gone, he'll feel safe enough to land, and your provisions will be off-loaded. Captains! Take charge of your companies and lead them back to camp!"

The officers fell out and issued orders to their respective companies to fall in. They were led back to camp.

As Moffett and his company of newly formed musicians filed past the colonel, he stopped the sergeant. "Sergeant Major, I realize you boys have been marching for ten straight days in this hot sun and dust, living off nothing but doughboys and sassafras tea, but I want your company to stay here and help the teamsters load their wagons."

Moffett saluted and asked, "One favor, sir? After we finish, may we ride in with the wagons?"

"Of course," said Bishop.

They exchanged salutes, and Bishop rode off to catch up with his regiment.

Moffett turned to his company. "Okay, boys! You heard the man! Let's go!"

With much grousing and grumbling, the men turned back to the river's edge. They sat and waited for the boats to dock. As usual, John, William, and Vandyke worked as a team.

John was fuming with anger. "Work, work, and more work. I thought Pa was a mule driver, but this is crazy! I'm so angry, if I ever got my hands on a Reb, I'd tear him to shreds right now!"

William nodded. "I'm with you. This is not what I signed up for." Vandyke grumbled along with them. "Maybe that's the whole idea. They work us to a frenzy point where we don't care if we live or die, then set us loose on the enemy. We sure would fight like devil dogs then, wouldn't we?"

John agreed, "Yeah, we sure would, but they are not going to let us musicians into a fight."

"Don't be too sure about that. I hear Grant is breaking up all the musician companies in the entire western army and sending them home," replied Vandyke.

William scoffed. "So you've been saying, but they just formed a new regimental band."

Vandyke had an answer again, "Well, not everyone is going home. Only those who play in the band. Drums and bugles stay for communications, and a few regiments will keep their bands for entertainment and official parades, but they must be the best in the army, or they are out! At least that's what I overheard from Moffett."

William was not convinced. "Oh yeah? I say that's a rumor."

Vandyke was on top of it. "Nope, it's true. That's the word. We are to be transferred to the signal corps."

John now perked up. "Out of our state regiments into the regular army?"

Vandyke answered with certainty, "No. All regiments will have a separate signal corps company. We'll still be together."

"I'll believe it when I see it," said William.

Vandyke continued, "We may have to learn the signal flag Morse code, though."

John, now angered, slammed down a crate. "Why can't they just put us into the battle line? I am so sick of this kind of work with no end in sight."

"You'll be eighteen in less than a year. You can transfer in then," said Vandyke.

William nodded in agreement. The boys rolled the last of the barrels and crates down the ramp, then headed for the wagons and hopped on, making room for as many who could squeeze themselves on board. Moffett, John, William, Vandyke, and a few other soldiers sat on top of the crates, barrels, and sacks that they had loaded onto the wagon. The wagon wheels squealed as it bucked along a dusty Kentucky road.

John calmly asked of his Sergeant, "What's the news, Sergeant?"

Moffett sighed as he rested his back on a barrel. "A couple of days in camp to rest, then back on the steamers and up to Louisville again."

"Any news from back home?" asked John.

Moffett shook his head. "You all know about the Indian revolt, so nothing more there."

William joined in, "What about the old First? We haven't heard from our Pa in weeks."

Moffett set his mind at ease. "Seems they got into it a bit during the Peninsula Campaign but came out fairly well. We haven't seen a casualty list yet. I'm sure he's okay. As you can see, these teamsters get to play it safe."

Vandyke now joined the conversation, "What about the old Third Regiment?"

Moffett answered, "After they got surrendered, they went back home to help put down the Dakota. Word is they redeemed themselves well enough to join the ranks again as soon as they get exchanged for some of the rebs we took."

Vandyke appeared anxious. "If I get cut out of the regiment with the musicians, can I go back and join up with them? I mean, with all the musicians being discharged and all."

Moffett calmed him down. "Let's see how things shake out first. So far, I haven't any word on losing our music company, and I heard

Grant has taken a fancy to us. But I'll leave that up to you if it comes to having to lose the company. You can get out after we get to Louisville, or I can transfer you into this company. With the regiment thinning out as it is from disease, I'd like to keep you with us."

William lit up with joy. "Yeah! Do it, Otto!"

Vandyke smiled at the sound of his first name. "Otto? Nobody has called me that since I left Ohio."

Moffett shook his head. "Otto, hmm... With all the Ottos in the state, last names are better for the roster. Think about it, and while we are on the subject of Louisville, Simmons—"

"Which one?" remarked John.

"Simmons 2, I'm putting you in the hospital there so you can convalesce," said Moffett.

A wide smile came across William's face. Moffett added, "You feel good about that?"

John nudged his brother. "He thinks he has a girlfriend waiting for him."

William then shoved his brother aside. "Well... I get more mail from her than anyone. Maybe she will come and sit with me."

John laughed.

William continued, "You don't know anything about it, John!" The wagons finally reached their camp, where all the tents had been set up and food and new supplies were being distributed. The boys made their way to their tent and prepared for dinner. They got settled around a fire and were now wearing clean clothes and new boots. William rolled some wet dough around the end of a steel ramrod, then roasted it over the fire.

John eyed the roll of dough without expression. "I don't care if the colonel calls them dough gods, I'm gettin' kind of sick of eating these things."

William held out the roll to him. "They're doughboys, not gods."

John pushed it away. "The same thing, I guess, but what would an officer know about our dinner fare? I bet he's got himself a full plate of taters and pork right now."

Vandyke took the doughboy from William. "We'll get ours in Louisville."

William prepared another. "If not, I've had half a notion to roast me a doughboy for every officer in the regiment and shove it up his bung."

After a good laugh, the boys returned to their cooking.

The next few days were filled with the usual drill and replenishing of supplies. William's dysentery began to act up after a few more days even though the regiment was now at rest. Moffett then became true to his promise, and as the regiment was called on to parade through Louisville, Moffett saw to it that William was released from duty and had him assigned to the hospital for complete convalescence. At this time in the war, all men who had sided with the Confederacy had moved south to join regiments in states that had already seceded. Though Bragg was intent on reinforcing his army with Southern sympathizers from Kentucky, he found few. Louisville still raised the Union flag every day, and the city had many buildings converted into Union hospitals during the Civil War.

William was confined to one of the more splendid buildings overlooking the Ohio River. Compared to most Civil War military hospitals of the time, this facility had a full staff of nurses, cooks, and surgeons all operating in a clean and organized manner. After William was admitted to the hospital, John and Vandyke stayed with him for the first few hours to make sure he was well taken care of. They would visit every chance they got; and after a few days, William looked content enough, well-rested, and healthy enough for a young man who had just marched hundreds of miles on little food under the worst of conditions. A military surgeon by the name of Dr. Smith would be taking care of him, and to William's surprise one sunny morning, William was woken by the young and beautiful Mary. She sat on the edge of his bed and gently stroked his hair until he woke. Dr. Smith was standing nearby overlooking the two young lovers. "Well, Mary, is this the young man you are concerned about?"

William, upon recognizing Mary, sat up in bed to give her a good look. "How…how did you find me? How did you know I was here?"

Mary took a damp cloth and wiped his brow of sweat. "Quite easily. I saw in the newspaper that your regiment was returning to the city, and I got a ride to the camp and just asked where you were. John told me."

William was still in disbelief. "Your last letter said you were working in the Jefferson Barracks Hospital."

Mary shuddered in mock horror. "Oh, that place is just too horrid. It's all wounded. I asked for a transfer."

Dr. Smith gave his opinion of that, "She demanded it."

Mary continued, "All those poor gutshot boys, the amputations, the smell, and gore were just too much for me to stomach. I much prefer taking care of the sick instead of the wounded."

There was a wink and a nod from the doctor as he approved of her choice.

"And we find, the more pretty the nurse, the quicker the boys are up and out of here so we can make room for more of all you sickly ones."

Mary took his hand.

William, though shocked by this sudden move on her part, stuttered to find the words. "I'm sure glad to see you."

The doctor tapped her on her shoulder.

Mary rose to leave. "As I am to see you. I'm just grateful you are not in that other place."

The hospital was quite clean considering the standards of the time. Within the hospital, a large kitchen with all the needs were operating at full speed. African American freedmen and freedwomen rushed about preparing meals.

Dr. Smith motioned for Mary to stay at William's bedside. "I'll leave you two to catch up. It appears you have a lot to talk about. And, Miss Mary, see to it this boy gets regular good meals for the next couple of days so we can get him corked up and on the road to recovery."

Mary smiled, then spoke to William, "What have they been treating you with up until you got here?"

William grimaced. "The regimental surgeon had blue mass, but as you know, it doesn't work all that well."

Mary tucked in his blanket. "You'll get none of that here. Good food, fresh air, and plenty of sleep in a real bed are all you need."

William leaned back to rest. "Fresh air we got plenty of, but a soldier is always in need of sleep and good food."

Mary leaned over and touched his forehead. "Any fevers lately or blood in your stool?"

"Not since I got here," said William with a grin.

Mary checked his forehead for a fever. "That's a good sign. Just lie back and try to sleep. I'm going to go get you your lunch. Go to sleep. We can talk all about your adventures later."

"Okay, thank you," said William.

Mary headed off to the kitchen as William dozed off to sleep.

LITTLE CROW

*The Treaty of Traverse des Sioux, July 23, 1851, and
the Treaty of Mendota, August 5, 1851. With these
two treaties, the Sioux would lose most of their land
in a cash buyout. Little Crow would be blamed for
this. By 1862, only a small ten-mile strip of land
on the south side of the Minnesota river belonged
to the Dakota.*

Six hundred miles northwest of Louisville in Mendota, Minnesota,
the situation in the summer of 1862 turned violent. Most Dakota
families were desperate; annuity payments were late due to the US
government's priority in financing the Civil War. Some traders and
officials at the Indian agencies refused to extend credit for food and
supplies until the Dakota had cash to pay their debts, and crop failures
and poor hunting had left many Dakota families hungry. Due to these
and other factors, tensions within Minnesota's Dakota community
reached a breaking point. The Indian revolt that Sibley and others
had hoped would never materialize did; and it started that August at
the same time when the Second Minnesota Regiment was tramping
through Tennessee, Mississippi, and Kentucky.

Many other regiments that had been mustered in after the Second
Regiment and were now in the Western Theater of war were now being
called back to help put down the revolt. The Second would not be
called back, but the news that the Third Regiment had already been
sent home was already known to the men in the Second. The Third
Regiment had been surrendered at the battle of Murfreesboro. They

had been humiliated, and though they fought well, their officers gave up the regiment to Southern cavalry against the protests of the ranks. Now back at Fort Snelling, they were anxious to redeem themselves. Governor Ramsey had cashiered all the officers responsible for the humiliation, and he put Sibley in charge of settling this Indian war.

In August of 1862, Dakota chief Little Crow met with some of his subchiefs for a war council to determine what might be done about the situation of unpaid annuities. Below the walls of Fort Snelling in the Dakota camp, four leaders of the Dakota nation sat in a conference. Chief Little Crow, Big Eagle, and Traveling Hail— all men in their forties—had grown up in a time when the Dakota and their neighbors, the Chippewa, had fought over territory and hunting grounds. They knew about war and were cautious to start another one. Little Shakopee was in attendance as well, but he was still young at twenty and was considered a firebrand anxious to fight the Whites.

Little Crow currently was not the chief of the Dakota. He had lost the election to Traveling Hail, but he was still respected and considered to be a great warrior and war chief, if it was to come to that. Little Shakopee did not hold much respect for his elder and would continue to debate him as to why Little Crow had lost the election. The war council started by addressing the election.

Big Eagle opened the discussion, "Little Crow, we understand your disappointment in not being elected chief."

Little Shakopee considered Little Crow a traitor. "Why did you sell off the upper ten miles of the upper agency back to the Whites? It cost you the election and the respect of the younger braves, you fool!"

Little Crow was slow to answer. "Traveling Hail will make a good chief if it is a war you seek."

Big Eagle spoke again, "He has always been against war. Even as a young man, Little Crow understood the risks of it."

Little Shakopee insulted Little Crow, "He has always been a coward."

Then Chief Traveling Hail came to the defense of his friend, "That is not true. He and I were on many war parties together, along with your father. He is as brave as any of our tribe. He killed many Chippewa long before you were even born."

Little Shakopee scoffed at this statement. "The Chippewa are cowards too."

Little Crow laughed at the ignorance of the younger man. "Is that why you ran in your first battle with them?"

Little Shakopee became heated. "We are not here to discuss that… If we are to get our lands back and live the life of our fathers, then now is the time to strike."

Now Chief Traveling Hail stood up for the younger man. "Shakopee has a point… The half-breed Indian farmers are doing well, as are the cut hairs, but those of us who want to live by the old ways are starving. The treaty was a joke. Ten miles on either side of the river and now Little Crow has given away the upper side? This is no way to live."

Big Eagle now joined in, "I'm against a war with the Whites, but I hear the South has been getting the best of the North. It is so desperate they have even called up half-breeds to fight."

Little Shakopee thought he had now found common ground with two of his elders. "Yes, I heard there is a full company of cut hairs from Renville County calling themselves the Renville Rangers who are about to be sent South soon."

Big Eagle spoke again, "Maybe you should join them if you are thirsty for blood. Traveling Hail, you are chief now, so how do you vote?"

He answered, "I will lead you into war or peace. It is your choice."

"*War!*" shouted Little Shakopee.

Big Eagle shook his head and responded quietly, "I stand with Little Crow. I'm against it."

Little Crow looked to Shakopee but said nothing.

Shakopee pointed his finger at his superior. "Still the coward? Everybody! Think about it! We are starving. Our women and children are getting sick. I overheard Sibley say that the agencies will receive no more government money until the war is over. The Whites are spending all the money on their war. Now is the time to hit them!"

Little Crow faced Shakopee with intent. "I'm still against it. They have made many promises, but they have kept only one. They promised to take our land, and they did. Therefore, I will die with you and lead you into battle if that is what you want."

Shakopee looked up in joy. "Finally the old man has come to his senses!"

Chief Traveling Hail rose to dismiss the meeting. "I will visit the Indian agent Thomas Galbraith one more time and try to get our annuity. I prefer peace over war."

Little Shakopee was not through. "Galbraith is a cheat and a fool. We know he has a storehouse full of our government food and supplies, but if we complain that we are starving, he just hands out little bits here and there. He has no concern that all the land left to us has been hunted out and this past winter destroyed all we had left of our supply."

Now Little Crow rose to leave. "And I will visit the chiefs of the Chippewa, Winnebago, Wabasha, and Sisseton to see if they will assist us."

As Traveling Hail departed, he turned to Little Crow. "Very well. Little Crow? Will you lead the war party if the time comes?"

Little Crow nodded as Little Shakopee let out a loud war whoop. "Kill the White man! Kill them all!"

The four Dakota leaders had traveled to the Lower Sioux Agency warehouse near the village of Redwood Falls. The agency was located about a two-day horse or buggy ride from Fort Snelling. Traveling Hail and Little Shakopee entered the building to find a long line of other Dakota Natives standing in wait of Andrew Myrick, the trader and official officer in charge of the agency supplies.

Myrick and his Dakota Indian wife stood behind a counter as a young warrior Runs When Crawling asked Andrew about getting his annuity.

"We are very hungry, and we beg you one last time to extend credit to us so we may feed our families."

Myrick brushed him off as if he was just a nuisance. "Let me tell you again what I said at the council meeting when you were all claiming that the treaty had been broken. You people said at that time for the agency to not cut your grass as your animals needed the feed."

Runs When Crawling interrupted him, "And you told us, if we were hungry, we could eat our grass or our dung."

"That's correct, and as far as I am concerned, you still can."

Little Crow had now made his way through the crowd and approached Myrick. "Is it true that the wife of your president spent all the annuity gold on decorating her White House?"

Myrick replied respectfully, seeing that he was confronted with the former chief whom he had a great deal of respect, "The rumor has it that she spent the entire four-year allotment. Congress has refused to replenish the allotment."

Little Shakopee was upset by this rumor and now reacted, "Has your president no control over his woman? You may think this is no concern of yours, but your concern is to see to it that we get what has been promised."

"And if I don't?" countered Myrick.

Little Shakopee snapped back, "Then you get what *we* promised at the council meeting. War!"

Myrick's wife, now shocked and scared, came to her husband's side.

Myrick replied, "Do you think your reservation savages can hold your own against the US military?"

Little Shakopee would not back down. "It seems you give us no other choice."

Myrick pointed to Traveling Hail. "Your chief assured me he was against any war."

Now all the Indians in the building had turned their attention to the verbal conflict.

Traveling Hail spoke, "It is true. I'm against it. There is no good cause for it, and I have been to Washington and know the power of the Whites and that they will finally conquer us. We might succeed for a time, but we would be overpowered and defeated at last."

As tensions calmed, Myrick got in the last word. "Follow your chief, and when the war with the South is finished, you will get your payments."

Disappointed once again, the Natives turned and exited the warehouse. The following day, the Dakota leaders mounted their horses and followed the Minnesota River back downstream to Fort Snelling. They made their camp there again and once more took up a conference in their war tepee.

Big Eagle opened the discussion, "The war talk has settled a bit from the younger braves."

Traveling Hail looked to Little Crow. "Maybe they have come to their senses."

Little Crow responded, "I think they are still hungry for blood."

Now Little Shakopee would speak, "Yes, we are, and it won't take much to push us over the edge."

Traveling Hail looked at the young man with regret. "I still stand by my words. We may get a quick victory or two, but we'll never get all our land back."

"Then you won't lead us?" snapped back Little Shakopee. Traveling Hail shook his head.

Big Eagle now confronted Little Shakopee, "This is not a war council. I am only giving my opinion, but if you want war, it is almost certain we will lose. Therefore, I am against it."

Little Shakopee, now frustrated, stood up to leave. "Even though you were elected chief, many of your band are now against you. In their eyes, you have become a coward. You are afraid of the White man. Now is the time to strike, when the blue-suit White man is busy fighting the gray-suit White man. What do you fear? Look to their fort. Snelling is empty. There is no army here to fight us. They have taken all their rifles and even their big guns." Shakopee now turned for support from Little Crow.

"Little Shakopee, your father was a great leader, and he was for the White man. He had a great influence on them. He would oppose you making war, but in some way, I agree with you. You are a young warrior, and you need to prove yourself in battle… If Big Eagle will not lead you and his band is against him and he will not stand up for his nation, then he must be shunned for being a traitor. Then you can select another leader."

Big Eagle had now taken offense. "So this is how you intend to become chief? This is your revenge for losing the election? I should have guessed you two were in on this together."

Shakopee was very pleased with what he was hearing. "We are planning a war council in the soldiers' lodge. If Big Eagle or Traveling Hail will not lead, then we will hold a new election."

Big Eagle spoke again, "Traveling Hail and I will not lead you into a war with the Whites, but we are not cowards. We will fight with you and die with you."

Shakopee turned to Little Crow. "How do you stand?"

"I do not wish to lead you into a war I know you will lose, but I believe as you do that, if there will ever come a time when we will have the advantage to take back our land, it would be now. I will die with you too," answered Little Crow.

Little Shakopee then asked, "So if it comes to a new election in the council, you will lead us?"

Little Crow nodded. "Yes, but try to control your braves. Don't do anything that will provoke the Whites into a war neither of us wants."

"I will do my best," responded Little Shakopee as the meeting was dismissed..

THE UPRISING

*We have waited a long time. The money is ours,
but we cannot get it. We have no food, but here are
these stores filled with food. We ask that you, the
agent, make some arrangement by which we can
get food from the stores, or else we may make our
way to keep ourselves from starving. When men are
hungry, they help themselves.*

—Taoyateduta (Little Crow), 1862

The Sioux Indian revolt and massacre commenced on August 18.
Authentic information reached Saint Paul on the nineteenth, the same
evening the ex-governor Henry H. Sibley was appointed by the governor
of Minnesota to conduct a military force against the hostile Sioux, and
he started the next day with four companies of the Sixth Regiment for
Saint Peter. In compliance with the request of Governor Ramsey, General
Halleck on August 22 instructed General Schofield to send the Third
Regiment to Minnesota. The War Department announced on August
27 that the enlisted men of the regiment, as paroled prisoners, were
fully exchanged. A high value, even in their disorganized condition,
was placed upon their service in the Indian campaign; and their arrival
was anticipated with much interest. Rapidly marching until eleven at
night, they made forty miles.

Near Acton, Minnesota, close to the Lower Sioux reservation
along the Minnesota River, was the farm of the settler Mr. Robinson

Jones. On the hot, humid morning of August 17, four young braves all belonging to Shakopee's band—eighteen-year-old Brown Wing, twenty-year-old Breaking Up, twenty-year-old Killing Ghost, and eighteen-year-old Runs Against Something When Crawling—were hunting in a wooded area near the Jones homestead. They wandered up to a split rail fence that separated the woods from the farm. Brown Wing spotted a hen's nest with some eggs in it.

He reached over the fence rail to take them and exclaimed to the others, "I'm so hungry! I'm going to eat these."

Breaking Up reached out to stop him. "Don't take them. They belong to a White man, and we may get into trouble."

Brown Wing held fast to the eggs anyway and lashed out at Breaking Up. Angrily he dashed the eggs to the ground and yelled out, "You are a coward! You are afraid of the White man! You are afraid to take even an egg from him though you are half starved. Yes, you are a coward, and I will tell everybody so."

Breaking Up yelled back at him, "I am not a coward! I am not afraid of the White man, and to show you that I am not, I will go to the house and shoot him. Are you brave enough to go with me?" Brown Wing accepted his challenge. "Yes, I will go with you, and we will see who is the braver of us two."

Not to be left out, Killing Ghost turned to Runs Against Something When Crawling and said, "We will go with you, and we will be brave too."

"Yes, we will all go," replied Runs When Crawling Against Something.

The four braves, without any permission from their chief, then moved out toward the house of Robinson Jones.

Robinson Jones, a family man and settler in his early thirties, was resting in his cabin. Without any concern, he sensed something was amiss and headed for the cabin door to have a look outside. He opened the door and looked out across his property. Headed toward him were the four braves with rifles at the ready. Becoming alarmed at the sight and having heard rumors of unrest among the Dakota, Robinson reached for his rifle, which he kept loaded next to the door, and made a mad dash to the house next door. This was the home of his brother-in-law, Howard Baker.

He was greeted by a shocked Howard Baker, Baker's young wife, and the wife of another neighbor named Webster. Jones's wife and his fourteen-year-old daughter were also at the house. As Jones relayed what he had just seen outside his cabin, all the occupants of the Webster home rushed to the windows to see for themselves and were all horrified to see that the braves were now headed for the Webster house. A panicked Jones reached for his wife to comfort her. The startled neighbors could hardly believe what they were seeing.

Ester, Jones's daughter, ran to her mother's side. "They've got guns, Mama! What could they possibly want? Mama! I'm scared."

Jones looked to his wife and daughter. "I don't know what they want, but they sure don't look happy."

Howard was now panicked but tried to remain calm. "Okay, everyone, take cover. Webster, take my shotgun."

Howard lifted a rifle from its perch above the door, then handed the shotgun to Webster. The men prepared for the worst as the women cowered in a corner of the cabin. Webster handed a pistol to Mrs. Jones, and the men all took positions of defense at the door.

Within moments, the four braves had reached the entrance to the Baker house. In a shockingly quick time, they breached the threshold of the door without incident and immediately fired on the settlers. Before any of the defenders could get off a shot, the three men were killed. Mrs. Jones rushed to cover her child and was shot in the back. Ester was then pulled out from under her dying mother and raped by two of the braves. The other two rummaged through the cupboards and took whatever food stock they could find and stuffed it into a grain sack. One of the braves slit the throat of Ester, and with a loud whoop, they departed the house.

The four Indians rushed to the barn and stable to find a team of horses and a wagon. They hitched up the team and rushed off in the wagon. They cut across the open field and entered a wagon trail road.

Runs When Crawling Against Something wiped the blood from the knife he used to kill young Ester, then turned to Killing Ghost. "Where is Shakopee's camp?"

Killing Ghost, who had taken command of the horses, answered, "He's about six miles above the Redwood Agency."

"He'll be proud of how brave we are," said Brown Wing.

"Is he with Little Crow?" asked Runs When Crawling Against Something to nobody in particular.

Killing Ghost answered him, "I'm not sure, but I don't think Little Crow will find us so brave."

Breaking Up added to that comment, "Not after what you two did to that little girl."

Brown Wing tried to put on a brave face as he was now evidently not so proud of his actions in the death of Ester. "You know how angry Whites get when it comes to their children."

Runs When Crawling Against Something scoffed and put an end to this early chatter. "That's because they are weak, and so are their children. Always crying, for what? They already have everything!"

The carriage headed down the wagon wheel road, making haste for Little Shakopee's camp. Though the drive was less than ten miles, they had to ford many streams and rough terrain full of fallen trees and tangles of brush. They did not get to the camp until late evening. Before going to Little Crow's cabin, the four braves stopped to meet with Little Shakopee, thinking that maybe he would understand their violent outburst of the day against these innocent settlers and smooth the way for the meeting with Little Crow, who was not in this camp but had gone back to his cabin in Redwood Falls.

Shakopee and the four braves exited the tepee and walked across the campground, passing the Native dancers and drummers. It was a hot, humid night full of mosquitoes, which were common in this part of the Lower Sioux Agency. The swamps, wetlands, and Minnesota river itself were the big contributors to these conditions; but the smoke from the bonfire held back the infestation of flying insects, which made their walk to the stolen wagon more pleasant. The braves mounted the stolen wagon and headed out. Little Shakopee took the reins and snapped the horses to a gallop. The wagon pulled out onto the agency road. Their drive to Little Crow's cabin took them a little over an hour.

Little Crow, at this point in his life, had become a partially assimilated Native who, even though still kept his hair long, had learned to live by White comforts. As the braves and Shakopee arrived at his cabin, they let themselves in and found him to be sitting on the edge of his bed wearing a long nightshirt and nightcap. The guests were used to seeing him in his White condition and paid little attention. Little Crow was mildly put out by their abrupt intrusion, and his voice had the intent of a man who had just been disturbed from a restful sleep.

"If you are here for advice, why do you come to me? Go to the man you elected speaker and let him tell you what to do."

The new election had been held, and Little Crow lost again.

Shakopee answered, "It's true, Traveling Hail is our chief, but we see you as our war chief, so tell us what to do."

Little Crow sighed. "War must be declared. Blood has been shed. The payments will be stopped, and the Whites will take a dreadful vengeance because women have been killed. What did Traveling Hail tell you at the council? This is not what I wanted. I told you to control your young warriors, and now we must fight."

Little Shakopee answered, knowing he was being reprimanded, "He, Wabasha, Wakota, and others all talked of peace, but nobody wanted to listen… When these four came to the agency and told us of what they had done, there was much excitement, and the cries rose from all. Kill the Whites, and kill all the cut hairs who will not join us!"

Little Crow nodded in agreement. "There must be an official council before war can be declared… I suppose this could be our council now. So this is what I have to say to a war council. I would have liked all the chiefs from all the tribes who want to join us to be here, but if you, Shakopee, and these four fools want me to give the order, then so be it. We go to war in the morning! Begin the preparations. Form war parties now! That is my first order."

Brown Wing spoke next, "Shall we send scouts and word to the other tribes to join us?"

"Yes, gather as many as are willing. Start the women and boys cleaning the guns and preparing the weapons. Have the women run bullets. At sunrise, we attack the agency and kill all the Whites who are there or in our path."

With that final order from Little Crow, all of the men left his cabin and loaded themselves onto the stolen wagon. They traveled the wagon road the distance back to the Lower Sioux Agency camp and entered the central Native communal building. After a little discussion, Little Crow and the other chiefs set the people to work in preparation for war. As Little Crow's orders were being fulfilled, Big Eagle was off to the side talking privately to Traveling Hail. As they talked, women poured molten lead into bullet molds as boys cleaned the rifles and the girls prepared food and supplies.

Big Eagle turned to Traveling Hail. "I still don't want any part of this killing. Neither do my men, but I suppose, once it all starts, we will all take part in it."

Traveling Hail nodded in agreement. "I agree with you. This is an unfortunate situation. I know you have friends at the agency that you want to warn. I have a friend there as well, as do many of us. Not all of the Whites need to be killed."

With sadness in his heart, Big Eagle answered, "Yes, I will go along tomorrow, for that is my main purpose. I wish to protect them. But the order has gone out, and just look at all this excitement. It cannot be stopped now… Nearly every one of us here has a friend at the agency we don't want to see hurt, but who among us cares for another's friends? You cannot protect mine, and I cannot protect yours."

Traveling Hail shook his head in disbelief. "I'm afraid we are making a huge mistake."

Big Eagle pointed to Little Crow, who was helping to manage the preparations. "You know? Little Crow was at the White church this morning, and he was shaking hands with the very people he intends to kill tomorrow."

Traveling Hail led Big Eagle away from the group. "I'm surprised he has come around so quickly to take the lead in this foolish plan. I thought for sure he was becoming a cut hair and would soon leave us forever."

The excitement of the next morning's action had all of the compounds up until dawn finishing the preparations for the uprising.

Endless Marching and a Skirmish

"Take off your bedroom slippers. Put on your marching shoes," he said, his voice rising as applause and cheers mounted. "Shake it off. Stop complainin'. Stop grumblin'. Stop cryin'. We are going to press on. We have work to do."

—Barack Obama

The same day as the great Dakota war would begin, John, William, and the entire Second Minnesota Regiment marched out of Louisville. They were once again on the road to find Bragg's army. William had fully recovered from his illness but was now heartbroken over having to leave Mary behind. As the column of Union soldiers of the Second Minnesota Regiment marched along a muddy road in Kentucky, William Simmons took his post at the front of his company, tapping out a steady marching cadence for the men. His brother, John, ran up alongside him, excited to pass on some news.

"Did you hear?"

"Hear what?" answered William.

"Well, they are going to separate the musicians into pairs, give us rifles, and set us out into picket duty with the others in the company. This is it! We are about to see the elephant!"

William was not convinced, nor was he impressed. "I don't think skirmishing would be considered a real fight. It's about as dangerous and exciting as hunting rabbits, remember?"

"Anyway, we are headed into it. No more parades and concerts for the ladies of Louisville and no more of you blubbering over your Mary," said John.

"I rather liked all that attention we got from the ladies back there," William answered while keeping the cadence.

John waved it off. "Oh, they weren't all just looking at you. You certainly had no favors to pay them. What could a woman possibly see in a drummer boy when a real musician can be had?"

William stopped drumming and stared at his brother. "Is that what you think you are now?"

Colonel Bishop, who had left the regiment to return to Minnesota when he fell ill with dysentery, was now back from his convalescence.

He rode up next to the Simmons brothers and reprimanded John, "Bugler, fall back into ranks where you belong and leave this boy alone. You're disrupting the cadence."

John rushed off to take his proper place in line. William set the marching pace again.

Bishop looked down from his high horse and addressed William, "How you are holding up, boy?"

"Quite well. Thank you, sir."

"I bet you're missing the comforts of Louisville right now," continued Bishop.

"Yes, sir. This rain and mud are even worse than last year." "Well, Grant and Sherman have Johnny on the run now," said

Bishop with a disarming grin.

"Is it true they have them surrounded in Mississippi? Is that where we are headed?" asked William.

"I couldn't tell you even if I knew. Don't mind the mud. Just keep up that steady beat. It calms the men and keeps them focused. I'm sure you'll find out soon enough where we are headed."

William saluted his superior as Bishop galloped off toward the head of the column. Soon William and John would find themselves placed in a skirmish line facing an enemy they had been tracking for over a year. Back home in Minnesota, the Third Regiment was about to face a completely different foe, but this was not on the minds of John or William. On the morning of the twenty-eighth of August, the same day the Third Regiment would meet the Dakota in battle, a platoon of the Second Minnesota Company K, the company William and John were now part of, was spread out in skirmish formation and was sweeping across an open field that was at the base of the foothills of a mountain somewhere in Kentucky, west of Louisville. The field was teeming with apple and peach trees. John and William were among the men making up the line. Though they were supposed to be keeping intervals of ten yards between them, John once again broke ranks to come to his brother's side.

It was a hot, humid, and muggy day in August; and the boys were dripping in sweat.

John whispered to William, "Let's load up on these apples and peaches. These will be a great addition to that hindquarter of hog you got off that fella in the Thirty-Fifth Ohio."

William nodded in agreement but kept his eyes peeled ahead for any trouble. "Yep. They've been some good foragers, and we should pay them back with a little fruit. Hey, you better get back into formation before the sergeant sees you!"

John laughed it off. "What for? When's the last time we contacted any rebs?"

William paused to catch his breath and wipe the sweat from under his cap. "Um, about a year ago, I guess, back at Mills Spring when we first got into this state. It seems we've been marching in circles ever since then."

John answered in agreement, "I believe we have. We've crossed into Georgia, Alabama, Mississippi, and back again, but all in all, except for Minnesota, I'd say this here part of Kentucky is about as pretty a place there ever was. Just look at all the crops and wildlife around here."

William gazed around at their surroundings. "And with all these rivers and creeks, they sure won't ever need fresh water. Kind of reminds you of home, doesn't it?"

John pulled a rag from his haversack and wiped the sweat from his neck before answering. "I sure would like to come upon one of those cold mountain creeks now."

As the boys marched along, they began to pull apples and peaches from the trees and stuffed them into their haversacks.

William nudged his brother. "Go on. Get back into formation before we get into trouble with Moffett."

John began to move back to his proper interval. "Just one more thing. Don't forget we have to send our pay home to Ma when we get back to camp."

"What news did we get in her last letter? I never did get a chance to read it," asked William.

John replied sarcastically, "Maybe if you would have spent more time worrying about your family instead of playing with your nurse, you would have. Anyway, nothing too special. Sara is in school again, and this year, the new teacher is an agency teacher, so she will be in school with all those cut hairs that have turned to farming on the south side of the river. And the news from Pa is I guess he had a terrible bout of dysentery along with most of the other teamsters, and luckily it kept him out of the big battles in that seven-day ruckus on the peninsula. He should have let us go with him. Let's hope he gets a medical discharge and gets back home soon."

On ending that discussion, John ran back to his place in the skirmish line, and the platoon continued out of the orchards and up a steep incline toward the top of the mountain.

Waiting at the top of the mountain was a skirmish line of Confederates forming up on the edge of a tree line. They were hidden from view of the Union line. A hand signal was given from an officer, and they started down the slope, muskets at the ready. They moved, but a few yards before, they spotted the Second Minnesota boys coming their way. They opened fire on them with a sporadic volley.

In an instant, the entire skirmish line of the Second Regiment went to ground. Bullets whizzed past the boys. John thought they were being attacked by bees until he saw the smoke from the Confederate rifles. During this first volley, William felt a tug on his haversack, which was riding high on his hip; and looking down, he saw a hole ripped through it. He immediately swung open the flap of the bag and pulled out half a peach.

Surprised, he mumbled to himself, "Well, that's a new way to pit a peach!"

He then shoved the half peach in his mouth, raised his rifle, and fired off a round, then dropped back to the ground. John ran up next to him and went to hug the ground as well. The rest of the company was doing the same, firing and taking cover on the ground as best they could. They continued to load and fire from their prone positions.

John grabbed William by his belt. "Are you okay? I saw you get hit!"

"I'm fine. They just got my bag," William explained as he reached back into his haversack and pulled out the other half of the peach, handing it to his brother. "Here. They're good and ripe."

John shoved the peach into his mouth and mumbled while chewing, "Well, I'll be damned if it ain't."

The boys enjoyed this moment of refreshment. The Confederates seemed to be having the same bad luck in not being able to hit anybody while firing from such an awkward lying position as their counterparts were. The Union fire died out, and the rebels cautiously began to rise one by one. They moved forward and, within moments, were standing within a few yards of the boys from the Second Minnesota, who had also stopped firing and were now standing. Calmness and silence hung over the men from both sides. They stared at each other cautiously until a rebel NCO pulled out a white hanky and waved it at the Union platoon.

An NCO of the Second Regiment Company K returned the gesture, and both sides stepped forward to greet one another. Both sides then realized there would be some trading to be done. John and

William foolishly were the first to break ranks and step up to greet their counterparts. They extended hands to a couple of young rebels.

A young rebel boy about the same age as William asked, "What news you blue bellies got?"

William responded with a smile, "Not much. I suppose you heard we whipped you real good out at Shiloh."

The rebel boy nodded, "Yeah, we heard. Were you there?"

John answered, "Nope. We never made it in time. We got there just in time to clean up the mess and put you boys under."

A second young Confederate now spoke to William and John, "You should be glad you missed it. That was some terrible fight, and I'll admit you got us good."

The first young rebel now asked of William, "Got any coffee? We got tobacco."

William answered, "A little. We got that and some beans we'll trade you for some chewing tobacco if you got it."

The second rebel boy asked, "Sure 'nuff… You all got any newspapers? We don't hear anything."

All along the line, men were exchanging goods.

John handed over a can of beans to the boy, then asked him, "Is there a nice cool creek around here we can fill our canteens and get a bath?"

The boy turned and pointed. "Yep. Just head to the top of this hill. Go east about a quarter mile, and there you'll find a nice little waterfall and a rocky creek full of ice-cold mountain water that feeds right into the Tennessee River. You got anything on our way down this valley?"

William answered, "Plenty of fruit as you can see, but about a mile or so, you'll run right up on a full division, so be careful."

"You boys be careful too. We got plenty of ours hiding all over these hills."

"Thanks for the tip, blue belly," said the boy standing across from John.

John responded in kind, "Likewise, grayback."

The two opposing skirmish lines finished up their fraternizing and crossed through each other and continued their separate ways. This was not the exciting combat William and John was anxious to experience, but they had at least fired their rifles at the enemy for the first time in the war.

Pursuing a northward march, the Second Regiment arrived at Nashville on the seventh of September and encamped at the edge of the city. Most of the army had already crossed the Cumberland River, but it was given out that their brigade would remain at Nashville.

They did for a week while their divisions north of the river were watching Bragg's movements. By the fourteenth, his army was across the river at points higher up the river and farther north than Nashville, and the race back to Louisville began. Their brigade left Nashville on the fourteenth, crossed the river, and encamped just north of Edgefield. They received five days of rations of flour, coffee, and sugar only. No clothing or shoes, which were especially needed. In the next three days, they marched on the hard, dusty pike seventy miles to Bowling Green. Here, on the eighteenth, more rations of flour were issued; and they crossed the Barren River, in which they found the first supply of drinkable water since leaving the Cumberland. On the nineteenth, they marched twenty-five miles and, on the twentieth, overtook their other divisions and, passing through their camps, came up to the enemy's rear picket line near Cave City. Here they extended their line of battle to right and left and posted their picket line confronting theirs. This was the seventh day of the march, which was without a parallel in the regimental experience thus far. It was the dry season of the year, and in this part of Kentucky, there was no living water except the Barren River between the Green and Cumberland Rivers.

William and John were continually posted on skirmish duty during this march, but nothing much happened of any note. The regiment never engaged with the enemy at this time. The news did reach them, though, of the Dakota trouble back in Minnesota; and this concerned many of the men in the regiment who had families and friends in the places that were under attack. At this time, the Third Regiment under General Sibley was engaged with the Indians.

ANTIETAM CREEK

The fighting was so severe at Antietam that one soldier claimed it appeared as if the entire landscape had turned red. At twenty-five thousand casualties, it would come to be the bloodiest day in US history. To equate this to a modern-day equivalent, imagine that, for twelve hours starting at 6:00 a.m. and ending at 6:00 p.m., every ten minutes, a fully loaded 747 jetliner crashed into the twelve-square-mile field that made up the battlefield on that September day in 1862; and you would know the horror what those soldiers faced.

In the Eastern Theater, First Minnesota was part of the great slaughter at the battle of Antietam. Dan was not wounded, nor was he involved in the fight. The Army of the Potomac had just had its medical corps updated with new ambulances and a system for getting wounded off the field and to a tent hospital as quickly as possible. Dan was now part of the new ambulance corps and had been issued a new Letterman-style ambulance and two horses. The ambulance was equipped to carry six wounded on stretchers and had with it two litter carriers and one driver. News of this had not reached William or John or, for that matter, anyone back in Mendota. Unfortunately, even with this easy duty, Dan had become a casualty of the most dreaded affliction of the army: dysentery. But through the heat and humidity of Maryland's summer of 1862, Dan still carried on with his duties.

A few days after the great battle, Dan drove his ambulance to the top of a ridgeline overlooking the Antietam battlefield. He dismounted and walked toward an open-air hospital. Row upon row of soldiers from both sides was laid out in the cuts of a cornfield. The grand hospital tent that was promised never arrived, and these men suffered under whatever protection comrades could slap together for them. Surgeons and attendants walked among them, tending to the wounded and dying.

A surgeon noticing Dan and his ambulance walked up to him to ask him about his load of wounded. "How many more you got this time?"

"A baker's dozen," answered Dan with a painful grimace. "Are they all living?" asked the surgeon.

"Yes, most, I think," said Dan.

The surgeon pointed in a direction down the hill. "Unload them here, but take the dead to the end of this road. You'll find graves registration down there. I'll have my orderlies here to help you unload. I can see you are in no condition to do that alone."

The surgeon whistled, and two Black men came running up.

Dan stared at them in disbelief.

One of the men, looking annoyed, stared back at Dan. "What's the matter with you? Never seen a gravedigger before?"

Dan was taken aback. "Uh…no, no, no… Just…" "Just what?" asked the digger.

Dan, caught off guard, answered, "Just never seen any darkies before."

The second digger responded, "We ain't darkies. We freemen. You're in a border state now, White boy. Better get used to seeing new things. Where you from up North?"

"Minnesota," Dan answered.

"It gets cold up there?" asked the digger.

Dan nodded and wiped the sweat from his brow. "Yeah, most of the time."

Now all the men including the surgeon were wiping sweat from their faces and reaching for their canteens.

Dan gestured to the scene before him. "Been pretty hot work here, it looks like."

One of the diggers responded, "Guess, drivin' that wagon, you don't get to see too much of the fightin'."

Dan nodded. "Not much but seen enough…seen enough to know I don't need to see anymore."

The second Black man took a pull off his canteen, then made a sweeping gesture out over the field. "Looking at this is the worst of what war has to offer, and we gravediggers got it worse. We not only have to see it, but we must also smell it too."

At that, Dan passed gas, and they both shared a light laugh. "Okay, well, let's get this done before I soil myself again. Go easy on the ones who are hurtin' the most. Some of these boys were just picked up today. They were lying out there in the sun for two days now."

One of the diggers looked back over the field. "Those poor devils lying in those cornrows have been there longer. It rained the other night, and those rows filled with water, and some of the worst wounded drowned in the mud."

Dan shuddered at the thought. "My God!"

The orderlies set forth to off-load the wounded and carried them over to the cornrows and gently laid them in the field. The moaning, crying, and suffering was more than Dan could handle. He bent over and gripped his stomach.

The surgeon noticed. "Hey, driver! You okay?"

"Yeah, just another cramp. Virginia Quickstep. Been going on for over a month now."

The surgeon called back to him, "I'll have my orderly get you some blue mass."

Dan waved him off. "That stuff hasn't worked at all."

"Would you like to stay here in the hospital? I can get you out of your regular duties until you feel better."

"This hospital? If that's the best you can do, no, thanks. I'll tough it out," said Dan as he mounted his ambulance.

He then led his team and ambulance of the dead down the road to graves registration.

Mid-September 1862 would find the Simmons men spread out across the Midwest and the Eastern United States. General Sibley was the commander of Minnesota troops in the battle against the Dakota, and the citizens of Mendota were living in fear of their lives as White settlers were being killed and/or captured and enslaved by the Natives who were rebelling.

Along the banks of the Minnesota River, Little Crow and his bands had been engaged with skirmishes with some of the volunteer militia made up of settlers who had joined in the fight with Sibley all through August and now into late September. The uprising started mid-August after a brief meeting between Little Crow and Big Eagle, when they discussed that the only choice was to now fight for their freedom as they knew the Whites would not tolerate what those four braves of Little Shakopee had done. The rape and murder of a child and women would not sit right with the Whites. Now the Indians were not just fighting for their rightful due, but in the eyes of the White settlers and army, they were simply criminals. When caught, there would be no mercy shown to them. So the uprising continued. The citizens of the new state and those settled near the fort, agency, or reservations were most concerned for their lives.

Nearing the end of September, the Dakota had killed or captured 1,500 Whites, 300 of whom were held in captivity. Sibley knew that his first mission would be to find these captives and negotiate a release. In the village of Mendota, Louise and Sara Simmons spent the evening of September 22 sitting in the relative comfort of their small cabin. Autumn was coming early, and Sara placed a couple of logs that her father had split before he left into the fireplace. In her mind, she could see her brothers and father and wondered what they were doing this evening. She longed for them to be home, especially since the Natives in the camp on the other side of the river were once again celebrating their victories over the White settlers.

Sara covered her ears to block the sound of the drumming, chanting, and continued annoyance of the tribe. She knew that, in that Indian camp, some of the captured White women and children were being held and could only imagine their suffering, especially after what she knew of the first mother and daughter that had been killed on the first day of the uprising. Her cut-hair teacher from the agency school had told the students what would be done to those captives, and Sara thought it was the cruelest thing any teacher could say to any classroom of students. Sara noticed her mother wince at every drumbeat or high-pitched yelp coming from across the river.

"Oh! How much longer? That noise is driving me crazy! Oh! When will this stupid war be over? I want Dad and my brothers back at home!"

Louise tried to comfort her. "Me too, honey. Me too."

"That hooting, howling, and drumming has been going on for three days now. Nonstop! What is the army doing about this?" said Sara with tears in her eyes.

"I don't know. All I can say is there were some words that the Indians killed more settlers, and they are about to go on another rampage. How I wish we could at least get some news straight from General Sibley so we could at least put our minds to rest."

Sara sighed. "Oh, I don't think we'll be seeing him for quite a while. Let's go talk to Mrs. Sibley tomorrow, and maybe she can tell us something. I want to hear from her about what happened. I don't trust what my teacher has said."

Louise nodded, and the two tried to put it all out of their minds.

The very next day, Dan checked himself into the tent hospital that had finally been established near the Antietam battlefield. A surgeon's orderly helped him to lie down on a bed made of straw, which, though not very comfortable, was far better than lying in a muddy cornrow exposed to the elements of nature. Fortunately for Dan, his situation appeared much better than the others. He at least had half of a canvas tent to cover him.

As he lay under the shelter half, the orderly spoke to him, "How long have you been having the trots?"

"Since we fell back at White Oak Swamp in June."

"My God! This started during the Peninsula Campaign?"

Dan nodded. "Yes, going on nearly three months now. And nothing has seemed to work, but I'm certain a decent home-cooked meal would help."

The orderly wrote something down in a notebook. "Yes, I'm sure it would, but that's not about to happen for a long time, I'm afraid. Do you say the fever started in earnest this afternoon? And you have been passing blood too?"

Dan groaned and nodded yes to both questions.

The orderly took a good look at Dan and could see his misery was more than just someone slacking duty. "Okay, I'm going to write this up and recommend to the surgeon that you be moved to the hospital in Washington. If you don't recover there, I suspect you will be discharged because of illness."

The orderly left the tent but not before Dan could ask where he was going.

"I'm going to fetch you some fresh water. We'll try to break that fever of yours. In the meantime, just rest as easy as you can."

"I don't think I can make it to the sinks if I have to go again," answered Dan.

"I'll hurry back," said the orderly.

"One more thing," asked Dan. "When you get back, could you write a letter for me to send to my wife?"

The orderly nodded his head.

Though the Dakota uprising was now well into its second month, details of the conflict had not been revealed in any honest telling to the folks in Mendota. Jane Sibley was the one in closest contact with her husband, and she did get regular mail from him explaining in explicit terms what had transpired from August 17 until this late date in September.

Louise and Sara made the climb to the top of the hill to visit Jane in her fine stone house. They were determined to hear it all. Jane cordially greeted them and offered coffee and cake.

As they sat together, Louise opened the conversation, "Please be honest, Jane. What do you know about this Indian situation?"

Jane settled back, preparing herself for a long story to be told. "On the seventeenth of August in Meeker County, there was a family murdered and horses stolen. Nobody we'd know. Three men and two women, one a girl of fourteen... Rumor has it she was sullied by two of the Native boys... The mother was shot in the back running to her aid, and the girl's throat was slit."

Sara felt weak at hearing this and held fast to her mother. "Is this the truth?" asked Louise.

Jane answered, "This is the first report I got from Henry. One of the agency men told him as he heard it from one of the Natives who came in to collect his annuity. After that, word had it Little Crow led a war party. He knew the army would be looking for those horse thieves, and he knew they would all be hanged as criminals and not as people fighting for their freedom. The next day, Henry got his commission as general to lead troops against these Dakota savages. Though the Dakota has made an official declaration of war, there is no official declaration of war by Governor Ramsey. Therefore, these Indians in revolt will be considered common thieves, murderers, and rapists and will be treated as such."

Louise now looked to Jane with real worry. "What shall we do? I have no men left at home, and neither do any of the other women in this valley."

Jane answered, "Henry doubts they will cross the river. But if it comes to that, you are welcome to stay here with me until this all passes. Henry has five thousand soldiers with him, and I'm sure these savages will be put back in their place soon enough."

Before Sara and Louise departed for their own home, Jane told of all the other battles that had taken place in the past month.

But what she did not know was what the chiefs thought that day. Before the attack, Chief Big Eagle sat grandly atop his horse. He and his band of thirty to forty braves overlooked the battlefield. What they saw was Little Crow on the battlefield directing operations. Bodies were scattered about the grass, and it appeared most of the killing was already finished by the time Big Eagle and his band arrived. Buildings were already ablaze. Women and children were being gathered up and herded along as Indian prisoners. Chaska, a handsome-looking warrior of about thirty years old, sat on his pony next to Big Eagle.

He asked of Big Eagle, "Aren't we going to join in?"

Big Eagle shook his head and brushed him off. "What's the point? The killing is already finished."

Chaska was not pleased. "Then what was the point in us even coming here? You know I was against this from the beginning. The only reason I am here and you are here is because we have White friends down there and we came here to protect them. Am I right?" Big Eagle grunted his approval. "That's true. I have known George Spencer for a long time, and he is a good man. I think every man here in my band has a friend down there. Maybe we should ride down and take a closer look to see who is still alive."

Big Eagle signaled to his band to move forward. They rode down from the ridge into the middle of the battle. A few shots were still being fired from both sides, but Big Eagle's band rode through without incident. The horses moved cautiously among the dead and dying. Chaska and Big Eagle dismounted and continued on foot, talking and inspecting the dead Whites as well as dead Indians. They came across the bodies of the agency trader Andrew Myrick, who had earlier taunted the Indians by telling them to eat grass. Now he and his Indian wife were lying dead on the ground, and Myrick's mouth was stuffed with grass.

Victorious Natives danced around the Myricks' bodies, chanting, "Myrick is eating grass himself! Let him eat grass!"

Moments later, all was quiet, and Little Crow led his celebratory warriors from the field.

While General Sibley and his troops rallied farther up the Minnesota River to protect the settlers that would most likely be hit next, Dan was lying restlessly in his bed of straw near the Antietam battlefield. His two sons were still stomping through Tennessee in pursuit of Bragg;

and though they were worn out, tired, and hungry, they still had their health. Dan, on the other hand, now struggled to sit up and get words out as the regimental surgeon's orderly transcribed a letter to Louise.

The orderly wrote while Dan spoke, "My very dear Louise, I have been as sick as a man can get ever since the campaign on the peninsula. I am now in what is said to be a field hospital but, in truth, is nothing more than a bloody field in far-off Maryland near the town of Sharpsburg along the Antietam River. The surgeon here, though kind, has not been able to give me much relief, and I fear I may pass before ever seeing you again as so many of the other boys have also gone up with this terrible dysentery. The orderly writing for me has said that I am to be moved to a proper hospital in Washington City as soon as I can be moved."

Dan did not have the energy to go on and fell back exhausted as the orderly caught up on his writing. "There I am assured of rest and a proper diet, which should relieve my suffering. If I do not get well enough to continue my duties, I will be discharged for medical reasons and return soon to you. I have not heard from the boys for some time. Please tell them to write."

The orderly then wiped Dan's brow and helped him to take a drink from his canteen. "Is that all?"

Dan sighed and finished his letter. "Almost… All my love to you, Sara, and the boys. Your loving husband, Dan."

Do No Harm

*It may seem a strange principle to enunciate as the
very first requirement in a hospital that it should
do the sick no harm.*

—Florence Nightingale

The war with the Dakota was hardly over. It would last well on into
the next decade and evolve into what would become the great final
acts of the wars against the Indian nations. While General Sibley was
about to lead his troops into the final battles that would eventually
push the Sioux out of Minnesota and into the Dakota territories, the
great Civil War in the east was still very active. News reports of the
Sioux Uprising were slow in making it into the eastern newspapers.
This Indian conflict would be pushed to the inside pages as the combat
actions taking place in the Western Theater and Eastern Theater made
all the headlines. The South, up to this point in the fall of 1862, seemed
to be winning all the major battles, except for the battle of Antietam,
which was considered a draw. By most accounts, the Union Army was
not doing very well. Only in the western campaign with Grant and
Sherman in command was there any good news for Washington and
supporters of the Union cause. Grant had secured victories along all his
routes into Kentucky, Tennessee, and Mississippi. Now he was getting
ready to move on to Vicksburg.

Meanwhile, Dan was being transferred to one of the best hospitals
in Washington, DC. Instead of driving an ambulance, he was now a

passenger. In the final week of September, the regimental surgeon at the Antietam battlefield wrote up orders for Dan to be moved. He climbed aboard one of the new Tripler US army ambulances that made up a mile-long train of the same wagons loaded with sick and wounded heading toward the nation's capital. The Tripler ambulance was a new design that could seat up to six walking wounded and carry four stretchers bearing wounded.

In comparison to Dan's supply wagon and his most recent Letterman ambulance, this was a luxury vehicle. Dan was seated in the rear of the wagon along with the other walking wounded. On a rack before him was a wounded man by the name of Sam, an older soldier of about twenty-seven who had had his right leg amputated. Sam saw something familiar about Dan and introduced himself.

"Hey, pard! You coming out of Antietam?" said Dan.

"Yes. You? Did they keep you lying in that ditch of a hospital long?" Sam turned on his side to get a better look at Dan.

"Five days. How about you?"

"Only three for me. Your accent sounds familiar. What regiment you with?"

"First Minnesota. You?" asked Dan.

"No kidding! Me too! Say, aren't you one of our teamsters? I thought you looked familiar."

"I sure am, or was," said Dan.

Sam reached out to shake Dan's hand. "Nice to finally meet you. We don't see much of you guys when things get hot."

"No…no, you don't, and we like it that way." "Where'd you get hit?" asked Sam.

"I didn't. Got the shits. Going on four months now." "That's rough," answered Sam.

"Not as rough as you."

Sam turned on his side to ease his pain. "I thought it was painful soon after I got shot, but, I tell ya, the suffering didn't start in earnest until after they took it off."

Dan moved closer to him and asked quietly, "Has it been festering? I hear that's a good sign. They say, if the puss flows, you'll survive. If it turns black, you're dead."

"That's encouraging."

Dan was slightly embarrassed by his remarks. "Sorry, didn't mean to—"

Sam shrugged it off. "It's okay. By the way, where you from back home?"

Dan was encouraged that the conversation was taking a different route. "Mendota. You?"

"Stillwater."

"I hear it's nice there," said Dan.

"It's pleasant enough. Hey! Have you heard the news? The Dakota have taken up arms and are massacring everyone along the Minnesota River valley."

"Haven't heard any details other than a few settlers have been killed and Little Crow seems to have taken command of the Native bands," replied Dan.

"Yep, and your local man there, Sibley, the governor put him to the task. Made him a general, I read. All regiments forming up from number 5 on are being left in the state to put down the rebellion."

Dan was surprised and delighted. "No kidding? He's my neighbor. Great. Now we got two wars to contend with. What else did you hear? Any fighting in Mendota?"

"As far as I know, everything is happening north of the Minnesota River. So your kin should be well out of harm's way."

"Thanks for the update. I've got two boys who ran off with the Second Minnesota—and I have no idea what they're into—and a wife and daughter at home that I've been worried sick about."

"That's rough, not knowing. The Second was supposed to be with us out here, but they got diverted in Kentucky and are in the Army of the Ohio now. Too bad they aren't with us, but then again, maybe they are better off."

"I knew that much. They're musicians, so I expect them to be doing okay," said Dan with a sad tone.

The ambulance hit a rut and jostled the occupants very hard. A long moan rose from the wounded in the ambulance.

"I hope you handle a team better than this guy," said Sam.

"I try to, but I have to admit I probably did a terrible job when I was assigned to haul the dead and dying off that field at Antietam."

Sam winced in pain as the wagon rumbled on. "I didn't even get that luxury. The rebs got me first, and then I was exchanged after the first day. Worst of it, though, was…" Sam choked up with emotion, then regained his composure after a moment. "My…my best friend, who was to be my future brother-in-law, was killed right in front of me. His body was hung up on a fence, and I had to look at him like that for a good twelve hours or more. Watched him bloat up so big he burst the seams on his uniform."

Dan was overcome as well. "My God! The things we've seen.

Not like any of the war pictures they have in the Bible, is it?"

"Not like anything I ever imagined. It's horrible. Hey, did anyone give you an idea of where we are going?"

"Yeah, I asked the driver before I got on, and he told me we are going to the best hospital in Washington called Amory Square," answered Dan.

The two men chatted on for the remainder of the trip, which took the better part of a full day and night. With only the rations they had managed to scrounge for themselves and no fresh water, they were feeling much worse by the time the wagon rolled into the outskirts of Washington. Dan leaned over and looked out of the ambulance as it began to make the final few blocks toward their destination. His stomach let out a loud rumble. He gripped his gut and moaned.

"Stinks something awful out there. We must be getting close," he said as his stomach erupted again.

Sam asked if Dan was okay.

Dan replied, "Yeah, sorry, but I can't hold this in any longer." Dan then bent over and pulled off one of his army-issue boots.

He pulled open the tongue, then stood to drop his trousers. He then squatted over the boot and then relieved himself in it. Those in the wagon who were able heckled and jeered him.

Sam was more sympathetic in his response. "Clever trick. I'll have to remember that when I can't make it to a sink."

"Yeah, it's a dandy trick, all right, but the worst part is not having a place to wash your feet afterward," said Dan with an embarrassed grin.

"I'll make a mental note to write the Sanitary Commission and tell them they need to put slop buckets on these new ambulances," replied Sam, "with some clean water as well."

The ambulance was making its final approach to the hospital. They had reached the inner circle of Washington, DC proper. Some of the roads were of cobblestone, but most were still unpaved and full of ruts and potholes. The wounded were bounced around as the ambulance rolled to a rough stop. Orderlies from the hospital threw open the backflaps and dropped the tailgate. In their haste, they began to unload the stretchers.

An orderly spoke up, "Okay, all who can walk, follow us." Dan and the others who were able started to move.

Dan put out his hand to Sam. "Didn't get your full name, pard." "Sam, Sam Bloomer. You?"

"Dan Simmons."

"Good luck to you, Dan. I'll be looking out for you in there." "Likewise. Good luck to you too. Hope you make it home before Christmas."

Sam smiled at his new friend. "That would be nice."

The men shook hands and nodded a farewell for the moment. Sam's stretcher was then lifted out of the wagon, and Dan stepped out into the hot and oppressively humid air as he followed the stretcher bearers into the hospital.

The Armory Square Hospital was a pavilion hospital constructed in the summer of 1862 and was located on Seventh Street across from the grounds of the Smithsonian Institute, just beyond the canal. Today this is on the Washington Mall, where the Smithsonian Air Museum is located. At this time, the canal was an open sewer, which rendered this location rather undesirable. The old city canal was a "fetid bayou" filled with floating dead dogs and cats and all kinds of putridity and reeking with pestilential odors. Dan tried to move into the hospital, but exhausted and panting, he was forced to lean against the wagon until he regained his strength. He lifted his head to get a whiff of the putrid air, nearly gagged, then gathered his strength and headed toward the entrance to the hospital. He reached the front entrance to the building and paused to look at a stack of arms, legs, hands, and feet that were piled up on a cart.

Next to the cart were, stretched out, the naked bodies of the dead who had been taken out of the hospital and laid out in the open on canvas shelter halves and rubber blankets. Sam reached out to Dan as he was carried into the hospital.

"Oh, hey, Sam. I think I see your leg in there."

The orderlies halted as Sam gazed into the amputation pile. "Nope, not there. These are too fresh."

Dan doubled over and gripped his gut as he asked one of the orderlies, "Where are the sinks?"

The orderly pointed. "Far opposite end of the building." Dan sprinted for the entrance, holding his trousers up.

The orderly called out to him, "Hey! You may want to run around back and go in that rear entrance. You don't want the crowd to hold you up."

Dan ran along the outside of the long pavilion-style temporary building. He reached the back of the structure and came to a quick stop. As he ran up to the edge of the creek that spilled into the DC swamp, he paused to look. What he saw made him vomit. After he vomited into the creek, he quickly ran into the building.

Then he called out to the first orderly he saw, "Where are the sinks?"

The orderly pointed. "Behind that wall."

Dan rushed behind the wall, and anyone nearby could hear him do his business most disturbingly. As Dan walked out from the sinks into the open area of the hospital, he was impressed with what he saw.

The hospital interior was pristine for the general condition of hospitals at that time. It had ample space and was well ventilated though it was overflowing with nurses, walking wounded, doctors, and visitors. There were beds lining the walls and room for about two hundred patients. A male nurse, a partially recovered wounded soldier, hobbled up to Dan. He looked Dan up and down.

"Let me see your ticket."

Dan pulled a patient tag out of his tunic breast pocket and handed it to him.

"Um, dysentery, huh? Not wounded. Not surgical. Okay then, section 2." He then pointed the direction out to Dan. "Find an open bed along that wall, and we'll get you checked in as soon as we can."

"When will that be?"

"Take a look around. It's a never-ending supply of guys like you. Probably sometime after dinner."

"And what's for dinner? I'm starving."

The male nurse answered, "The same fair as what you get in the field. Two hardtacks, a handful of beans, a half cup of sugar, and coffee."

"No meat?" asked Dan.

The nurse gave him a sarcastic reply, "Where do you think you are, pard? This ain't Buckingham Palace. You might get some salt pork on Sunday if those cuss-talking, stupid, lazy teamsters can get their wagons here on time." The nurse then got a good whiff of Dan and nearly fainted. "If you need a bath, the creek is right out the back door. We ain't got no soap, though. You're on your own for supplies. Most of the men here find something to barter with. The creek flushes out fairly well after a storm, and we get plenty of them this time of year."

Dan was in no mood to chitchat. "Thanks. I'll pass for now. I'll see myself to my bed. Thank you."

"Yes, please do. You look awful."

Dan headed toward the area he was directed to and, in doing so, saw Sam lying on a comfortable-looking cot. There was an open cot next to him. Dan took it.

"What you doing in this section? This is for the sick, not the wounded."

"They say I'm just sick and well on my way to recovery," replied Sam.

Dan looked at Sam's bandaged stump and leaned in to smell it.

Sam moved away, embarrassed. "I wouldn't if I were you. It's been putrefying and festering pretty bad."

"Yeah, you smell about as sweet as I do. I guess you are sicker than wounded," said Dan as he recoiled back into his bunk.

Dan then called out for a nurse. A beautiful young Black female nurse heard him and jogged over to see what the trouble was. She was a slender girl of about eighteen.

She stepped between the two bunks and looked at both men. "My name is Jill. This is my section of the ward, and I'll be your nurse for as long as you are here. Now what's the problem?"

Dan looked her over and gave her a nod of acceptance, then introduced himself and Sam, "Well, my name is Dan, and this here is my pard, Sam. As you can see, his stump needs some attention. I think he needs to have some more surgery, and maybe he should be moved to the other side closer to the doctors."

Jill leaned in to take a closer look at Sam. "I'm sorry, but as you can see, the doctors don't have time for those who don't need immediate attention."

Sam protested to Dan, "Dan, no, no. I'd rather stay here. No more butchers for me. I can tend to it myself."

Jill looked at Dan. "If he's your friend, then you can surely help, can't you?"

Dan pointed to Sam's ragged bandages. "I suppose, but can we at least get some clean bandages? These smell pretty bad."

Jill turned to leave. Other patients were calling.

"I'll see what I can find. I'll bring a pan and a knife so you can drain that wound too."

"Thank you, miss," said Dan.

"You're welcome, and you may call me Jill or Nurse Jill," she replied as she left to attend other soldiers.

Sam now turned to Dan. "You ever drain a wound this big before?"

"I've doctored hogs in worse shape than you, and they lived long enough to produce a decent ham," he replied with a sly smile.

"Are you planning on having me for dinner?" asked Sam jokingly.

"If that's the only way I can get any meat, then yes." The two men were very tired and started to drift off.

Sam asked one more question from Dan, "Can you get to the sinks okay on your own?"

"Yes, I think so. If not, I'll let you call an orderly for me." "Okay. How about we get some sleep?"

That ended their conversation, and they both fell asleep.

Thunder and lightning cracked outside the hospital. A torrent of rain poured down. The canvas roof of the pavilion hospital was full of leaks, and water poured in on the sick and wounded. Nurses and attendants were running helter-skelter to place buckets under the leaks. Sam was feverish and tossing and turning in his bunk, obviously in a great deal of pain.

Dan woke up to Sam's moaning. "Hey, pard? You all right?" Sam shook his head not all right.

Dan rose from his bunk and looked for a nurse. "Hold on. I'll fetch that nurse. What's her name? Jill."

Dan, not doing very well himself, slowly lifted himself out of his bunk and took one of Sam's crutches that was leaning against the wall. He steadied himself with it and moved slowly across the hospital floor looking for Jill. He found her on the opposite side of the room, where she was busy helping a doctor in surgery.

Dan abruptly interrupted her, "Nurse? Nurse Jill?"

Jill spun around, obviously annoyed. "What is it now?"

"My friend, he's suffering something awful. Is there anything you have for his pain?" asked Dan ever so politely.

Jill barked back at him. The amputation the surgeon was performing was not going well. "No! Not now! I told you you'll have to drain that wound for him and redress it. In case you didn't notice, I put a pan and knife at the end of your bunk."

"What about his pain and fresh bandages?" asked Dan.

"We have nothing to spare for his pain. Give him something to bite on. That will have to do." Jill then pointed to a string of bandages that were hanging off the end of the surgical table. "You can use those."

Dan reached for a bandage and inspected it. It was caked in dried blood. "This is so stiff it will hardly fold."

Jill then pointed to a large cast-iron pot of boiling water, which was sitting atop a potbellied wood-burning stove. "Just throw them in that pot over there."

"You want I should boil these bandages?" asked Dan, curious as to why this was a good idea.

Jill nodded and went back to paying attention to the poor soul lying on the table about to have his arm cut off. "It will make those bandages more manageable. I'll bring them to you as soon as I'm finished here."

Dan dropped the bandages into the pot, thanked her, then left to return to Sam's side.

Jill returned to her work helping the surgeon with the amputation.

The doctor wiped a bloody surgical knife on his apron and then proceeded with this fresh amputation. "Nurse, tighten that tourniquet."

Jill turned the screw on the device. The doctor proceeded to slice around the patient's arm above the elbow, and in one quick flash, he had cut through to the bone. He ordered Jill to hand him the bone saw. Jill handed him the saw, and the doctor was through the bone in a few seconds. He dropped the arm at his feet, where an orderly would deposit it outside later.

"Record time, Doctor!" exclaimed Jill with pride.

The doctor then pulled the flap of flesh over the bone end and opened wound and prepared to stitch it closed. "Nurse? Do you have silk and needle ready for me?"

"I'm sorry, sir. We've run out of silk."

"What do we have? I can't hold this much longer," the doctor replied in a very stern manner.

"I'm boiling some horsehair. It will be good and flexible in a few moments. I'll prepare the first suture now," said Jill, trying to appease the surgeon.

Jill then immediately fished around in the boiling pot and pulled out a long strand of horsehair. She threaded it through the large leather worker's curved needle, then handed it to the surgeon.

"Thank you. Now watch closely how I tie this off. You may have to do this yourself soon."

"Yes, sir," replied Jill.

The surgeon put in the first stitch and handed the needle back to Jill. "Again, and a dozen more should do it."

Jill continued to supply him with sutures until the wound had been closed. Jill finished the surgery by fully bandaging the stump. All the procedures from the time the patient was placed on the table until the entire surgery was completed took less than ten minutes. The surgeon wiped his bloody hands on his apron and looked around. He looked at another soldier who was suffering from a stomach wound.

The surgeon waved them off. "There's nothing we can do for him. Take him to the dead room."

The orderlies removed the man and hurried off with his body. The cries and moaning from the sick and wounded filled the air, and the misery that was so suffocating was only made worse by the heat and humidity of the autumn heat wave that was covering Washington and the mid-Atlantic region.

An afternoon thunderstorm relieved the suffering for a while. The city began to cool off, and to everyone's relief, the orderlies opened all the doors and windows that would let in the cool breeze that came after the storm. Dan had returned to his bunk with the bandages and saw sitting on the floor at the end of his bunk the pan and knife that Jill had left for him. He picked up the articles and seated himself next to Sam. He pulled back Sam's blanket to reveal his bandaged stump. He then gingerly began to unwrap the bandages. As he exposed the wound, he retched at the sight before him. The stump was swollen and festering badly. Puss was oozing out around the stitches and the partially healed wound. Sam grimaced. Dan held out a piece of the leather strap of his belt for him. Sam put it in his mouth and bit down hard, knowing full well what was about to happen. Dan patted the sweat off his friend's brow as Sam moaned.

"Sorry, pard. It's all we've got. Hold tight. I'm going to cut these stitches and drain this leg of yours."

Dan, overcome with a fever himself, began to pop one stitch after the other. As he released more, the wound opened, and the puss sprayed out and splattered at Dan and the bedding. Sam, relieved for the moment of the pain from the pressure buildup, groaned a deep sigh of relief and spit out the leather strap. Dan caught what he could in the pan.

Dan squeezed the hand of his friend. "That should hold you for a while."

Sam, near tears, could only thank him in the weakest voice.

As Sam settled back into his bunk, Jill walked up with the bandages and needle and horsehair thread in hand. "What do you think, Sergeant? Should we put you back together?"

Sam nodded. "Sure. Have at it."

"Okay. First I'm going to wipe some laudanum over that stump to ease the pain a bit, then I'll restitch it and put on these fresh bandages."

Dan looked over to Jill. "Do you know how to stitch up a wound?"

"Sure, just watch me," replied Jill.

Dan sat up to watch and handed the leather belt back to Sam, who put it back in his mouth and bit down hard again as Jill did her work.

With the wound now cleaned and put back in order, Dan and Sam discussed the news they had read earlier about the Sioux Uprising back in their home state. The *Harper's Weekly* newspaper of September 1862 had a detailed report of the events, along with a cartoon of the savage murders and raping of the citizens caught up in the ordeal.

The cartoon also mentioned that the uprising was supported by the Confederacy. This newspaper, as well as others that were found in the hospital, were somewhat out of date; but Dan and Sam were able to construct a very detailed account of what had taken place. The two men had known about the record of the Third Regiment and knew that they were about to be sent back to the Western Theater, but they had not known about the role the Fifth Minnesota Regiment had played in the revolt. Dan and Jill, who was one of the rarely found educated Negroes, would take turns reading to Sam the account of the battles that consumed Redwood, Fort Ripley, Fort Abercrombie, Fort Ridgely, New Ulm, and Saint Cloud. The dispatches from the state were spelled out. *Harper's* opened the narrative as such:

A recital of the horrible atrocities committed by those Indian devils, and the brutalities and terrible deaths suffered by many of the defenseless pioneers upon our then western border, is enough to curdle the blood and chill the heart of the hearer. That those horrors were not multiplied tenfold and additional thousands numbered among their victims is due in great measure to the service rendered by Companies B, C, and D of Fifth Minnesota.

ARMORY HOSPITAL

By the end of 1863, well-ventilated multiple-pavilion-style hospitals were being built in major cities, accommodating up to three thousand patients each. Letterman's ambulance corps was effectively functioning, and the wounded were timely removed from battlefields. Tent hospitals by the hundreds were prepared and set up at battlefields, such as Gettysburg, and at way stations, such as City Point. By the war's end, there were 204 Union general hospitals with 136,894 beds. During the war, over one million soldiers received care in Union military hospitals and perhaps a similar number in Confederate hospitals.

Dan and Sam were convalescing in the Armory hospital, and all the news they had read about the Indian revolt was good news in the fact that neither man needed to worry about their families. Autumn was closing in fast. John and William were still on what seemed to be an endless march in pursuit of Bragg and his Southern Army.

At the Armory hospital, Sam had undergone three more surgeries on his stump to relieve the festering, and he was now about to complete another. Jill, one more time, would work on draining and restitching Sam's stump. Sam struggled against the pain but toughed it out. Dan was dripping in sweat from fever as he watched from his bunk the procedures that were now becoming commonplace with Sam. On one such occasion, he was suddenly overcome with cramps, and he excused himself.

"Sorry, I hate to miss this show, but I have to trot off to the sinks again."

Dan left his cot and somewhat comically grabbed his bottom as he rushed off to the toilet. Sam let out a whimper as Jill put in another stitch.

"Sorry. Just one more and then I'll put on the fresh bandages." Sam nodded and winced once again.

Dan returned as Jill was tying off the last of the bandages to Sam's stump. He climbed back into his bunk, but he was very ill.

Dan motioned to Sam. "How you are doing there, pard?" "Almost finished. I'll be out of your hair in just a moment," said

Jill as she finished up her work. "There you go, Sergeant. A couple more weeks and you should be able to get up and move around with crutches," she said as she packed up her belongings and turned to Dan. Jill looked to Dan and saw he was trembling from a terrible chill and fever. "Have you been getting any better?"

"Not by a long shot."

Jill patted his hand. "I'm going to get you an extra blanket to fight that fever. Have you had your blue mass today?"

"Yes, and it hasn't done any good at all. I've been chugging down that awful cement for nearly five months now. Isn't there some other remedy? I've seen some folks do better with a little bit of tar and kerosene."

Sam shook his head in disbelief. "How about a proper diet?"

Jill answered Sam, "Sorry, but all of the choice servings are reserved for the top officers and government officials we have in here."

Dan, shaking with chills, asked Jill, "Well, could you at least get him some fresh linens? The smell of his old puss and that festering wound is enough to make me vomit."

Jill agreed to return soon with the fresh bedding.

Dan then asked her a surprising question as she was about to walk off, "By the way, Jill? Are you a freedwoman?"

She asked him why he wanted to know.

Dan replied, "Just curious. You seem to be good at your job here, and I would suspect that there would be a good nursing job for you in any big Northern city."

Jill thanked him and continued to her duties. "Maybe one day that will all come about. In the meantime, you try to get some sleep, and I'll see if I can steal some decent vittles from those rebel officers in the other ward."

As she walked away, Sam asked of her, "We got rebs in here with us?"

Jill told him, "This is a hospital. We don't discriminate against the sick. All people suffer the same."

Both men agreed with that. As Jill walked off, Dan took in a long gander at her. Sam asked what he was thinking, and Dan told him he thought Jill was a handsome-looking woman.

Then he said, "Never thought of a darky woman in that way."

Sam jokingly replied, "But I bet you have regarding one of your mules."

Dan nodded and forced a slight laugh. "Maybe…maybe… But I never would treat a mule any way like I've seen some folks treat their darkies down here."

Sam looked over to his friend and saw nothing but the sunken eyes of a man in dire straits. "Hey! If you want to get through the night alive, you'd better shut up and get some sleep. I've never seen a man as miserable-looking as you."

Dan tried to find some comfort and replied, "If I could find a mirror, then you could get a good look at real misery."

Jill returned with the linens and rolled Sam onto his side as she changed his bedding and made him as comfortable as possible.

"Did those bedsheets come out of that creek?" asked Sam to Jill. "Everything comes out of that creek, but don't worry. We've got good laundresses here and plenty of lye. I see to it that the bedding always gets hung out to air so the bad vapors don't spread any more illness."

On that, Dan let out a huge wet fart.

Sam pulled Jill close. "Speaking of vapors, can we do anything for him? Really?"

Jill pulled away. "We've got over two hundred patients in this hospital alone, and there are thousands more in DC. More than half are sick like him, and of that half, most will die. I'll do what I can."

Sam thanked her, and she continued with her chores.

Dan's condition faltered between days of relative relief to recurring bouts of misery, fever, and intense suffering at night. As Sam was regaining his health, Dan was slipping away. He did not look well at all. His weight loss and paleness gave him the appearance of a living skeleton. On one muggy night in early October, Dan was stricken again—for the worse. No longer able to control his bowels, he had defecated and vomited all over himself and his bedding. His fever had reached its peak. Delirium was setting in. He frantically reached out to Sam. Thunder and lightning were breaking outside, and another torrential autumn storm began.

With sunken eyes, Dan looked for help from Sam. "Get...get... me out of here... Help me get up. I don't think I can walk."

Sam reached for his crutch and gingerly lifted himself. He then moved to Dan's bedside and helped him to get up.

Jill came running over as she saw the two men struggle to get to their feet and make an escape. "Where do you two think you're going?"

Dan turned to Jill and pleaded, "Just let me stand in the rain one more time."

Jill took Dan's arm, and with Sam's help, they led him to the exit. The three stepped outside, and the hard rain soaked them. They stood there in the pouring rain, arms around each other. Dan looked up to the sky as the thunderclouds passed over and revealed a bit of the moon.

"Can my wife and children see this same moon tonight?" he whispered.

"I believe they are looking at it right now," said Sam.

Dan was losing his balance, and the other two struggled to hold him on his feet.

As his knees buckled, he breathed his last words, "Oh, how I love a good summer storm in Mendota... Time to go home..."

Dan then fell forward face-first into the mud. Jill knelt to cover him with his blanket. She checked his pulse, then looked up to Sam and shook her head.

"Gone up" was all she could say.

Sam was at a loss for words, but he knew what had to be done. "I'll write letters to his family."

Jill nodded and replied, "It's best a friend does it. Also can you see to it he gets shipped back home? The army has no place for the dead here. Okay now…you get back to bed. The orderlies will take it from here."

Sam hesitated to move. "Are we just going to let him lie here in the ditch?"

"They'll sort it out in the morning. Now off to bed for you before you bust open your stitches again."

Jill helped Sam back to his bunk, where he would spend a sleepless night dwelling on the loss of his new friend.

WAR AT HOME AND IN THE WEST

Man is the only animal that deals in that atrocity of atrocities, War. He is the only one that gathers his brethren about him and goes forth in cold blood and calm pulse to exterminate his kind. He is the only animal that for sordid wages will march out...and help to slaughter strangers of his species who have done him no harm and with whom he does not quarrel... And in the intervals between campaigns, he washes the blood off his hands and works for "the universal brotherhood of man"—with his mouth.

—Mark Twain, "What Is Man?"

Dawn in Eastern Kentucky in October of 1862 wasn't much better than in the nation's capital city. Heavy rain was falling on company K of the Second Minnesota as it neared a creek that was overrunning its bank. A team of horses was pulling a caisson and cannon that were stuck axle deep in the river's edge. John and William, along with the others in the company, pitched in to help push the artillery piece across the overflowing plank bridge.

As John took hold of a wheel spoke, he grunted out to his brother. "And so begins another lovely day on the march."

"Yep, just another bridge to nowhere, it seems," replied William as he put his shoulder into the wheel.

"We'll make contact one day. I heard the generals are all taking a break to examine the whereabouts of Bragg and his army," said Vandyke as he ran up to help.

"I thought Bragg and his boys were right in front of us," said William.

Vandyke heaved against the wheel along with the others. "That's what I thought too, but rumor today is seems like old Bragg has slipped back to Louisville."

"The circle never ends, does it? How many more times are we going to walk through that place?" replied John.

William answered pragmatically, "Just over one year since we left home, and this will make it our third circle back. I sure hope Mary is waiting."

The conversation then turned to past events.

"That little battle at Mill Springs was a fine welcome. And are we going to get a battle ribbon on the flag for Perryville?" asked John.

Vandyke answered, "I heard we are not. We weren't engaged long enough to earn one."

"So they said about Corinth, but I think both of those were as hot as Mill Springs."

"Corinth? Are you joking? We did nothing there. But they ought to give us a ribbon for having to put up with the stink at Shiloh," William said to his brother.

All the men, now engaged in freeing the cannon, had a good laugh.

Then William added, "Maybe Bragg will stop long enough so we can hit him hard."

John changed the subject again, "I wonder how Pa is doing out east."

"The old First has been in the thick of all of it. But no news from him is good news, I suspect," said the all-knowing Vandyke.

Suddenly one of the caisson wheels slipped off the edge of the plank bridge and was about to take the entire battery into the creek. The men jumped back out of the way of the falling equipment. The mules strained and whinnied against their yokes but to no avail. The driver jumped for his life. The cannon was lost into the rushing water.

"Great! Just great!" moaned William.

"Look on the bright side. At least we can rest while we march," said John.

Vandyke and William looked at him, puzzled by his comment.

But then John explained, "Interesting thing, isn't it? Seeing a man sleep while he is walking."

The other two agreed.

John continued, "Yes, sir! And if you don't mind, I think I'll fall in behind you this time so I can fall in on your pack."

Company K continued its march at a leisurely route step under a cloudy sky and heavy rain. John was marching directly behind his brother. The backpack held his head on top of William's backpack. His face was nestled into William's army blanket, and in fact, he was indeed sound asleep yet still plodding along with the rest of the company. William and Vandyke tapped out a simple beat to keep the men moving in their hypnotic state. They, too, appeared to be fully asleep.

The putrid creek behind the Armory Hospital was running somewhat clean as the heavy rain that fell on the night Dan died had flushed most of the debris down the creek and toward the Potomac River out to the sea. Sam and Jill wandered out of the hospital after taking a brief breakfast to look for Dan's body. They found his naked body stacked upon a heap of others. Sam stood next to Jill, and as tears came to his eyes, he asked of her what the proper procedure was for procuring Dan's corpse so that it could be sent back to his family. Dan had told him, if he was to die, to make sure he got back home; and this was a promise that Sam would uphold. Jill was familiar with the circumstances and had helped many other soldiers on their way back home, so she knew what to say to ease Sam's anxiety.

"I'll see to it that he is taken to the embalmer's tent in a few hours and that they prep his body so he can be sent home. Do you know if that's what he wanted? It will cost a couple of dollars. Can you spare it?"

"Yes, he left me all he had. I never asked, but that would seem the right thing to do. Would you mind helping me with getting letters off to his wife and boys?"

"Sure. I'd be happy to help." Jill then took Sam by his arm and helped him back into the hospital.

Dan's body would lie on the stack of dead bodies for another day, at which time orderlies upon Jill's direction took him to the embalmer, where he was registered for the official records of the army. The next day, Sam would leave the hospital on his own to tend to the business of sending Dan home. His stump was healing fine; and the surgeon had told him that there was a possibility that there would be no more infections and that, within short order, he would be fitted with a false limb.

Able to hobble about with just his crutches, Sam made his way to the embalmer's tent and was faced with a young mortician's assistant. The assistant was dressed like a civilian as the army did not have men like these in the ranks and all burial details were either seen by freed slaves or contracted civilians. Sam was asked what his business was, and he replied that he was there to collect his friend's body for proper shipment back home. The attendant asked if he was living or dead. Dan told him he was one of the dead and had died not of wounds but dysentery.

He then gave complete details, "Dead as of a few nights ago.

Dan, Dan Simmons. First Minnesota Volunteers."

The attendant shuffled through a file box and mumbled to himself just loud enough for Sam to hear.

He spoke with an Irish accent, "First Minnesota. Dysentery. Yes, I think I remember him. Right, so many with dysentery. This war will end just from men dying of the shits. Forget about the gunshots, shells, and other wounds. Okay, here we are." He then slid the file across his working table for Sam to read. "Go around the back. You'll see row on row of coffins waiting to be shipped. He's in aisle B, number 303. You're a good lad to make sure he gets home to his family. Too many end up in that stink hole of a creek or are buried in the swamps around here."

"I also have a couple of letters to go with him," replied Sam. "You'll see the postmaster's shack out there. Just hand them to him and tell him your details. They'll take care of it for you. By the way, how are you getting on?"

Sam was in a hurry but paused to thank the man and tell him he was doing fine and well on the way to going home himself. "Just fine. I was told I'll be getting fitted for my cork leg soon."

"Good, then I won't be seeing you back here anytime soon?" asked the attendant.

"I reckon not. I'm to be mustered out within the month. They tell me I might be home before Christmas." Sam continued on his way.

The attendant tipped his hat to him. "Let's hope so. Good luck to you then."

Sam followed the path to the stacked coffins, found Dan's box, and then delivered the letters to the postmaster along with the shipping instructions for Dan's body. He paid the fare, then hobbled back to the hospital and his bunk.

Once Sam was comfortable in his bunk, Jill came to him with a couple of letters from his family in Minnesota. "Here's some old news that has finally caught up with you."

The letters were from his sister; and folded within them were clippings from the local newspaper of Stillwater, Minnesota. The clippings were reprints of dispatches from one of the soldiers who had participated in the two battles at New Ulm, Minnesota, which took place on August 18 and August 23, 1862.

Back at the Armory Hospital, Sam was recovering at a good pace. He was no longer suffering from infections, and his overall pain was minimal. The surgeon in charge was preparing for Sam to be discharged but not until Sam could master with some skill the ability to walk alone with an artificial limb. Jill had now become his only source of care and friendship. He trusted her completely; and on the day she arrived at his bedside with the crude leather, cork, and wood artificial leg and asked him to expose the stump of his amputated leg, he obliged. She proudly presented the leg to him as if it were a trophy, and indeed to Sam, it did feel as if it were an earned award.

"Okay, Mr. Sam, the idea here is to roll this knit stocking over your stump for comfort and to absorb sweat. That helps keep the leg in place."

Sam presented his stump to Jill, and she rolled the knit stocking over it.

"Okay, now we are going to fit the leg. I'll set it, and you need to stand to force your stump in all the way. Do you understand?"

Sam nodded as Jill put the leg opening over the stump. "Okay, that looks good. If it feels all right, then get up."

Sam wiggled the leg a bit to set it more comfortably, then with the help of his crutches and leaning on Jill, Sam rose to fit his new leg. Jill buckled the leather belts that secured his leg to his thigh.

"Okay. There you go. You feel all right?" "Yeah, a little bit unsteady but not bad."

"Do you want to take your first step?" Jill asked.

Sam inched forward, dropping his crutches and taking Jill's hands.

"Yes, that's it. Just take my hands, and I'll steady you. Start with your good leg, then just drag the other up until you can set it."

Sam took his first awkward step, nearly falling, but with Jill spotting him, he managed a couple more.

"Very good! How do you feel now?" "Dizzy," said Sam.

"That's normal, but as you regain your strength, you'll be as good as new. And I think that's enough for today."

Jill helped Sam back into his bunk. He lay back to rest. "Can I leave it on for the rest of the day?"

"You can leave it on for as long as you like, but if it gets uncomfortable, just take it off and set it aside. But put it under the bed. We don't want anyone to steal it."

Sam was shocked that anyone would steal his leg.

Jill continued to explain, "You'd be surprised at what walks out of here. Soldiers going home will take anything they think they can sell."

"Speaking of going home, any final word on that?" asked Sam. "Yes. As soon as you can walk one hundred steps by yourself, you'll be released."

"How long does that usually take?"

"About three weeks. But that means work and exercise every day. Do you think you can do that?"

"Sure, I can."

"Okay then. Now get some sleep. I'll come to get you when the mess is served."

"What kind of slop are we getting today?" asked Sam. "Navy bean soup."

"Any bread with that?"

"I'm afraid just the usual three squares of hardtack. But you might be one of the lucky ones who finds a piece of ham in their bowl," replied Jill as she headed off.

Sam would indeed take a moment to examine if he was one of the lucky ones. He thanked Jill for all her help; she just replied by telling him it was just her job. As he eased back to sleep, his mind was full of expectations of being discharged as well as his fondness for his nurse Jill.

Indeed, it came to pass that Sam did learn to walk quite well with his new leg; and to his surprise, he was to be discharged on December 2, 1862. With luck, he would be in Minnesota before Christmas and be able to attend the funeral of his friend Dan, which was scheduled for just before the holiday.

Dan's body had arrived in Saint Paul, Minnesota, in late November and had been in storage at a local icehouse to keep him preserved until his funeral. Before Sam was discharged from the hospital, Jill had approached him with a letter from the surgeon general at Armory Hospital asking if Sam would be interested in reenlisting into the Veteran Reserve Corps, or Invalid Corps as it was commonly known among soldiers. It would give him the rank of lieutenant with the same pay as all junior officers in the army, $105 a month. He could also report for duty at the Armory Hospital if he wished.

Jill tried to encourage him to do it as she thought he would be an asset helping other soldiers who had lost a leg or two. Sam said he would consider it, and Jill passed that on to the surgeon general. Though Sam was still interested in serving in the military, foremost on his mind was getting home and settling back into civilian life. In December of 1862, the Invalid Corps was not yet fully realized; it would be a year or more before it was. This, thought Sam, was perfect as it would give him time to recuperate and see if he wanted to return to military life.

On December 4, Sam boarded a train out of Washington and began his journey home. His route was the same as when he had traveled east more than a year ago. Nine days later, at La Crosse, Wisconsin, he boarded the steamboat *Dunbar*, which took him to the dockage at Saint Paul. Surprisingly the river had not yet frozen over though there was some thin ice that the steamer had no trouble breaking through. When the riverboat tied up at the landing, it was greeted by the citizens of the city, who lined the dock and shore. Christmas decorations were hung from the telegraph poles and trees. The air was full of patriotic and holiday celebrations as the throngs of people cheered the arrival of furloughed troops and wounded or dead companions.

Sam Bloomer steadied himself on his artificial leg as he worked his way across the gangplank to the shore. On the dock waiting to receive him were Louise, Sara, and the casket of his friend Dan. Sam recognized them immediately and rushed as best he could to take the hand of Louise.

"You must be Louise?"

"Yes, that's right, and this here is Sara," replied Louise as she shook his hand.

Greeting Sara, Sam took her tiny hand and said, "Ah, the lovely Sara. I heard so much about you. You were the joy of his life."

Louise now turned to Sam. "Thank you so much for your letters, and especially thank you for taking care of him in his final hours."

Sam thanked her for saying so. "He did his share of taking care of me too."

"I'm sure he did. He liked helping others. Now let's be on our way and see to this unpleasant business, shall we?"

Overcome with emotion, Sara and Louise broke down, which then had the same effect on Sam.

"There will be a huge reception after, and we insist you be there."

"I would be honored, but I can only stay the day. I hope to get home to Stillwater before too long," said Sam.

Louise nodded between sobs. "Yes, I'm sure you have family. A wife? Children of your own?"

"Not really," said Sam.

Sara now wiped away her tears and spoke, "A sweetheart then." Louise reprimanded her, "Sara! Mind your manners!"

Sam kindly replied, "No, no, no, it's quite all right. Maybe there is. How about I tell you all about myself later, okay, Sara?"

Louise was preparing to see the loading of her husband's casket. "Well, come along then. Let's get him on a cart and off to home."

Among the confusion of the masses of people, Dan's casket was loaded onto an ox cart. Sam, Sara, and Louise climbed aboard as the driver slapped the reigns on the back of an ox. The cart lunged forward and up the hill of the levee. A regimental band struck up a martial song as the dry axle of the cart squawked along the muddy road, followed by furloughed and wounded soldiers.

Louise now settled back for the ride home. She turned to Sam. "The crossing is just a few miles up this road. I'm afraid Mendota will not have all the amenities and comforts you are used to in DC or the other fine places you've seen."

"I don't think you would have found any of those places so fine," answered Sam.

"But wasn't Washington grand?" asked Sara.

"I didn't get a chance to see much. I've only been able to get around on this peg leg for about ten days and only saw the fine points of the capital from a buggy. As much as I would have loved to see it on foot, it wasn't to be so."

Louise was becoming irritated by Sara's exuberance. "Sara! I won't tell you again. Don't trifle with Mr. Bloomer. He is our guest, and I'm sure he doesn't want to be reminded of his situation any more than we do."

Sara pouted. "I'm sorry, Mr. Bloomer."

"Don't be. I'll tell you all you want to know, later, okay?"

That ended the conversation until the cart reached the high road up from the levee that would lead to Fort Snelling. The ox knew this route as it was part of its daily journey of taking supplies to and from the fort and river. When it reached the crest, the ox was able to ease the cart's wheels into the ruts of the road; and from henceforth, the ride was as smooth as could be.

A NEW YEAR

We shall meet, but we shall miss him,
There will be one vacant chair:
We shall linger to caress him,
When we breathe our evening prayer.
When a year ago we gathered,
Joy was in his mild blue eye;
But a golden cord is severed,
And our hopes in ruin lie.
At our fireside, sad and lonely, Often will the
bosom swell At remembrance of the story, How
our noble Willie fell;
How he strove to bear our banner.
Through the thickest of the fight,
And upheld our country's honor
With the strength of manhood's might.
True, they tell us, wreaths of glory
Evermore will deck his brow;
But this soothes the anguish,
Sweeping o'er our heartstrings now.
Sleep today, O early fallen.
In thy green and narrow bed.
Dirges from the pine and cypress
Mingle with the tears we shed.

> *We shall meet, but we shall miss him,*
> *There will be one vacant chair*
> *We shall linger to caress him,*
> *When we breathe our evening prayer.*

—Henry Stevenson Washburn,
"The Vacant Chair"
Worcester, Massachusetts, November 16, 1861
Set to music by George F. Root

December 1862 in Kentucky was barely more comfortable than in Minnesota. There was less snowfall, but the rain and mud that consumed the marches of the western Union Army were relentless. The year was ending; and the Simmons brothers, along with the rest of their company, had seen endless marching, boredom, and misery. News of their father's death had reached the boys via the letter that Sam had sent from the Armory Hospital. Now William and Vandyke were given guard duty to oversee the stockade at the camp they were bivouacked at somewhere in the hills of Kentucky. William was sitting on the side of his drum next to a makeshift desk and was scribbling something into his diary. Vandyke was standing guard yet keeping an eye on his friend out of curiosity.

"How long have you been writing in that diary?" "Since the very day we left home," answered William. "Have you been keeping a record of everything?"

William told him that, yes, he was keeping a good record of most everything. Vandyke thought the idea of keeping a record of their boring rituals was boring enough and not worth writing about.

What is the point? he thought.

"Are you making up hero stuff so that someone might read it one day and not get bored?" asked Vandyke.

William said he was just keeping a record of the true life of his experience and didn't care if anyone ever read it in the future.

"Okay, so how many drummers did we start with last year?" asked Vandyke.

"Eleven. And now it's just us two, which is why we always get guard duty," answered William.

Vandyke scoffed. "I've been meaning to complain about that." William laughed. "What good would that do?"

"Probably nothing, but it sure would feel good yelling at somebody about it, like when you find somebody half your size who is aggravating you and you give him a good beating."

William laughed again. "I'm half your size. You want to try and lick me?"

"Nah, I've seen how you stand up in a fight. You're no slacker for sure. Besides, we drummers must stick together. Maybe I'll give your brother a lickin'."

William laughed again. "Okay by me! Try it!"

William then went back to his scribbling. He mumbled out numerical figures to himself.

Vandyke overheard him. "Hey! What are you figuring over there in your diary?"

William looked up a bit perturbed. "It's not a diary. Girls have diaries. This is a journal. And one day it might be a book."

Now Vandyke laughed. "Ah, who would ever want to read a book about this? We ain't done nothing much than walk all over a couple of states wet, cold, hungry, and miserable all the time."

William half-heartedly agreed, "Well, that's just it. I'm tallying up all the miles we marched in the past year."

"The entire year?"

"Yep, with New Year's just around the corner, I'd figure it would be a nice gift for the boys to know how far they walked in one year." Vandyke nodded and then took a more somber note. "By the way,

I've been meaning to tell you how sorry I am to hear about your pa." William thanked him as Vandyke paused.

"Stinking officers! You'd think the colonel could have at least given one of you two a leave to go home for the funeral. After all, it is Christmas."

William brushed it off as if it were just old business, which it was, and they had both been in the army long enough to know that complaining about it was of no use.

"Ah, it's okay. I guess it's more important I stay here and sound an alarm in case one of these criminals tries to make a run for it."

Vandyke took a seat next to William and watched him work on his figuring. "Almost finished?"

William scratched in a few more numbers. "Yep, just have this month to go. And there it is! It's 1,493 miles for all of 1862."

"But we still have two days left in the year."

"Then how about we get a bet started around camp to see if we can break 1,500?" replied William, excited by his idea.

Vandyke thought this was a good idea as well, something to break up their monotony. "Sure! We can break it down to tenths of a mile, and the one who gets the closest wins! I'll be the first to throw in."

"Okay, what you got?"

Vandyke wanted to know how many miles they had been averaging in a day.

William would not allow his friend any advantage. "No cheating! I'm not telling! Nobody gets an advantage."

Vandyke protested, "But…but…you and I are the only drummers left in the regiment. That must hold for something."

William held firm, "No buts. Make your bet."

Vandyke thought for a moment. "Okay then. Two bits say we hit 1,498.7."

William jotted it down in his book. After sunrise, the boys were off guard duty, and they spread out among the camp, taking bets from whatever men were interested. By evening, William had filled an entire small notebook. William, having real knowledge of the daily average of their marching, kept himself out of the pool as he felt it only fair.

Back in Mendota, a fire had been built over the ground which would become Dan's grave. It was common at this time of year as the ground would be rock hard and frozen and nearly impossible to dig into, so the hot coals of the fire were used to warm the earth so the grave could be dug. This would take almost the better part of two days. But it was ready when Dan's casket arrived. The grave was dug next to the tree stump that held the axe that Dan buried in on his last day at home.

A military honor guard sent over from Fort Snelling stood at attention along the edge of the grave. The casket holding the body of Dan was set on planks over the open hole in the ground. Sara, Jane Sibley, Sam, and Louise, along with some members of the community, stood to the side. Sara openly wept as her mother comforted her. The local preacher said the final words about Dan and his heroic efforts, then ended with a few words from the Bible.

"For the Lord himself shall descend from heaven with a shout, with the voice of the archangel, and with the trumpet of God, and the dead in Christ shall rise first."

An unseen bugler played out taps as the pallbearers lowered the casket into the grave. The honor guard fired off two rounds, which were the customary signal of a lost man. Then, from the parade ground at Fort Snelling across the river from Mendota, a gun crew waited for the muskets to sound. On hearing the second shot, they returned the final return salute with a shot from a small field cannon. The cannon shot was the signal that the missing man had been heard and help was on the way. With that, each person passed the grave and dumped a shovel full of dirt onto Dan's casket. The funeral broke up, and people walked up the hillside leading to the Sibley mansion. Guests filled the interior of the house for the reception. Food and drink were being consumed as people chatted in the background. From across the river the, faint sound of a slow drum roll could be heard.

Sara tugged at Sam's sleeve. "Mr. Bloomer? What is that beat? I used to help William with his rudiments, but I don't remember that one."

Sam, still choked up from the funeral, responded slowly, "Um, well, that one…that one is the death march."

Sara began to weep again. "Is he playing it for my dad?"

Sam was trying to control his feelings in front of the girl. "Well, he may just be practicing, or he may be playing it for all those who died in the Indian revolt, but I think he is playing it for everyone."

Louise was in the parlor talking to Jane. "Jane, I just can't thank you enough for all you have done. There was no way I could have paid to bring my man home, and the thought of him being buried in a common grave in some Southern soil is just too much to even consider. You have done us a great service making sure he can rest on his property among family and friends."

Jane took Louise by her hand to comfort her. "Don't ever think anything of it again. Henry insisted. He said he'll bring all the Minnesota boys back home if he must. You know he lost so many of his soldiers to the massacres."

Louise sighed. "When do you expect him home? Now that the rebellion has been put down and the Natives are in custody, is there any reason for him to still be in the field?"

Jane explained Henry's situation as briefly as she could, "Little Crow and some of the other leaders have headed for Dakota Territory and into Canada. He intends to chase them down in the Dakotas and destroy them all. So I don't now really know."

Sam then limped up to the parlor serving table, where he found Louise and Jane. He had heard of final dispatches sent to Jane by her husband of the events that finalized the Sioux Uprising and was anxious to read them.

After the proper salutations were said, he asked of Jane Sibley, "Mrs. Sibley, I understand you have dispatches from your husband regarding the end of the uprising."

She acknowledged it was true. "Yes, I have a report you could read if you like."

Sam said he would very much like to see it, and Jane left the parlor to fetch it. When she returned with it, Sam thanked her, then found a place to sit and read through it. What he read was Lieutenant Colonel Marshall's extensive report of the Battle of Wood Lake on September 23.

Sam was satisfied that he was now caught up on the news and returned the dispatches to Jane. Jane was grateful but felt compelled to talk to Sam anyway.

"Mr. Bloomer! How nice of you to have stayed with us these past couple of days. We so enjoyed your news of the war and your pitiful descriptions of that awful hospital. Oh! I just can't imagine the horror of all of it! And Louise, Henry, and I want to thank you again for all you did for Dan to ease his suffering and help him on his way." "But one question I have to ask," interrupted Louise. "Why haven't my boys come home? It's been over a year, and we were prom-ised they would all get a thirty-day leave within the year."

Sam answered as best he could, "That's a question you'll have to take up with their colonel. One thing I learned is you can't trust what the army says or does."

Louise turned an accusing eye toward Jane. "You'd think there was some special compensation for a mother who has sent all her men off to fight in this useless war."

Sam suspected there was some unsettled business between the two women that involved General Sibley and the Simmons boys.

He responded with "Not that it will do any good, but once I get settled back into my home, I'll send a letter to Ramsey and see if I can get special circumstances to get them out of where they are."

Louise thanked him for the effort.

Then Jane added, "Yes, Mr. Bloomer. I think Henry made promises to Mrs. Simmons, and he needs to keep them. I'll see he tends to this business when he returns home."

Sam nodded his approval and then said, "As you wish, but I intend to write the governor anyway."

Jane was shocked by this as she imagined Sam was set on getting her husband in trouble with the governor. "What in the world for?" "Nothing to do with your husband. I just wish to get a commission in the Invalid Corps."

Sara, who had been eavesdropping from a short distance away, now asked Sam what the Invalid Corps was.

Louise spoke up to explain, "Honey, I think he means the Veterans Reserve Corps. Remember? I read that clipping to you about the army corps they are thinking to form that will be organized so wounded veterans can still serve if they wish to."

Sara turned to Sam now. "Would it put you back in the fight?" "Not likely. The Invalid Corps or Veterans Reserve is for old cripples like me. Most would end up working in the hospitals, and if anything in this war needs some good military organization and help, it's those filthy places."

"So you'd like to return to DC then and work in that hospital you just left?"

"Yes, I think I could be of good use there. Lord knows I'm not of much use for anything else these days."

Louise changed the direction of the conversation and asked Sam what kind of work he had done before the war.

"I was a carpenter and part-time farmer with my brother, but I don't think I will be doing much carpentry with this peg leg holding me back."

Then Sara said, "Why's that? You look perfectly strong to me." "Well, for one thing, carpentry involves a lot of climbing, and though I can walk okay, I can't much get up a ladder or scaffold."

Sara pondered his response for a moment. "I see. Well, in the hospitals, who made all the fake legs and arms? Isn't that skilled work for a carpenter?"

"I'm not sure who makes them, but I suppose that is work a talented carpenter can do."

"Well then, with all those men returning without arms and legs, maybe you could open the first and best artificial limb company in Minnesota," Sara said encouragingly.

"Um, that's a very good thought, and I will consider it. But for now, I think an officer's commission in the Invalid Corps better suits my mind."

Sara said she did not understand.

"Well, Sara, war hurts a man more than in just his body."

Louise put an end to the conversation, "Leave Mr. Bloomer alone and go fetch us all a nice dessert."

Sara ran off to the serving table to see what was available as a treat.

Returning bodies and soldiers on leave to Minnesota may have been a nice reprieve for some soldiers and their families, but as for Company K of Second Minnesota, the new year of 1863 was not off to the start they had hoped for. Boredom was at its highest, marching at its most miserable, and morale was at its lowest. Company K of Second Minnesota was out front of the regiment. William, John, and Vandyke were in the lead rank of the leading column. Colonel Bishop galloped by on his horse. He slowed his horse to a slow walk as he inspected his men. The men of his lead company were more than threadbare. William was marching barefoot except for bloody rags that were bound around his feet. They were marching through a hard wind and blowing snow on a muddy road.

John called out to the colonel as he passed, wanting to know where they were headed.

Bishop brought his horse to a slow trot alongside the moving column and called back to John, "On to Nashville! We're going to catch that scoundrel Morgan in the act if we can. How does that sound to you boys? You all anxious to see some action again?"

A cheer for the colonel went up.

John called out back to Bishop, "Sounds pretty good to all of us, I reckon."

William yelled out too, "Beats drill and marching every time!" Bishop halted his horse to take a long look at William. "Boy?"

How long have you been marching with those rags on your feet?"

"Since before the new year, sir."

Bishop shook his head in disbelief. "Why is that? I ordered new brogans and winter wear to be dispatched to this regiment on Christmas."

Bishop looked down the line of soldiers and saw a mix of men dressed in full winter gear and others much like William still in ragged uniforms.

"What company is this? Why are the other companies in their proper dress?"

Vandyke spoke up, "Sir? Company K, sir." "And? Can you explain this?"

"Well, sir, when the clothing issue was given out, you had ordered our company to follow those four darkies we captured to locate those barrels of lard they said they had hidden, so we missed that day as we were out of camp."

"And how many barrels did those darkies have?" "Seventy-five in all, sir," answered Vandyke.

"Did all of those barrels go to the division?" asked Bishop. "No, sir. The division took only twenty-five barrels."

"Ah, yes, I remember now, and I kept you boys out on that river all night too?"

"Yes, sir. We loaded the remaining barrels on a flat barge that was sent to Nashville," continued Vandyke.

"Well, how about we get on down to Nashville and cut off old Morgan and take back those barrels before he grabs them up for the rebel army?" replied Bishop.

William yelled out, "That's fine by us!"

A cheer rose from the throats of the men in Company K. Bishop looked down at William and Vandyke. "Good then!

How about you drummers give me a nice, quick route step to get this column moving along at a faster pace?"

William saluted and asked if he wanted the cadence at the double quick.

"No, boy, I'm not out to kill you. I just want to beat Morgan.

Company K, is it?" William nodded.

"Good! You boys can have the honor of carrying the regimental colors into the city, and I'll call up a supply wagon to make sure you all get outfitted properly. I'm afraid we have a long winter of walking ahead of us. Bugler?"

John stood at attention and saluted.

"Fall out and get what's left of the division band to give us a tune. I'd like some music on the march. That constant drumming gets a little annoying."

John broke for the rear. Bishop galloped on ahead as William and Vandyke tapped out a steady, casual marching drumbeat. The column of soldiers straightened themselves, and a newfound pride and energy came over them as a martial tune rolled over the men from the divisional band.

THE LATE GREAT
THIRTY-EIGHT

*On October 11, 2020, protesters in Portland, Oregon,
tore down a statue of Abraham Lincoln, leaving
the phrase "Dakota 38" spray-painted at its base.
The attack took place during a protest called the
Indigenous Peoples Day of Rage Against Colonialism,
organized in opposition to the nationally observed
Columbus Day holiday on October 12.*

December of 1862 would see the largest war crimes trial ever in the United States. But before those trials could be put into action, one must review the final defeat of the Sioux Nation that took place in the late summer of 1862. There was one final battle where Little Crow had hoped to defeat General Sibley. At Wood Lake near Fort Ridgely in late September, Little Crow planned his assault. Little Crow and his chiefs gathered a few hundred braves for one final assault on Sibley and his troops near Wood Lake and Fort Ridgely, which was located near Morton, Minnesota. Little Crow conferred with Big Eagle in his tepee. Big Eagle asked if Little Crow had a firm battle plan.

"I think a quick ambush of Sibley's troops early in the morning before they rise is the best."

Big Eagle was not convinced an ambush would work.

Little Crow would explain, "We'll gather our men and let them hide in the ravines and tall grass. Then we'll sneak up on them as they sleep and then pounce on them without warning."

"But what if Sibley moves before we think he will?"

"One thing I know about White soldiers is they are lazy. They will prefer to sleep. He will not move."

Big Eagle was not convinced. "Sibley is not so stupid. He beat us both times at New Ulm."

"Maybe so, but his cannons did no harm. The noise just scared the dogs, children, and women, but none of our braves were hurt. Why do you think he will move early?"

"We hold 1,600 prisoners. He wants them back now. He will come to take them, and this time, his cannons will not miss. He will react foolishly to get at those prisoners."

"Let him try. We will still be waiting in the grass."

Big Eagle finally agreed, "Okay, I will place the bands in the field now. But we are still heavily outnumbered."

"He will not be able to recover so fast from a surprise ambush as this. Do not worry," said Little Crow.

So the final battle was set for September 23 in an open field surrounded by a high-grass-covered ridge near Wood Lake.

Long before sunrise, Little Crow's Sioux crept through the tall grass and concealed themselves from the camp of General Sibley, which was within a few hundred feet of their ambush position. The US troops of the Third Minnesota Regiment were just beginning to wake up. The sergeants of the many companies walked among the sleeping soldiers and quietly rousted them from their slumber. The soldiers rose and fell into formation. An artillery battery of four cannons was manned with the muzzles pointed in the direction of the field. Supply wagons rolled out of camp.

A corporal driving one of the wagons spoke to a private seated next to him, "Well, this beats that lousy duty in Nashville, right?"

The private was not humored. "I didn't sign up to fight Injuns."

"And I didn't sign up to have our entire regiment surrendered, be taken prisoner, and then sent back home to forage for food in an Indian war either, but here we are," replied the corporal.

"Yep, the good old Third Minnesota Regiment, the shame of the state," said the frustrated private.

"Look to the bright side. All we must do is lick these Dakota, and we'll be back on top. All that business down South will be forgotten."

"Sure, unless we actually get in a fight or even see an Indian, which, so far, we have done little of both."

The corporal had to remind him of the New Ulm battles. "Hold up now! I thought we redeemed ourselves well in those two battles at New Ulm."

"All we did was lob a few shells and shoot from behind some breastworks," said the private in disgust.

The corporal pulled the wagon to a stop. "I've got a feeling today is going to be different."

"How's that?" asked the private.

"Look around here. Nothing but an open field for miles."

If one had been an Indian warrior now lying in the grass, one could see the wagons approach. The wheels sliced through the tall grass and nearly rolled over some of the hidden braves. A couple of the Indians had to roll out of the way to avoid getting run over but then suddenly jumped up and fired on the wagons.

The ambush's element of surprise had failed, and the last battle of the Dakota war had begun. A bugler sounded the alarm, and within an instant, the remainder of the Third Minnesota Regiment fell into action. They advanced on foot in the standard battlefield formation. The artillery opened, and rounds began to explode over the heads of the Indians in the field. They rose in mass and began to fall back toward a tree line to take cover. From the tree line, the Indians put up a barrage of fire into the advancing soldiers. A few soldiers were hit and dropped, but the Indians were getting the worst of it. Musket fire and cannon shot tore into the tree line. The Third Minnesota Regiment charged into the tree line and surrounded the Natives, forcing them to surrender. The battle ended quickly, and Sibley rode up to Little Crow, who was also mounted on horseback. Sibley asked if Little Crow would now surrender his weapon.

Little Crow simply replied, "I told you our reasons for the war after the Battle of Birch Coulee."

Sibley held out his hand in a gesture of truce. "Yes, and I understood your reasons then as well as now. But you must realize by now that you can't win."

Little Crow held out his rifle to Sibley. "It does now seem impossible. Yes, I am ready to quit. Here is my rifle."

"Very well. Now let's set terms for you and your people."

While Little Crow was handing his rifle to Sibley, the soldiers set off to round up the Indians and put them in a military file to march them off the field as prisoners of war.

"For now, your men will be treated as prisoners of war. But before we take you back to Fort Snelling, you must release all of your White captives to me, or I cannot promise you a safe passage."

Little Crow was suspicious of any White man's promise. "Promises? When were your promises ever kept?"

Sibley ignored him and was more concerned about the release of the prisoners. He asked where they were being kept, and Little Crow answered that they were being held at the Lower Agency. Sibley then ordered his junior officers to prepare to march toward the Lower Agency, which they promptly did. With Little Crow leading the head of the column alongside Sibley, the soldiers and the defeated braves marched into the camp, where they found that the captives were made up of a few White men, women, and children, who came running out to greet the column of soldiers and braves. Most of the prisoners, though, were cut hairs who had refused to take part in the rebellion. Little Crow was greeted as a hero by the Indians in the camp.

Sibley gave him one order as Little Crow dismounted, "Set all of them free, then gather up all your women and children and put them in line with your captured braves. We'll move out immediately for Fort Snelling."

Little Crow asked how long they would be required to stay there.

Sibley answered, "As long as the US government determines. It could be days, weeks, months, or years."

On September 26, Sibley started his march toward Fort Snelling but stopped at the Indian encampment at the Hazelwood Mission near Granite Falls, Minnesota. It would then become known as Camp Release (later during the war crimes trials, it was changed to Camp Sibley) as this was where the Indian chiefs were holding close to three hundred settlers, both White and half-breed, captive. Sibley now demanded their release with generous provisions for the Indians.

"I have listened to what your chiefs have said about this uprising. Though I can feel sympathy for your reasons, I must now demand the immediate release of all White captives."

The Natives and half-breeds who had gathered began to mumble among themselves, not knowing what was taking place. Some moved away and headed for the compound which held the White captives.

Sibley continued with his order, "They must be delivered to me at once, or you will be fired upon with no quarter given to women or children."

A few of the cut hairs who were moving toward the compound opened the gate. Inside were 269 captives. Sibley walked forward to personally greet the captives and welcome them to move out of the compound, which of course they all did.

He then turned back to Little Crow. "Have all your chiefs relay this message. We will remain here for as long as it takes to set up an office in which to conduct war crimes trials. Any Natives who intend to escape will be pursued and killed. Until the trials are complete, this goes for all half-breeds too."

Little Crow's warriors immediately released 91 White settlers and about 150 mixed-blood captives and, within the next few days, released the rest of the captives. The total number of captives was 107 Whites and 162 mixed-bloods for a total of 269.

After this work was completed, Sibley held a council with Little Crow and his chiefs to tell them, "These trials will determine who is guilty of rape, murder, and mutilation and/or to what degree they participated in the war. As soon as all captives are released and put in marching formation with my soldiers, all of you Indians and captives will be marched to Fort Snelling, where you will be cared for until after the trials are completed."

Another column was formed. This consisted of soldiers of the Third, Fifth, and Seventh Regiments along with a few members of the Renville Rangers. They assembled the captives and others who were to be taken to Fort Snelling. Along this march, they stopped first at the Dakota camp at the Lower Sioux Agency. There was still confusion here as to who was a combatant and who was not.

All the warriors willingly gave themselves up during the surrender. It was not uncommon for the soldiers to point out Natives whom they believed were combatants and try to force them into a line of warriors that were being marched off to Camp Release to stand trial. In one instance, a sergeant from the Third Minnesota Regiment collared a Native man as he was heading toward the river.

"Hey, you!" he yelled out, startling the man. "Where do you think you're going?"

The man told him he was going to the river to fetch water for his family.

Approaching the Native, the sergeant said as he pointed to a line of Natives being herded up, "Haven't you heard? If you get in line with all your friends and neighbors over there—"

The man protested, "But those are prisoners of war. I didn't fight in the battles. I'm a farmer and a Christian."

The sergeant countered his protest, "Oh really? It seems to me I saw you in the second battle at New Ulm.

"*No*! It wasn't me. I didn't kill or hurt anyone."

The sergeant continued, "That line is not the line of criminals. That's the line that is going off to collect their annuity."

The Native paused for a moment to think the situation through. "Really? Our annuities have arrived?"

"Yes, that's right. Just follow them, and you'll get all that is owed you."

The duped Indian jogged up to the line and fell in with the other Dakota prisoners.

In one of the only buildings left standing after the Dakota Uprising, the trials began. Reported in local newspapers was as follows:

> The trials of the Dakota were conducted unfairly in a variety of ways. The evidence was sparse, the tribunal was biased, the defendants were unrepresented in unfamiliar proceedings conducted in a foreign language, and authority for convening the tribunal was lacking. More fundamentally, neither the Military Commission nor the reviewing authorities recognized that they were dealing with the aftermath of a war fought with a sovereign nation and that the men who surrendered were entitled to treatment under that status.

Sibley, along with five officers chosen by Sibley and with the reverend Stephen Riggs as an interpreter, was to decide which warriors were guilty of taking part in the uprising.

Sibley began the proceedings, "Gentlemen, I have a dispatch here from General Pope regarding the recent outrages against the White community." Sibley opened the letter and began, "The horrible massacres of women and children and the outrageous abuse of female prisoners, still alive, call for punishment beyond human power to inflict. There will be no peace in this region by treaties and Indian faith. It is my purpose utterly to exterminate the Sioux if I have the power to do so and even if it requires a campaign lasting the whole of next year."

Sibley paused to take a look around the room and stared into the faces of the accused.

He then continued to read the letter from General Pope, "Destroy everything belonging to them and force them out to the plains, unless, as I suggest, you can capture them. They are to be treated as maniacs or wild beasts and by no means as people with whom treaties or compromises can be made."

Grumbling and moaning arose from the crowded room.

Sibley finalized reading the letter. "So there you have it, from the general himself. This is to be a war tribunal, and though we have no jurisdiction to prosecute you as civilians, those of you found guilty of any crime of violence against the citizens of this state will be executed."

The surrender ended with about 1,200 Indians being taken into custody, with many more taken in as they later surrendered. Eventually nearly 2,000 Indians were captured. They were eventually tried within mass trials at the Camp Release headquarters. With the Natives and returned captives under Union soldier guard, they were all led along the river's edge in a long, slow procession marching southeast, toward Fort Snelling and the village of Mendota. The White captives could return to their homes on their own; but below the fort on the banks of the Minnesota River, directly across the water from Mendota, a prisoner camp had been set up in which to concentrate all the Natives who had surrendered.

It was late October by this time, and as the leaves were changing and cold weather set in, the Indians would soon suffer the hardships of starvation and disease. All they could do as they awaited the verdicts of their crimes was to mill about their tepees seeking whatever comfort they could.

The trials were eventually played out at Fort Snelling, where there was much more room than at Camp Release. Also all of those on trial were being held in the concentration camp at the fort so it was made for convenience when an accused or witness was called. As weeks passed, cases were handled with increasing speed. On November 5, the commission completed its work: 392 prisoners were tried, 303 were sentenced to death, and 16 were given prison terms.

Within the confines of the fort, the trials of the Native warriors had reached their end. Sibley presided over the sentencing. Colonel Crook and recorder Issac Heard were at his side to witness and take the written notes.

In the final statement from Sibley, he addressed Heard, "Mr. Heard, from your knowledge and interrogations at Camp Release, we were able to justly accuse sixteen men of crimes of murder and rape.

Yet as of today, we have over three hundred men whom we can most certainly send to the gallows. Is that correct?"

Heard nodded in approval.

"And you agree with Reverend Stephen Riggs, the missionary from the American Board of Commissioners for Foreign Missions, who had worked with the Dakota since 1837."

Heard then replied, "Yes, sir. Between the two of us, we have reviewed all of the confessions and accusations made by the accused and witnesses. We can execute 303 prisoners with the evidence we now have."

"And these crimes include only rape and murder of innocents?" asked Sibley.

"That is correct, sir."

Colonel Crook then interrupted, "If I may, sir. The recent dispatches from General Pope." Crook paused as Sibley sat back to hear what was in the dispatch. "The president will be reading all the proceedings of this trial and will make a final decision on executions."

Sibley asked if that was the extent of the dispatch.

"No, sir. He also has written that, if the Natives cause any more mischief and do not abide by the president's final decision, he, General Pope, will order you to destroy all of them without regard to age or sex."

Sibley then asked if the court may proceed with sentencing. "Mr. Heard, will you read the sentence of the accused?"

Issac stood to read the pronouncement. "We, the members of this military commission of the United States of America, find 303 Sioux Indians guilty of the crimes of rape, murder, and other outrages against the peaceful White settlers of the state of Minnesota. The name of those to be executed will be posted on the fort wall for all to see, and their names will be read as they ascend the gallows."

Sibley then spoke, "Very well then. Colonel Crook?" "Yes, sir?"

"I would like you to muster a provost guard company from the Fifth Minnesota Regiment and have them load the accused onto wagons and send them to Mankato."

"Mankato, sir?"

"Yes. We will hold the execution there. It is central enough to all of the battlefields of this brief war and will be easy for the press and local spectators and those who were so violated by these men to reach and be witness to justice."

Crook saluted and began to dismiss himself.

Sibley stopped him. "One more thing. After I receive word from Washington, I will instruct you on the construction of the gallows. Plan on staying in Mankato until this has all been resolved."

"Yes, sir!"

Issac then spoke, "General Sibley, sir? Should I take these names to the Dakota camp on the river and announce the accused and their families?"

Sibley agreed, "Yes, but you'd better take a couple of half-breed guards with you for protection and translators."

Heard acknowledged, and Sibley then dismissed the proceedings. The courtroom emptied, and there was a mad rush of spectators and reporters to the door.

Near the middle of December, just after the burial of Dan Simmons, General Sibley was able to return to Mendota to spend a few days with his wife. General Sibley, Jane, Sara, and Louise gathered in the Sibley home and rested after having a fine preholiday meal. It would soon be Christmas, but as the future was uncertain, they decided to best celebrate now. The meal was prepared by the half-breed servants who had been hired to care for the Sibley home while the general was off doing his duty on the prairie.

Jane settled back to taste the dessert of fresh apple pie. "Can you believe it, Louise? Only five more days until Christmas."

"Yes, it's hard to see the three empty chairs one more year at Christmas."

Jane then turned to Sara. "Sara? What do you want for Christmas?" "Well, Dad is home but dead, so I guess I wanted my brothers home for good."

"Sorry. Stupid question for me to ask." "No, that's okay. What do you want?" "My husband at my side as well."

Sara looked concerned. "But won't you be here, Mr. Sibley?" The general responded, "No, Sara, I'm afraid not."

Sara asked why.

"Well, the execution is set for the day after Christmas in Mankato."

The execution had been on everyone's mind since the trial had ended. The final report had come back from Washington, but some details were not clear.

Jane looked to the floor, not wanting to appear too forward. "What was the final toll on that again?"

The general answered, "Lincoln approved thirty-nine for hanging, but I've found new evidence to acquit one more, so we are down to thirty-eight now. A half-breed, one of our sergeants, claimed to have been at New Ulm was found to be innocent of all charges. He never left his farm on the reservation."

Louise was shocked. "My God! Thirty-eight. That's still a lot."

"Indeed. It will rank as the largest single mass hanging in the

United States, and though that may be nothing to be proud of, it will certainly put Minnesota on the map."

Sara now had some harsh words. "If you mean to kill all the Indians, why can't you just take your soldiers out of the fort, go down to the riverbank, and kill them all? I'm sick of looking across the river and seeing their tepees and smelling their fires."

Louise then reminded her daughter that she was a Christian and should not speak that way. She asked Sara, "What would Jesus do?"

Sara said she did not know but added, "I heard more than half have already died from disease and starvation since they arrived, and probably more will before summer gets here, so I suppose Jesus would just let them die."

Sara was angry, and her anger was probably based on the stress and fear of the past year's events.

Jane now spoke for Louise, "Sara, I think what your mother is trying to tell you is maybe we should be more like our Lord and feed them and shelter them."

Sara was having none of it. "After what they did? They can all burn in hell!"

It was now time for Louise to silence her daughter. "All right now! No more! Watch that language! You're a guest here, and you need to behave yourself."

General Sibley calmed the situation. "It's quite all right. I understand her frustration. Louise, are you still getting weekly letters from your boys?"

Louise shook her head. "No, not regularly."

Sara spoke again, this time with more kindness, "William writes to me a lot."

Louise nodded. "That he does, and I'm grateful for that. I did receive the last letter from Dan the day after his funeral."

Sibley then asked Sara, "And Sara? How are your brothers doing? Have they been staying out of the fighting?"

"From what William says, they are bored most of the time and just seem to be marching around in a big circle covering all of Kentucky and Tennessee. For the most part, I don't think they've seen any real fighting at all."

Sibley continued, "From what I heard, the Second Regiment performed quite well at the Battle of Mill Springs, so much so that the ladies of Louisville made the regiment a new silk flag."

Sara smiled and knew of the accounting of the flag ceremony. "William did mention that a girl caught his eye and he may be in love with her."

Jane scoffed at this and pulled out a hanky to cover her mouth as she mocked vomiting. "Oh, Louise! How dreadful. Can you imagine your boy taking up with a horrid, filthy Southern harlot?"

Louise was upset at the thought of this too. "He can bring whatever trophies home from the war he wants, but there will never be a Southern girl crossing my threshold."

Sara defended her brother, "Oh, but, Ma! Haven't you seen *Harper's?* Those Southern belles have all the best dresses and hairstyles. They're all so pretty."

Louise and Jane scoffed.

Then Louise said, "Pretty until they open their mouths. Even the savages around here speak better English."

There was a short laugh from all, and then the women rose to clear the table.

As the dirty plates were handed off to the Native servants, Sara pulled general Sibley aside. "Mr. Sibley? Why did you give a reprieve to that one savage?"

Sibley explained, "He had been accused from the testimony of two German boys, one of whom said the Indian shot his mother and the other that he killed a German at Beaver Creek while he was on his knees in the act of prayer."

"Shouldn't he hang for that?"

"Initially yes, but it has since been proven that the man who did these deeds is on the run with Little Crow and all the others who escaped capture."

"Where did they escape to?" asked Sara.

"We think they went to Devils Lake, but some we know went to Canada, and most went to the Dakota Territory."

Sara asked if he was going to hunt them down.

"I'm still waiting for orders from Washington as to what is to be done with this situation."

Christmas came and went without any further disturbances. General Sibley had left for Mankato on December 23. He arrived late the next day and inspected his troops, prisoners, and the gallows. The instrument upon which the extreme sentence of the law was to be performed was constructed in a very simple yet most ingenious manner. It was erected upon the main street, directly opposite the jail, and between it and the river.

The shape of this structure was a perfect square. The base of the gallows consisted of a square formed by four rough logs, one foot each in diameter and twenty feet long. From each corner of this square rose a heavy round pole running up to a height of twenty feet while from the center came another but heavier timber rising to about the same height. At an elevation of six feet from the ground was a platform so constructed as to slide easily up and down the corner pillars and with a large opening in the center around the middle mast or post. From each corner of this platform, a rope or cable was fastened to a movable iron ring that slid up and down the middle mast employing a rope fastened to one of its sides. This rope was taken to the top of the mast, run through a pulley, returned to a point between the ground and the second frame or platform, and made fast.

The mechanism of the whole thing consisted in raking the platform utilizing the pulley and then making the rope fast when, by a blow from an axe by a man standing in the center of the square, the platform falls; the large opening in its center protects the executioner from being crushed by the fall. About eight feet above the platform, when in its raised position, was another frame like the ground square mortised into the corner pillars. Into these timbers were cut notches, ten on each side of the frame, at equal distances; and a short piece of rope was passed around the beam of each notch and tied securely. Descending on this again was the fatal noose. And now having described and seen the scaffold, Sibley confirmed it ready for its victims.

In thirty-seven days of fighting, 77 American soldiers, 29 citizen-soldiers, approximately 358 settlers, 49 half-breeds, and an estimated 29 Dakota soldiers had been killed. This was nothing compared to the slaughter that was taking place in the Eastern or Western Theaters of the Civil War. But for the sparsely populated state of Minnesota, this was an outrage against the settlers. The trials had been held, and verdicts had been secured. Now General Pope had to send the information to President Lincoln because prevailing federal statutes required the president's approval before the sentences of death could be carried out although Sibley and his immediate superiors had initially been unaware of that requirement.

By November 10, Major General Pope had forwarded to Lincoln the names of the condemned men; Lincoln responded by requesting the complete record of their convictions and a careful statement indicating the more guilty and influential of the culprits.

Pope forwarded the transcripts on November 15, preceded by a letter in which he urged the president to execute all of the condemned, claiming, "The only distinction between the culprits is as to which of them murdered most people or violated most young girls." He warned that the people of Minnesota, perhaps combined with some of the soldiers, would take matters into their own hands and kill all the Indians—including old men, women, and children—if the president did not allow all the executions to go forward. If the president proved reluctant to decide, he suggested the condemned could be turned over to the state government. Minnesota governor Ramsey left no doubt what decision he would make if given the opportunity, writing to Lincoln to urge execution of all the condemned.

A great public outcry arose in Minnesota in response to reports that Lincoln might not carry out the full sentence of the military commission. The *Stillwater Messenger* demanded the extermination of the Dakota: "Death to the Barbarians! is the sentiment of our people."

Minnesota's senator Morton Wilkinson and representatives Cyrus Aldrich and William Windom wrote to Lincoln, reciting stories of rapes and mutilation "well known to our people" and protesting any decision to pardon or reprieve the Dakota. If the president did not permit the executions, they said, "the outraged people of Minnesota would dispose of these wretches without law. These two people cannot live together. We do not wish to see mob law inaugurated in Minnesota as it certainly will be if you force the people to it." An open letter to the president from the citizens of Saint Paul called the actions of the Dakota wanton, unprovoked, and fiendish cruelty, predicting further violence by "these Indians" if an example were not made by executing the convicted and predicting vengeance by the settlers if the government did not act.

Others expressed doubt about the proper response. Commissioner of Indian Affairs William P. Dole, visiting in Minnesota, suggested that execution of the sentence would partake more of the character of revenge than of punishment. Reverend Riggs and Bishop Henry Whipple urged clemency for men involved in battles or plundering rather than in murdering women and children. Some in the East, more removed from the scene, expressed sympathy for the imprisoned Dakota.

Lincoln was torn between the cries for vengeance and his concerns about potential injustice to the accused.

On December 1, he wrote to Judge Advocate General Joseph Holt, asking his legal opinion, "If I should conclude to execute only a part of them, I must myself designate which, or could I leave the designation to some officer on the ground?"

Holt replied that the decision to pardon could not be delegated. On December 5, hoping to force the president's hand and prevent sympathetic appeals from shaking his purposes, Minnesota senator Wilkinson introduced a resolution requesting that the president give an account to the Senate of the events in Minnesota and the evidence upon which the commission ordered the execution.

Meanwhile, Colonel Stephen Miller, commanding officer of the regiment holding the condemned prisoners, repeatedly reported unrest among the citizens and soldiers, which he feared would lead to mob violence against the Dakota. Indeed, as the wagon train of prisoners moved through New Ulm on its way from Camp Release to Mankato, a crowd of men, women, and children pelted the shackled Dakota with bricks and other missiles, seriously injuring some prisoners and guards. A mob attacked the rest of the Dakota friendly community on their way to Fort Snelling; one baby was snatched from its mother's arms and beaten to death.

After being moved from Camp Release, the prisoners were held in an open field near Mankato, where they were easy objects of attack. On November 16, Miller reported the existence of an extensive secret organization including men of character in all this upper country and many soldiers who would attempt to take charge of the prisoners unless they were executed within a week.

"I was informed only yesterday," Miller said, "that the sheriff was very busy exciting the citizens upon this subject."

On the twenty-second, twenty-third, and twenty-fourth, Miller warned again of possible mob violence, particularly if word spread that the prisoners were to be moved from Mankato or pardoned.

"It is daily hinted to me," he went on, "that too many of the soldiers participate in this feeling and determination."

Miller was making plans to build a log prison to hold the men more securely and thought that he could get the prisoners safely into town but that getting them out would require a small army.

At 11:00 p.m. on December 4, several hundred civilians armed with clubs, hatchets, and knives attacked the new camp. Miller reported that the mob had planned to meet with two thousand other people the next day and intended to murder the prisoners. The soldiers surrounded, arrested, and disarmed the civilians, then permitted them to return to Mankato after receiving promises of good behavior. The soldiers had acted rapidly to put down the attack with good results; but Miller continued to warn of a general, fearful, and bloody demonstration if the prisoners were moved or if a general pardon were issued.

In response to the attack on the camp, Governor Ramsey issued a proclamation urging the people of Minnesota to act with restraint and to obey the law. The proclamation was a double-edged sword, however; it suggested that Lincoln ultimately would agree to execute the prisoners and warned that the state courts and legislature would take action if the federal government did not.

On December 6, Lincoln finally issued his decision. In his message to the Senate, he explained that he had been "anxious to not act with so much clemency as to encourage another outbreak on the one hand nor with so much severity as to be real cruelty on the other." He had accordingly ordered a review of the transcripts to order the execution of only those who had been proved guilty of violating females. Lincoln indicated that, contrary to his expectations, only two men had been convicted of rape; so he determined to draw the line by executing those who had participated in massacres as distinguished from those who had participated in battles. Of the forty men fitting this description, he said one had been recommended by the commission for clemency, leaving thirty-nine to be executed on December 19. He ordered that the remaining prisoners be held "subject to further orders, taking care that they neither escape nor are subjected to any unlawful violence."

Officials in Minnesota worried that a violent reaction would follow the president's decision to execute only thirty-nine prisoners. Sibley immediately requested that Lincoln postpone the execution for one week, writing to Miller that he needed time for due preparation and for the concentration of the troops necessary to protect the other Indians and to prevent a fearful collision between the US forces and the citizens. As of December 17, the prisoners had not been told of the president's decision. On that date, Reverend Augustin Ravoux wrote to Sibley, requesting they separate the condemned men from the others and inform them of their fate at least one day before the planned execution to let them prepare themselves "for the awful judgment of God." The condemned men were finally moved on December 22. Later reports suggest that, because of the similarity of several of the Dakota names, some errors were made in identifying the thirty-nine condemned individuals from the larger group of those convicted; but

Sibley denied this claim.

After the division was made, Reverend Riggs addressed the condemned prisoners, translating to them the president's order and a statement prepared by Miller: Their Great Father at Washington, after carefully reading what the witnesses testified to in their several trials, had concluded that they had each been guilty of wantonly and wickedly murdering his White children. And for this reason, he had directed that they each be hanged by the neck until they were dead on next Friday, and that order would be carried into effect on that day at ten o'clock in the forenoon. Good ministers would be there, both Catholic and Protestant, from amongst whom each one could select a spiritual adviser who would be permitted to commune with them constantly during the few days that they were yet to live.

Reverend Riggs (well known to the Indians in his missionary capacity) spoke first, "Say to them now that they have so sinned against their fellow men, that there is no hope for clemency except in the mercy of God through the merits of the Blessed Redeemer, and that I earnestly exhort them to apply to that as their only remaining source of comfort and consolation."

The prisoners received the news of their impending execution with equanimity according to Dakota tradition. Several Indians smoked their pipes composedly during the reading; and one in particular, when the time of execution was designated, quietly knocked the ashes from his pipe and filled it afresh with his favorite kinni-kinnick while another was slowly rubbing a pipeful of the same article in his hand, preparatory to a good smoke.

On December 23, the president suspended the execution of one of the condemned men, Tatimima, after Sibley telegraphed that new information led him to doubt the prisoner's guilt. Preparations proceeded to hang the remaining thirty-eight. The settlers in the region took great interest in the hanging, and Colonel Miller feared violence from many of those arriving uninvited to view the execution. To help keep the peace, Miller declared martial law would be in effect from the morning of December 25, the day before the scheduled execution. Meanwhile, the troops constructed the previously mentioned scaffold large enough to hang all thirty-eight at one time.

Having accepted their fate, the condemned prepared themselves for the execution. On the evening of December 23, the prisoners danced and sang together, probably to demonstrate their calmness and to honor each other and their relatives. On the twenty-fourth, they were permitted to meet with male relatives and friends also confined at the camp to say goodbye and send messages and words of comfort to their families. These meetings were reported to be sad and affecting, with many of the prisoners moved to tears.

Tatimima, not yet informed that his execution had been stayed, sent word to his relatives not to mourn him and that he died innocent of any White man's blood and hoped his friends would thus consider his death as simply a removal to a better world.

Reflecting a belief that more of the prisoners would later be executed, he said, "Tell our friends that we are being removed from this world over the same path they must shortly travel. We go first, but many of our friends may follow us in a very short time. I expect to go direct to the abode of the Great Spirit and to be happy when I get there, but we are told that the road is long and the distance great. Therefore, as I am slow in all my movements, it will probably take me a long time to reach the end of the journey, and I should not be surprised if some of the young, active men we will leave behind us will pass me on the road before I reach the place of my destination." On the twenty-fifth, Christmas Day, the condemned met with female relatives who had been working as cooks for the prisoners. These interviews were reported to be less sad. The prisoners sent messages to their relatives and friends, advising them to bear themselves with fortitude and refrain from great mourning; they also distributed personal items and locks of hair for the women to give to those outside. Shortly before the time for execution, Hdainyanka (Rattling Runner) dictated a letter to Wabasha, his father-in-law, one of the leaders who had counseled against the fighting and had helped negotiate the surrender to Sibley:

Wabasha,

You have deceived me. You told me that, if we followed the advice of General Sibley and gave ourselves up to the Whites, all would be well; no innocent man would be injured. I have not killed, wounded, or injured a White man or any White person. I have not participated in the plunder of their property, and yet today I am set apart for execution and must die in a few days while guilty men will remain in prison. My wife is your daughter; my children are your grandchildren. I leave them all in your care and under your protection. Do not let them suffer; and when my children are grown up, let them know that their father died because he followed

178

the advice of his chief and, without having the blood of any White men, was made to answer for to the Great Spirit. My wife and children are dear to me. Let them not grieve for me. Let them remember that the brave should be prepared to meet death, and I will do as becomes a Dakota.

The thirty-eight condemned men were led through town. They were shackled together and shuffled along as best they could. A local White preacher followed alongside them and begged for them to confess their sins.

The preacher nudged one of the half-breed prisoners. "Confess, my son, and take Jesus into your heart. James, I know you have converted to Christianity, but what you did on that battlefield was not within the rules of war, and if you do not accept Jesus and confess your sin right now, you will find yourself in hell before the sun sets." "No, thank you, brother. I will die as a good Indian and go to the Dakota heaven. I have done nothing wrong."

As the procession moved through town, White folks stepped up and insulted the prisoners. Some spit on them. Others hit them with sticks and shovels. A small White boy ran up and kicked one of the prisoners.

They finally reached the gallows, and as their names were read off, they climbed the stairs to the top and took their place in line.

Instead of any shrinking or resistance, all were ready and even seemed eager to meet their fate. Rudely they jostled against each other as they rushed from the doorway, ran the gauntlet of the troops, and clambered up the steps to the treacherous drop. As they came up and reached the platform, they filed right and left, and each one took his position as though they had rehearsed the program.

Standing around the platform, they formed a square, and each one was directly under the fatal noose. Their hoods were now drawn over their eyes and the halter placed about their necks. Several of them feeling uncomfortable made severe efforts to loosen the rope; and some, after the most dreadful contortions, partially succeeded.

At the appointed time for the execution, there were more people at Mankato than ever were there before at one time. Every convenient place from which to view the tragic scene was soon appropriated. The street was full, the housetops were crowded, and every available place was occupied. There were from three to five thousand persons present. The reports of a probable attempt by a mob to take possession of the remaining 275 prisoners and inflict summary punishment upon them induced the authorities to provide a large military force for protection. Accordingly the Sixth Minnesota, Colonel Averill; the Seventh, Colonel Miller; and Ninth, Colonel Wilkin—in all, about 1,500 men—were detailed for special duty at the execution. Major Buell, with a company of cavalry, did efficient service in keeping the crowd back from the proximity of the awful scene. The infantry formed three sides of a hollow square, starting from each side of the jail and enclosing the scaffold, the front of the jail thus forming the fourth side of the square. From the door at the extreme northern entrance to the place where the culprits were confined to the steps at the foot of the gallows, two companies were drawn up, one on either side, forming a gradual path through which the prisoners would have to pass to the scaffold. As the prisoners waited for the moment of the axe to drop them, one of the prisoners started to sing the Dakota death song. The others joined in. It was the most mournful sight.

The local newspaper reported:

> Precisely at the time announced—6:00 a.m.—a
> company, without arms, entered the prisoners'
> quarters to escort them to their doom.

Several of the Christian missionaries stayed with the condemned through that night. They reported that the prisoners were cheerful and contented and had asked the missionaries to tell their wives and children how cheerful and happy they all had died, exhibiting no fear of this dreadful event.

At 7:30 a.m. on December 26, the iron manacles were removed, and cords were used to secure the prisoners' arms. The men continued their songs and conversation, and each shook hands with the soldiers and reporters present to wish them goodbye. Father Ravoux led them in prayer, after which white hoods rolled up to reveal their face paint were placed on the prisoners in preparation for the execution. The head coverings were a source of shame—the Dakota would have wanted to show that they faced death without flinching—and after being hooded, the men became more subdued.

At exactly 10:00 a.m., soldiers led the men out of the prison and to the scaffold. As they ascended the scaffold, watched by a throng of spectators, they began to sing loudly what was variously reported as a death song or a hymn. One of the men sang of his deeds in battle, mocking the crowd regarding a mutilated body at New Ulm.

The signal to cut the rope was three taps of the drum. All things being ready, the first tap was given, when the poor wretches made such frantic efforts to grasp each other's hands that it was agony to behold them. Each one shouted out his name that his comrades might know he was there. The second tap resounded on the air. The vast multitude was breathless with the awful surroundings of this solemn occasion. Again the doleful tap broke on the stillness of the scene. Click went the sharp axe, and the descending platform left the bodies of thirty-eight human beings dangling in the air. The greater part died instantly. Some few struggled violently, and one of the ropes broke and sent its burden with a heavy, dull crash to the platform beneath. A new rope was procured, and the body was again swung up to its place.

It was an awful sight to behold. Thirty-eight human beings suspended in the air on the bank of the beautiful Minnesota River. Above, the smiling clear blue sky. Beneath and around, the silent thousands hushed to a deathly silence by the chilling scene before them while the bayonets bristling in the sunlight added to the importance of the occasion.

They were the following:

1. Ta-he-do-ne-cha (One Who Forbids His House)
2. Plan-doo-ta (Red Otter)
3. Wy-a-tah-ta-wa (His People)
4. Hin-hau-shoon-ko-yag-ma-ne (One Who Walks Clothed in an Owl's Tail)
5. Ma-za-bom-doo (Iron Blower)
6. Wak-pa-doo-ta (Red Leaf)
7. Wa-he-hua
8. Sua-ma-ne (Tinkling Water)
9. Ta-tay-me-ma (Round Wind)
10. Rda-in-yan-ka (Rattling Runner)
11. Doo-wau-sa (The Singer)
12. Ha-pau (Second Child of a Son)
13. Shoon-ka-ska (White Dog)
14. Toon-kau-e-cha-tag-ma-ne (One Who Walks by His Grandfather)
15. E-tay-doo-tay (Red Face)
16. Am-da-chi
17. Hay-pe-pau (Third Child of a Son)
18. Mah-pe-o-ke-na-jui (Who Stands on the Clouds)
19. Harry Milford (half-breed)
20. Chas-kay-dau (Firstborn of a Son)
21. Baptiste Cambell (half-breed)
22. Ta-ta-ka-gay (Wind Maker)
23. Hay-pin-kpa (The Tips of the Horn)
24. Hypolite Auge (half-breed)
25. Ka-pay-shue (One Who Does Not Flee)
26. Wa-kau-tau-ka (Great Spirit)
27. Toon-kau-ko-yag-e-na-jui (One Who Stands Clothed with His Grandfather)
28. Wa-ka-ta-e-na-jui (One Who Stands on the Earth)
29. Pa-za-koo-tay-ma-ne (One Who Walks Prepared to Shoot)
30. Ta-tay-hde-dau (Wind Comes Home)
31. Wa-she-choon (Frenchman)

32. A-c-cha-ga (To Grow Upon)
33. Ho-tan-in-koo (Voice That Appears Coming)
34. Khay-tan-hoon-ka (The Parent Hawk)
35. Chau-ka-had (Near the Wood)
36. 36 Had-hin-hday (To Make a Rattling Voice)
37. O-ya-tay-a-kee (The Coming People)
38. Ma-hoo-way-ma (He Comes for Me)

The Dakota convicted by the commission but not executed continued to be held as prisoners since no general pardon was issued. The rest of the Dakota community also remained under restraint, most of them in the internment camp at Fort Snelling. Beginning shortly after the trials concluded and extending well into 1863, Sibley and others continued to collect evidence to determine if they should bring any other Dakota to trial or have any more of the sentences carried out, but no further executions or trials occurred.

In February 1863, John Nicolay, President Lincoln's secretary, wrote to Sibley, requesting his opinion about what to do with the remaining condemned men. Sibley still hoped for further executions but suggested that the government send those not hanged to a military prison in Illinois or, in some other way, remove them from Minnesota, where public sentiment still ran strongly against them. Finally, in late March, the decision was made to send the convicted men to Camp McClellan in Davenport, Iowa.

Meanwhile, Congress had enacted a statute providing for the removal of all members of the four bands of Dakota from Minnesota, leaving the president to select an appropriate place for a new reservation. In April 1863, the men who had been acquitted and the fifteen or twenty women who had served at the prison in Mankato were reunited with the 1,600 Dakota still held at Fort Snelling. The convicted prisoners were transported to the new prison camp in Iowa while the rest of the community was moved to a reservation at Crow Creek in South Dakota.

THE LONG DAYS DYING

*I've been a soldier all my life. I've fought from the
ranks on up. You know my service. But, sir, I must
tell you now, I believe this attack will fail. No 15,000
men ever made could take that ridge. It's a distance
of more than a mile, over open ground. When the
men come out of the trees, they will be under fire
from Yankee artillery from all over the field. And
those are Hancock's boys! And now, they have the
stone wall as we did at Fredericksburg.*

—Lieutenant General James Longstreet
to General Robert E. Lee after the initial Confederate victories on day one
of the Battle of Gettysburg in *The
Killer Angels* by Michael Shaara

As the Dakota war came to an end in late September, the First Minnesota
Regiment, which had now taken part in all the major conflicts in the
East had a brief period of relaxation at Bolivar Heights, West Virginia,
overlooking Harpers Ferry. There had been a minor battle here just
preceding the great battle at Antietam. It was another Confederate
victory, but after the draw at Antietam, Union troops now in pursuit
of Lee's army would catch the time when and where they could to rest
and recuperate.

A week after the battle of Antietam, a company of soldiers from the First Minnesota Regiment was bathing in the Shenandoah River. After their long march from the Antietam battlefield, they were in rough-looking shape. Their deeply tanned faces and hands contrasted their blindingly white bodies that had been protected from the sun by their heavy wool uniforms for so long. Two young soldiers, Alonso and Harold, discussed the latest events as they passed a bar of lye soap between them. Neither man was over twenty and had so far survived the war without a scratch or disease. Their lives on the frontier had turned them into rugged individualists used to hard work and very capable of surviving under the harshest of conditions. As their platoon swam and bathed in the river, a conversation of the regiment's performance came to the mind of Alonso.

"What was the final tally of casualties at Antietam?" he asked Harold.

"One hundred forty-seven." "Did we lose our flag?"

"Don't know," he said. "I saw Bloomer go down with it, but I didn't see any rebs take the flag."

"Hope he made it out all right."

"I hope so too… Hey! I heard, though, that we are finally getting some of our boys back from the hospitals who dropped out during the Peninsula Campaign."

"That'll help," replied Alonso.

Harold then asked if he had heard the news about their most recent colonel, Sully. Alonso said he had not heard anything. Harold said that he was being promoted to general and would be heading back to Minnesota to help subdue the Dakota Indians.

"No kidding? I hope he is not being punished for our awful performance at Antietam."

Harold scoffed at the remark. "Oh, it wasn't that bad."

"If you call getting hit by enfilading fire on our flank and almost having the entire line turned, then I suppose not."

"Well, our line held, and we were one of the only regiments that retired from the field in good order."

"So say you, but if that makes a general, then we should all be promoted."

Harold ducked underwater for a moment and then came up with "Well, I'm going to miss the old guy."

Alonso asked who the new colonel would be.

"Morgan," replied Harold. "He'll do, but I'd prefer Colvill,"

Harold told him, "Colvill will be next in line, and the way things are shaking out, they might not have to wait much longer. What don't you like about Morgan?"

Alonso scrubbed the soap from his face. "He never cusses. How can you trust a man who doesn't cuss during a fight?"

Harold thought about that for a moment. "Good point! How about we get out of this river and get some mess?"

The platoon soon split up and headed back to their camp and prepared for dinner. For the remainder of the autumn, the regiment would be part of the Army of the Potomac stalking Lee's army south. They would not see their next action until late December. Skirmishing and disease would take their toll, and every day bodies would be collected for delivery to graves or hospitals.

At the Armory Hospital in Washington, DC, it was business as usual. Sam Bloomer had just returned from Minnesota and was now posted in the hospital, waiting for his commission as a lieutenant in what was to be called the Invalid Corps. Though the Invalid Corps would not be official until April, Sam had taken up the duties he was to fulfill and was wearing the light-blue wool uniform that would distinguish members of the Invalid from the regular army.

Sam sat at a desk in a small office, where he was now serving as a hospital clerk. He leaned back in his office chair with his legs propped up on his desk.

His friend, the mulatto nurse Jill, poked her head into the office. "Lieutenant Bloomer is it now?"

"Ah, my favorite nurse. Sam. You can still call me Sam. The commission will not be formal for a few more months. I prefer you just call me by name. I was hoping you'd find me."

"I saw your name on the roster of new helpers." "Was that a surprise? I told you I'd be back."

"People tell me lots of things. That doesn't mean they're true." Jill then noticed Sam's leg propped up on the desk. "So this is how our new clerk is going to work?"

"Sorry. It just feels a lot better when I put no weight on it."

Jill knelt beside him to inspect his leg. Sam pulled up his trouser leg to expose his prosthetic leg.

"Let's have a look. That's not the one you left here with."

"No, ma'am. That government-issue leg had too many faults, so I took it upon myself to make a new one. I should get plenty of more miles out of this one. Knock on wood." He knocked on his leg with his knuckles. "Solid oak. Hand whittled. Sheepskin lining for comfort and oxhide harness. Should last the remainder of my life."

Jill was impressed. "Maybe you should apply for a patent." "With everyone, it seems, fighting to get a government contract, I would think by now someone has beaten me to it."

Jill nodded knowingly, then lightened the conversation. "Do you miss your old regiment? I'm sure there were several of them here after the last campaign. You should check your files and see if we still have any here."

Sam briefly flicked through his file box. "I will. Later. But first how about we get out of here and find us a good meal in the city?"

Jill responded shyly, "My shift has just begun. I don't think I should."

"I could order you. I do outrank you even if it isn't yet official."

Jill blushed. "Let's not forget who was wiping your bottom just a few months ago."

"I haven't, which is why I want to treat you."

Jill was hesitant to accept. "But if we go out into the city together, well, I'm Colored, and you're White."

Sam did not seem to care at all.

Jill continued, "This may be the nations' capital, but we are still on Southern soil, and there are still slave hunters out there."

"But you're a freedwoman. Nobody will think anything of it.

They'll just see an officer in the Invalid Corps and you, a nurse."

"Maybe we should just eat here with the regular mess," Jill countered.

"Nope! No more army mess for me. I've got a half dollar in my pocket. It's a beautiful night, and I haven't had a stroll with a lovely lady in a very long time."

Jill blushed again. "Lovely lady?"

"Don't forget. You were the angel on my shoulder. Yes, lovely lady." Sam shuffled to his feet and put his arm out for Jill to take.

"Hold on. I have to check out with my supervisor."

Sam dipped a quill into an ink bottle and signed a pass for Jill. "You just did."

Jill smiled and took his arm. They then walked out of the office together.

While Sam was getting settled in his new job at the hospital, his former comrades of the First Minnesota Regiment were planning to settle in for a long winter along the banks of the Rappahannock River in Fredericksburg, Virginia. It was common for fighting to halt during the cold months. Both sides were short on ammunition, food, and other supplies. General Burnside had recently been given command of the Army of the Potomac by Lincoln, and though he did not want this command, he was now faced with Lee's Confederate Army that had taken possession of the town. Burnside had planned to move his army out of their winter camp by mid-November, but because the necessary pontoon bridges did not arrive in time, he had to wait until December 11.

The First Minnesota, along with the rest of the Union Army, would cross under fire and take the city on the eleventh. On the thirteenth, the Union assault on the heights would take place as regiment after regiment would be sent to their slaughter. The Fist Minnesota, by order of Commander Sully, was placed in position on the far right of the line and escaped the worst of it. This was the very day exactly one month before Sam would arrive in Washington to take up his new posting.

The Confederates were pushed out of town and took control of the high ground on Marye's Heights. They would now have control of the battlefield and were well prepared for the next day's assault. From this position, they spent the next couple of days sending artillery shells into the city as Union soldiers looted and made themselves as comfortable as possible in the homes of the local citizens. As shells passed overhead, many of the Union soldiers set up small fires for heat and cooking in the main street of Fredericksburg. This included men of the First Minnesota.

Four men from the First Minnesota Regiment—Alonso, Harold, Lieutenant Heffelfinger, and Corporal Irvine—huddled around a small campfire that they had made in the street. They fueled the fire with articles they had taken from the homes of the Confederate-held city. The sounds of skirmishing musket fire rang out at the front, and a constant firing of rebel sharpshooters gave continuous annoyance to the Union troops in town. Though the Confederates spared the buildings in the town, whenever any considerable number of soldiers appeared in the streets, they sent shells down the streets leading toward Marye's Heights, which had been the scene of that day's great slaughter of Union forces.

Corporal Irvine, seated on a liberated footstool before the fire, winced as shells flew overhead. The other three soldiers looked across the street. Walking along the boardwalk of Princess Ann Street, a young female citizen of considerable bravery caught their attention. She was between the age of twelve and sixteen and a modest, respectable and very well-dressed young lady. She was the only woman to be seen in such a place walking along the sidewalk toward the river. A squad of Union soldiers coming up from the river with full canteens crossed the street a few yards in front of her. Instantly a half dozen shells came ricocheting and bursting down the street past her. The soldiers ran for cover, but the girl kept her pace with perfect calmness, giving the matter no heed whatever.

This caught the admiration of Private Irvine. "Well now, I guess those rebel gals do have some pluck to them after all."

His friend Alonso agreed, "Maybe you should court one and take her back home after all this war ends."

"I don't think so. She might be able to handle hotshots and shells, but those frozen lakes and hard prairie living, I'm afraid, would put her under. No, thanks. I'll find me a strong fat German or blockheaded Nordic gal from back home if you don't mind."

Lieutenant Heffelfinger now joined the conversation, "Why not just get you a fat Chippewa squaw? I hear if ole Sully has his way, when he gets back home, he and Sibley got orders to kill all the Natives in the state and Dakota territories."

"Is that so?" said Harold.

The lieutenant nodded. "That's so. I saw it writ up in the *St. Paul Pioneer Press*."

Harold looked at the officer with skepticism. "Now where and when did you ever see a recent newspaper from home?"

"Remember that teamster we lost at Antietam?"

Alonso now joined back in. "Simmons? The one who got the shits at White Oak Swamp and never recovered?"

"Yeah, that's the one. He was from Mendota. Has two sons in the Second out West," added Irvine.

"Lieutenant, what became of him?" asked Alonso.

"Not sure, but he's no longer on the muster sheets. I believe he must have gone up. But his wife had sent him a copy of the newspaper back in early September, and it was full of the Dakota war news." "That's right. I saw it too. General Pope passed the order on to Sibley to kill 'em all! And Sibley requested more troops and officers to take the war into the territories before they all escape into Canada," said Irvine with a thrill in his voice.

"Well, after General Sully saved our asses today, I hate to see him go," replied Harold.

Irvine added to that, "Lieutenant? Why did Sully hold us on that flank so far out of the action?"

"You all saw the same as me. It was an assault nobody could survive. The entire Irish Brigade and Iron Brigade were nearly wiped out."

Alonso agreed, "I never saw anything so stupid. To order a charge like that was nothing short of wholesale murder."

Harold then asked where the regiment would be placed the next day.

"I'm not sure, but the corporal and I are about to go find out." Irvine looked at him in dismay. "We are?"

"Yep. You just volunteered." "For what now?"

"To reconnoiter the center of the line. After the failed assault, General Howard went to see Sully, and he told him, 'General, the First Minnesota never runs. I want you in the center of the line tomorrow to lead the first wave and take those heights.'"

"Those were his exact words?"

"Yeah, so get off your arse, and let's get up there and see what there is to see."

Corporal Irvine reluctantly got up and followed his lieutenant. Dusk turned to night, but the Confederate shelling never ceased. When there was a break in the shelling, the Union soldiers could hear the Confederates digging in. When Heffelfinger and Irvine reached the place in the stone wall where the greatest destruction of the day took place, the corporal volunteered to crawl forward and reconnoiter. After a brief time, the lieutenant came back to report to the colonel that the labor they were hearing was on the enemy's rifle pits at a little distance.

Corporal Irvine had been discovered by a sentinel, pulled over the wall, and captured. Colonel Morgan, at once, sent back for picks and shovels. By working most of the night, the regiment made a serviceable trench and breastwork along the line, which else would have been untenable after daylight; for besides the rifle pits a stone's throw away and the entrenched lines behind them, there were several buildings nearby occupied by the enemy's sharpshooters.

The following morning, the First Minnesota was placed on the right of their brigade and joined by another brigade, extending farther to the right, also entrenched to some extent. In the afternoon, the enemy placed a battery on a height near the river above the town, where it got an enfilading fire along their line and endeavored to sweep the Union trenches, sending solid shot and shell with great rapidity bounding along the line.

The 127th Pennsylvania, a new regiment, on the right of First Minnesota, at once broke and ran from this frightful danger except its left company, which joined the First Regiment. And the contagion carried after it two veteran regiments on its right. This uncovered the right of the First Minnesota, exposing it to other obvious dangers besides the enfilading fire, which continued with apparently increasing fury. The regiment, however, stood firm and, by its conduct, held the balance of the line in its place. General Howard, with his brigade commanders, occupied a house in the rear overlooking the line and saw with alarm the retreat of the three regiments one after another.

Seeing the First Regiment stand fast, Howard exclaimed, "Sully, your First Minnesota doesn't run!"

Sully, who had felt no less alarm for the credit of his favorite regiment than about the danger of the situation, now reassured, answered calmly, "General, First Minnesota never runs."

General Howard was extremely gratified at the conduct of the regiment on this occasion and complimented it in general orders and in a brief address to the regiment a few days later. The line was held until night, when they were withdrawn under darkness, crossed the river, and returned to their camp back at Falmouth on the other side of the Rappahannock, taking up again the routine of drill and picket duty in winter camp.

Winter passed easy enough in Washington. Both armies settled in for the winter, and the war seemed to have settled into a truce though it was far from anything like a truce. In April of 1863, the name of the Invalid Corps was officially changed to the Veteran Reserve Corps as the abbreviation for the Invalid Corps was IC and it confused many officials as this was the same stamp that was put on goods unfit for the military, "Inspected. Condemned." At this time, Sam would be officially commissioned as a lieutenant in the army. In May, Lee's army was defeated in a second battle at Fredericksburg and chased out. Burnside would shadow him in what became known as the Mud March.

Burnside would lose his generalship over the command of the Army of the Potomac, and he would be replaced by Lincoln with

General Hooker. "Fighting Joe" Hooker, as he was known, didn't prove to be much of a fighter, though; and he was defeated at the Battle of Chancellorsville. Once again, the Union Army was humiliated and set back on its heels. Lee moved farther north as the Union Army shadowed his movements. Lee was preparing for his second invasion of the North. If he could lick the Union Army on its ground, he would win the support of the British and most likely win the war. Washington was within his grasp.

The situation at the Armory Hospital had not changed much other than it was now filled with many veterans working as nurses, orderlies, and clerks. Sam was put in charge of supplies and any other duties that suited him. He was free to do as he wished for the most part. And one thing he wished was to take Jill out to dinner as he had promised her back in December.

She was reluctant up until mid-May, when the spring air and warmth of the season made her feel less conscious of her situation. She finally agreed to go out with Sam. By now, Sam had been well acquainted with the city and had found a restaurant he liked. There was an inconspicuous pub near Willard's Hotel that was frequented by Union officers that Sam thought would be perfect. It was not too high class but had a good selection on the menu, and as far as he knew, it would welcome a person of color. The pub was within walking distance from the hospital, and as the night was pleasant, they decided to stroll there instead of taking a cab.

Upon reaching the establishment, they entered and took seats at the bar. An immediate hush fell over the room as the two entered. Jill's stomach tightened as the all too uncomfortable fear of the patrons staring at her was overwhelming. She gripped Sam's hand for support, which only brought more raised eyebrows and undertones of criticism from the people in the pub. The regulars in the bar gave them the cold shoulder and the evil eye.

The bartender stepped up to Sam. "What can I get you, soldier?" "Can we get a table and something to eat?" Sam could see that the young man was unnerved.

"I can get a table for you but not the Negress."

Sam raised his voice, "She happens to be in my charge, and we would like a table."

"Are you her master?"

"She's a free woman and happens to be a nurse at a hospital here."

Onlookers were now taking an interest in where this debate was headed.

"Sorry. It's against the law to serve darkies here." "Whose law?" countered Sam.

"The law of this establishment."

Sam now leaned in. "You listen here, boy! I lost my leg a few days before Lincoln's Emancipation Proclamation at Antietam battlefield, and this woman saved my life."

The barkeeper stood his ground. "As I said, if you want to eat, you can have a table for yourself, but the darky either eats outside or in the kitchen. Whatever laws that ape Lincoln passed don't apply here." The bartender then reached under the bar for a club. "I suggest you keep your voice down and take a look around you."

Sam looked behind him and saw angry patrons getting ready to defend the bartender.

Jill tried to calm him and lead Sam out the door. "It's okay, Sam. Let's leave."

"Not until we get what is right."

Overseeing all of this was a Union major who was sitting alone in the rear of the room. He put down his utensils and approached Sam and Jill.

"Is there a problem here, Lieutenant?"

"This slacker here refuses to serve us," answered Sam.

"Oh, don't mind him. His daddy has pull with all the copperheads in town. He's no threat. You two can join me at my table if you like."

"Thank you. We would like that very much." Jill protested, but Sam led her to the table.

A waiter who knew the major quite well stepped up. "Charles, please bring me two more menus for my quests."

The waiter bowed and said he would be right back with the menus.

"So, Lieutenant, I overheard you lost your leg at Antietam." Sam nodded.

The major continued, "Such a wonderful and horrible day." Sam asked if he had been there.

"I'm afraid not. My job is here in DC. Legal affairs mostly. Sam asked if he was a lawyer.

"Not quite. I work in supply."

Jill now took curiosity in the major. "What kind of supply?" Sam now realized he had not properly introduced Jill and himself. He set about doing that before the conversation continued. "It's very nice to meet you both. I do whatever the army feels it needs, and I have to find sources to provide those needs. And what is it you do?"

Sam answered, "My job is to oversee the needs of the Armory Hospital."

The major nodded and said that he had heard stories of the conditions there.

"Unless you see it, you can't imagine it," said Jill.

Sam thought now would be a good time to pry the major for supplies for the hospital. "Please come by and visit us. We have some serious needs. To begin with, there is no fresh water and little or no bandages. The food is rotten most of the time."

Jill added, "We could give you a list of a hundred things we desperately need."

The waiter returned with the menus.

"Hold those thoughts and let Charles take your order. I'd recommend the beef stew tonight."

Sam and Jill went along with the major's recommendation. Sam also ordered a beer, and Jill asked if she could get cold buttermilk. Charles wrote down the order and left the three to their conversation. The major accepted their invitation to visit the hospital and said he would write a report to be included in his monthly dispatch to the quartermaster's office and see what help might be given to the medical corps. The dinner ended amicably, and Sam and Jill thanked the major for his decency and dinner, which he paid for. Sam and Jill left the pub with harsh remarks in their ears.

As Sam and Jill strolled along the gaslit streets of Washington, DC, they were harassed with scowls and snide remarks of passing soldiers and pedestrians. Jill's face was filled with panic as Sam did his best to ignore the situation. They walked arm in arm, which, for any other couple, would have been scandalous enough; but for a Colored woman with a White soldier, the sight must have been most disturbing to any Southern sympathizer, which Washington was full of.

Sam tried to ease Jill's anxiety, "Don't let them get the best of you."

"How can I not? You can't imagine the humiliation." "Ignore their words. They're just talking about my bum leg."

"So that's what a peg leg is called now? Black harlot? What were you thinking of by taking me out in the first place? I was perfectly comfortable staying at the hospital. You didn't need to bring me out here to remind me of how cruel and unfair the world is." Jill could see that Sam was now ashamed of his mistake.

He tried to reconcile, "The major was a decent enough fellow, though. Not everyone is the same. But you're right. You see enough cruelty in the wards every day, and I should have known better. I'm sorry."

"True enough. I'm sorry too, but let's not do this again, okay?" Sam said he had learned a good lesson. They agreed to try and forget about the evening's unpleasantness. They unlocked their arms and walked silently and solitarily.

Jill finally broke the silence. "Do you ever wonder where or what your old regiment is up to?"

"Sure. I think about them all the time."

"There's been talk about Lee moving into DC after those terrible defeats at Fredericksburg and Chancellorsville."

Sam said he had heard the same rumors and hoped that was all they were. "And we are still getting casualties from those two big battles, one more so close to here, and what will we do? I doubt we could handle the load."

At that moment, a carriage passed with a group of young sailors. One of the sailors called out as it rolled past the couple, "Hey, Lieutenant! Can we use your darky wench when you're through with her?"

Jill rushed to Sam's side.

"Ignore them. They're just a bunch of drunken sailors on leave." "I'm sorry, but this is too much. Can't we just hurry back?" Sam immediately hailed a cab. They hopped in; and the driver, under orders from Sam to rush them to the hospital, slapped the horse into a gallop. They reached the security of the hospital in short order and without further incident. The days passed as they usually did, but casualties were surmounting. Surgeons and everyone were overwhelmed for days.

It was well into June of 1863. The Amory Hospital was full and then some. The government was taking over any available buildings they could get to turn into temporary hospitals. Sam had settled into his work schedule quite easily. Jill depended on him to help with soldiers who were amputees, not so much with the wounds of their body, but more with the wounds of their minds. One morning, as Sam was sitting at his desk paging through invoices, Jill entered with his lunch. She also carried the most recent copy of the local newspaper and tossed it on his desk.

"Bet you haven't seen one of these in a while." It was the news of that very day.

Sam opened the paper to the front page. "Um, 'Lee moves North. Army of the Potomac follows.' That's not good news."

"Well, here's something that is! Navy bean soup." She set the bowl along with a loaf of freshly baked bread on his desk.

Sam poked around in the soup bowl with his spoon. "Is that a ham bone I see in there?"

"Sure is. Only the best for our favorite clerk. The cooks wanted to thank you for following up with that major on his promise to bring some fresh meat in here."

Jill then pulled up a seat next to Sam. "Sam, I need to ask you a favor."

"Sure, what is it?"

"We've got a boy in here from New York, a young Irish kid. Maybe eighteen if that. Lost both his legs at Fredericksburg. He's all healed up and ready for his new legs."

"Yeah? So what's his problem?"

"He told me he won't let no nigger nurse help him to learn to walk on no stinking army peg legs."

Sam was shocked. "He called you that?"

"Yes, that and a whole lot more. I won't take any cursing from anyone, especially when they are blaming all their troubles on Jesus."

Sam scoffed and began to shovel in his soup. "Sure. Just point him out to me after lunch, and I'll set him straight."

Jill thanked him and then left to go back to her duties.

About this same time, on June 26, the First Minnesota Regiment was back on the march. They crossed the Potomac River at Edward's Ferry and halted near their old camp. After a couple of days there of sending out scouts and pickets, they struck camp on the morning of the twenty-ninth and continued the march, screening Lee's Confederates on their push into Pennsylvania. Lieutenant Heffelfinger, Alonso, and Harold helped each other settle into their knapsacks and bedrolls as they prepared for the long march. Soldiers from other divisions and corps marched out ahead of them, and the other long line of regiments kicked up dust on this very hot and humid summer day. The men hadn't even started moving, and some were already appearing to be suffering from heatstroke. Heffelfinger was concerned about the heat and knew that his men would need lots of water to get through the day.

"Did you boys fill extra canteens for yourselves as I told you?"

Alonso and Harold swung around to show their officer that they were burdened down with extra water.

"Good! Colonel says we may be putting in a good twenty-five or more miles today, and in this heat, I don't need you boys passing out on me."

Alonso turned to Heffelfinger. "So tell us again, Lieutenant. How was it you lost Irvine?"

"I didn't lose him. I know exactly where he is. With any luck, he's in a Confederate prison camp."

Alonso replied, "Just promise us that, if we are sent out to reconnoiter with you, you don't leave us behind enemy lines."

"Like I've told you all over a hundred times, we weren't behind enemy lines. Our lines were nearly touching, and when I went back to call up help to entrench our line evidently, they just pulled him over to their side."

Harold now asked, "How do you even know they got him?"

Heffelfinger gave up. "When I came back, he was over there just hollering away for us to come and save him. Ah, get off my back, you two, and fall in line before the entire company leaves us behind."

The three fell in with the rest of the marching column and trudged along.

On the evening of July 1, the entire Union Army had the road jammed with equipment and men, all heading north to Gettysburg. The heavy sound of distant artillery fell upon the regiment like an approaching thunderstorm. They knew trouble was just up ahead, but they continued in the direction of the noise. The roar of conflict increased as they drew nearer; and then they were put upon by the retreating crowd of men from the Eleventh Corps running along with supply trains, sutlers, and civilians all fleeing south in terror with their frightening tales of utter defeat and rout. As most of the soldiers wore the crescent badge of the Eleventh Corps, which was held in little respect since Chancellorsville, they received but taunts and jeers from the sturdy veterans of the Second Corps, which the First Minnesota was part of.

As the sun was setting and with evening coming on, the regiment was halted and ordered to bivouac many miles outside of Gettysburg. Lieutenant Heffelfinger, Alonso, and Harold, all now beyond human exhaustion, flopped down onto the ground into one pile.

The lieutenant addressed his men, "Gentlemen, you may put up your shelter halves, make dinner, and get some sleep."

Alonso said he was too tired to prepare a meal or even put up his shelter half and preferred to just sleep where he fell.

Harold agreed, "Me too… I'm going to flop right here, Lieutenant. Wake me if you need to, but I'm about as played out as I've ever been."

"If that's the case, I'll join you here in the dust and dirt. But maybe we can all mess for breakfast then?"

"Sure," said Alonso, "if you make the fire."

Heffelfinger passed a canteen to the other two. "May as well finish this off."

They all took one final draw of water and then flopped back onto their knapsacks and were out stone-cold asleep within seconds. General Sully had returned home to Minnesota in the winter of 1863. He and General Sibley, who was now settled back in his house in Mendota, would have regular meetings in the officer's wardroom at Fort Snelling, which would once again become the operating base out of where the war against the Dakota would be determined. In early summer, the two generals devised a plan, the first of what was to be called the punitive expeditions. This was to be launched in Dakota Territory in the summer of 1863. A two-pronged attack was planned to drive the Indians farther west, which would also have the purpose of opening new territory for settlement, which was already well underway in the eastern parts of the territory.

General Sibley would lead one of the columns, and the other would be led by General Alfred Sully. Both would march north from the Missouri River. During their final meeting of the plan of attack in late June, Sibley and Sully discussed the final preparations. Sully wanted confirmation from Sibley that their plan had been approved by Governor Ramsey and General Pope, the two men most responsible for the continuation of the war against the Dakota.

"General, then we agree with General Pope and Governor Ramsey's order?"

"Yes, sir. And I think your plan is excellent."

Sully was overjoyed. "Good! Then we will embark on these so-called punitive expeditions immediately, sticking to my two-pronged attack, if you agree with that."

Sibley said he was indeed in agreement.

"Fine then. We will each lead a column north and push the savages out of the Dakota territories and as far west as we can or until they can be settled without too much bloodshed on reservations."

Sibley then asked where their forces would rendezvous.

Sully answered, "I'll go north. You head south. We'll both follow the Missouri River until we meet at Fort Pierre and wait for our steamboats there to resupply."

Sibley reminded him of the drought they were experiencing and that boats might not be able to get along on the river. He also wanted a date for the rendezvous.

"July 25. If the drought hasn't lifted by then, we'll take supplies overland by wagon and continue the chase."

Sibley double-checked on what units Sully would be marching with.

"I'll have the Second Minnesota Cavalry, Brackett's Minnesota Cavalry Battalion, and also the Eighth Minnesota Infantry and the Third Minnesota Light Artillery Battery."

Sibley felt he needed more troops and asked for them. "May I have the galvanized Yankees out of that prison camp in Rock Island, Illinois?"

"Sure, if you don't mind fighting alongside former Confederates."

"They're veteran soldiers. I'll take them!" answered Sibley.

General Sibley would start marching first. He left Fort Snelling in early July for the Dakota Territory.

While he was moving his men west, what was left of the First Minnesota Regiment would find themselves in a situation that would crown them in glory like no regiment before them. The regiment left their camp outside of Gettysburg early on the morning of July 2. After a long, hot, dry, and dusty march, the exhausted men arrived on the Gettysburg battlefield in the afternoon. They were not immediately put in a line of battle but were to be held in reserve on the left and rear of Cemetery Ridge. Colonel Colvill, who had been placed under arrest during the march, was now relieved of arrest and rejoined to take command of the regiment.

Lieutenant Lochren would write of the events of July 2:

> July 2, we arrived on the battlefield; and the Second Corps was placed in position on the line to the left of the cemetery, being joined on its left by Sickles's Third Corps, which extended that line to the vicinity of the Little Round Top. For some reason, the First Minnesota Regiment was not placed in this line but apparently in reserve, a short distance to the rear.
>
> Early in the morning, just after we reached the battlefield, Colonel Colvill was relieved from arrest and assumed command of the regiment; and Company L (sharpshooters) was detailed to support Kirby's battery near the cemetery and did not rejoin us during the battle. While lying here, one man was killed, and Sergeant O. M. Knight of Company I was severely wounded by shells from the enemy. Sometime afternoon, Sickles advanced the Third Corps half a mile or more to a slight ridge near the Emmitsburg Road, his left extending to Devil's Den in front of and near the base of Little Round Top; and Company F (Captain John Ball) was detached as skirmishers and sent in that direction.
>
> Soon after, the remaining eight companies of the regiment, numbering 262 men (Company C was also absent, being the provost guard of the division), were sent to the center of the line just vacated by Sickles's advance to support Battery C of the Fourth United States Artillery. No other troops were then near us. We stood

by this battery in full view of Sickles's battle in the peach orchard half a mile to the front and witnessed with eager anxiety the varying fortunes of that sanguinary conflict until at length, with the gravest apprehension, we saw Sickles's men give way before the heavier forces of Longstreet and Hill and come back, slowly at first, and rallying at short intervals but at length broken and in utter disorder, rushing down the slope by the Trostle house, across the low ground, up the slope on our side, and past our position to the rear, followed by a strong force, the large brigades of Wilcox and Barksdale in regular lines, moving steadily in the flush of victory and firing on the fugitives. They had reached the low ground and, in a few minutes, would be at our position on the rear of the left flank of our line, which they could roll up as Jackson did the Eleventh Corps at Chancellorsville. There was no organized force near to oppose them except our handful of 262 men. Most soldiers, in the face of the near advance of such an overpowering force which had just defeated a considerable portion of an army corps, would have caught the panic and joined the retreating masses. But First Minnesota had never yet deserted any post and had never retired without orders, and desperate as the situation seemed and as it was, the regiment stood firm against whatever might come.

The men of the regiment were lying in a prone position along the ridge in front of Cemetery Ridge. In front of them, the Union line had been advanced into a desperate position which it could not hold. The line was breaking under the pressure of the overwhelming Confederate forces advancing on them.

Alonso rolled on his side and nudged Harold as he saw their colonel Colvill approach. "Lookee there, Harry! Here comes ol' Colvill."

"Well, how about that? We must be in a fix for him to be released early from the stockade," Alonso answered.

"He never should have been arrested in the first place," Harold agreed.

Both men felt a surge of strength now that their beloved colonel was back to lead them.

Colvill called the regiment to attention. "First Minnesota! Rise!"

The regiment rose as one and fell into a long battle line. Colvill then gave commands to his company captains to lead his regiment forward to a new position forward toward the front. Alonso and Harold were always in line next to each other, and now they watched as the Union line in front of them gave way before the heavier forces of the Confederates.

Just then, General Hancock, with a single aid, rode up at full speed and, for a moment, vainly endeavored to rally the retreating forces. Reserves had been sent for but were too far away to hope to reach the critical position until it would be occupied by the enemy unless that enemy was stopped. Quickly leaving the fugitives, Hancock spurred to where the First Minnesota stood and called out as he saw Colvill standing in front of his regiment.

"What regiment is this?"

"First Minnesota!" Colvill proudly exclaimed.

Hancock knew the desperate situation his army corps was in and barked out the order to Colvill, "Charge those lines!"

At that moment, if one were to see the expressions on the faces of the men in the regiment, it would be clear that every man realized in that instant what that order meant, death or wounds to all, the sacrifice of the regiment to gain a few minutes and save the position and probably the battlefield. Every man saw and accepted the necessity for the sacrifice; and responding to Colvill's rapid orders, the regiment, in a perfect line with arms at right shoulder shift, was in a moment sweeping down the slope directly upon the enemy's center. No hesitation and no stopping to fire though the men fell fast at every stride before the concentrated fire of the whole Confederate force directed upon them as soon as the movement was observed.

Silently without orders and almost from the start, double quick had changed to utmost speed, for in utmost speed lay the only hope that any of them would pass through that storm of lead and strike the enemy.

As the men broke into a full run, Colvill called out the order that would now strike fear into the hearts of the enemy, "Charge bayonets!"

Colvill gave the order as they neared the first line; and the men, in unison, leveled their bayonets and broke into a full sprint. The surprise bayonet charge was opened with a full-on volley of musket fire and so shocked the Confederate front line that it collapsed on itself and fell back into the second and third line, disrupting the entire Confederate advance and stalling the entire movement, thus saving the Union position.

The First Minnesota Regiment then poured in their first fire and availed themselves of such shelter as the low banks of the dry brook afforded and held the entire force at bay for a considerable time and until reserves appeared on the ridge they had left. Had the enemy rallied quickly to a countercharge, its great numbers would have crushed the small regiment in a moment and would have made but a slight pause in its advance. But the ferocity of their onset seemed to paralyze the Confederates for the time; and although they poured upon the First a terrible and continuous fire from the front and enveloping flanks, they kept at a respectful distance from the bayonets until, before the added fire of the fresh reserves, they began to retire and the regiment was ordered back.

What Hancock had given them to do was done thoroughly. The regiment had stopped the enemy and held back its mighty force and saved the position. But at what sacrifice! Nearly every officer was dead or lay weltering with bloody wounds, their gallant colonel and every field officer among them. Of the 262 men who made the charge, 215 lay upon the field, stricken down by rebel bullets. Forty-seven were still in line, and not a man was missing. The flag went down several times but went back up again, never to be taken by the enemy. In the hand-to-hand struggle with the enemy, Alonso and Harold were both killed. Colvill was seriously wounded as was Heffelfinger. Of the 262 men who made the charge, only 47 were able to report for duty at roll call on the evening of July 2.

THE YOUNG CUT HAIR

"The wearing of long hair by the male population of your agency is not in keeping with the advancement they are making, or will soon be expected to make, in civilization," Jones says in the order. "The wearing of short hair by the males will be a great step in advance and will certainly hasten their progress towards civilization."

—Commissioner of Indian Affairs
William Atkinson Jones, 1902

July 1863 in Mendota was a month of continued drought for the state, especially in the southeastern portion. One of the driest summer months ever observed in Minnesota before or since confronted the state for the first time with a possible calamity from drought. The coolest temperatures that prevailed, however, kept agricultural consequences less than what they might have been, had the high temperatures that frequently coincide with drought been more prevalent. No measurable rain fell the entire month in Mendota or Saint Paul, just sprinklings on several days of no account.

Over the agricultural areas of the southeast, greater falls fortunately occurred near the close of summer. Significant crop damage was confined only to late-sown wheat. On the rivers, reports of record-low water levels and progressively less boat traffic came regularly. Brooks ran dry, mills were forced to stop operating, and the Mississippi dwindled to a respectable creek. A marked cooling, however, then followed, with Saint Paul only in the fifties on the nineteenth and twentieth of June. After the nineteenth, all forms of commercial navigation were suspended on the Minnesota River. The Mississippi, on the twenty-seventh, opposite at Saint Paul was reportedly one and a half feet lower than it had ever been since the city was settled in 1848.

Wood was now becoming scarce as it couldn't be floated down in any quantity from the upper Mississippi country. Fort Ripley reported, "The grass upon the prairie nearly or quite dried up." A bizarre sight around mid-July in the Saint Paul vicinity was the cattle seen wading across the river above and below the city. The temperature in July would rise to the upper nineties during the day, and by the end of the month, the nights found frost on the ground in regions just outside the city limits of Saint Paul.

On the weekend after the battle of Gettysburg, news finally reached Fort Snelling of the sacrifice of the First Minnesota Regiment and traveled quickly across the river to the Simmons cabin. Sara was enjoying what she could of her break from school. It was supposed to be the time of year when children stayed home to help with chores in preparation for the harvest and the coming winter. On this second Saturday of July, Sara had just placed flowers at the base of her father's headstone, which was at the base of the tree stump where the axe he embedded upon the eve of his leaving for the war was. Sara was interrupted by the noise of someone approaching up the gravel lane to the Simmons house. She rose to see a Native Chippewa boy by the name of Robert Two Arrows. He was one of the local cut-hair Native boys who was being educated in the same school as Sara, and they had become friends.

Sara turned to greet him. "Oh! Hi, Robert! You surprised me!" "Hi, Sara. What are you doing?"

"Oh, nothing much. Just putting some flowers out for my father like I do every Saturday. What about you?"

"Ah, I've been down by the river's edge trying to catch some fish for my mother. I thought, with the water so low now, it would be a good time to club catfish."

"Any luck?

"Yeah, I saw some big old granddads in the shallow spots down there among the rocks. I was hoping you might have an old wagon wheel spoke I could use as a club to hit me a couple with."

"Sure. I think Pa had a couple in the shed. I'll go look."

Sara ran off to fetch the spoke. Louise had heard the commotion and exited the house and walked up to Robert as Sara ran off to fetch the spoke. Louise walked up to Robert.

"Hello, Robert."

"Hello, Mrs. Simmons… It sure is a hot one today, isn't it?" "Yes, hot and humid as all heck, and this drought isn't helping matters either."

Robert nodded in agreement, then asked a peculiar question, "Can we say heck? They don't let us say heck in church."

"They don't?"

"No, ma'am. We get a beating for that one."

"Well, that's not right. *Heck* is not such a bad word. I don't think the Lord will punish us for that one."

"That's what I think too."

Just then, Sara returned with the wagon wheel spoke. "Here it is! Shall we go?"

Louise held them up for a moment. "Where are you two off to now?"

"Just down to the river to get some catfish for Robert's mother." "Get me a couple too if you can, okay?"

Robert said he would do what he could to bring back a couple of fat fish for Louise.

She thanked him and then sent them on their way. "You two be careful down there, and, Sara? Stay out of those mushroom caves! I don't want you getting lost in there."

Robert told Louise not to worry and that they would be back before sunset. Looking west to the sky, he noticed black clouds filling the sky and said he thought that rain would be coming soon. Louise said she would welcome the relief.

"Okay, Robert. I'm counting on you. All my men are gone. You're in charge. Get me a couple of big fat, juicy catfish for dinner, and I'll send you home with some of those sugar-fried donuts your mother and sisters like so much."

A huge smile cut across Robert's face. "Thank you, ma'am. That would be great!"

The two children jogged along the path down to the river's edge. When they reached the river, Robert found a spot that he could wade into and, with the large wooden wagon wheel spoke, began searching for catfish as they swam about in the shallows of the river rock. He clubbed at them as he saw them and snatched them out of the water after he killed them. He managed to haul in five of the biggest and best. He gave two to Sara, who was very pleased.

Then she asked, "Have you heard?"

Robert did not know what she meant and said he had not heard any news of importance other than what had happened at Gettysburg.

Sara continued, "General Sibley and General Sully are on their way to the Dakotas."

Robert was surprised to learn that Sibley had been promoted. "Are they going after those stinking Sioux?"

"I don't know. Why do you hate them so much?" answered Sara. "Why do you hate the Southerners so much?" asked Robert.

"I don't know. I guess we're just supposed to."

"Yeah, but we were fighting the Sioux for a long time, like forever Don't know really why we hate them. Just over land and stuff, I guess. But one thing is sure about the Sioux. They are the most brutal and mean of all Indians. We have an old saying. If the Cheyenne, Crow, or Blackfeet are coming, prepare for war, but if the Sioux are coming, prepare to die. They show no mercy to anyone."

Sara shrugged it off. "Hey! Want to get some mushrooms?" "Sure, but your mom said to stay out of the caves."

"I won't tell if you don't."

"But won't she see the mushrooms?"

"Not if you take them all for your mother." Sara then ran off ahead of Robert and headed toward one of the local caves. She called back to him, "Ah, come on. What are you? Chicken?"

"I'll show you who's chicken. Follow me."

They were about to head into a cave, but Robert came to an abrupt halt as he spotted a shrub.

"Hold on. I promised I'd pick some kinnikinnic for my mother."

"That's not kinnikinnic. Kinnikinnic doesn't have five-pointed leaves like that. What does she want that for anyway? No kind of tobacco grows in the North. She should know that."

"I know it's not, but she smokes it for her headaches, and I have to get some, so just wait a minute, okay?"

"Sure. I'll meet you inside. But don't take long."

Sara entered the cave as Robert gathered the weed. Once inside, they found an open area with a smooth dirt floor that had signs that other people had made themselves at home in this cave. Sara asked if Robert had brought his fire-starting kit with him. Of course he had as this is something every young man or boy living on the frontier did as a survival tool. Robert was curious as to what Sara was thinking. The sound of thunder bounced off the cave walls. Robert poked his head outside the cave as he heard the thunder, and large raindrops began to pelt the shoreline. A summer storm was moving in.

"It's cold and dark in here. We could build a fire, make a torch, and explore way back where nobody been before, or…"

"Or what?" asked Sara. "Fry us a catfish?"

Robert gave her a stern look. "No way! We'd get skinned alive if we don't bring back any food! But we could…"

Sara waited for him to continue.

"Wait out this storm by the fire and smoke up some of Ma's kinnikinnic and see what all the fuss is about."

"You don't think they'll smell that on us?"

"Not over the smoke of the burning logs, no way," replied Robert.

"All right then, if you think it's okay."

"Nothing to worry about. It's the same stuff they put in the peace pipe."

"Really?" asked Sara.

"No, not all the tribes or all the time, but some of them anyway if nothing else can be found to make a good mixture."

Robert, with Sara's help, made a good fire in the cave. They huddled up close to each other. Robert put his arm around Sara in a more than friendly manner, but it was still innocently childish. He carved a simple pipe out of a piece of wood, and they took turns puffing off it as he packed it with the weed. As the inhalation of the smoke hit their brains, they giggled at nothing and talked about school, the recent Dakota war, and the plans that General Sibley had for his continued pursuit of the Dakota.

"So that cut-hair Ruth Little Tree didn't turn out to be such an old hag of a schoolmarm after all."

"I never imagined she would be okay," said Robert. "But she follows the orders of the mission church, so I guess she's okay with them anyway even though she is half Sioux."

"I like her just fine."

"You mean, you like her just fine as for a half-breed," said Robert with some bitterness.

"I didn't say that. She's a nice woman, and so is her pa even though he is still sitting in that prison camp over there under the fort." "Well, what do you think of your friend Sibley now? I suppose you think he's great too even though he's out hunting to kill all the Sioux in the Dakotas right now."

"What do you care about the Sioux? I thought you Chippewa hated them. That's what you've always told me," said Sara.

"I've changed my mind. Not anymore. Not since you Whites took all the Indian lands wherever they were. We're one people now."

Sara was handed the pipe and took another drag off it. "So do you hate all Whites now?"

For some reason, Robert felt humor in this and could not contain his laughter. "No, I don't hate all Whites. Do you hate all Indians?"

Sara joined in on his infectious laughter. "I never said that. I just said I think General Sibley is a good man. And even though you are a cut hair, you're my friend, and I hope you'll be my friend for a long time."

Robert passed the pipe to her again.

She turned it away. "No. The storm has passed, and I think we should get home. Our mothers will be worrying soon."

Sara got up feeling a little unsteady and Robert put out his hand to help her. They both had a good laugh.

"I can see why your mom likes that stuff," said Sara as they left the comfort of the cave and headed off in their separate directions.

The Punitive
Expeditions

I hope you will not believe all that is said of Sully's "successful expedition" against the Sioux. I don't think he ought to brag of it at all because it was what no decent man would have done. He pitched into their camp and just slaughtered them, worse a great deal than what the Indians did in 1862. He killed very few men and took no hostile ones prisoners...and now he returns saying that we need fear no more, for he has "wiped out all hostile Indians from Dakota." If he had killed men instead of women and children, then it would have been a success, and the worse of it, they had no hostile intention whatever. The Nebraska Second pitched into them without orders while the Iowa Sixth was shaking hands with them on one side. They even shot their own men.

—Samuel Brown, a language interpreter during Sully's expedition, 1863

On May 27, 1863, Little Crow and the dozens of Dakotas still with him marched through the gates of Fort Garry in Canada. This was a fort similar to Fort Snelling. They marched proudly through the gates in high style, with the British Union Jack being prominently displayed. Over the next three days, Little Crow negotiated with Governor Alexander Grant Dallas, a British official who wanted nothing more than for Little Crow to turn around and go away. Dallas was the administrator of 1.5 million acres held by the Hudson Bay Company, but he had little influence or power over those in or near Fort Garry. Given a decent contingent of British soldiers, Dallas would have forced Little Crow back to the US on that very day.

Little Crow saw that there was very little chance of success in terms of being granted sanctuary in Canada, but he kept negotiating, swearing hatred for the US and peaceful friendship with Dallas and Britain. Increasingly desperate, Little Crow brought up the agreement his grandfather had made with the British over fifty years before. To Little Crow, that agreement might as well have occurred yesterday; but to Dallas, it was ancient history and irrelevant. Even after a second meeting, Dallas made his position clear to Little Crow that he should return to the US. Little Crow responded that, if he was sent back, he and his followers would be forced to fight to the last man. Little Crow suggested that it would be to the advantage of Dallas and the British if they negotiated an agreement with General Henry Sibley that would allow Little Crow to peacefully return to Minnesota. All that accomplished, however, was that Dallas could now make empty promises to get rid of Little Crow.

After the last fruitless meeting with Dallas on May 29, 1863, Little Crow knew that he would no longer be in a position of leadership among the Dakota that followed him to Canada. In June 1863, Little Crow returned to the US with only eighteen Dakota in tow, and he moved quickly to avoid conflict and/or capture. In early June 1863, Little Crow was able to get an item in a Saint Paul newspaper, which told Sibley and the rest of the authorities in Minnesota to look for him soon in the Lower Agency along the Minnesota River. Great curiosity and conjecture followed, with the fears of the Whites in southern Minnesota once again stoked to a frenzy. Little Crow was truly returning to Minnesota but with very few Dakota still following him.

For the Dakota that weren't hanged at Mankato or imprisoned at Fort Snelling, they would experience a sort of the Long Walk via steamboat to a reservation in Missouri that was the rough equivalent of Bosque Redondo, all courtesy of the outgoing secretary of the Interior Caleb Smith.

In June 1863, General John Pope's punitive expedition started, months after Little Crow thought they would do so. Pope now operated like General George McClellan (cautious and playing not to lose), not as the bragging general he was before the Second Battle of Bull Run (a.k.a. Second Battle at Manassas) in August 1862. Pope was obsessed with the idea that Little Crow had well over a thousand warriors and was ready to invade Minnesota and that they would even threaten Saint Paul. Pope was still in Milwaukee, so it wasn't very difficult for Governor Alexander Ramsey to fuel Pope's fantasy by insisting that Little Crow still posed a significant threat to the state.

Under Sibley's command, three thousand soldiers would execute a pincer movement in western Minnesota, cross into the Dakota Territory, and advance toward Devils Lake. Sibley's orders were to capture, kill, or scatter the masses of Dakota warriors. Sibley would kill over one hundred Dakotas from every band of the eastern Dakota during his trek west, but few of them were warriors.

In July 1863, Little Crow crossed back into Minnesota, and his small band split: some wanted to attack Whites while others wanted to steal horses. Little Crow and his son headed for the Big Woods. On July 3, 1863 (which was the last day of the Battle of Gettysburg), Little Crow and his son were picking raspberries north-west of Hutchinson, very near the site of the largest pitched battle of the Dakota War eleven months earlier.

Suddenly Little Crow was shot in the midsection, badly injured, but he got back up on a knee and started to return fire on a White father-son duo. Little Crow wounded the father, but soon the son of the White father shot Little Crow in the chest. After doing just enough to ensure his father's successful transition to the afterlife, Little Crow's son, Wowinape, fled. Little Crow was dead. What happened next was morbid but not unusual. After the news was brought back to Hutchinson, the newspaper finally reported a few weeks later:

> The search party callously removed the dead Indian's scalp and went back to town. Later that day, the body was loaded on a wagon, brought into Hutchinson, and there tossed it into the refuse pit of a slaughterhouse, like an animal carcass. About a week later, some local ghoul pried the corpse's head off with a stick and left this gruesome object lying on the prairie for some days, the brains oozing out in the broiling sun. No one knew at this time who the victim was. He appeared middle-aged. He had curiously deformed forearms, and he had the physiological oddity of a double row of teeth. Although several Hutchinson residents thought that the man looked familiar to them, no one seemed able to identify him positively.

The paper also noted:

> His body was dragged down the town's main street while firecrackers were placed in his ears and nose.

Another thing worth knowing, the bodies of the Sioux executed after the war in 1862 were dug up and used for medical study. William Worrall Mayo, who had been an army surgeon during the uprising and father of the brothers who founded the Mayo Clinic, received the remains of Mahpiya Okinajin (a.k.a. He Who Stands in Clouds and a.k.a. Cut Nose) and reportedly kept them in a rendering kettle in his home and used them to teach his sons anatomy.

General Sibley had reached a point in the Dakota Territory, where he had enough of the pursuit of Dakota warriors and returned to Minnesota after ironically his advance scouts had captured Wowinape in late July 1863 at Devils Lake trying to cross into Canada. An interview with Wowinape appeared in the *St. Paul Pioneer Press* on August 13, 1863, with the death of Little Crow prominently featured. No more rumors. Little Crow was dead.

Wowinape was put on trial, and four of the six White jurors agreed that he should be hanged. Sibley set the date of execution for November 20, 1863, pending approval from President Lincoln. Ironically Pope interceded and stayed the execution, saying that a violation of military due process had occurred under the Articles of War. To Sibley, Pope's decision to obstruct the execution of Little Crow's son sullied the hangings of the thirty-eight Dakotas, making them in his eyes illegitimate. But by late 1863, the Whites in Minnesota didn't care if Wowinape was executed or not. In their eyes, the threat of a Dakota invasion ended when Little Crow was killed.

Veterans at Last

The nicest veterans... the kindest and funniest ones,
the ones who hated war the most, were the ones
who'd really fought.

—Kurt Vonnegut, *Slaughterhouse-Five*, 1969

The great chase to push the Sioux Nation out of Minnesota and the US and onto reservations was just beginning. Governor Ramsey was on his way to northern Minnesota currently to make a treaty with the Red Lake Chippewa. He would cross paths with the Minnesota regiments that were being sent South. In total, the Sixth and Seventh Regiments had marched 1,200 miles in eighty-nine days in their pursuit of the Dakota bands. They had fought well and had endured the hardships of any other Union regiments in the war.

William and John of the Second Minnesota could say they were veterans of some of the fighting in the Western Theater, but when it came to boredom and marching, they had nothing on these men who were assigned to the prairie wars. All that was left of the First Minnesota Regiment had departed the Gettysburg battlefield crowned in glory, and after a brief assignment in New York City to put down the draft riots that had inflamed that city, they soon rejoined the Army of the Potomac and were once again in pursuit of Lee's army.

Summer in Washington, DC, can be a miserable time. It is typically hot, humid, and oppressively muggy. In August 1863 at the Armory Hospital, it was a time of suffering for not only the sick and wounded but also every person who worked at the hospital. There was no ice; the water was putrid and the air stagnant. The general misery of the suffering wounded and uncomfortable conditions put most everyone in a state of anger and outbursts that led to arguments and fights.

Jill and Sam had their hands full in more ways than one. Relief only came from the occasional thunderstorm at which time those who could manage it would sprint from the hospital to sit in the showers outdoors. Weather also ravaged a regiment's health while they were in the field. New cases of typhoid fever and the effects of malaria arrived at the hospital every day. Jill had complained to Sam that the boys were suffering from the change of climate and water as much as anything. The excessive heat contributed to debilitating wounds. It was midsummer: gangrene and erysipelas (a skin infection) attacked the wounded, and those who might have been cured of their wounds were cut down.

Aside from this, Jill still had to contend with soldiers who were on the mend, and one in particular was the Irish boy from New York who had lost his legs at Fredericksburg. His name was Pat Kelly. Over the summer, she and Sam had tried to work with this young boy to first get him to accept his condition and then accept the fact that he would have to deal with it. Progress was slow. He was resistant to nearly everything Jill had to say. When Sam was helping, he would remain somewhat calm but still had a fair share of fine cuss words for Sam. When Jill first introduced Pat to Sam, she was polite as possible, but Pat only complained about Negros that would be taking over all the jobs once he was released to go back home and how his life was now useless. Pat's wounds had healed, but his disposition had not.

It was now late into the dog days of August, and Jill and Sam sat by Pat's bedside trying once again to get him up and into his new legs. "Private Kelly, Lieutenant Bloomer and I are going to give you one more attempt at this. Today we are going to be helping you with your new legs."

"But he's only lost one. I've lost both of mine. How's he going to help me with that? How many times do I have to argue with you? I can't do this!"

Pat broke into another fit of cussing at Jill and blaming her and all "darkies" for the cause of the war and his condition.

Sam tried to comfort him. "Pat, I can see by your stout build that you were probably a short man."

Pat nodded in affirmation. "Yes, I stood only five feet three when they shanghaied me off the boat to join this stupid army."

"How would you like to stand as tall as Lincoln?"

"That ape is freeing the slaves, and now I hear he's even allowing them into the military as well. I don't know about being as tall as that darky lover."

Jill added, "But women love a tall man."

Pat grinned a half smile. "Well, if I was as tall as my brother, then that would be okay."

"And how tall is he?" asked Sam.

"About five feet nine, I think. And he's always got himself a gal."

"I think we can manage that, can't we, Sam?" said Jill.

Sam said that, with a few adjustments, it would be no problem. He then left to go to the carpenter's shop to see about adjusting the height of the legs. When Sam was gone, Jill questioned Pat about his life and how he ended up in the US Army. He told her how bounty men were waiting on the docks at New York harbor offering three hundred dollars for every man who would take the place of a rich man who had been drafted. The bounty men told him he would also receive his thirteen dollars a month and a guarantee of citizenship after the war or his discharge, whichever came first. He told Jill that now he realized how he had been duped like so many others and only wished he could get back on his feet and find a job to support himself. Jill told him that he had to listen to Sam and all his dreams would come true. Soon Sam returned, carrying a new set of legs. He set them on the bed.

"Okay, I found a new pair that should do the job. Are you ready to give this a try?"

Pat shrugged but said he'd at least try.

"Okay then, let's do this. One step at a time and one day at a time. But first we must get you fitted."

Pat was having none of it. Anger rose in him as he saw the inspection mark on the prosthetic legs. They were government inventory marked IC.

"No, sir! I'm done with those! Nothing fits as it should!"

Pat then picked up one of the legs and threw it against the wall in a rage that startled all around him, including Jill.

"You see what I mean? He's so full of anger we just can't get him to settle down and try anything."

Sam motioned for Jill to leave. "It's okay, Nurse. Can you give me some time alone with him?"

"Gladly," she said. Jill walked off to attend to other patients. "All right then, Private, let's start from the beginning. I'm assuming you were drafted straight off a boat or you were paid the three hundred dollars substitute fee."

"Right. I took the fee."

"And you have a family waiting back home?"

"Yes, sir, a wife and daughter in a New York slum. But now look at me. I'm not even a man anymore. I'll never be able to support them, and that three hundred dollars won't even get us through one year, let alone support their needs."

Sam then asked what regiment he was with. Pat told him he had been with the Twenty-Eighth Massachusetts.

"Second Corps, Irish Brigade?" Sam asked.

"Don't ya know it? Were ya there yerself? Antietam, I mean?" "Yep. Second Corps, Second Division, the old White clubs even though we had not got that distinction yet. We saw you guys go into it at the Sunken Road and catch hell."

"You lose your leg there?"

Sam told him of how he lost his leg in the battle and how he lay in the cornfield for a day before a Confederate surgeon cut off his leg.

"That must have been hell," winced Pat.

"Not like the hell you faced at that wall in Fredericksburg." After many more minutes of sharing their military experiences,

Pat had calmed down.

"Well, so do you think I can walk again?" he asked.

"I do, and I think we can make a good set of peg legs for you.
Jill tells me you were quite the craftsman back in Ireland."

Pat went on to tell Sam how he had been a master leatherworker
and saddlemaker.

"That's perfect," said Sam.

"Perfect for what?"

"For your new business."

Pat was now more puzzled than ever. "My new business?"

"I should have said 'our new business,'" replied Sam, going on to
explain. "That's right. We're going to design and make the best artificial
limbs in all of America and set up a shop in your new hometown of
New York so you can serve all those returning veterans who need hands,
arms, feet, fingers, toes, and whatever."

"You think we can do that?"

"Why not? Somebody must do it, and the government isn't going
to do it, or at least they won't do it right. We've already seen that. So
how about we get started?"

Finally, after months of resistance, Pat had found new hope. "I
guess so."

"Okay. I'm going to get your nurse back in here, and we're going
to give it that old Fighting Irish try again, okay?"

Pat was agreeable. Sam went off to locate Jill. She returned with a
wheelchair, and Jill wheeled Pat outside of the hospital where he could
get some fresh air. Sam followed them out carrying the prosthetic legs.
He stood next to them, overlooking the hospital creek.

He lit up a cigar and offered one to Pat. "I find good cigar smoke
covers the stench."

Pat thanked him and lit up his stogie. While the two men talked
among themselves of the war and casualties, Jill was able to get Pat into
his legs and helped him to stand with the aid of crutches.

"Private, do you think you can take more than a few steps today?"
"If you let me use the crutches, I think I can do the complete one
hundred."

Jill turned to Sam. "What do you think, Sam?"

Pat was a little bit shocked at the informality in Jill's speech to her superior. "Oh! Sam, is it? You two better be careful. People are starting to talk."

Jill said that she was already aware of that, and Sam added that they had done nothing to be ashamed of or inappropriate.

Pat decided he should remind them of the delicate situation they were putting themselves in. "Just because she's a free woman and there are some new free laws don't make this a free land or a free world. I'd be careful, Lieutenant."

Pat took a couple of shaky steps.

Sam reached out to spot him in case he was to fall. "Private, you just be careful you don't fall on your arse and hope you make your hundred steps so we can keep you out of this chair and get you to full-time walking again."

A wagon train of ambulances interrupted their conversation as it rumbled past the hospital.

Jill nervously wiped her hands on her apron. "Oh, oh…the never-ending rush. I thought that the Gettysburg battle ended over six weeks ago."

"Sure, it did, but you know by now it takes them months to clean up the mess. Look at our boy Pat here. He went down in December, and it was February before he came here, and it's August now."

Sam helped Pat as Jill headed back into the ward. The ambulance wagon train rolled on.

"What do you think, Patty? Let's get your legs on and get your walk complete for the day, then go check on the new boys and see how many Second Corps we got this time. That okay with you?"

Pat said it sounded fine to him. He was becoming very exhausted anyway and felt he needed to lie down. The hospital was full, so only a few of the wagons from the mile-long train of ambulances could off-load patients at the Armory Hospital. The remainder were sent on their way to other temporary facilities that had now filled the city. Sam and Pat checked the roster of new patients. They found no one familiar.

The next morning began a sequence of events that would be repeated every day to come until Pat had mastered his walking skills. Jill and Sam would start the morning by reaching behind Pat's wheelchair and hauling out his legs, then after helping him put them on, they would hand him his crutches and help stand him up and then set him on his way. Pat would spend all his time before breakfast meandering along the wooden plank sidewalk that surrounded the hospital perimeter. As the days passed, more and more amputees would gather outside to see the awkward parade of men like Pat struggling to regain their self-worth. Every time Pat or any other amputee made a solo lap, a cheer would rise from the spectators.

It was obvious to all that Jill and Sam were becoming close. Pat had become their special charge, and after they set him off on his own for the day, the two would walk to the river's edge to spend some time alone.

One morning, as Sam was lost in thought, Jill leaned in close to him. "What are you thinking about?"

Sam said his thoughts were on the rivers back home. "Bet it's nothing like this one."

Sam nodded.

"Bet it runs clear and clean."

"Yes, ma'am, all day, every day. Step right in. Wash your clothes. Have a drink. Take a bath. Pull catfish out by the dozen."

Jill smiled as she remembered her home. "Ah, I loved the way my mama prepared catfish."

"Where was it you said you were from?" "Cairo. Cairo, Illinois," answered Jill. "Yes, now I remember."

"Oh, you do, do you? You remember now?" teased Jill. "Yep. In fact, I looked it up on a map."

Jill was curious as to why he would do that.

Sam told her, "Just to see how long it would take me to get to you in case I wanted to get a catfish dinner made with your mama's special recipe."

"And how long did you figure?"

"Well, it's about 650 miles by canoe from my house, so it would take some time, I suppose."

Jill was enjoying where this banter was heading. "And did you suppose I'd be waiting for you?"

"Well, I didn't suppose it, but I did imagine it."

Jill snapped back to reality. "Well, Mr. Sam, you can just keep on imagining those things, but that's not the world we live in, and right now, we'd better move away from this stink and go find our boy."

They walked off together in search of Pat.

Corralled at Chickamauga

The Rock of Chickamauga is the only Union general who never lost a battle. But being Southern-born and from Virginia when states mattered more than nation, he was never trusted by Grant, Sherman, or Lincoln and therefore received little credit for his deeds.

—Blake Stilwell, We Are the Mighty, 2019

The summer of 1863 would be the turning point of the war. Lee had been turned back at Gettysburg, and the threat of another northern invasion would most likely not be attempted again. Grant had taken Vicksburg and secured the Mississippi River for the North. Colored troops had proven themselves in battle in the swamplands of South Carolina. The US Navy had grown from three battleships in 1861 to over one thousand vessels by 1863 and now had the South blockaded at all ports from New Orleans around the Gulf of Mexico and as far north as the coast of Virginia. Winfield Scott's "anaconda plan" for choking off the South by blockade was beginning to work.

England would no longer be a threat after the defeat at Gettysburg. New York City nearly destroyed itself over a week of rioting that stemmed out of the draft lottery. Regiments were still being held in Minnesota to pursue the Dakota, but with the North now having the advantage,

Sibley did not have to worry about losing his command to the battles being fought in the south or west. The Second Minnesota was now part of the Fourteenth Corps under the command of generals Rosecrans, Sherman, and Grant. William Simmons had been keeping his daily log of miles marched but now found time to write in his journal the events leading up to the great fight that would take place at Chickamauga.

The Battle of Chickamauga fought on September 18–20, 1863, between US and Confederate forces in the American Civil War marked the end of a Union offensive in southeastern Tennessee and northwestern Georgia—the Chickamauga Campaign. It was the first major battle of the war fought in Georgia and the most significant Union defeat in the Western Theater and involved the second-high-est number of casualties after the Battle of Gettysburg. William's narrative began thus:

> On the sixteenth of August, our pleasant camp at Winchester was broken up, and we marched eastward about a mile under a blazing sun, then two miles in a terrible thunderstorm. Then finding the road full of troops and trains entitled to precedence, we encamped. The next day, we marched three miles farther, reaching the foot of the Cumberland Mountain range, over which our route lay to reach the Tennessee River. Here we found the heavy wagon trains toiling up the steep, narrow, tortuous road, ascending the western slope of the mountain; and the slow progress of the last two days was explained.
>
> On the eighteenth, we found the road clear and marched up the mountain to University Place, on the summit, where we spent the night. Here the cornerstone of a magnificent university had been laid by Right Reverend Bishop Polk, now a general in the Confederate Army. An endowment of three million dollars had been pledged, and

the foundations of the several buildings had been constructed when the war interrupted the enterprise with an adjournment it has since died.

On the nineteenth, we marched down the eastern slope of the mountain range and encamped at the foot of Sweden's Cove, remaining there the twentieth. Since leaving our Winchester camp, we had found plenty of green corn, and the roasting ears had made a considerable item in our subsistence. On the twenty-first, we moved to the north side of the Tennessee River, at the mouth of Battle Creek, about six miles above Bridgeport, where the railroad bridge had been destroyed and was being rebuilt by our engineer forces. The river here was broad and deep, and the enemy's pickets lined the south bank.

They, for the first few days, kept popping their guns at our men whenever they approached the river. Occasionally the bullets would reach the camps, but we picketed the north bank with better marksmen. After a competitive trial of skill, the men on this duty came to an agreement to save their ammunition and thereafter amused themselves by debating the war with each other by yelling across the river. The men of both armies not on duty came down freely to bathe on their respective sides of the river, and soon it got to be the practice for a couple of good swimmers to meet in midriver to swap lies, newspapers, etc. while the pickets kept watching to see that there should be no foul play or breach of confidence.

Colonel George rejoined us here on the twenty-fourth from a long absence on sick leave and left us again on the twenty-seventh, promising to be back, if alive, in time for the expected battle. He kept his promise, returning to the regiment on the eighteenth of September, the day before the Battle of Chickamauga.

Meanwhile, Company F of our regiment, composed mostly of rivermen and raftsmen from the St. Croix / Stillwater lumber region, had been quietly at work in Battle Creek out of the enemy's sight, constructing rafts and rude scows in which four of our companies affected a crossing in the evening of the twenty-ninth and got possession of the south shore. The enemy, not expecting an effort to cross here, had left only a few men to watch the river, not enough to make any serious opposition.

By noon of the next day, our entire brigade was over, and the two other brigades of our division (Brannan's) completed the crossing on the thirty-first. Meantime, the other divisions of the army were crossing simultaneously at several points above and below us, and our trains and artillery were sent down to Bridgeport to cross on the new bridge when it should be ready. On the first day of September, we moved out about three miles to Graham Spring, near the foot of Raccoon Mountain and the monument marking the corner of the three states— Alabama, Georgia, and Tennessee.

On the fifth, our trains and artillery having arrived, we marched on the Nickajack Trace, as the ravine is called by which the road ascends the western slope of Raccoon Mountain. After marching four or five miles, it was found that the road needed so much repair and the wagons so much help that it would be impossible to get them to the summit that night, and we were obliged to go back two miles to find water for a camp.

On the sixth, we completed the ascent and encamped on the summit and, on the seventh, descended the eastern slope into Lookout or Wills Valley and encamped at Boiling Springs, about three miles below Trenton. Here we remained two days, learning on the ninth that Bragg had evacuated Chattanooga on the eighth and was retiring southward. On the tenth, we marched through Trenton and up the Lookout Valley about thirteen miles. On the eleventh, we started in the morning; but as the road in front of us was full of trains and artillery toiling up the mountain, we only made three miles and halted at the foot of a steep grade. Orders reached us at 7:00 p.m. to start at once and pass the trains as the enemy had been encountered on the other side of the Lookout Mountain. But these orders were soon countermanded, and we bivouacked again.

The next morning, we started at five o'clock, crossed the mountain, and halted in Chattanooga Valley at 10:00 a.m. At 2:00 p.m., we made a reconnaissance, returning to our position at seven o'clock. Here we remained the thirteenth and fourteenth while troops were moving around and behind us in a way that then seemed mysterious and without any definite or intelligible purpose. On the fifteenth, our brigade moved to Lee's Mill, on or near the Chickamauga Creek, and bivouacked in line of battle in apparent preparation for a fight. We remained there, standing to arms

at four o'clock in the mornings of the sixteenth
and seventeenth, expecting an early attack.

On the seventeenth, the heavy clouds of
dust extending along the eastern slope of the
Chickamauga Valley showed that the enemy's
columns were in motion northward; and about
eight o'clock, we took arms and commenced our
march by the left flank, abreast of and less than
a mile distant from the enemy's parallel march
by his right flank. Our progress was slow, the
day hot, and the road ankle deep with fine dust,
with which the tramping feet filled the air as the
column moved along.

At ten o'clock, we had got about three miles
from our starting point when some scattering
musket shots were heard in our rear, and presently
an order was received from Colonel Van DeVere
commanding the brigade for Second Minnesota
to return as far as the Pond Springs to see what
was the matter and rejoin the brigade. We unslung
and piled our knapsacks, leaving a few men with
them, and, in less than an hour, retraced nearly
the whole forenoon's march. As we came in sight
of the springs, the two leading companies were
deployed forward, and men were detailed from
each company to take all the canteens and fill
them at the springs as promptly as possible upon
our arrival there.

Approaching the place, we found the springs
in the possession of a detachment of the enemy's
cavalry who were resting in unsuspicious comfort,
many of them dismounted. They had been
worrying about our train and, having been
repulsed by the guard, had halted there for

reinforcements. They were promptly attacked and routed by our advance skirmishers; and while we halted, maintaining ranks, the canteens were filled and distributed. Then we reversed our march, returning by the left flank to our brigade, which had not moved during our absence, and soon bivouacked for the night. The light from the enemy's campfires was visible all night to the eastward, and we slept on our arms ready to be attacked if he was so pleased.

We remained here all day on the eighteenth while troops and artillery and trains were moving behind us to the left and northward, and about 5:00 p.m., we joined in the procession. We moved about a quarter of a mile per hour during the whole night, halting every few rods just long enough to get stiff and cold but never long enough to build fires and get warm. Many of the men would fall asleep, sinking in the road and some standing on their feet, but strict orders were given not to leave the column and to follow closely those leading us.

As the day began to dawn, we could see the brigades and batteries leaving the road from time to time and moving off in a line of battle into the woods to the eastward and toward the Chickamauga Creek, and we knew that the army was taking a position for the great contest so long anticipated. We could now understand how this had been going on during the night and how slow and difficult had been the construction of the grand line of battle in the darkness, and our tedious and halting progress was accounted for.

We had been all night in moving less than five miles and were now on the Lafayette-Chattanooga

Road and had passed in the darkness near General Rosecrans Headquarters at the widow Glenn's house; and at eight o'clock, our brigade halted, filed out of the road near Kelly's house, and stacked arms while the word was passed down the line, "Twenty minutes for breakfast" In five minutes, hundreds of little fires were kindled, and hundreds of little coffee cans were filled with water from the canteens and set to boil. In ten minutes, the boiling coffee was lifted off, the luscious bacon was nicely browned, and the ever-toothsome hardtack had been toasted when came an aid at a furious gallop down the dusty road. A brief order was delivered by him to our brigade commander, and each regiment got orders to take arms and march immediately.

Of course, some urgent and peremptory necessity was supposed. Arms were taken; and we filed out into the road, now clear, and briskly moved off northward in a cloud of choking dust. After making about a mile, we halted near McDaniel's House, whence a road, or rather a narrow wagon track, led through the open oak woods eastward to Reed's Bridge and the ford on the Chickamauga Creek.

It may be here explained that the extreme left of our general line of battle rested in the woods about opposite the midway point between Kelly's and McDaniel's houses; the position of the line, extending southward and facing eastward, was about midway between and parallel to the woods and the creek. So as we faced the eastward and marched in brigade order of battle along Reed's Bridge Road, we were detached from and nearly half a mile to the left of the left division (Baird's) of the established line.

Our orders were said to have been given on information by Colonel McCook, commanding a cavalry brigade on the left, that only one Confederate brigade had crossed to the west side of the Chickamauga and that he (McCook) had destroyed the bridge (Reed's) behind it and we were to take and hold the ford and prevent further crossing by the enemy while our First and Second Brigades were to find, attack, and capture the enemy's supposed isolated brigade. This information, if given, proved entirely erroneous, nearly the entire Confederate Army being in position between our lines and the creek; and their brigades were not hard to find when we came to look for them.

Our brigade was formed with Second Minnesota on the left and the Thirty-Fifth Ohio on the right of the front line, with Smith's battery in the road between them. The Eighty-Seventh Indiana was in the second line behind the Thirty-Fifth Ohio; Ninth Ohio was detached with the division ammunition train. So we commenced our march, a few skirmishers preceding our front line. Proceeding along the road, which seemed to follow a low ridge through the woods and while yet to the left and rear of Baird's division whose exact position we did not know, we heard musketry to our right and front. Changing our direction to face it, to the southward, we moved off the ridge and down an easy slope and soon met the enemy in force; and the firing began at once. In a few minutes, the enemy retired, then rallied and attacked again and was again repulsed, this time retiring out of our sight. We gathered up our wounded and carried them back over the ridge to the northern slope in our rear, replenished our cartridge boxes, and readjusted our line, the Eighty-Seventh Indiana meantime changing places with the Thirty-Fifth Ohio on our right. In a few minutes, the firing again broke out in our front; but while the bullets dropped in among us, we were, on account of the trees and underbrush, unable to see any men for a time. Then the firing approached, and the big guns joined in for a few rounds, then a burst of cheers and the rebel yell.

The artillery ceased, and the rattling musketry came nearer and the bullets thicker.

Our men were ordered to lie down and hold their fire until they could see the enemy.

Presently, to our astonishment, a straggling line of men in our uniform appeared, then more of them, running directly toward us, their speed accelerated every moment by the yelling and firing of the exultant enemy behind them. Our men got ready and waited while the stampeded brigade, officers and men, passed over our lines to the rear, then, as the enemy came in view, gave them a volley that extinguished the yelling and stopped their advance. They rallied, however, and stood for a few moments, receiving and returning our fire and then wavering, and broke and ran out of sight.

Just now, Ninth Ohio arrived, having abandoned the ammunition train when the firing broke out and followed our trail to the front.

The firing had ceased when Colonel Kammerling rode up and vociferously demanded, "Where dem got dam rebels gone?"

Someone pointed in the direction they were last seen, and away went Ninth Ohio over our front lines, disregarding Van DeVere's order to come back. We could hear them yelling and cheering in both languages long after they disappeared. About a quarter of a mile distant, they found and recaptured the battery (Guenther's), which the enemy had taken half an hour before. The enemy's troops about the battery made a fight for it, and Kammerling lost a good many men in getting it and was even then obliged to leave it when recalled by a peremptory order to rejoin the brigade, which he did not receive or obey too soon.

During the first fighting, our band men, as they had been previously instructed, were busy with stretchers, picking up the wounded and carrying them back up the slope and over to the north side where our surgeon, Dr. Otis Ayer, had established a temporary hospital and was giving them as much attention as circumstances permitted. It soon happened that some of these men were shot the second time while being carried back, and the carrying was suspended until the firing should cease. There was much confusion and activity on this part of the battlefield. Confederates had made a huge advance on the Union lines and had pushed them up the ridge where they had held at a loss of many men wounded and killed.

Sergeant Major Moffett was seen running about giving orders to his musicians.

"You there! Simmons 1! Simmons 2! Vandyke! Gather up any other musicians or slackers, teamsters, or cooks you can find and get some litters!"

William and Vandyke obeyed immediately. John asked what they should do about the dead.

"Leave 'em. Don't waste your time," commanded Moffett.

The boys gathered a crew of litter carriers and went about the business of collecting the wounded. As they pulled the wounded off the field, the rebel forces made another charge at the Union line, and a volley of lead spattered around the boys. A round ripped through John's cap, tossing it high in the air. William noticed and immediately ran to his brother's side. Noticing he was not hurt, they carried on with the unpleasant business they were assigned.

Later that evening, William would add to his journal:

> Our skirmishers soon reported the enemy moving around our left flank; and our regiment, by facing left and filing left, changed front to face the east. The enemy attacked us in this position, which was repulsed by our regiment alone; and then by the same maneuver, we changed front again to face the north, the enemy having passed a large force around our left flank during the last attack, which was probably made to cover the movement.
>
> *We were now* on the road again and on the right of our brigade, on a line nearly parallel to our first position but facing the opposite direction; and the movement had brought our left company next to the battery, which, without changing position, had exchanged the places of its guns and caissons and now also faced the north. The other regiments of our brigade had formed on the

left of the battery, and for a moment of silence, we awaited the onset. Here on the ground now before us lay our wounded men who had been carried back from the first line of the fight and were now between the opposing lines. But here they came, ranks after ranks emerging from the sheltering trees and underbrush and approaching us with the steady tramp and desperate silence.

Our men were cautioned now to "shoot to kill," and we opened with file firing that soon broke up the orderly march of the first line, whose men hesitated and then commenced firing wildly. Their second and third lines were promptly moved up, and all pressed on in the charge. Our big guns were loaded with canister, which opened great gaps in the enemy's columns at each discharge, while the withering fire of our infantry was thinning their ranks at every step of their advance.

They greatly outnumbered us, and it seemed a question for a time whether we could so reduce their numbers and their nerve as to prevent an actual collision, in which they would have the majority. But they began to waver at sixty yards.

At forty, they broke and then ran, every man for himself leaving, alas! Hundreds of brave fellows prostrate in helpless suffering before us, some of them intermingling with our own wounded who had been carried there from the first fight in the morning.

This assault and repulse ended our part of the battle for the day; we now refilled our cartridge boxes, gathered our wounded men and sent them to the field hospital at Cloud's house, and collected our dead for burial. Our regiment had commenced the battle with 384 men and officers, of whom 8 had been killed and 41 wounded, none missing. While waiting here for orders, we heard from time to time the roar of battle along the line to the southward but saw nothing more of the enemy in our vicinity, thus ended the first day of battle. We fell back to make camp and resupplied for the next day's turmoil.

On the morning of the twentieth, the regiment was moved into position along the top of a ridge known as Snodgrass Hill. They were put here to defend an artillery battery. During the day, the battle pitched back and forth with both lines of either Union or Confederate having the advantage. By midafternoon, the men of the Second Minnesota could see and hear that the rebel army was closing in on their brigade. William wrote that, at first, they could see stragglers of wounded Union men breaking out of the woods headed in their direction, followed by shirkers who were just running away like cowards. Behind them, a full brigade of Confederate had broken through and was advancing and rushing up Snodgrass Hill.

The Union artillery battery next to the Second Minnesota battle line loaded their cannons with canister shots, which essentially turned their weapons into huge shotguns. The Confederate line was within a few hundred feet and closing with bayonets dropped, and though the Union line stood fast for the bayonet charge, they would be hard to stop. Fear set in along the entire line of the Union brigade. Few men were made that could stand up to the cold steel of leveled bayonets. They were on the edge of breaking.

Moffett ordered his crew of musicians back into line, "Okay! You boys set those wounded men down. Find yourself some rifles and fall in with Company K! Now!"

They reacted with haste and soon were in the battle line along with the other survivors of the first day's battle. William, John, and

Vandyke had taken their place in the front rank of Company K. They were locked and loaded and stood ready for the fight.

The artillery captain gave the order to fire. The first rank of Confederates evaporated in the smoke as if they never existed, but the second rank continued to come on. The cannons loaded again and fired canister after canister at will. The order was then given for the entire regiment to fire at will, and they opened with one solid volley, which halted the movement of the Confederate line. They then followed that up with nonstop sporadic firing accompanied by the constant booming of the canons.

The Confederate line, after many brave attacks, finally broke and retreated in disorder down the hill. The Union line on this portion of the battlefield had been saved. But the two days of fighting had left the Confederate Army still holding the ground, and the battle ended in the first defeat of the western army of the United States. After the battle, Moffett walked along the line looking over his musicians. He was full of pride as he recognized that finally his boys had turned to men.

"Well, boys, something to finally write home to Mom about other than slogging through mud." He then pointed to a rip in Vandyke's trouser leg.

Blood was seeping out. "What's that, Vandyke?"

Vandyke said he did not know as he had felt nothing during the height of the battle.

"You better get that looked at. You other two okay?" he asked of William and John.

They both acknowledged that they were fine.

"Good then. Get back to your duties. There are still others out there who need attention."

The boys handed off their rifles to the corporals of the company and ran off in opposite directions to continue their duties as litter bearers.

The summer of 1863 was ending. At the Armory Hospital, Pat had finally mastered the use of his new legs but was dissatisfied with how they were constructed, and he and Sam set out on their mission to design and construct more suitable prosthetics. Many regiments were coming up at the end of their three-year enlistments, and those who would choose not to reenlist would be discharged.

News of the war was filtered across the river from Fort Snelling to Mendota daily. Generals Sibley and Sully were well entrenched in their pursuit of the Dakota and were building temporary forts in the Dakota Territory with plans to make these forts permanent structures to contain the Indians and continue the war on them after the Confederates had been defeated, which was now looking like a real possibility for the first time. The South could not match the North in industry nor men in which to fight the war. More and more, it was appearing to many Southerners that they were fighting a lost cause.

In the village of Mendota, Jane Sibley found herself to have only one friend to confide in, and that friend was now Louise Simmons. Sara was growing up to be a fine young lady. A new year of school was beginning. She and Robert Two Arrows remained close friends, but their friendship was being tested by those who still saw the Natives as inferior to the White settlers.

Under the incompetent leadership of General Rosecrans, the Union Army had been defeated at Chickamauga, and this gave Bragg and his Southerners a new hope and redemption. Without the quick tactics of General Thomas, the Union Army may very well have been destroyed. Bragg's Southerners had now pushed the retreating Union Army back to Chattanooga, where Sherman and Grant would build up a defensive line. The Second Minnesota had fought well at Chickamauga and had nothing to be ashamed of. They had lost several men who had been killed, and a number had been wounded, including Vandyke.

The hospital in Louisville was full as usual. Nurse Mary was still receiving letters from William, but they were dated weeks in the past. Most troubling to her now was what she had been reading in the local newspapers. Casualty reports were listed every day, and she anxiously read these lists every morning looking for the names of the men from the Second Minnesota. To her relief, she never saw William's name but did see the name of Vandyke, so she knew that William must have been involved in some form of combat. She knew that Vandyke and William were inseparable friends.

On an early November morning at the Louisville Hospital, Nurse Mary sat in the shade of the veranda of the hospital porch. She was rereading one of William's many letters when Dr. Smith took a seat next to her.

He saw the concern in her face and spoke gently to her, "I hope you won't be much longer, Mary. Good news, I hope."

Mary folded the letter and put it back into her handbag. "It's very old news, but yes, I'll be right along, Doctor."

"You look troubled," Dr. Smith added. "Is it that Yankee boy you took a shine to?"

Mary nodded and wiped a tear. "Yes, the western one. They just came out of a big battle in Georgia. I'm afraid though I don't see his name on any of the lists." She paused to pronounce the name of the great battle.

"Chickamauga?"

"Yes, that's it. Though I can hardly pronounce it."

Dr. Smith took her hand to comfort her. "It's been in all the papers. Terrible fight. Bad as Gettysburg, I read. I'm sure he is okay, though. If you don't see his name listed by now, he's fine. Don't give it another thought."

Mary looked at the doctor for more reassurance. "Yes! Thank you. But his friend isn't, and his regiment took some awful casualties." "Are they headed back this way to convalesce?" asked the doctor. "Not likely. From what I've read this morning, Bragg has pushed the Union Army back to Chattanooga, and in one of William's last letters, he wrote that they have fought with old Thomas long enough, and now he thinks they will be put to the task with Sherman."

"Ah, Thomas. The Rock of Chickamauga, they've named him. So your boy has been in good hands, and Sherman ain't no slacker either though they say he's crazy. But then who isn't these days?" The doctor helped her to her feet and escorted her back indoors. "Come on, child. Let's get back to work. No need to fret on your boy now.

Nothing we can do here. He's held up to shot and shell for over two years. I'm sure he'll be okay. We've got more just like him in here who need us right now."

OVER THE TOP AT
MISSION RIDGE

I was the first fruit of the battle
of Missionary Ridge.
When I felt the bullet water my heart
I wished I had stayed at home and gone to jail
For stealing the hogs of Curl Trenary,
Instead of running away and joining the army.
Rather a thousand times the country jail
That to lie under his marble figure with wings,
And this granite pedestal
Bearing the words, "Pro Patria."
What do they mean, anyway?

—Edgar Lee Masters, *Spoon River Anthology*

By the late summer of 1863, the campaign to control Chattanooga and eastern Tennessee resulted in some of the war's heaviest fighting. On September 19–20, the Second Minnesota clashed with General Braxton Bragg's Army of Tennessee at the Battle of Chickamauga in northern Georgia. On the second day of the battle, a federal tactical error led to a Confederate breakthrough that swept half the Union Army from the field. The Second Minnesota and their comrades took up a defensive position to delay the Confederates. From midafternoon until dusk, they held their position in the face of repeated attacks. This brave defense earned their corps commander, Major General George H. Thomas, the nickname "Rock of Chickamauga." The battle was a Confederate victory.

The Federals retreated to Chattanooga, and Bragg's army took a position on the heights surrounding the town, including Lookout Mountain southwest of the city and Missionary Ridge (Mission Ridge) to the east. In mid-October, Major General Joseph Hooker came west with a detachment of the Union Army of the Potomac. General Ulysses S. Grant arrived to assume overall command of the Union forces. He gave General Thomas command of the Army of the Cumberland. In mid-November, Major General William T. Sherman arrived with his Union Army of Tennessee.

On November 24, 1863, Hooker's soldiers attacked and defeated the Confederates on Lookout Mountain. The next day, the Federals advanced on the main Confederate line on Missionary Ridge. General Grant gave the Army of the Cumberland a passive role in the center while Hooker's and Sherman's troops prepared to do all the real fighting on the flanks. These attacks stalled, and Thomas's men were ordered to assault the first line of Confederate works. Second Minnesota led their brigade in capturing this position.

Soon afterward, General Grant watched in amazement as the entire Army of the Cumberland, without orders, assaulted the main rebel line atop the ridge. A stunning Union victory resulted. The Minnesotans captured two cannons at the climax of the assault. On that morning of November 24, the regiment was being held in a position along with the rest of the entire divisions of Thomas's brigade ready to assault the Confederate works at the lower slope of Missionary Ridge. At the top of the ridge were Confederate gun emplacements, which, under ordinary circumstances, would be insurmountable. Orders had only been given for Sherman to take the first line of defenses and go no further.

Vandyke had been returned to the ranks and was in line with his friends once again as they lay low behind a log breastwork. William welcomed Vandyke back to the company. Vandyke's wound had been minor, but given the conditions of the day, even a simple infection could lead to death. In his case, he healed without incident.

"How's the leg?" asked William.

"Fine. A little sore but it wasn't much to begin with."

"Nice to have you back," added John as he came to settle in line next to his messmates.

Vandyke rested his rifle against the breastwork. "I'm surprised they put us back in the line."

William nervously checked the cartridges in his cartridge box. "It's only for this big push. Then we're back to litter duty and signaling commands."

Vandyke asked how many rounds they had been given. Both William and John answered that they each had sixty rounds. Vandyke said he had the same and, with everyone having full cartridge boxes and twenty extra to put in their pants pockets, they "must be expecting a hell of a show."

John then added, "Well, the skirmishers sure have been poppin' them off." John then popped his head over the breastwork to see Moffett crawling toward them. "Shh, here comes Moffett."

Moffett then stopped to address his boys. "All right, you three, listen up. Look out there. You see that dip in the slope about four hundred yards out?"

They all nodded.

"That's their first line of defense. It's fully lined with infantry, breastworks, encampments, you name it. Every obstacle we have, they have. That's what you'll face."

John then asked when they would step off.

"It's going to be a while, so relax. Eat something. Take a nap. Write a letter. Word will be passed a half hour before we go. You know the drill."

William asked why they were given so many rounds.

"We've got hundreds of skirmishers out front, and so do the rebs, so this is not like a massed assault. We are going in as a large skirmish line attack. We'll fire at will the entire way. Take the position and hold it."

Vandyke wanted to know how long they were expected to do so. William was concerned about the artillery on top of the ridge, which was only a quarter of a mile from the first entrenchment they were supposed to hold. "With their guns so close, they could smash us to bits."

Moffett put on a brave face. "And what's the accurate range of your Springfield?"

William answered that it was a one-quarter mile.

Moffett settled in with his three favorite musicians. "Then maybe it's about time you Northern sodbusters start showing these Southern swamp slugs who's the better shot."

The four hunkered down behind the breastwork as they waited for the assault to begin. John, Moffett, and Vandyke shared a breakfast of hardtack and coffee. William scratched out a letter to Mary.

John nudged William. "Do you believe she even gets your mail?" William pushed back. "Of course she does."

"Oh yeah? When was the last time you got a reply back from her?"

"I don't know. Two months ago maybe." "And that's enough to keep you going?"

William said it was and that he was pleased enough with their correspondence.

John stopped his teasing as Moffett looked at his pocket watch. "Okay, boys, pack it up. Get ready. Half hour. I'm going in with you."

The boys squared up their equipment and uniforms and readied themselves for the attack.

As silent orders were passed down the entire Union line, the army rose, then stepped forward as one.

Moffett, leading his boys, turned around to face them and quietly gave them orders, "Hold your fire until all NCOs and officers are back in line and we have reached that ridge just in front of their breastworks. Now fix bayonets and make sure you've got one round down and on safe."

William, walking next to his brother, turned to him and handed him his haversack. "If anything happens to me, you know what to do."

John said that William was acting stupid and not to worry, then asked him specifically what he wanted him to do.

William was shaking so badly he could barely respond. "I've never been so scared. This is not like the other battles we've seen. I just know something terrible is in store for me. Send a letter home to Ma and this last one to Mary and then finish my journal."

John took his haversack and could now see the true fear in William. "Well then, you do the same for me."

William managed a lighthearted laugh. "You don't have a journal or a girlfriend, but I will write to Ma. And be assured I'll also keep your pay."

They both laughed loud enough for Moffett to tell them to hush up and pay attention.

As the Union line moved forward through the tall grass and rough brush, the Confederate soldiers broke from their duties to rush to their defensive positions as they saw the Union forces move toward them. They readied themselves for the attack. With muskets leveled on top of the breastworks, they aimed. These were the same soldiers who had so roundly beaten these same Union forces just a few weeks prior, and they were full of confidence that the result would be the same today.

From somewhere on the right of the Union line, a bugle call swept over the entire line, signaling the men to a full charge. Everyone knew that they were supposed to fire at will, so there was continuous sporadic fire being poured into the Confederate trench line as the boys in blue advanced at the double quick with their bayonets leveled. Colonel Bishop, who was in the rear line of his regiment, now gave the order for his men to charge.

Raising his sword, he yelled as loud as he could, "Charge, Minnesota! Charge!"

Over the thunder of the shot and shells, Moffett called out to John, "Now, John! *Now!*"

John reached down to take hold of his bugle, which had been hanging off his hip. He stopped running for a moment to sound out the bugle call for the general charge. The bugle enlivened the regiment, and in an instant, what had been an anxious fear turned to fury. They dashed forward with newfound confidence and energy. From on top of the highest ridge, Confederate artillery opened fire, and shells began to drop within range of the charging Union forces. Some of the men in blue began to scatter and fall, but the overall line remained intact. The rebels in the first trenches opened with a volley of musket fire. Bullets whizzed past the boys in the regiment and slapped the ground around them. Some got hit and went down, but the majority continued.

Within a few moments, the Union line was on top of the Confederate breastwork and, without orders, fired a volley into it, then dove in to fight the rebels bayonet to bayonet and hand to hand. It so disrupted the Confederates that they had no time to react, and the Union soldiers jumped into the trench and were upon them with a shock that sent them reeling back out of their trench.

The Confederates were chased out of their trench and ran for the top of the ridge and the protection of the artillery emplacements. Now the Union had the advantage and the protection of the trench, but the Confederates had the advantage of the high ground and could easily use it to pick off Union soldiers and make good use of it. This is where sharpshooting from both sides came into play. The orders of the day were for the Union Army to hold at this point.

Within a few minutes, though, somewhere within the Union line, a disgruntled Union soldier decided he had enough and was not content to sit under the shelling and sporadic musket fire; so he took up his regiment's flag and moved out of the trench and headed up the slope. His regiment had no choice but to follow the flag, which it did. This sent a general wave throughout the entire Union Army, and now the whole of the army followed one regiment after the other into a general charge up Missionary Ridge.

Generals Grant and Sherman, who had been watching this through binoculars far in the rear, were shocked because this was not part of their plan of attack. Grant turned to Sherman and told him that, if this turned out badly, someone would have to pay for it. The regiments moved up the steep slope in disorder as the hill was covered in entanglements of all kinds. The troops pushed forward, their heads bent down as if running into a hailstorm, dodging their way through the brush and undergrowth as well as the continued barrage of artillery fire and musket fire laid down on them from above; but they moved on as one angry mass.

The individual regiments assembled on their colors as best they could but reached the crest generally intermingled; and when the brigade finally crowned the enemy's works at the crest of the ridge, the regimental and even the company, organizations had become completely merged in a crowd of gallant and enthusiastic men who swarmed over the breastworks and charged the defenders with such promptness and vigor that the enemy broke and fled, leaving their artillery batteries and barely getting away. Portions of the caissons and limbers and six twelve-pound Napoleon guns were thus captured by the brigade, two of them by the men of the Second Minnesota Regiment.

Hardly had a lodgment been made in the works when the enemy's reserves made a furious counterattack upon the men yet in confusion. This attack was promptly met by a charge en masse by the crowd, which, after a few minutes of desperate hand-to-hand fighting, cleared the ridge, leaving the place in undisputed possession of the Union Army. Between two to three hundred prisoners were captured in the melee. The captured artillery was turned upon the retreating enemy and manned by volunteers from the different regiments, but darkness soon closed over the field, and the firing ceased. During this confusion of the returning rebels to attempting to regain their guns, John, William, and Vandyke had been caught up in the hand-to-hand melee. William, being overpowered by two rebel soldiers twice his size, was thrown about quite easily; and though John and Vandyke tried to rescue him, they failed in their attempt. William was unceremoniously dragged off down the opposing side of the hill as a prisoner. The sun set on Missionary Ridge with a decisive Union victory, and once again Bragg's army was in a full retreat into the heartland of Tennessee.

After the battle at Missionary Ridge, the Second Minnesota retreated to its camp at a place called Hospital Hill in Chattanooga, where they would relax for two days. Colonel Bishop sent this dispatch to Fort Snelling regarding the regiment's performance at Mission Ridge and the pursuit of the enemy after the battle, where it was then passed on to Governor Ramsey, who then released it to the press:

> On the morning of the twenty-sixth, we drew rations for four days and, at noon, marched in pursuit of the retiring enemy, a distance of about eight miles to the crossing of Chickamauga Creek by the Rossville and Graysville Road, where we bivouacked for the night. On the twenty-seventh, at 4:00 a.m., we marched again, passing through Graysville and arriving at Ringgold, Georgia, about 10:00 a.m. about eleven miles. Here an engagement with the rear guard of the enemy was in progress, and we formed in line of battle in readiness to act as occasion might require.
>
> At noon, the enemy retired; and at night, we bivouacked, remaining in the same position until noon on the twenty-ninth, when we marched for Chattanooga, arriving at 6:00 p.m., eighteen miles.
>
> Of the conduct of the officers and men of the regiment, under the hardships and privations of the week's campaign in severe and inclement weather with insufficient clothing and scanty rations, and especially of their gallant bearing under fire in the operations of Wednesday, I am incompetent to speak in terms that would do them justice. The regiment being brought into action deployed as skirmishers, there was better scope for individual acts of heroism or of cowardice than would otherwise have been afforded; while I witnessed many of the former, I am proud to say

that none of the latter has come to my knowledge. A list of casualties is hereby transmitted.

I am, Captain, very respectfully, your most obedient servant, J. W. Bishop, lieutenant colonel commanding Second Minnesota Volunteers.

The brigade commander, Colonel Ferdinand Van DeVere, in his official report, stated:

My total force engaged at 1,679 officers and men and his total casualties at 161 killed and wounded. Separating the Second Minnesota force and casualty reports from those of the brigade, I found that the average loss of the other six regiments was a little more than 8 percent while that of the Second was as before stated over 21 percent. This disparity followed naturally from the brigade commander's judicious plan for the attack, which assigned to our regiment the duty of carrying the first line of breastworks "if we could" before exposing the other six regiments to the enemy's fire. Doubtless the aggregate loss of the brigade would have been greater and our attack would have failed had not our men made so cool and steady an advance across the open field, reserving all for the final rush.

The brigade commander acknowledged the gallant service of the regiment in the following language, which was quoted from his official report:

Especial credit is due Lieutenant Colonel Bishop for the management of his regiment when skirmishing in front of the brigade and for the gallant manner in which his command carried the rifle pits at the foot of the ridge.

VETERANIZED

*I offer neither pay, nor quarters, nor food; I offer only
hunger, thirst, forced marches, battles, and death.
Let him who loves his country with his heart, and
not merely his lips, follow me.*

—Giuseppe Garibaldi

Two days after the assault on Missionary Ridge, the Union Army
celebrated their victory in their camps surrounding Chattanooga. This
was the same day that President Lincoln gave his Gettysburg address
and was the day he declared there would be a national day of thanks.
This very first Thanksgiving went without notice in the Union camps.
Even if it had been an official holiday, John, Vandyke, and Moffett had
no reason to be thankful. John was left with his brother's belongings,
and there had been no official word passed through the lines of who
was captured or killed. All they knew was that William had not reported
for muster the night after the assault. John and Vandyke assumed he
was in captivity as they saw him being pulled over the ridge by the two
huge Confederate soldiers who had fought him during the taking of
the Confederate guns.

The regiment was encamped on a hill on the outskirts of Chattanooga.
It was just two days after the big battle that secured the Union Army's
occupation of Tennessee and the Cumberland Valley. The regiment
was comfortably settled in. Vandyke and John had now partnered up
without William. They shared a dog tent and messed together. Moffett

was now spending most of his time with the junior officers. John had done as his brother wished and was continuing to record everything of interest in William's journal.

As John was completing the evening's passage in the book, Vandyke broke his concentration as Moffett approached their shelter. "Have you heard the news?"

John inquired to Vandyke what news that could be, hoping it was good news about his brother.

"Next week, on the tenth of December, Companies F and G are being sent back to the ridge and Chickamauga to bury the dead." "Good," replied John. "Let them wallow in that stink for a bit.

Any word on what they have planned for us musicians?"

Vandyke replied that all he heard was that they were to stay in camp. Moffett walked by, then took a seat in the wet grass with his boys. John gave him an anxious look.

"No word yet, Simmons. I'll let you know as soon as there is any notice of prisoner exchanges."

John thanked the sergeant major.

Moffett continued, "Oh, before I forget. After those battlefields are cleaned up, we are to be veteranized."

Vandyke looked confused and asked what that meant.

"It means the regiment has completed two years in service. You can reenlist or get out."

Vandyke asked what the advantage of reenlisting would be. "For one, you'll get a thirty-day leave back home and come back with a pay raise and a rank promotion. Two, you won't be in the band anymore."

John brightened. "So that means no more dirty duty. No more digging graves and hauling bodies, chopping down trees, and building bridges and roads, right?"

Moffett said that indeed that was so. Vandyke asked if this meant they would be placed in the battle line and become regular combatants and, if so, if it would mean they would no longer have to take orders from him.

Moffett simply smiled and nodded.

"One month leave, you said. And if we don't reenlist?" asked Vandyke.

"Then you're done. Out. Your war is over."

John said he would have to think on it and consider what William would do if he had a choice; though going back home to his mother and sister seemed great, he could not possibly leave William to fend for himself if there was even the slightest chance that William would be exchanged back into the regiment.

"But what will the others think? What would Will think if he knew I didn't sign up again? Because I know he would."

"We promised each other we see the war out together," added Vandyke.

Moffett told the two they would have a couple of days to make up their minds and, if they could live with the shame of leaving the regiment, then it was fine with him to let them go. John filled the pages of William's journal with this accounting of the veteranizing as it was to happen. He later copied the portions into a letter to his mother along with the details of William's capture, which he included in William's journal:

> Having returned to our camp on Hospital Hill in Chattanooga on the evening of the twenty-ninth of November, we enjoyed a comfortable night's rest under shelter after the week of bivouacking, marching, and fighting. On the thirtieth, Companies F and G, having been on detached service, cutting timber for and aiding in the construction of bridges and pontoons, rejoined the regiment. The weather was getting cold and wintry; but with fair supplies of clothing, blankets, and food, and with comfortable huts and plenty of fuel, the situation was quite tolerable.
>
> The enemy, some twenty miles away, seemed to be perfectly willing to let and be let alone.

About the tenth of December, large details were sent out to the field of Chickamauga to gather and bury the dead, who had thus far been neglected. About this date, the announcement was received from the War Department that regiments having been in service two years or more were invited to reenlist for three years and, upon so reenlisting, would be sent home on thirty days' furlough. This announcement was eminently wise and timely under the circumstances.

The three years' term of many of the regiments would expire in the summer of 1864, and it had become evident that the war would not be ended within that term. Recruits and new regiments were coming out slowly, and it had moreover come to be understood that a veteran regiment was much more than equal to a new and inexperienced one.

The proposition was read to the regiment at dress parade. We were briefly informed by the lieutenant colonel commanding that, for himself, he intended to continue in the service to the end of the war if he should live so long; that the question of reenlistment was a personal one; that every man should, with due consideration, decide for himself and that, having so decided, his position would be respected, whatever his decision might be; and that there should be no distinction or discrimination made or permitted between the men who did and those who did not reenlist.

The question was taken up by us men, and a good deal of earnest discussion was had among us during the next ten days. We were, after two and a half years of service, perfectly familiar with the restraints and hardships and dangers of war and were not to be enticed into reenlistment ignorantly. We longed to return to our homes in peace, but we were as loyal and patriotic as when we first responded to the call to arms. We well knew that our services were now as much needed and more efficient and valuable than they were in '61.

On the twenty-fifth of December, the regiment was reported to headquarters as reenlisted—80 percent (about three hundred men) including myself and Vandyke having so decided. This was one of the first regiments in the Army of the Cumberland to so reenlist, but several days elapsed before the proper rolls could be obtained and made for the muster out and in, which took place on the twenty-ninth of December.

The payment of the troops and procuring transportation and other preparation for going home consumed several days. The nonveterans, numbering about seventy-five men, were formed into a temporary company; and Captain John Moulton and lieutenants M. Thoeny and Charles Rampe were detailed to remain with them. This detachment was assigned to duty during the absence of the regiment as provost guard at division headquarters.

On the eighth of January 1864, the regiment embarked at three o'clock in the morning on the small steamers *Dunbar* and *Kingston* and arrived at Bridgeport in the afternoon, a distance about forty miles by river. Here us men were loaded into a train of boxcars and arrived at Nashville on the afternoon of the next day. This trip, without exercise or fire or warm food in midwinter, was a severe one; but we were yet in the war country and going home. There was little grumbling or complaint.

At Nashville, at 7:00 p.m. on the fourteenth, a train of empty boxcars was again assigned to us, in which we had another cold and uncomfortable journey of eighteen hours, arriving at Louisville about noon on the fifteenth; and we were quartered in the military barracks. Here all needed clothing was supplied for their midwinter trip to Minnesota, and we took advantage of this opportunity to turn in our old Enfield muskets, which we had been obliged to carry since our second equipment exchange in '62.

Arrangements having been made for this, we had a parade march on the seventeenth from the barracks to the ordnance building, carrying for the last time the arms and equipment with which we had fought Tullahoma, Chickamauga, and Mission Ridge. Our arms were stacked, the equipment unslung and hung on the bayonets, and we returned to the barracks forty rounds lighter and feeling perhaps more like furloughed men than before.

Our orders for transportation to Chicago were here obtained over the Louisville, New Albany, and Chicago Railroad upon the assurance of the superintendent that we should have comfortable coaches and quick passage. We, at first, thought that boxcars were good enough for soldiers; but our officers now insisted upon proper transportation as it was paid for and they felt we had a right to it. Finally we were notified that, on Monday morning, the eighteenth of January, our train would be ready; and we crossed the Ohio River to the New Albany depot to find a train of box and cattle cars, some of them bedded six inches deep with frozen dung, backed down to the platform for our accommodation.

The superintendent was conveniently absent, but he was informed by telegraph that the cattle train would not answer the purpose and that we would return to Louisville and ask for transportation by some other line if passenger coaches were not promptly provided as promised. The weather was intensely cold, with wind and driving snow, and it was a shameful thing to propose to transport human beings in such weather and such cars as had offered us.

After some delay, a message came that the cattle cars were all a mistake and that coaches would be ready in the afternoon, and so we waited. About five o'clock, the train was made ready; and we started in warm, comfortable cars for Chicago, expecting to arrive there the next morning. Such transportation as that would, however, have been too good for soldiers; and we did not arrive there until the morning of the twenty-first.

After breakfast at the Soldiers' Home, we started again by rail for La Crosse, arriving there at 3:00 p.m. on the twenty-second, where we were hospitably entertained. Henceforward our transportation was to be by sleighs by the stage company, but only conveyances for half the regiment were ready. Major Davis, with the

band and four companies, was forwarded the
same evening and arrived at Saint Paul early
Sunday morning, the twenty-fourth of January,
140 miles in twenty-two hours, which was a
considerably better time than we had made on
the New Albany Railroad.

The lieutenant colonel commanding, with
the remaining six companies, left La Crosse twelve
hours later and—except the three companies A,
B, and C—furloughed at Winona and arrived
at Saint Paul Sunday evening.

The ladies of Winona gave a hot breakfast
to the first detachment and a hot supper to the
second, and the people of all the river towns
along the route improved every opportunity to
show us boys we were welcome. On Monday, the
twenty-fifth, we dispersed for our homes, each
with thirty days' leave of absence, which time we
doubtless enjoyed as we deserved to.

The officers, instead of receiving furloughs,
had been ordered on recruiting service and were
aided everywhere by the enlisted men, who all
felt interested in filling up the regiment, now
reduced to less than half the standard strength.

Headquarters were reopened at Fort Snelling
on the twenty-fifth of February; and as the men
came in rapidly, the regiment was mustered for
inspection and pay on the twenty-ninth, showing,
besides the 300 veterans, about 150 recruits. In
the afternoon of this day, on the invitation of
the ladies of Saint Anthony, prominent among
whom were Mrs. and Ms. Van Cleve, the wife
and daughter of our first colonel, the regiment
marched from the fort to that place where a grand

reception, supper, and ball were given in its honor at the then-vacant Winslow Hotel building. The ball lasted all night and ended with a hot breakfast at seven o'clock, after which we boys marched back to the fort, eight miles, arriving quite rested and refreshed.

When John and Vandyke had reached the Simmons house, they found themselves feeling very out of place. Louise and Sara, of course, were upset and heartbroken that William was not among the furloughed men but were relieved that John was home and took in Vandyke as a welcomed guest as he did not wish to return to his family in Ohio for reasons he never explained. News had not yet reached Fort Snelling regarding whether William was safe in a prison camp or dead. He was only listed as missing in action. Louise was beside herself with remorse and anger at herself and General Sibley. She broke off all contact with Jane and Henry Sibley as soon as she had received John's letter explaining what had happened to her youngest son.

Louise was concerned about John's health. In the time he had been gone, he had lost so much weight she almost didn't recognize him when he ran up to meet her at the Fort Snelling reunion set up by the local ladies' aid society. John would be nineteen years old soon. He had grown a beard and grown another five inches in height. He was now nearly as tall as Vandyke, and both boys appeared as if they could be blown over by the slightest breath of wind. Sara was overjoyed to have her oldest brother back and was entertained by the presence of Vandyke, whom she took an immediate liking to. Now safe at home, John was also shocked to see how much Sara had grown. He could hardly believe that she was nearing fourteen years of age, only two years younger than Mary, the girl William had taken a fondness for and whom he had a secret fancy for.

Sara and Louise had received full reports from William in his letters about this young girl in Louisville. Sara was overcome with curiosity about her and continued to pester John with questions about the young lady, and in doing so, John inquired as to her being interested in any young man that may have been courting her. This provoked some anger between Sara and her mother, which led to an argument on one of the first nights that the family was together. Louise was still upset about Sara and her innocent retreats with her Chippewa friend Robert.

It was mid-February, and this was a time when the citizens of Saint Paul and Mendota would celebrate the hopeful early coming of spring. The young people of the communities had planned a party to be held on a frozen section of the Minnesota River that had been cut off and surrounded by land. It was known as Lake Pickerel, and it was so shallow that it would freeze to the bottom into one solid block of ice. It was from this lake that men from Mendota and soldiers from the fort would cut ice blocks and store them in an ice house for use in the summer.

On the night of the planned celebration, Louise and Sara got into a verbal fight over Sara's disobedience toward her mother.

As John prepared the family dinner, he could see the tension between Louise and Sara rise. He knew how frustratingly lonely the Minnesota winters were and that being trapped for months in a one-room cabin could easily affect one's nerves. Though a fire raged in the hearth, ice had built up on the window and door sills, making the home feel even more like an inescapable prison.

Sara stood by a window and pleaded with her mother, "Oh, Mother, please, can I go out?"

Louise told her most directly, "No!"

Sara begged to know why. Louise told her that she knew exactly why she could not go out or go to the celebration.

Sara stomped her feet in protest. "That was months ago, and nothing happened."

Louise countered, "I just don't want you hanging around any Indian boys."

"But why not? He's a cut hair, a Christian. We go to school together. We have the same teacher. Our teacher, Miss Big Head, is a civilized

Chippewa. She'll be there. She grew up with Mr. Sibley's daughter. Nothing bad will happen, I swear it!"

Louise had reached her limit. Just the sound of Sibley's name turned her red with hate. "I don't care. They're all the same! *No*!"

Sara shot back, "But there's going to be a big buffalo-hunting dance tonight on the river, with a bonfire and everything!"

"You mean a powwow and that damn drumming! Oh, I can hear it now! Just like the summer of '61, and you know what that led to. No! You're staying in. Those savages can dance all they want for all the buffalo in the world, but they're trapped in that prison below the fort, and as far as I'm concerned, they can all starve to death."

John joined in now in support of his sister, "Ma? Why not let her go? She has to grow up sometime. You can't keep her locked up in this shack forever."

"No, sir! I let you and your brother go, and now look where we are at. Your father is dead, your brother missing, and you, of all the stupid things, reenlisted. I thought you were the smart one. What did that army do to you anyway?"

Louise now broke into tears again, something she did often since the war had started. Sara tried to comfort her mother but was pushed away.

"You just go sit right back over there and put another log on that fire, and don't say another word."

Sara returned to the hearth and set a log on the fire. She grumbled to herself.

John sat next to his mother and tried to reason with her, "Look, I'll take her down to the lake party and make sure she's okay and nothing happens to her."

Louise pushed back. "Oh, sure, just like you said you'd look after your brother?"

She was crying uncontrollably now, and John moved to his sister and whispered in her ear. He would go against his mother and escort Sara to the celebration.

The following day, a corporal under orders from General Sibley was sent across the river to Mendota. He had with him a copy of a telegram that had been sent through various channels from the Confederate prison camp at Belle Isle in Richmond, Virginia. The dispatch had arrived via Governor Ramsey and then forwarded to Sibley at his post in Fort Snelling. Sibley had already once tried to speak directly to Louise but was so put off by her that he felt that any news regarding her boys should come from an unbiased messenger.

The messenger arrived at the Simmons house early on this cold February morning. He was greeted by John. John read the dispatch and then read it out loud for Sara, Vandyke, and his mother to hear. It simply stated that William had been captured and was now being held at Belle Isle and that he was being well taken care of. The dispatch also stated that he would be exchanged when the generals in command of the Union Army determined that an exchange of prisoners was timely. The dispatch had been signed by the Confederate colonel in command of Belle Isle and was nearly three weeks old.

The news was a relief for Louise and Sara, but John and Vandyke showed little joy. They knew that, with the current conscription of men into the army and with reenlistment rates at over 80 percent, the Union Army did not need to do a prisoner exchange. Grant, Sherman, and Lincoln all felt that keeping Confederate prisoners in the Union prisons would benefit the war effort more than releasing them back into the ranks of the rebels. The tide of the war had turned.

John took the ferry back across the river with the corporal who had delivered the message. He felt he'd like to visit with General Sibley and get caught up on the news of the Indian war. He knew his mother would not approve of the visit, so he left without telling her where he was going. Sara walked with him to the ferry, and they talked about the winter celebration on the river. Sara was pleased that, when she introduced Robert, John did not object and found the young Chippewa to be clever and trustworthy. Sara asked many questions about his experiences in the war; but John was in no mood to reveal much other than the whole thing was a dirty, lousy mess. One day, she could read William's journal when all of this had passed into history.

When John arrived at the fort, he had to get special permission to see General Sibley and finally gained it after it was made clear to the general who John was. They had a cordial visit lasting the better part of the afternoon. They shared a simple soldier's lunch, and when John asked about the punitive expeditions into the Dakota Territory, General Sibley let him read the news of the final battle that took place in the previous September at a place called Whitestone Hill in Dakota Territory.

BELLE ISLE

In a semistate of nudity…laboring under such diseases as chronic diarrhea, scurvy, frostbites, general debility caused by starvation, neglect, and exposure, many of them had partially lost their reason, forgetting even the date of their capture and everything connected with their antecedent history. They resemble, in many respects, patients laboring under cretinism. They were filthy in the extreme, covered in vermin… Nearly all were extremely emaciated, so much so that they had to be cared for even like infants.

—Lucius Eugene Chittenden
US treasurer during the Lincoln adm-
inistration in describing the dreadful
and horrifying conditions Union soldiers found at Belle Isle in late 1863

After his capture at Mission Ridge, William was packed into a cattle car along with other Union prisoners of war. They were forced to stand shoulder to shoulder with not even enough room to turn around. The only warmth they had was from their body heat. Snow and wind blew in from the wide gaps between the wooden planks that made up the walls of the car.

William nudged the soldier next to him. "Any idea where we are headed?"

The other prisoner, who was older and more robust than William, shrugged. "Instinct tells me south. Weather says north."

William asked where and when he had been captured. They had both been captured on the same day near the same spot on Missionary Ridge. The prisoners then told each other which regiments they were from. The other man was from the Fifteenth Indiana; it made sense that they were in the same area of the fighting as both regiments had been in the same brigade for quite some time. The other prisoner asked if William was a drummer as he looked so young.

William said that he had been for most of his service and said, "It shows, huh?"

The prisoner replied, "Yeah. You look a little young, but I see, by the powder on your face, you've been chewing off cartridges, so they must have let you loose with a rifle yesterday."

William told him he had also fought at Chickamauga.

The prisoner responded with pride, "Now that was a proper battle, wasn't it?"

William wasn't in agreement. "I don't know. I kind of liked that run up the hill yesterday much better."

"Well, congratulations kid, you're a real veteran now." "And a prisoner on top of that," added William.

They both laughed it off, then properly introduced themselves. The other prisoner's name was Otis Nelson from a small farming town in Indiana.

"Nice to meet you, Private William, if you don't mind me calling you by your new-earned rank."

"No, not at all. Nice to meet you, Corporal Otis."

Forty-eight hours later, the train rolled over the cityscape of Richmond, Viginia. It passed over the bridge that spanned the James River, then came screeching down to a landing at Belle Isle, where a prisoner-of-war camp had been set up directly on the rocky banks of the river. The river was partially frozen over and covered with snow.

As the train rolled to a stop, Confederate guards ran up to unlatch the doors of the car. The disheveled Union prisoners were herded off the car under gunpoint en masse and forced into two lines, then ordered to march toward the camp entrance. William and his new friend Otis marched side by side. William was accidentally pushed out of line by one of the prisoners behind him. A guard shoved him back into place.

"Hey! Watch where you're stepping!" yelled William.

"Shut up, blue belly, and stay in line." The guard pushed William back in line with his rifle.

William was not amused. "You could at least tell us where we are."

"You'll find out soon enough," answered the guard.

Otis now spoke out against the guard. "The boy is right. Where's all this Southern hospitality you're supposed to be so famous for?"

"Okay, right. I'll tell you. You're at Belle Isle, in Richmond, Virginia, the capital of the Confederate States of America. And we are about to whip your Yankee asses once and for all. How's that for Southern hospitality?"

William then sarcastically thanked the guard for his kindness.

They were led to the iron gates of the prison.

The guard pushed them in. "All right, now shut up. Get inside and pay attention to what the captain has to say, and maybe you'll live to get back home to your filthy, whoring, godless women and children."

The prisoners were marched through the gates and into the prison. The gates were closed and locked behind them. A cold wind blew light snow across the open campground. The prisoners lay or stood about shivering. They had little for clothing and certainly nothing for winter wear. Some were shoeless. Most were threadbare, and there was little around to give any evidence of shelter from the cold. Small fires were the only source of heat. Fortunately William's regiment had been resupplied within the past few months, and his wool fatigue jacket and trousers were in fair condition. No evidence of food was to be seen. A young soldier by the name of Al spotted William's divisional blue acorn patch that was stitched to his uniform and ran up to him, shivering. He was very excited.

"You…you…you're…you're Fourteenth Corps." "Yes, that's right," said, William.

"Me…me too… What regiment?"

William told him, and then Al asked him from what part of the state he was from. William explained he was from Mendota, which was across the river from Fort Snelling. Then he inquired about where Al was from.

"Sure. I know where it is. I'm from Saint Peter, with the Fourth. They got me at Mission Ridge."

Al introduced himself as Albert Masterman. William then introduced himself, and Al asked about food. His teeth were chattering.

William told him how he gave his haversack to his brother. "I had some rations in my haversack, but I passed it on to my brother before the attack to take care of for me, and he gave me his, but he never likes to take food into a fight with himself. Sorry."

Al said he understood and then explained the situation, "I've only been here two days but haven't gotten one bite yet, and some guys have been here for over six months and haven't had hardly one meal a week."

They both talked about how they enlisted as drummers but found themselves eventually as combatants.

Soon the guard approached and pushed them along with his rifle. "Okay, you two. No talking and move along. The captain has a report for all of you fresh fish."

The boys hustled along to a gathering spot around a large fire, where the captain was standing on a large river boulder waiting to address his new arrivals.

"Gentlemen! I am Captain Black, and I am the commander of Belle Isle prisoner camp. As you may know, Belle Isle is one of the oldest Confederate prisoners-of-war camps in the South and, my opinion, the fairest and most civil. If you behave yourselves and do as you are told, you will be treated fairly and humanely. Because your gorilla president Lincoln has decided to blockade our ports, we no longer can attend to your medical needs and no longer have the surplus food supplies to give out the ample rations we had at the start of hostilities two years ago. You may take that up with ape Lincoln after we have defeated you."

Otis yelled out, "What about prisoner exchanges?"

The colonel answered in the harshest tone, "Because monkey Lincoln has decided the niggra can take up arms against his White master, we have decided to stop prisoner exchanges. Instead we are constructing a beautiful new prison facility in sunny Georgia, where soon we will move you and any new prisoners to reduce our over-crowding, where you will be well fed and looked after by the finest Southern doctors and nurses."

Otis yelled out again, "When?"

"After the first of the year! By February, we predict a grand opening," answered the captain.

This was William's first impression of the camp, and he felt lucky that he was not among the men who had spent months here. He would later write in his new journal:

> No wooden structures were furnished for the prisoners at Belle Isle. If they were lucky, several men could be crammed into thin canvas tents, but most were forced to construct their drafty shelters. The lack of substantial and adequate shelter compounded the prisoners' plight on Belle Isle and increased the amount of death and suffering brought on by disease and exposure. The new arrivals were given paper and pencil and ordered to write to their families and/or sweethearts to tell them they were safe and well cared for.
>
> Autumn passed and winter settled in. Al Masterman of the Fourth and I had become best of friends as we shared our experiences of life back in Minnesota. We agreed that winter wasn't half as harsh as it was back home, but it was bad enough.

The James River never fully froze over and was always in a state of the constant onrush of ice and rushing water. The large boulders that made up the riverbed caused heavy-running rapids. Some prisoners saw a way to escape would be to swim the river and make for the woods on the other side. Few made it. Most drowned or were shot. Once I watched as one man tried to skip over the large rocks. He slipped and fell into the rapids. He went under and was never seen again. Near Christmas of 1863, Otis, Al, and I were sent to a large brick building that sat on the edge of the riverbank. It was an arms and munitions factory. The Union prisoners were forced to work there under slave conditions with the promise of better rations. No rations ever came. We suffered there through January, waiting for that promised day when we were to be removed to the new camp in Georgia.

ANOTHER KIND OF
PRISON CAMP

*Cavender-Wilson sees the fort as "very, very bizarre.
It's very disturbing on a political level, but on an
emotional level, it's trying," she comments. "If I
look down [from the Round Tower], I can see the
concentration camp. This is where the cannons
were; this is where the soldiers started from when
they descended into the camp to rape our women
and children."*

—The *Twin Cities Daily Planet*, July 29, 2010

In March of 1864, General Sibley returned to Fort Sully. He would begin
to prepare his troops for the continuation of the punitive expedition
that had ended with General Sully the previous fall. Sibley had been
informed by General Pope that an important impetus to the upcoming
summer's military campaign against the Sioux was the desire to protect
lines of communication with recently discovered goldfields in Montana
and Idaho. The lifeline for the American gold miners were steamboats
plying the Missouri River through the heart of the Sioux territory.
During the winter of 1863–1864, Sully's superior, Major General
John Pope, ordered Sully to establish several forts along the Missouri
River and in the eastern Dakotas to secure the communication routes

to the goldfields and to eliminate the Sioux threat to the settlers east of the Missouri River.

Now, in early spring, Sibley was standing in the fort his men had finished the past October. His major Logan was at his side. Logan was scanning the horizon with binoculars. After having a good look, he handed the binoculars to Sibley, who asked Logan what his Crow scout had told him.

Logan replied, "He thinks the Dakota will stay across the river on that land for as long as we leave them alone. He said their chiefs have agreed to leave the White man be if we leave them in peace. The Dakotas are full of buffalo and other game, and they can live okay. Just go back to Minnesota, and there will be no more trouble forever."

Sibley responded, "Tell your scout to send a message back to the Dakota chiefs that this may not be acceptable to Washington. In the meantime, I'll send word back to General Pope to get his response. We'll have to wait."

And wait they would. It would be July before Sully had returned with fresh troopers and new orders to eliminate the Dakota threat. Of utmost importance now was to see to it that all gold in the Black Hills, Badlands, and territories west of there did not fall under the protection of the Dakota. Settlers were moving in to mine the gold, and it appeared another gold rush like the great rush of 1849 was imminent. Washington had a very expensive war on its hands in the south, and the industry that fueled it needed to be paid.

Sibley was glad to be away from Fort Snelling. His job there over the winter of 1863–64 was to oversee the care of the Natives who were still in the concentration camp at the base of the fort on the riverbank. Many Sioux had been killed by White settlers when they were marched to the fort in November of '62. A census taken on December 2 stated only 1,601 Natives had made it to the compound alive.

Though many were killed on the march to the fort, Fort Snelling proved no less dangerous. Less than a week after their arrival, the Dakota had established a camp in the river bottom below the fort. One evening, a Dakota woman who was out gathering firewood alone was attacked and raped by a group of soldiers, Saint Paul newspapers reported. Military leaders ordered a wooden stockade built in the river bottom to protect the prisoners from White antagonists as much as it was to confine them. Armed guards patrolled the stockade day and night, and no one was allowed in without a pass.

The three-acre enclosure encompassed between 200 and 250 tepees behind its fourteen-foot walls. The Dakota did have a few friends among Minnesota's White population. Local clergy made frequent visits to the stockade, who tried to force Christianity upon them. Episcopalian bishop Henry Whipple became an advocate for the prisoners, raising money for their care and arranging for the release of several. The reverend John Williamson, who had lived among the Dakota his entire life, would join them at the concentration camp and remain with them for the rest of their ordeal. An article in the *St. Paul Pioneer Press* reported:

> The enclosure also had its share of gawkers, taunters, and those who came simply relieved to see the Dakota confined. Among them was one of the mission teachers, Harriet Bishop, who was disgusted to learn that the government was spending $1 a day per prisoner to maintain the camp rather than putting those funds toward the care of White settlers victimized during the war. The streets were receptacles of all the offal of the lodges, where barefooted women and children splashed around in the filthy snow slush.

These conditions left the Dakota vulnerable to diseases like measles. Gabriel Renville, a half-Dakota man imprisoned at the camp, later recalled in a memoir that "we were so crowded and confined that an epidemic broke out among us, and children were dying day and night." Renville added, "Amid all this sickness and these great tribulations, it seemed doubtful at night whether a person would be alive in the morning." The total number of deaths that first winter was likely between one hundred and three hundred. After the bodies of several dead Dakota were exhumed and mutilated by Whites, the captives began burying the bodies of loved ones in the floors of their tepees. The reverend Stephen Riggs later wrote:

> In early May 1863, the army loaded the 1,318 captives who remained at the concentration camp onto a pair of riverboats to be exiled to the Dakota Territory. As they streamed past the levee at Saint Paul, a crowd gathered along the river and pelted them with rocks. At Saint Joseph, the Dakota were loaded onto a single overcrowded steamer for the final leg of their journey up the Missouri River. Many more would die before they reached their destination. A month after departing Fort Snelling, the survivors disembarked at the Crow Creek Reservation, a drought-stricken waste-land. They were soon joined by the Ho-Chunk (or Winnebago) of southern Minnesota, who were also exiled to Crow Creek despite having no part in the conflict between the Whites and the Dakota.

The reverend characterized this as a naked land grab by the state and federal governments. But the stockade at Fort Snelling would not remain empty for long. As the hundreds of Dakotas who fled to the plains after the war were captured or surrendered between summer 1863 and spring 1864, the fort became a way point on their journey to Crow Creek. Included among them was the family of Little Crow, who remained at large until he was killed near Hutchinson for a five-hundred-dollar bounty offered by the State of Minnesota.

HALFWAY TO PARADISE

I was not an anthropology student before the war. I took it up as part of a personal readjustment following some bewildering experiences as an infantryman and later as a prisoner of war in Dresden, Germany. The science of the study of man has been extremely satisfactory from that personal standpoint.

—Kurt Vonnegut

William had been in Belle Isle prison camp for less than a week. He had made a few friends and, having a few dollars of good Federal money, which he had hoarded since his capture, purchased a small blank book and intended, as long as he was a prisoner of war in this Confederacy, to note down from day to day, as occasion may occur, events as they happened, treatment, and ups and downs generally. It would serve to pass away the time and may be interesting in the future to read over, or so he thought. His first entry was thus:

> December 1, 1863. Very cold weather. Four or five men froze to death last night. A large portion of the prisoners who have been in confinement any length of time has been reduced to almost skeletons from continued hunger, exposure, and filth. Having some money, I indulged in an extra ration of cornbread for which I paid twenty cents

in Yankee script, equal to two dollars Confederate money, and should say by the crowd collected around that such a sight was an unusual occurrence and put me in mind of gatherings I have seen at the North around some curiosity.

We received for today's food half a pint of rice soup and one-quarter of a pound loaf of corn-bread. The bread is made from the very poorest meal—coarse, sour, and musty. It would make poor feed for swine at home. The rice is nothing more than boiled in river water with no seasoning whatever, not even salt, but for all that, it tasted nice. The greatest difficulty is the small allowance given to us. The prisoners are blue and downcast and talk continually of home and something good to eat. They nearly all think there will be an exchange of prisoners before long, and the trick of it is to live until the time approaches.

We are divided off into hundreds, with a sergeant to each squad who draws the food and divides it up among his men, and woe unto him if a man is wronged out of his share—his life is not worth the snap of the finger if caught cheating. No wood tonight, and it is very cold. The nights are long and are made hideous by the moans of the suffering wretches.

William went on to explain how Otis had found a company in a very large tent and had promised him space as soon as one was available There were twelve men in the tent; and he promised it would not be long as, every couple of days, one would pass on. He only had to wait three days before there was a vacancy. The day before he could take the place of the perished man in the tent, Otis sacrificed his comfort to spend William's last night on the open ground with him, which made for a more comfortable night than those before. On December 3, the prisoners were getting two meals a day, which was still not much at all; and in William's entry in his journal, he wrote:

> Old prisoners say it is fully a third more than they have been getting. I hardly understand how we could live on much less. But less was the usual fare. From fifteen to twenty-five prisoners die every day and are buried without coffins or ceremony. They were simply wrapped in canvas and buried at the river's edge. A squad of men amounts to one hundred, and every day they were given eight sticks of four-foot pieces of wood to divide among themselves, which does nothing to warm the men. Two or three will put their wood together and boil a little coffee made from bread crusts. The sick are taken out every morning and either sent over to the city or kept in the hospital just outside the prison and on the island. None are admitted unless carried out in blankets and too far gone. There is not much chance of recovery. Medical attendance is scarce.

On December 20, William wrote about his new friend Al Masterman from the Fourth Minnesota Regiment:

> Al is a very slight boy with almost-effeminate mannerisms and a high, squeaky voice. The rebel guards took some pity on him as he was so small and frail. He was given a job in the cookhouse. Otis, who is now the senior in the tent of twelve men, promised Al a spot in the tent as soon as one opened on condition that Al steals as much

food as he could from the cookhouse storeroom and bring it to the men in the tent. There is a storehouse next to the cookhouse, which is full of hog heads and other meats, which has been sent south to Richmond by the US Sanitary Commission intended for Union prisoners; but seldom does this food ever get to the prisoners as the rebel guards take it all first.

From his journal, he continued:

December 23. Almost Christmas, and we are planning for a Christmas dinner. Very cold. The rebels are testing their biggest guns on the opposite shore of the river and fairly shake the ground we stand on. We can see the shells as they leave the guns until they explode, affording quite a pastime for us watching their war machines. Militia in sight drilling over in Richmond. A woman was found among us as a prisoner of war. Someone who knew the secret informed Lieutenant Bossieux, and he immediately had her taken outside when she told him the whole story—how she had "followed her lover a soldiering" in disguise and, being of a romantic turn, enjoyed it hugely until the funny part was done away with. Madame Collier, from East Tennessee, found herself facing a very long prison sentence. Nothing to do but make the best of it and conceal her sex if possible, hoping for a release, which, however, did not come in the shape she wished. The lieutenant has sent her over to Richmond to be cared for, and she is to be sent north by the first flag-of-truce boat. She tells of another female being among us, but she has not been found out.

December 24. Must hang up my stocking tonight for habit's sake if nothing else. I am enjoying splendid health, and prison life agrees with me, or so that is what I wrote home to say today.

December 25. And Christmas. One year ago, today I sat in camp and wrote out our total mileage marched in that past year. Today I am a prisoner and wished I could step back in time. Little dreaming what changes a year would bring around, but there are exchange rumors afloat and hope to see White folks again before many months. All ordered out to be squadded over again, which was quite a disappointment to our mess as we were preparing for a grand dinner, gotten up by our outside hand, Al. However, Al made good before our mess was desquadded.

We had our good things for supper instead of dinner; and it was a big thing, consisting of cornbread and butter, oysters, coffee, beef, crackers, cheese, etc. All we could eat or do away with and costing the snug little sum of two hundred dollars, Confederate money, or twenty dollars in greenbacks. Lay awake long before daylight listening to the Richmond church bells as they rang out Christmas good morning, I imagined they were the bells from the Fort Snelling chapel in Mendota. Little do they think as they are saying their Merry Christmases and enjoying themselves so much of the hunger and starving here. But better days are coming.

December 26. News of exchange and no officers came over from Libby Prison to issue clothing though we did get an extra quantity of wood. Rebels are all drunk and very domineering. Punish for the smallest kind of excuse. Some men tunneled out of the pen but were retaken and were made to crawl back through the same hole they went out of; and the lieutenant kept hitting them with a board as they went down and then ran back and forward from one hole to the other and, as they stuck up their heads, would hit them with a club, keeping them at it for nearly an hour. A large crowd of both rebels and Yankees collected around to see the fun.

December 27. Colonel Sanderson and Colonel Boyd came over from Libby Prison this morning in a great hurry and began to issue clothing very fast, saying an exchange had been agreed upon and they wanted to get rid of it before we all went away. Pretty soon, the news got inside; and the greatest cheering, yelling, shaking of hands, and congratulating one another took place.

Just before dinner, five hundred were taken out, counted, and sent away. Everybody was anxious to go away first, which of course they could not do. Two of our rebel goons, sergeants Hight and Marks, stood at the gate with big clubs, keeping order, letting them out two at a time, and occasionally knocking a man down; and it was seldom he got up again very soon. Some, on the outside, went; and the rest go tomorrow. It is a sure thing, a general exchange, and all will be sent away immediately. Everybody is in good spirits. Guess Northern folks will be surprised to see such odd-looking objects come among them. They are the worst-looking crowd I ever saw. An extra ration of food and wood tonight, and I am anxiously waiting for the morrow.

December 28. For some reason or other, no more being taken away and more despondent than ever. Very cold.

December 29. Nearly as cold weather as I ever saw up North. All the supplies were brought by hand over the long bridge, owing to the river being frozen over yet not strong enough to hold up. Rebel officers are all drunk during the holidays. Snow, an inch deep.

December 30. No rations were issued yesterday to any of the prisoners, and a third of all here are on the very point of starvation. Lieutenant Bossieux sympathizes with us in word but says it is impossible to help it as they have not the food for us, yet they eat like kings from the rations sent from the North that was marked for us. This is perhaps true as regards edibles, but there is no excuse for our receiving such small supplies of wood. They could give us plenty of shelters, plenty of wood, and conveniences we do not now get if they felt so disposed. How hard would it be to send work parties of prisoners under guard to forage these supplies, one wonders?

December 31. It is still very cold, and no news encouraging. Rebels are very strict. One prisoner found a brother among the guards who had been living in the South for a good many years and lately conscripted into the Confederate Army. New Year's Eve. Man wounded by a guard shooting, and the ball broke his leg. Might better have shot him dead, for he will surely die. Raw rice and cornbread were issued today in small quantities. *Richmond Enquirer* spoke of the five hundred who left here day before yesterday, and they have reached Washington. Good news for them but leaves those of us left behind very disheartened.

January 1, 1864. A great time this morning wishing one another a happy New Year. Al stole from the storehouse a dozen apples and gave us all a treat. Nothing but cornbread to eat and very poor quality. Dr. F. L. Lewis, veteran surgeon, Ninth Michigan Cavalry, came in today. He was captured at Dandridge, East Tennessee, where one of our tentmates' regiment had a severe engagement. Tells us all the news. Colonel Acker wounded, etc., etc. Thinks it is a queer New Year trip but also thinks we will be exchanged before many weeks.

January 2. Rebel Congress about to meet, and the people of Richmond demand through the papers that the prisoners confined here to be removed immediately as there is hardly enough for themselves to eat aside from feeding us "Northern hirelings." We hear of bread riots and lots of trouble across the river. A big fire last night in the vicinity of Libby Prison.

January 3. I received a letter from Mary today. She says she is well. The hospital is full of sick Union boys, and it is not quite so cold yet disagreeable weather. Nine men from our tent were bucked and gagged at one time on the outside, two of them for stealing sour beans from a swill barrel. They would get permission to pass through the gate to see the lieutenant and instead would walk around the cookhouse to some barrels containing swill, scoop up their hats full, and then run inside; but they were caught and are suffering a hard punishment for it.

January 4. Some ladies visited the island to see us bluecoats; laughed very much at our condition; thought it so comical and ludicrous the way the prisoners crowded the bank next to the cookhouse, looking over at the piles of bread; and compared us to wild men and hungry dogs. A chicken belonging to the lieutenant flew up on the bank and was snatched off in short order, and to pay for it, we are not to receive a mouthful of food today, making five or six thousand suffer for one man catching a little chicken.

January 5. Succeeded in getting Dr. Lewis into our tent, who is rather under the weather, owing to exposure and hardship. Al, Otis, and I spend the evenings together; and we have fun times talking over better days—and are nearly talked out. I have said all I can think and am just beginning to talk it all over again. All our stories have been told two to three or four times and are getting stale. We offer a reward for a good new story.

January 6. Still prisoners of war without the remotest idea as to how long we are to remain so. Some of the paroled Yankees on the outside of the gate curse and treat the inside prisoners crueler (when they have a chance) than the rebels themselves. Blass, a Spaniard, who has been a prisoner for over a year and refuses to be exchanged, is now the rebel lieutenant's right-hand man. He tied up a man a few days ago for some misdemeanor and whipped him. He is afraid to come inside, knowing he would lose his life in a jiffy. He also raises the rebel flag at the island every morning and lowers it at night. It is a dirty rag, and the appearance of it ought to disgust any sensible person.

January 7. Rainy, cold, and disagreeable weather. Henry Stilson, a fellow who was captured with me, was carried out dead this morning. He was diseased when taken and fell easy prey to their cruelties. A good deal of raiding is going on among the men. One Captain Moseby commands a band of cutthroats who do nearly as they please, cheating, robbing, and knocking down—operating principally upon new prisoners who are unacquainted with prison life. Moseby is named after the rebel guerrilla, his real name being something else. He is from New York City and is a regular bummer.

Nothing much changed over the next couple of months. Rumors of prisoner exchanges never ended until some new prisoners coming gave notice that the US had officially suspended exchanges. The commander of Belle Isle Prison still promised that the prisoners would be soon transferred to the new prison being completed in Georgia. Word was that all the prisoners that had been in captivity for over six months would be transferred.

This was the only "good news" that the men in William's tent could look forward to. Nearing the end of February, William added to his journal:

Everything runs along about the same. Little excitements from day to day. The weather is fair and, taken all together thus far this winter, has been very favorable to us as prisoners. Lieutenant Bossieux lost his dog. Some Yanks snatched him into a tent and ate him up. Bossieux is very mad and is anxious to know who the guilty ones are. All he can do is to keep all our rations from us one day, and he does it. It seems pretty rough when a man will eat a dog, but such is the case.

Too much exertion to even write in my diary. Talk of getting away by escaping but find no feasible plan. Rebs are very watchful. Some mail today, but nothing for me. Saw some papers. A new prisoner brought with him a New York paper, but not a word in it about an exchange. I am still outside almost every day. Al Masterman is still at work in the cookhouse cooking rations for the prisoners. He comes down where I am every day and hands me something to take inside for February 20, 1864. Being in this place brings out a man for just what he is worth. Those whom we expect the most from in the way of braving hardships and dangers prove to be nobody at all. And very often, those whom we expect the least from were proving to be heroes, every inch of them. Notably one of these is Al Masterman, who is nothing but a good-looking, effeminate boy and fit, you would say, to be going to school with a mother to look after him and for not much else. But instead he is brave, cheerful, and smart, watching every chance to get the best of Johnny Rebs. His position in the cookhouse has given him a chance to feed, I presume, hundreds of men.

Al has managed to get up a board in the cookhouse floor, where he can crawl fifteen or twenty feet under the storehouse and up through that floor. By this Yankee trick, he has stolen, I presume, one hundred hams and gets them inside where they belong. This is very risky on his part, for should he be discovered, it would go very hard with him. He is about as unselfish a fellow as you can well find. This is only one of his plans to outwit the rebels for our benefit. His head is all the time, too, planning some way of escape. Well, we all hope he won't get caught. All shake in our boots for him.

Was on guard last night outside over the clothing. There is so much clothing stolen by the rebels that Bossieux put a guard of two over the boxes through the night; and if any of the rebs come around to steal, we are instructed to wake up the lieutenant, who sleeps nearby in a tent. I was on duty last night with Al, and Otis came where we were and unfolded a plan for escape which he had been working up. It is a risky affair and had best be thought over pretty thorough before putting it into execution. Robinson, another of our tentmates, has been found out as a lieutenant and taken over to Richmond to be placed with the officers in Libby Prison. We are sorry that we must lose him.

February 23. More prisoners came today and said there was to be no general exchange during the war and we were to be sent off into Georgia immediately. Stormy and disagreeable weather, and everybody downhearted. Very still among the men, owing to the bad news, hardly a word spoken by anybody. The least bit of anything encouraging would change the stillness into a perfect bedlam.

This morning, I investigated a tent where there were seventeen men and started back frightened at the view inside. What a tableau for a New York theater! They were all old prisoners nearly dead, very dirty, and poor—some of them sick lying on the cold ground with nothing under or over them and no fire—and had just been talking over the prospect ahead. All looked the very picture of despair with their hollow eyes, sunken cheeks, and haggard expressions. I have before imagined such scenes but never realized what they were until now. And such is but a fair sample of hundreds of men fully as bad.

February 25. No officers over from Libby for a few days past. Nearly all the clothing issued. A few days more will close up the clothing business, and then probably all the outsiders will be sent inside. For fear, such will be the case we have decided upon tomorrow night for the escape (which I have not said much about in my diary). The nights are dark and cloudy. Otis and Al both sleep outside now, and I must manage too, both tonight and tomorrow night. I have been two weeks trying to get a map of Virginia and have at last succeeded. A Negro brought it to me from the city. It has cost over thirty dollars, Confederate money—at the North would have cost twenty-five cents. I would not take for it unless I could get another one, one thousand dollars in gold. We are well rigged, have some food saved up to take along, are in good health, and are determined to get away.

Lieutenant Bossieux suspects and today took the pains to say in our hearing that he knew an escape among the outsiders was in view and, as sure as there was a God in heaven, if we tried it and got caught—and we surely would be—he would first shoot all he could before catching us and the balance would be tied up and whipped every day until he got tired as long as we lived. We must expect trouble. It does not change us in the least; if anything, it makes us more determined to escape. Tonight we are to start, and I will write down the plans we have, running the risk of the rebels getting hold of it.

At a few moments past eleven and before midnight, the guard will let us cross his beat and go to the water's edge. We all have rebel clothing, which we are to wear, furnished partly by a Negro and partly by the guard who helps us off. We take the quartermaster's boat, which we unlock, and, having been furnished the countersign, give it to the picket, who will pretend that he thinks we are rebel guards going over to the city in case we are caught, which will screen him in a measure.

Having passed him, we get into the boat and row across the river, give the countersign to the guards on the other side of the river, and talk with them a little, being ourselves posted on general information regarding the place. To quiet their suspicions, if they have any, we then start up into the town and, when out of sight of the guards, take a turn to the left and go straight to the Richmond jail, taking care to avoid patrols. We will then meet with a Negro who will guide us ten miles up the river and then leave us in charge of friendly Blacks who will keep us through the next day and, at night, pilot us farther along toward our lines. If possible, I shall steal the rebel flag, which is kept nights in the lieutenant's tent, and a few other relics to take along with me.

The big bell in Richmond strikes six, and I close my writing, hoping never to look upon it again until we return to free our fellow prisoners with the glorious army of the North. Now I leave my diary to finish preparations for the flight for freedom. May God aid us in this land of tyranny, where we have met nothing but suffering. Goodbye, Belle Isle and prison. Hail! Freedom, home, friends, and the grand army of the old flag! What is in store for us in the future?

February 26. Our escapade was a grand fizzle, and all hands have been punished in more ways than one in the last few days. Bossieux suspected something going on among us and had us secretly watched.

Bossieux confronted Otis after their capture. "You know I suspected something from you three long ago and have had my most trusted prisoners spying on you for weeks."

Otis was taken aback, as was William. "Who was it that gave us up? I'd love to get my hands on him," countered Otis.

William calmed things. "It doesn't matter now."

"That's right. It doesn't matter. What matters is how I'm going to punish you three," said Bossieux threateningly as he presented a box of evidence before the men. "Do these things look familiar? Confederate uniforms, packed food for travel, and a broken boat lock?"

"This proves nothing," said William.

"Don't push me, boy! I also know this other little friend of yours has been stealing food from the storehouse."

Al finally spoke up, "But that food is meant to be distributed to Union prisoners."

"By whose order?" growled Bossieux.

Al snapped back, "Abe Lincoln and his generals, I suspect." "Food shipped south from a foreign nation belongs to the South now."

Otis ended the debate, "So what's our punishment?"

"Well, seeing as you seem to be anxious for it and are the largest of the group, I think two days of hanging by your thumbs should be a good start," answered Bossieux.

"What about the other two?"

"Well, I'm not an evil man, and I don't wish to hurt mere boys, but to start, you will be bucked and gagged twice a day for an hour each, and then for four hours of the day, you will carry this large timber up and down in front of the main gate under the watch of my guards."

"Your two most sadistic guards?" interrupted William. Bossieux continued as he pointed out the large timber, "Yes, and if you walk too slow, they are under orders to move you along with the bayonet."

Otis was inflamed now. "Let's get this over with."

Bossieux replied, "You asked who it was who gave you away?"

Otis nodded. "Your tentmate Robinson." Al was shocked. "Corporal Robinson?"

"Now that was one of your first mistakes. He's not a corporal.

He's a captain from a Pennsylvania regiment." "A captain?"

"Yes, and he and I made a deal when I first found out about it." "What kind of deal?" asked Otis.

"If he were to spy for me, I promised I'd get him out of here." William then asked where he was now.

"Halfway to his old regiment, I assume."

Al shook his head in disbelief. "I thought all exchanges were canceled."

"Special arrangements are still made for officers." Otis was fuming. "I knew he was a lying snake."

Bossieux looked around the guardhouse they were all standing in and his tone softened a bit. "You know I'm a reasonable man. Your punishment won't last forever."

"How long before we go back to our squad?" asked William. "One week of daily hard labor and punishment and six nights in this damp, dark, cold hole, and if you survive that, then I'll see what's next for you, but at the moment, you can all rot in here for all I care as I no longer have any trust in you." Bossieux then called a guard to take them away to begin their punishment. He then added, "Just one more thing. I do not blame you for trying to escape. You are very brave indeed, but I must punish you to set an example for those who may be thinking like you."

On the first day of their punishment, Otis was brought out to a platform set up in the center of the camp for all to see. He was hung by his thumbs and left there for the bulk of the day. A guard spoon-fed him river rice swill twice a day. Al and William were bucked and gagged on the same platform but were released every day to do their four hours of marching with the timber at the gate.

After six weeks of this punishment, the men were allowed back to their tent to find to their surprise that everything was in order.

In early March of 1864, William, Al, Otis, and Dr. Lewis were moved to a temporary prison designed for prisoners who were to be shipped farther south to the new prison. It was a warm day when they were forced to walk across the long bridge into the business district of Richmond. Here they were confined to the third floor of an old tobacco warehouse, which would be called Pemberton Prison. This converted tobacco warehouse became Richmond's Pemberton Prison.

William's journal explained what happened next:

> March 1. All sorts of rumors afloat, but still we stay here. Strange officers come over and look at us. Bossieux away considerable, and something is up. Anything for a change. My health is good and as tough as a bear.

March 2. None have been taken away from the island for several days. Have heard that a box came for me and is over in Richmond. Hope the rebel that eats the contents of that box will get choked to death. I wrote to the governor of Minnesota, Ramsey, who is in Washington, DC, some weeks ago. He has known me from boyhood through General Sibley. He always visited the neighborhood at Mendota when he had business at the fort or the Sibley house. Asked him to notify my family of my whereabouts. Today I received a letter from him saying that he had done as requested, also that the Sanitary Commission had sent me some eatables. This is undoubtedly the box that I have heard from and is over in Richmond. Rebels are trying to get recruits from among us for their one-horse Confederacy. Believe that one or two have deserted our ranks and gone over. Bad luck to them.

March 4. Was removed from the island yesterday. It was a warm day, and it was a long walk indeed. Came across the Long Bridge, and it is a long bridge. I was not sorry to bid adieu to Belle Isle. We were searched last night, but our mess has lost nothing. We are now confined on the third floor of the building, which is a large tobacco warehouse.

The men were so ravenous when the rations were brought in that the boxes of bread and tubs of poor meat were raided upon before dividing, and consequently some had nothing to eat at all while others had plenty. Our mess did not get a mouthful and has had nothing to eat since yesterday afternoon, and it is now nearly dark.

The lice are very thick. You can see them all over the floors, walls, etc. Everything is covered with them; they seem much larger than the stock on Belle Isle and a different species.

We talk of escape night and day and are nearly crazy on the subject. No more news about an exchange. Papers state that Richmond is threatened and that Kilpatrick's cavalry is making a raid on the place to release us and burn the town. Unusual bustle among the locals and rebs. Excitement among the Johnnies, flying around as if the Yankee army were threatening Richmond. We cannot learn what the commotion is but hope it is something that will benefit us.

Later the occasion of the excitement among the rebels is that Dahlgren is making a raid on Richmond, acting in conjunction with Kilpatrick, to liberate prisoners. We are heavily guarded and not allowed to look out of the windows. Nevertheless, we manage to see about all there is going on.

Al, who was always resourceful enough to find a newspaper, responded to the commotion outside, "Papers state that Richmond is threatened and that Kilpatrick's cavalry is making a raid on the place to release us and burn the town. The citizenry is in all a panic."

Otis mentioned that this was good news, and William nodded in agreement.

Al continued, "The paper made mention of Dahlgren working with Kilpatrick's cavalry in making a raid on the prisons."

Otis pointed out that more guards were being posted at the windows so that the prisoners could not look out. William said that he would much prefer to be back in the open-air prison of Belle Isle as the lice were too thick in the old tobacco building.

William asked of Al, "Do you think we will be sent back to the island?"

Al said there was not much chance of that as the paper made note that everyone in Pemberton was selected to go to the new camp in Georgia.

He then continued to comment in his journal on their current situation, "The food is bad. The water is good, weather admirable, but the vermin are still in control of our Astor House mess."

Dr. Lewis, who had found a comfortable place for himself in a corner, now crawled over to the other three and joined in, "And this trouble with the thieves disgraces the name of Union soldiers. They are the most contemptible rascals in existence."

William added to his complaint, "It's shocking how they walk up to a man and coolly take his food and proceed to eat it before the owner."

"And if the victim resists, then a fight is the consequence, and the poor man not only loses his food but gets licked as well," said the doctor.

Otis looked at Dr. Lewis and continued, "Surprisingly we are all in good health, except for Dr. Lewis."

The doctor then pointed out a boy from Ohio. Bill Havens was his name; and he, too, had been a drummer boy.

Al asked what was wrong with him.

The doctor answered, "I don't know. He just has a terrible fever which won't break, and he spends all his time under that threadbare blanket cursing and moaning."

Otis mentioned that he looked like a boy who had had a privileged upbringing and was probably missed by his mother. Dr. Lewis told them that Havens had said he ran away from home to become a drummer boy at age fifteen.

"That's a familiar story around here," said Al.

The doctor continued to talk of the boy, "He's been in numerous battles and wounded twice and now a prisoner and sick as I've ever seen. One of his old wounds may have caused sepsis throughout his entire body, I fear."

William and Al said they would keep an eye on him, and then Al asked if they should add him to their mess.

Dr. Lewis added, "He's in no condition, I'm afraid, and will be of no good to us anyway until he recovers a bit, but we should do what we can to help him."

William was grateful for their continued good health. "I'm glad we have all stuck to our sanitary regulations. As a consequence, we are in much better shape than most."

"That was very smart of you all to start such behavior on your first arrival," answered the doctor.

The last group of prisoners released in the exchange from Belle Isle had now made their way north. Many had been dropped off in Louisville, where they were to await boats to take them farther on to their western homes. The illest of this group was brought to the military hospital in Louisville.

Dr. Smith and Mary sat at the bedside of a young musician, a member of the Second Minnesota regiment who had just been brought into the hospital. He was a sixteen-year-old boy by the name of Frank Peterson. The doctor had just finished his preliminary examination of him, and he was moved to the ward that Smith and Mary tended.

Dr. Smith spoke to him first, "Well, son, we are going to try and get you back your strength and back to your regiment. When was the last time you ate?"

"The morning before they put us on the train in Richmond," the boy responded.

Mary was shocked. "My Lord! That's been more than a week!"

"We did get plenty of fresh water, though," Frank answered. Dr. Smith then asked had he not been given any food at all.

Frank answered, "A few kind folks at rail stops would throw bits of bread at us, but I was never fortunate enough to get any. The bigger guys always got the most."

Dr. Smith responded in kind, "We'll do what we can, but it may take a long while to get you back in any condition to join your regiment.

I'll go fetch something for you now. In the meantime, my nurse here would like to talk to you."

Frank thanked the doctor and then turned to Mary, whom he could see was anxious to ask him something.

"I see from your papers that you are fifteen and a member of Second Minnesota."

Frank corrected her, "Yes, but you must have information from my mustering in papers. I'm almost seventeen now."

"Where were you captured, and how long were you at Belle Isle?"

"I was captured just before the battle at Chickamauga. I fell asleep on the march. I thought I could take a nap in the woods when a rebel scouting party found me. Nearly six full months in the prison," Frank answered.

Mary smiled and held his hand. "You're very lucky then. I hear that you boys are the last to be exchanged from there."

Frank asked if that was true.

Mary continued to quiz him, "Yes, so it seems. By the way, do you know William Simmons? Drummer with your regiment?"

Frank lit up and answered in excitement, "I sure do! We trained together at Fort Snelling, but when they disbanded the musicians, I had a chance to go home or reenlist."

"I bet you'd like to take that choice again."

"Yes, ma'am! I sure would. That prison was hell without the fire."

Mary now asked the question that was really on her mind, "Did you know if William is at Belle Isle now?"

"No, I don't think I ever saw him there, and even if I did, I don't think I would have recognized him."

Mary asked why that was.

Frank told her, "Unless you see them the first day they come through the gate, after three weeks in that place, everyone looks like walking death. Nothing but sunken eyes, cheeks, and covered in filth."

Mary's heart sunk to a new low. "Sorry, I was hoping to get some news about him."

Frank seemed delighted. "Hey! You're not his girl, are you? I know he took an awful lot of ribbing from the boys over a Southern belle he met in Louisville."

Mary cheered up a bit. "Yes, I'm afraid that is me."

Frank could see she was heartbroken. "Well, I'm sure glad to meet you, but sorry I can't give you any good or bad news about him. Try not to fret over him too much. He was one hard nut to crack."

Mary said she was glad to meet him and thanked him then she got up to leave, telling him, "Now let's see if we can get a couple of big spoonfuls of soup into your belly and start building you up again. I'll be back shortly."

Frank thanked her, then immediately drifted off to sleep.

Back at Pemberton Prison, William continued adding to his journal. On March 7, he wrote:

> And now we are getting ready to move. The Lord only knows where. One good thing about these old prisons, we are always ready for a change. I have made many new acquaintances while here in Pemberton and some agreeable ones. My boy Havens has fever and chills. He is rather better today. It is said we move tonight. Minnesota Indians confined here and several sailors and marines.
>
> I am quite a hand to look at men, sometimes for hours, and study them over, then get to talking with them and see how near I was right in my conjectures. It is almost as good as reading books. The Astor House mess is now composed of but four members—Bill Havens, F. L. Lewis, Otis, Al, and me. We still adhere to our sanitary regulations and, as a consequence, are in better health than a majority of those here, except for Havens who is still doing poorly.

Otis may be said to be at the head of the mess (we call him Dad) while Lewis is a sort of moderator and advisor, with Havens, Al, and myself as the rank and file. We are quite attached to one another and don't believe that either one would steal from the other. I certainly wouldn't take anything short of pumpkin pie or something of that sort. Of course, a man would steal pie, at least we all say so; and Lewis even declares he would steal dough cakes and pancakes such as his wife used to make. We are all well dressed, thanks to the Sanitary Commission and our ingenuity in getting what was intended for us to have. Today there was a false alarm of fire.

THE ROAD TO HELL

If there are a million roads into hell, there's not one road out.

—Leonard Ravenhill

On March 7, the prisoners in the old tobacco factory (Pemberton) were roused out of their slumber at around midnight. They were counted off and prepared to march off to the railhead of the Richmond and Danville Railroad station. William and his newfound prison comrades stood in line with the crowd of other Union captives.

The sergeant of the guard called out to them, "All right, you Yankee pigs. Line up in columns of two and follow orders from the corporals who will lead you to the train depot."

Otis, always one to speak out of turn, called out, "Are we being exchanged?"

The guard walked up to him and poked him with his bayonet and then, in a loud voice so all could hear, said, "How many times do we have to go over this? You are being moved to a bigger and better facility. Richmond can no longer keep you. You are an eyesore and a burden to the Confederacy."

Then the corporal of their column gave the command to move out. The prisoners shuffled off to an uncertain destiny. When they reached the station, they found waiting for them empty cattle cars, which William described in his diary as having just been emptied of the cattle occupants, all except for the manure.

After the boys got settled into one of the wretched cars, the train whistle blew, and the train pulled out. William, Otis, and Al leaned against each other to absorb the warmth of their shared bodies. Early March nights in Virginia could be as cold as any late winter night in the far North.

The next morning, when the train had been pulled off to a siding track to wait for another passing train, William began his journal entries again with the accounting of the first night in the cars:

> March 7, 1864. Started southward to some portion of Georgia, as a guard told us. We passed through Petersburg and other towns that I could not learn the names of. Cars run very slow, and being crowded, we are very uncomfortable—and hungry. Before leaving Richmond, hard-tack was issued to us in good quantity from the Confederacy. I have not had much chance to write. Bought some boiled sweet potatoes off the guard, which are boss.
>
> Otis noticed the sweet potato. "Are you going to share that?"
>
> I held it out for all to see. "Yes, but we should save some large pieces for the doctor and that Havens boy, now that he is part of our mess."
>
> Al had found a knothole to look out of and reported the movement of the train, "We're headed south all right."
>
> When we were well out of the city, I commented, "I'd have to say my time in old Virginia leaves a lot to be desired."
>
> The guards watched us closely to see that none escaped, and occasionally a Yank was shot but not in our car. On the first day, the train was pulled over to a sidetrack to allow another train

to pass. In the interim, prisoners from another car were let out to relieve themselves.

Al gave details of what he saw, "It appears they are going down the line opening one car after another so we can get out and do our business."

Finally a guard opened the door to our car, and the prisoners rushed out to take advantage of the fresh air and a chance to rest. One of the prisoners suddenly made a break for it. He ran across the tracks and headed for the woods. A shot rang out. A guard had shot him dead. Otis was angered and lashed out at the guard.

"You didn't have to shoot him! You could have just as easily chased him down and brought him back. What's wrong with you people anyway?"

The guard snapped back, "Shut up and take this rest as you can. We have to make thirty miles today, and if you don't want to end up like him, you'll mind yourself!"

Al and I had to jump in to restrain Otis. We were soon herded back onto the train and it slowly moved out again. Once again, Al had his eye to the outside. As night fell, the train was pulled off onto another sidetrack.

They did not run over thirty or forty miles per day, stopping for hours on sidetracks, waiting for other trains to pass them. William continued in his journal:

March 8. Under heavy guard, we prisoners were rousted out of the cars and set in an open field, where we could stretch our legs and eat as much hardtack and any other foodstuffs we could acquire from the guards. Dr. Lewis and the Havens boy were too weak to move on their own and had to be carried off by the others. The edge of a wooded area was just beside the track, and soon we stretched out and fell off to sleep.

The guard walked up to where our boys were sleeping and kicked Otis awake. "I'll have no trouble out of you five tonight or any other night. Do you understand?"

Al asked if we were going to be spending all the nights outside. The guard said that we were. Dr. Lewis then asked if it was okay to make a fire. The guard asked why we needed a fire.

The doctor explained, "We are smothered in lice and would like to set some twigs to coal so we can burn them off ourselves and our clothes."

The guard paused for a moment. "It's okay by me, but keep it under your blankets. You don't want the sergeant of the guard to catch you."

We got a fire started and began the process of lice removal.

When we awoke in the early morning, we were met by an unusual sight. Rebel citizens and women had swarmed around us to get a good look at some real Yankees. A few of the more compassionate women passed out fresh fruit and other eatables to the men. We were fed passably well for once and then forced back onto the train cars.

For the nights of the eleventh and twelfth, we kept a constant watch for a chance to escape but found none. March 13, the train ran very slow through the night; but we were now in the vicinity of Macon, Georgia, and were told we were to reach the new prison late at night or early morning. During the morning of the thirteenth, room was made in the car for Dr. Lewis and the Havens boy so that they could lie down. Both were feeling very poorly. I knelt between them.

Dr. Lewis barely had the strength to speak but he asked of me, "William? What day is it?"

I told him it was the thirteenth of March.

Bill Havens then raised his head and asked, "Is there any food today?"

I answered, "Al was told we will all be getting a full pone of cornbread apiece courtesy of the belles of Georgia to celebrate our arrival."

"Are we in Georgia now?" was Havens's weak response.

"Yes, we crossed the border when you two were asleep. There were a host of ladies at the border station waiting with the pone," said I.

Dr. Lewis now took my hand and whispered, "Give my portion to the boy. I fear for him, and I fear I won't need it. I fear two more days of riding like this will kill us."

I informed them that they would arrive at camp by early morning or late at night.

Al was then scratching himself madly. "These lice are going to eat me alive before two days. I could use a kerosene bath."

One of the guards struck Otis during our last night in the car. We had been talking on the all-important subject of escape, and the guard hearing us chatting away to ourselves snuck over into the crowd where the noise came from and hit Otis in the back part of his head. He didn't speak for a minute or two, and Al was afraid it had killed him.

"Otis? Otis? Wake up!"

Otis soon came to and stood to confront the guard. "What was the meaning of that? We were just talking!"

The guard responded violently, "Who said you could talk in my car?"

Otis shouted back, "I've seen the machine casting marks on this car, and it was built in Indiana, so I'd say it was more my car than yours!"

"Shut up, Yankee swine! One more word out of you and I'll blow your head off."

The train rattled on through the night. Heavy rain fell along with the temperature, and the roof of the car leaked cold water onto us. Standing shoulder to shoulder, we shivered.

March 14. We arrived at our destination at last and immediately saw what a dismal hole it was. We got off the cars at two o'clock in the morning in the cold rain and were marched into a pen between a strong guard carrying lighted pitch-pine knots to prevent us crawling off into the dark. We could hardly walk having been cramped up so long.

As we dragged ourselves along, I complained to Al, "I feel like I'm 110 years old."

Al countered with "I'm doing better than you. I feel only one hundred."

"Can you believe we have been standing the entire time we rode in that car?"

"I'm cold and wet to the bone," said Al. "Nothing to eat since that pone this morning, and I fear there will be nothing for the rest of the night," said I.

Al responded with the obvious, "For many months, the officers and guards back in Richmond and Belle Isle had been telling us of the grand new prison being constructed for our pleasure and comfort. The truth now comes clear. They lied."

Come, See Paradise

Through the clever and constant application of propaganda, people can be made to see paradise as hell, and also the other way round, to consider the most wretched sort of life as paradise.

—Adolf Hitler

March 15, at about 2:00 a.m., William and Al could stand up no longer and lay down in the mud and water. The prison was not yet entirely completed. One side was left open, and through the opening, two pieces of artillery were pointed. About two thousand Yankees were there now. Colonel Piersons commanded the prison at this time. He rode in to meet the newest arrivals. William and Al were lying in the mud trying to get some sleep. They exchanged glances as they heard Piersons speak. "Welcome to the new Andersonville Prison. We have about 1,800 of you here as of now, more will be coming, but we intend to have a prisoner exchange very soon."

William looked over to Al. "Well, we know that's a lie."

"We've heard that for far too long. I'm not buying it," answered Al. William tried to rise and stand. "I'm so weak. I can hardly stand. How about you?"

"Same. But the mud is at least soft."

"Sure, but are you sure it's just mud, or are we sleeping in a latrine?"

Andersonville was situated on two hillsides, with a small stream of swampy water running through the center, and on both sides of the stream was a piece of the swamp with two or three acres in it. The prisoners lived mostly in holes they had dug into the ground and covered with anything they could find. The more industrious ones had created shelters out of stacked logs covered with pine or canvas roofs. These were called shebangs. Each shelter had its mess, which constituted the men in it. They were responsible for keeping themselves healthy and alive. In William's shebang, the mess was Al, Otis, Dr. Lewis, Havens, and William. They had been settled in for a few weeks when Al stumbled into their shebang with some news. As weak as he was, he remained as animated and excited as ever.

"I've found someone from home!" William was shocked to hear this.

"Yes! Herman Dickerson from Saint Peter and the Fourth Minnesota. We were friends."

"Was he part of the six hundred that arrived yesterday from our old home in Belle Isle?" asked William.

"No, he was sent directly here. Can we take him in? He has no shelter at all."

William looked to Otis, and they both looked to Haven and Dr. Lewis. Both were in such bad condition they appeared minutes away from death.

Otis spoke in a low tone, "I'm sure there will be room soon enough. I'm going out to try and scavenge some food for our mess," then left the shebang.

Al was sure this was the answer he wanted. "Great! I'll bring him later."

"You may want to wait a few days," said William. William then left with Al.

"Let's go out and try to find some wood. With these cold and damp nights, it's not surprising twenty to thirty are dying every day." Al shrugged and followed William. "It's crazy. We put on all the clothes we have at night, and then in the day, we have to take them all off if the sun comes out."

On March 16, William continued to write in his journal:

Colonel Piersons commands the prison and rides in and talks with the men. He is quite sociable and says we are all to be exchanged in a few weeks. He was informed that such talk would not go down any longer. We had been fooled enough and paid no attention to what they told us. Our mess is gradually settling down. Have picked out our ground, rolled some big logs together, and are trying to make ourselves comfortable in our new shebang. I am in the best of spirits and will live with them for some time to come if they will only give me one-quarter enough to eat—and they are doing it now—and am in my glory.

March 17. Get almost enough to eat, such as it is, but don't get it regularly, sometimes in the morning and sometimes in the afternoon. We have plenty of wood now, but it will not last long. They will undoubtedly furnish us with wood from the outside when it is burned up on the inside. A very unhealthy climate. A good many are being poisoned by poisonous roots, and there is a thick green scum on the water. All who drink freely are made sick, and their faces swell up so they cannot see.

March 18. There are about fifteen acres of ground enclosed in the stockade, and we have the freedom of the whole ground. Plenty of room, but open spaces are filling it up. Six hundred new men coming each day from Richmond. Guards are perched upon the top of the stockade. They are very strict, and today one man was shot for approaching too near the wall. A little warm today.

Our Al Masterman found a friend of his from the Fourth Minnesota today, Herman

Dickerson from Saint Peter, who was captured recently and sent directly here. He is well and talks encouragingly. We have no shelter of any kind whatever. Eighteen or twenty die per day.

Cold and damp nights. The dews wet things through completely, and by morning, all nearly chilled. Wood getting scarce. On the outside, it is a regular wilderness of pines. Railroad a mile off, and can just see the cars as they go by, which is the only sign of civilization in sight.

Rebels all the while at work, making the prison stronger. Very poor meal and not so much today as formerly. A young German boy who was in our squad at Belle Isle and was sent to the hospital about the time we left Richmond has been delivered to us today. Shall be glad to hear of his recovery. The prevailing conversation is food and exchange.

March 19. A good deal of fighting going on among us. Many sailors and marines are confined with us, and they are a quarrelsome set. I have a very sore hand, caused by cutting a hole through the car trying to get out. I must write with my left hand. It is going to be an awful place during the summer months here, and thousands will die no doubt.

March 21. Prison gradually filled up with forlorn-looking creatures. Wood is being burned up gradually. Every day, I find new Minnesota men, some of them old acquaintances but most from the Western regiments as only one regiment is serving in the Eastern Theater.

March 23. Stockade all up, and we are penned in. Our mess is out of filthy lucre—otherwise, busted. Sold my overcoat to a guard, and for luxuries, we are eating that up. My large blanket, which I purchased from my original captors at Mission Ridge, keeps us all warm. There are two more in our mess. Daytimes the large spread is stretched three or four feet high on four sticks and keeps off the sun and, at night, taken down for a cover.

March 24. Digging a tunnel to get out of this place. Prison getting filthy. Prisoners are somewhat to blame for it. Good many dying; and they are those who take no care of themselves, drink poor water, etc.

March 25. Lieutenant Piersons is no longer in command of the prison, but instead a Captain Wirtz came inside today and looked us over. He is not a very prepossessing-looking chap. He is about thirty-five or forty years old, rather tall, and a little stoop-shouldered; skin has a pale, white-livered look with thin lips. Has a sneering sort of cast of countenance. Makes a fellow feel as if he would like to go up and boot him. Should judge he was a Swede or some such countryman. Otis thinks he could make it warm for him in short order if he only had a chance.

Wirtz wears considerable jewelry on his person, a long watch chain, and something that looks like a diamond for a pin in his shirt and wears patent leather boots or shoes. I asked him if he didn't think we would be exchanged soon.

He said, "Oh, yes, you would be exchanged soon."

Somehow or other, this assurance doesn't elate us much; perhaps it was his manner when

saying it. Andersonville is getting to be a rather
bad place as it grows warmer. Several sick with
fevers and sores.

Havens and Dr. Lewis were getting worse, and Al had suddenly become constantly depressed even though he had his old friend by his side to encourage him to carry on. William tried to comfort Al by taking his mind off their situation.

"Have you noticed how quickly the new ones die off?"

"Yes, but do they have to bury them right inside the perimeter of the camp?"

William nodded in agreement. "They don't even have the decency to put us in a pine box,"

Al added to that, "It's one thing to be buried on the battlefield like that, but…just do me a favor, will you?"

William answered he would do anything for him.

"Thanks. Before they drag me into one of those pits, make sure you leave some identification on me just in case there is a reburial one day."

William responded, "You're not going to die now. We've both come too far."

Al said he didn't think he could bear it any longer and wanted out of his misery.

William tried to comfort him. "Come on! Suicide is not the answer if that's what you are proposing."

"No, but it's easy."

"How easy?" asked William.

"All one has to do is cross the deadline, and a guard will put you out of your misery in an instant."

William saw Al was serious and tried another tactic. "Heaven won't take those who commit suicide."

"Could hell be worse than this?" replied Al. "Besides, it's all murder anyway. Whether they shoot us for trying to escape or starve us to death, it's murder, not suicide."

William had heard enough. "Don't mention that again. I don't want to hear of it. We are getting out of here together!"

Al looked over to the Dr. and Havens. "We can't all make it." "Enough. I'm going out to get our rations," William said as he rose to leave.

William left the shebang to fetch the daily food fare. They were issued to each once a day about a pint of beans, or more properly peas (full of bugs); three-quarters of a pint of meal; and, nearly every day, a piece of bacon the size of two fingers, probably about three or four ounces. These were very good rations taken in comparison to what they had received before. The pine which they used in cooking was pitch pine, and a black smoke arose from it. Consequently all looked black as Negroes.

William returned with the mess for each man in his shebang and distributed it.

Otis tried to feed the doctor and Havens but had no luck in doing so. "I doubt they last through the night."

William changed the subject, "Do you know what the date is today?"

"Well, let's see… That bastard captain Wirtz took over command on the twentieth of March. Lieutenant Peirsons left the next day, and that was five days ago as I count. Why?"

William grinned. "My birthday was on the twentieth." "Is that right? How old are you then?"

"I am fully a man six days now at eighteen."

Otis took a hard look at William. "Um, appearances would seem to indicate that you are thirty or thereabouts."

"And you, my friend, could pass for seventy. I thought that, when a man became of age, he generally became free and his own master as well."

Otis laughed and then said, "I'm afraid you are quite away from free, my young man. Besides, I recall you telling me your birthday was July 4."

"I did? I don't recall anymore what day it is.

Al perked up for a moment but was still depressed. "The only freedom is crossing that deadline."

William got back to his news. "A curious thing happened in the mess line."

Otis asked what it was.

"I came across Sergeant Bullock, of my regiment, whom I last saw on Belle Isle. Gone from a fat, chubby young fellow. He is now a perfect wreck. Lost his voice and can hardly speak aloud."

Al reached for his portion of the mess. "Point him to the deadline."

Otis and the others ignored him.

William continued, "Nothing but skin and bone and black and ragged. Never saw such a change in a human being. Cannot possibly live, I don't think. Still he is plucky and hates to die. Goes all around enquiring for news, and the least thing encouraging cheers him up."

Otis then asked, "Did he have any news that he gathered up?" "He says that scamp Mosbey from Belle Isle of the raiders is in here now and up to his same old tricks." Otis asked for more info on the raiders.

"He's formed a new gang with those swamp-rat marines and sailors. But he also said that he is a rather intelligent fellow and, if you keep on the right side of him, he is very helpful and polite and will not bother you with his murderous ways."

Al now continued with his depression. "He can murder me for all I care."

William continued in his journal:

> March 27. Sometimes we have visitors of citizens and women who come to look at us. There is sympathy in some of their faces and some a lack of it. It makes me think of my dear Mary left in Louisville, whom I have not received a letter from since Belle Isle. I wonder if she thinks of me. The deadline composed of slats of boards runs around on the inside of the wall about twelve or fourteen

feet from the wall, and we are not allowed to go near it on pain of being shot by the guard.

March 28. We are squadded over today, and rations are about to come in. It's a sickly, dirty place. Seems as if the sun was not over a mile high and has a grudge against us. Wirtz comes inside and has begun to be very insolent. Is constantly watching for tunnels. He is a brute. We call him the Flying Dutchman.

March 29. Raiders getting bolder as the situation grows worse. Often rob a man now of all he has in public, not attempt concealment. In sticking up for the weaker party, our mess gets into trouble nearly every day, particularly Otis, who will fight any time.

March 30. The gate opens every little while letting some poor victims into this terrible place, which is already much worse than Belle Isle. Seems as if our government is at fault for not providing some way to get us out of here. The hot weather months must kill us all outright. I feel myself at times sick and feverish with no strength seemingly. Dr. Lewis worries, worries, all day long; and it's all we can do to keep him from giving up entirely. Al Masterman has recently been more depressed than usual and talks of his death continually. Otis sputters around, scolding away, and generally is a combatant to anyone who slights him in the least. I'm afraid a guard will kill him just for the fun of it.

The summer of 1864 in Andersonville prison camp saw the most suffering of any prisoner of any war that any US soldier had been into up to this time. Captain Wirtz was a tyrannical and abusive commander.

Maybe he was a genuine sadist; or maybe it was because the South had, by now, been so thoroughly depleted that he could not care for his prisoners at all and secretly wished they would all just die, which actually, by William's view, appeared to be the case.

More raiding groups were formed, and they did the devil's work just as good as Wirtz himself. The raider called Moseby now had many men under his command and made a life for William and his squad hell. Fortunately the squad had Otis, and in the camp, other older men did stand up to the raiders. When conflicts led to fights, the raiders could be easily driven off. William's diary continued this way for his remaining time in this hellhole.

During a conversation one day, Herman Dickerson informed William that William had been listed as presumed dead in the regimental muster. When this news came out, John wrote to his mother to inform her as well as Mary. In some way, this was a relief to William as now he felt as though he would not have to worry anymore about those he loved. In this sense, being dead to his loved ones made him free.

His journal continued:

> Rebels say they have no medicine for us. Herman has been telling me about himself and his family at home, and his case is only one of a great many good, substantial men of families who must die in Southern prisons as victims of mismanagement. The poorer the Confederacy and the meaner they are, the more need that our government should get us away from here and not put objectionable men at the head of exchange to prevent our being sent home or back to our commands.

The conditions at Andersonville would only get worse. Into the fall of 1864, thousands had already died. Most of the men from William's squad had passed. Al and Otis were still alive, as was William, and he was the healthiest.

Late into the night on what had been a very hot August day, William was woken by a dreadful moan coming from Dr. Lewis. He woke Otis, and the two of them rolled over to check on the doctor as well as Havens, who himself was near death for days. When they reached the two men, they saw that Havens had already passed on.

The doctor spoke in a halting whisper to Otis, "I'm afraid the boy has gone up."

Otis nodded that they knew.

"I'll be joining him soon, but before I go, see to it that this letter makes it back to his family." Doctor Lewis handed Otis a letter. Doctor Lewis's breathing was becoming more erratic now. "He gave it to me when we first got on the train. He knew his time was up even then."

Otis said that they would see to it, and then William asked if there was anything they could do for him.

The doctor pushed a tin container toward him. "In this tin is everything you'll need to see to it my remains are recovered one day and justice is done."

William asked what kind of justice.

"Justice for us all. I have a written testimony in there of how we have been mistreated, especially from that madman Wirtz."

William asked if there was anything else to be done.

"Don't drink the water, and give up our spots to some nice boys."

Al now crawled over to join the group. He closed Havens's eyes, then took Dr. Lewis by his hand. "I'll be joining you soon."

Dr. Lewis simply whispered no, then quietly took his last breath.

As the sun was rising, Otis, Al, and William prepared the bodies of Dr. Lewis and Havens as best they could and then dragged them out of the shebang. They left them lying in the mud outside.

Otis turned to the others. "When do you want to take them to the ditch?"

William answered, "Wirtz only opens the gate for a few minutes after our first mess."

Al added, "Yes, but remember, we have to pay off to Moseby to pass through."

William looked confused. This was something new.

Al explained in brief, "Wirtz is using the raiders to gain wealth for himself. He's been trading with them."

Anger grew in Otis. "Great. One can't even die and escape this hellhole with any dignity at all. What's next?"

The train whistle blew, and William reached to lift the body of Havens.

"Right on schedule," Otis replied.

"Yep, more rotting meat for the Grim Reaper." William and Al picked up Havens's body.

Al turned to Otis. "Can you take the doctor by yourself?" Otis lifted the doctor and put him over his shoulder.

Al continued, "Let's make it to the gate with these two now as Wirtz will have to open the gate to let the new boys in."

Otis thought they were putting one over on the raiders. "Good idea. We'll sneak these two by and avoid paying that crook Moseby." They took their friends toward the gate and walked through without any confrontation. The raiders were nowhere to be seen near the gate, and the guards just saw a couple of corpses coming through and waved them on. The train stopped at its usual spot near the gate.

New prisoners were unloaded and marched toward the entrance to the prison. The boys paused to watch the latest prisoners unload.

Otis commented, "Well, now there's a healthy-looking lot."

William said that they must have just been captured to appear to be in such good health.

Otis slung the doctor over his shoulder again. "Okay, let's get these boys on through and over to the ditch."

The gate was held open by two guards as the new prisoners were escorted in. Otis pushed his way past one of the guards, nearly knocking him down. The guard recovered quickly and pushed back on Otis.

Otis gave him a dirty look and grumbled, "Watch it, buddy. We have to get our friends to the ditch."

The guard taunted Otis, "You better watch it, or you'll end up in there with them and soon!"

William tried to calm Otis, "Otis, you can't keep sputtering off to these guards."

Otis scoffed. "Why not?"

"Because I'm afraid they'll shoot you, and Al and I are too weak to carry you to this ditch."

They made their way to the ditch and rolled the bodies into it.

A few of Moseby's raiders were shoveling dirt over the bodies of the dead.

One of them walked up to Otis. "You boys want to earn some extra grub?"

Otis shoved the man aside. "If the filthy lucre you steal from us all is being exchanged for food, then no, thanks."

The raider pushed back. "Are you calling us thieves?"

Otis said he was calling them worse than that. This was enough for the raider to take a swing at Otis. Otis blocked his punch and dove into him. They tussled in the dirt. Guards rushed over and broke up the fight.

William calmly intervened, "Come on, Otis. Let's put our boys to rest."

Otis, Al, and William took shovels and started throwing dirt over the bodies of their pals.

Later that day, William felt another bout of dysentery coming on and dashed to the sinks. The Andersonville latrine, or sinks as they were called, was placed at the downstream end of the Stockade Branch, where there was a small stream that flowed through the prison. The plan was to drink water from upstream and use the downstream end as the latrine or sinks. The problem was that the stockade walls slowed the flow of the water, so the sinks often backed up and formed a disease-filled sewage swamp.

William was taking his turn at the sink. It was another hot, muggy late summer day. Walking toward him was a new inmate he had not seen before but was sure he recognized. The new prisoner squatted a few men downstream from William.

William looked over to him and called out, "Hey, you! Yeah, you! New guy, do I know you?"

The man turned but shook his head. How anyone would have recognized William would have been a miracle anyway. After nearly a year of captivity, he was merely a bag of bones hardly able to walk or move.

William was certain he knew the man and called to him again, "It's me, William Simmons, musician from the Second Minnesota. You're Henry Bush. I remember you."

The man finally replied, "William? Is that you? Sorry I didn't recognize you. How long have you been here?"

"Since early March, but I was in Belle Isle for six months before that."

Henry Bush was a fellow musician when William first enlisted and was mustered into Company A. He was a tall, straight dark-complexioned man, about nineteen years old now. He was discharged in '62 when the musicians were sent home as a group but, in '63, was bountied out as a draft substitute for three hundred dollars and became a runner for the company. He was captured carrying dispatches from Knoxville to General Burnside, had been a prisoner two or three months, and was in Pemberton Building when William was there though he did not see him until sent here. He was a tough, able-bodied man, but from what William could tell from his experiences in captivity, Bush was one of those who were silent but continually paced around like a caged animal.

William tried to engage him, "Have you found a mess yet?" Bush just shook his head and grumbled to himself.

"Great, then come stay with us. A couple of spots opened in our shebang last night."

Bush thanked him as William rose to hitch up his trousers.

William turned away. "I'll wait for you to finish and then take you over to meet the others."

Bush soon finished, and they headed off together. They arrived at the shebang, and introductions were completed. Bush was accepted into the mess.

Otis welcomed him, "Well, you look healthy enough to still have some fight in you."

Bush said he was not so sure about fighting anymore. Then Otis added, "I'm sure you know about the raiders."

"Sure, I do. They're led by that scoundrel Moseby from back in Richmond."

"Yes, and we are forming a group of regulators to take them down, mostly made up of new prisoners."

"And you think I'm fit for that?" asked Bush.

"Look around. Al here is ready to step across the deadline. William is so sick with dysentery he can hardly walk, and I—" Bush interrupted, "Yes, I remember you as that mean old bastard from Richmond. Can you still handle yourself?" "Barely, but we need strong backup."

Bush turned away, uninterested.

William came to the defense of Otis, "One just has to remember those raiders are as sick as us."

"They are quite cowardly. Even Al here has chased them off just by raising his voice at them," continued Otis.

Bush thought for a moment, then made up his mind to join. He asked who was in charge. Otis said he was and set down the rules of the mess.

"Okay then, let's see what you have to trade," William asked if he got out of Pemberton with anything of value.

Bush replied, "A few greenbacks."

Otis continued, "Great, the guards are good for food if we have greenbacks. But we all share equally here. Got it?"

Bush agreed.

Al slowly got up and leaned on William to steady himself. "I've got my final escape plan."

Otis rolled his eyes as Al was always coming up with a new plan sure to fail. "What now?" said Otis sarcastically.

"Tonight I play dead. In the morning, you all take me out to the dead ditch. Throw me in. Dump a few scoops of dirt on me, just enough to fool the guards, then at night, I crawl off into the woods and make my way to the rail line."

William looked at his friend sympathetically. "You may make it to the woods. They're only about fifty feet from the ditch, but you'll never get up on a train."

Otis added, "Even if you did, how do you know where it's going?"

Al was determined. "Don't matter just as long as it's out of here." For the most part, the boys were in better health than most. William attributed that to Dr. Lewis. The doctor had told William as far back as Belle Isle that he must only drink boiled and purified water, get plenty of exercise, eat fruit when he could get it, and, above all, stay clean. William, Al, and Otis stuck to this behavior; and all seemed to fare better than the others.

William had purchased a block of lye soap from a guard in June of '64, and during every thunderstorm, he made sure to take a soapy shower in the rain. But conditions changed in the winter of '65. In late November of '64, the Confederacy had finally sent the names of all prisoners, dead and alive, at Andersonville, north to Washington, DC. Word was sent from there to the proper regiments. John now received the true news of his brother.

Otis was suffering from a fever; and he also now had bouts of dysentery though he continued to sputter around, scolding away, and generally stayed in a combative mood to anyone who slighted him in the least. Bush took things as they came in dogged silence but continued to pace around aimlessly like a caged lion.

The final news from Captain Wirtz was that there would never be an exchange of prisoners, or at least not until the war was over, and the cold weather made all the men ill. Otis, Al, and William all came down with dysentery and dropsy and became so weak they were all taken outside the gate and lined up with the dead. Only when a guard heard William cough did they check to see that two of these men were still alive and were then taken to the hospital, where gradually they were nursed back to health. Al was left for dead, and it seemed his escape plan was working.

As Otis and William were lying in the hospital trying to recover, Al had made his way to the railhead on the night that they had all been thrown in the ditch. It took him hours to crawl to the rail stop. There he lay for another twelve hours until the usual prison train stopped to drop off the most recent captured Union troops. A guard unloading prisoners saw him move and poked him with his bayonet. Al was captured once again and, this time, sent directly to the hospital. He was admitted and laid down next to his two friends.

Otis turned over to look at Al. "So I see you didn't make it."

Al told him he got as far as the train. William asked what happened next.

"The guards decided, if I wanted to die so badly, I could do it here with you two."

William said it was nice to see him back.

Otis was not so welcoming. "And maybe now you learned your lesson?"

"How's that?" asked Al.

"It's not your time. God has a bigger plan for you." "Since when did you believe in God?"

"Since I started shitting gallons of blood," replied Otis.

"I still pray to God every day that we are all going to get through this together," said William.

Otis laughed. "He does."

Al then said he had some good news, and both Otis and William were anxious to hear it.

"Wirtz plans to let us all go as soon as the war ends."

Otis chuckled at the ignorance of the statement. "Well, doesn't he have to?"

"Not really. He could kill us all before the end," said William. Al responded in kind, "That seems to be on his mind. I overheard the guards talking when they were dragging me back here." Otis and William perked up.

"Wirtz is afraid, if there are any survivors, that the US government will maybe blame him for mistreatment."

"As they should," replied William.

"Sounds like the rebs are on the run," added Otis.

Al continued, "Yeah, they seemed sure that they are all but used up completely. Many of the guards have already deserted, and the ones I overheard were talking about it."

Otis said he was worried about other stuff. William and Al were a little confused.

"The shebang and everything in it." "Raiders?" asked Al.

"Exactly. We've all seen what they do to those who abandon their place."

Al said that they had Henry Bush to watch over their things, and then Otis told him the news about Bush as he had not heard any news about him.

"He was shot through the thigh when he got too close to the deadline."

Al gasped.

Otis continued, "They brought him in here after his leg turned to gangrene but said they had no medicine to treat him. He died right there where you are lying now."

William added, "Didn't last but two days in here. There was nothing we could do for him."

William was returned to the Andersonville Prison in late March of 1865. New prisoners exchanged news of the most recent events in the war. Though William had regained most of his health, he was still unable to walk without assistance. Otis was released from the hospital a few days before, and he fashioned a crutch for William so he could be mobile while he continued to convalesce. Al would be released a few days later, and once again, the original "Belle Isle boys" were together again.

While they were in the hospital, the raiders had made off with every article that the three had left behind, including William's prized large blanket which had served them so well as a shelter. Now they had nothing and resorted to digging out a hole and living in it like rats. They covered it with timbers that they scrounged from around the camp. The men were so weak that they could barely talk, eat, or do anything without completely exhausting themselves to the point of collapse. The three had been reduced to living skeletons, hobbling together around the yard.

NEVER FOREVER

When the prison doors are opened, the real dragon will fly out.

—Ho Chi Minh

The ice had not come out of the two rivers that met at Mendota. It was late March of 1865, and it had been a cold winter, more so than usual. There was still some river traffic by horse-drawn sleigh that ran from the lower levee at Saint Paul to the fort at Mendota. Normal steamboat river traffic would not begin regular schedules until mid-April at best. General Sibley was in command of a full garrison of regular soldiers at Fort Snelling; but with the Indian war having moved farther into the Dakota, Colorado, and Montana territories, the fight to "pacify, Christianize, and civilize" the Natives would be put into the hands of other generals who were now being released from their service in the fighting to end the rebellion. Sibley's only duty now would be to oversee the trials of Medicine Bottle and Shakopee III, as well as overseeing a smooth mustering out of returning veterans.

Nobody talked much about the war coming to an end, but reports from army dispatches made it clear that the Confederacy was on its last legs. Desertions were at an all-time high as Sherman's bummers swept through Georgia and the Carolinas, not only stripping the land of food supplies for the Southern Army, but also giving proof to the rebel soldiers that they were no longer a match for the Northern industrial might. The South could no longer supply its soldiers, and with homes and farms being burned, even the most determined of Southern soldiers thought it better to desert home to protect their families than to stay and fight on in a lost cause.

Grant had a lock on Lee's army of Virginia and refused to let go. Though Northern casualties were at an all-time high, Lees' army was on the verge of collapse. It was now just a matter of days before the end.

At the Simmons cabin, Louise had asked Sara to invite Robert and his mother, First to Dance, to join her and Sara at the cabin to celebrate the hopeful return of her boys and the peace that had now come to the riverbanks of Fort Snelling. With the concentration camp now closed and the inmates moved west, Louise felt it time to make peace of her own. First to Dance had made some fry bread for all of them, and they were enjoying their time together.

First to Dance passed out the sweet cakes to all. "I want to thank you for the sugar to make these flat cakes."

Louise thanked her for making them and for teaching Sara how to make them. "I'm glad you showed Sara the proper way of making these. They will be a wonderful treat for my boys when they return."

"What have you heard about your boys?" asked Robert. "John is someplace in the Carolinas with Sherman." "And what about William?"

Sara answered, "We finally got an official message from the army that he is in a camp in Georgia."

"I hope he's getting better treatment than what those poor Dakota got at the fort camp," said First to Dance.

Louise was surprised that a Chippewa woman would have much sympathy for a Sioux, given their past violent history toward each other. She asked if First to Dance hated the Sioux. Robert said that those days were in the past.

Louise commented on her true feelings, "It's a shame how some of the settlers around here and the soldiers who were to guard them treated the prisoners. When Sara told me what she and Robert found, I had no idea! I may still have some harsh feelings about the Dakota war, but I certainly don't agree with how the government is expanding the mistreatment of these people. This is not the Christian way."

First to Dance and Robert nodded in agreement.

Sara spoke up, "If every Indian could convert like Robert and his mother, we could all have peace."

"Do you think that is true, Sara?" asked First to Dance. "Not really, but I hope it's true one day."

Louise interjected, "The key is friendship. It's hard to hate someone if you are friends."

"Yes, that I believe. I look at my son and your daughter, and I see friends… I doubt they could ever bring harm to one another."

Louise confessed, "I'll admit I was skeptical at first of their being together. I was raised to hate anyone who wasn't White and Christian."

"That's a sad thing, and we need to stop all this sadness now." "But the war goes on. My boys are not yet safe, and General

Sibley and Sully and others continue their so-called benevolent war on the Natives."

The war came to an end in April of 1865, but it was a full two months before the entire Confederate armies and navies would surrender and the official closing of the war would be announced. In late April, Mary waited for word from William. At the Louisville Military Hospital, Dr. Smith and Mary were enjoying their morning break together.

The doctor picked up a newspaper and began to read out loud. "Mary, I want to read you something here in today's paper."

Mary asked what it was.

"I read it earlier and found it most distressing. A report from Washington on the prisoner situation. I hope it's not too upsetting for you."

"Everything here is upsetting. Please go ahead."

Dr. Smith read aloud, "Out of a little more than 40,000 men imprisoned there in 1864, 13,647 were buried there, fully one-third."

Mary asked if this was about Andersonville.

The doctor nodded. "Yes and more. Do you want me to go on?" Mary said that she wanted to hear it all.

Dr. Smith continued, "And numbers unaccounted were buried in other prisons, to which they were removed from Andersonville, such as

Florence, Millen and Charleston, and in hospitals and also those who fell by the wayside after being exchanged and before they reached home."

Mary looked disturbed. "Sorry, I'll stop."

"No. I want to know it all."

The doctor continued, "The survivors looked death in the face, not for a glorious hour or day of battle such as all soldiers look forward to, but for days, weeks, and months until familiarity bred contempt and death had less terror than life in Andersonville."

Mary removed a handkerchief from her blouse and wiped away a tear. "Oh, Lord. He better come home safe."

"Let's pray he does… Let's pray that they all do."

It was late April 1865; and more than two thousand tired, sick, and injured men wearing dirty and tattered clothes filed down the bluff from Vicksburg to a steamboat waiting at the docks on the Mississippi River.

The city of Vicksburg was ravaged by the American Civil War, and so were the men who were about to board the steamboats there at this exchange point. Almost all were Union soldiers who had survived the battlefields only to be captured by Confederate troops and sent to prison camps in Alabama, Georgia, and Mississippi.

The prison camps were dirty, disease-ridden places, and food and medicine were in short supply. This was true of prison camps on both sides, but life in the Southern camps got considerably worse toward the end of the war when the Confederacy was having trouble feeding and caring for its soldiers and citizens. Thousands of men died in the prison camps of starvation and disease. At the Alabama camp at Cahaba, the Alabama River jumped its banks, and the flood forced the men to stand in waist-deep water for a week in winter.

By May of 1865, however, the war was officially ended; and the opposing armies agreed that it was time to release their prisoners and send them home. This was the best news the prisoners could hear. Soon they would be back home close to their loved ones, with plenty to eat and a bed of their own to sleep in—everything they had dreamed of during their military service and captivity.

After the prisoners were released, they had a hard time making their way west across the South to Vicksburg, where, they had been told, steamboats would carry them to their homes in the North.

Traveling north from Vicksburg on the Mississippi River, boats could reach the Missouri, Ohio, and Tennessee Rivers and, from there, the towns of the American Midwest from which the soldiers had come. But to get to the Mississippi River at Vicksburg, the soldiers had to travel by boat, by train, and on foot. Because they were so weak from their war and prison experiences, some of them died along the way. Making matters worse, some of the trains derailed due to the damaged railroad tracks—many of the railroad tracks had been destroyed by the war. In 1865, there were no highways and not even many good roads.

Rivers were then the best way to travel. They could be considered the interstate highways of the nineteenth century. After the recently freed prisoners reached Jackson, Mississippi, they had to walk the rest of the way to Vicksburg, which was then about fifty miles on the old road. Many of the men had no shoes, and their feet were bleeding by the time they reached the Big Black River, just east of Vicksburg. They were also extremely hungry.

The Big Black River marked the dividing line between the part of Mississippi held by the Union Army (which included Vicksburg) and the part held by the Confederate Army (which included the area closer to Jackson). By then, the fighting had ended, but only after they reached the area held by the Union Army were the recently freed prisoners truly free. There, after crossing the Big Black River, they were given clean clothes and food at Camp Fisk, a neutral holding pen for prisoners of war. While arrangements were being made to transport them north on the Mississippi River, they stayed in the camps outside Vicksburg without tents or even blankets, and many got sick while waiting to board a steamer.

One reason for the boarding delay was that the owners of the steamboats were competing to see who could arrange for the most freed prisoners on their boats. The steamboat companies were paid as much as ten dollars per person to transport soldiers and freed prisoners, which was a lot of money in 1865, and some of the company employees bribed army officials in Vicksburg to make sure they got as many passengers as possible.

When word finally reached William that he and his squad were to be exchanged and sent home, he was so weak he could barely respond. Except for a slight smile that came across his face that forced tears from his eyes, there was no response whatsoever. On their final night in camp, Otis, Al, and William decided they would sleep on the ground in the open air. It was a comfortable, clear night. The prison had been emptying over the past week. The raiders no longer bothered anyone as a court was held within the prison and they were all hanged to death. The guards had turned friendly, some to the point of offering food, water, and other goods to help ease the transition from prisoner to free man.

William lay awake for the better part of the night. Many thoughts ran through his mind that kept him from a restful slumber. It seemed, as soon as he was about to dose off, another train would pass the camp. Now that the war was over, trains were moving along at more regular intervals. As the wheels rolled along the metal rails, they hammered out a regulated hum that, to William, sounded like "Never…forever." This he repeated in his mind until the train would come to a stop.

When a train stopped to refuel the locomotive, William woke Otis and Al. "Can you hear it?"

"Hear what?" asked Al.

Otis finally woke. "I don't hear anything other than steam being let off, and that, to me, is the sound of freedom."

"No, I mean, can you hear the train talking to us?"

Both Al and Otis looked at William as if he had finally lost his mind.

"The wheels are talking."

A sarcastic grin came across Otis's face. "Oh yeah? What are they saying?"

"Just listen when they start up again." "Otis, his mind is gone," said Al.

The train pulled away from the stop and, within a few minutes, was back up to its normal speed. The wheels on the rails made the same rhythmic sound again.

"Hush! There it is again. Listen."

Al rolled over to go back to sleep. "I don't hear any words." "There it is. Never…forever."

Al lifted his head for a moment. "Never. Forever. Yeah, maybe." William nudged Otis. "Otis? Do you hear it?"

"All I hear is you two keeping me from my dreams."

Al listened more intently, then mouthed the words to himself. "Yup, I like it."

The three finally fell fast asleep.

The Belle Isle boys were fortunate. As they were already near death, they were transported by train and once again herded onto the same cattle cars that had brought them to Andersonville. Now they were being brought out under similar conditions. They did not complain, though, as sympathetic Southern women supplied the men with food and fresh straw to lie on for their journey west. In fact, for the first day, they never even spoke to one another. They were lost in their thoughts about what to expect on their homecoming.

A couple of days later, the train pulled to a final stop at its destination at Jackson, Mississippi. The prisoners were unloaded and lined up for a march to the old road that led to Vicksburg. Otis was the only one of the three survivors from Belle Isle who was still able to walk on his own. William managed okay with his crutch, but Al had to be carried the entire length by released prisoners who had the strength to do so. Of course, these men had only been in Andersonville for a few days, so they were still quite able bodied. Otis and William walked along beside Al, who looked up to Otis walking at his side.

"Where are we headed?"

"A place called Camp Fisk," answered Otis. William asked where the camp was exactly.

"I'm not sure, just somewhere on the other side of the Big Black River."

Al asked if that was in Vicksburg.

"Yeah. It's the official dividing line between the two armies.

Camp Fisk is in the part held by the Union." William asked if this was another prison.

A Confederate guard walking nearby answered, "Not a prison, just a common holding pen. That's where the exchanges are being made."

William asked if there was any food there.

The guard shrugged. "I suppose there is. You Yankees seem to have plenty, and I'm sure they'll give most to you all."

Al asked what else he knew.

"I've seen it, and it looks about as comfortable as any prison I've worked."

Otis took a defensive stand. "Did you work Andersonville?"

The guard said he had been there for a few months before he was transferred to Charleston.

Otis said he did not recognize him.

The guard nodded and then laughed a little. "Yeah, well, I remember you. You're that ornery SOB that threatened to kill us all after you got out."

"That's probably true, but I see you still hold the guns," replied Otis.

The guard pointed it at him. "And it's loaded." Otis just nodded and replied, "Aren't they always?"

William wanted to know what they were to expect on their arrival at Camp Fisk.

"Men are dying in there." "Still?" asked William.

The guard spoke again, "Yep. No blankets, tents, or any kind of organization I could tell. Like I said, it'll be familiar, except for you'll have niggra guards."

Otis said he had heard about Colored troops but never saw any in action.

The guard scoffed. "I suppose they finally found the job that suits them."

Otis had a puzzled look.

Then the guard added, "Looking over Lincoln's nigger lovers should suit them just fine." The guard began to drift back toward the end of the line. He parted with these words, "Try to stay healthy there."

Otis asked one more question of him, "How long a wait are we going to have before we get a boat?"

"I have no idea. All I know is there have been delays." "Delays?"

"Now that the war is over, the profiteers are trying to skin your government."

"That never changes, does it?" said William.

The guard parted with "Same on both sides. Boat owners are getting up to ten dollars a head to haul you scum upriver and eight dollars a head to take our boys downstream, so many boats are overloading just to make extra cash." The guard fell back to herd more men forward.

William sighed. "Is this ever going to end?"

Al tried to speak, but only a whisper came out of him. "Never... forever."

With Lee's surrender of the Army of Northern Virginia to General Grant at Appomattox on April 9, 1865, the city of Washington, DC, broke into a wild celebration. As telegram wires carried the news across the nation, other cities and communities broke out in celebration. Lincoln had done what no other man could have. He had kept the Union intact. The patients, orderlies, surgeons, and visitors at the Armory Hospital were celebrating the end of the war. All of Washington was in a celebratory mood. Those who were fortunate to have regained their health were being prepared for being discharged and a ticket home. Pat, Jill, and Sam celebrated with pastries and wine. They had a table to themselves near the kitchen and talked about their futures.

Jill raised her glass to her two cohorts. "Pat? I hope you carry on this business."

"Do I have a choice?"

Sam cut into a blueberry pie. He shook his fork at Pat. "Actually no. You now have a duty."

Pat asked whom he now had a duty to with the war all but over. "A duty to those like us, veterans who are still suffering," Jill commented.

"Will that ever end?"

Sam agreed that it was never ending.

"One would think that the government would care for you boys."

Pat responded sarcastically, "There's been some talk of that, but you know how fast Congress works. They want to be sure they get their kickback first. And how are they going to decide who is deserving or not?"

"Call me before Congress, and I'll tell them," said Jill.

"Do you think anyone from Congress would dare speak to a Colored, in particular, a Colored woman?"

"We're all free now."

"That's what they told us Irish Catholics too. Fight for the Union, and we'll make you a citizen. Yeah, and shit and two are eight!"

Sam joined in, "We may all be free, but we'll never be equal to those who control the purse strings."

Pat pointed his finger at Jill. "The only thing you darkies have been freed to do is work for slave wages and fight in their wars."

Jill said she had seen enough of war and would never partake in any war again. Sam agreed with her.

Pat changed the subject, "Sam? When do you head back to the farm?"

"As soon as I get my papers in order."

Pat leaned back and sighed. "We could stay and march in the big parade next month."

"I don't think they are posting a spot for VRC members, and we can't rejoin our former units for the parade if we have been invalided out," said Sam.

"In that case, come with me and partner up in business." Sam asked Pat where he planned to do this.

"New York."

Jill shook her head. "And last week, it was Boston."

"Sorry, but my wife makes the decisions about where to live... Besides, New York has more veterans."

"And labor riots, which is just another kind of war," added Jill. "What about you, Jill?" asked Sam.

"I'm going back downriver to get some of Mom's home cooking."

Sam looked saddened. "Well, you are going to be profoundly missed, both of you."

Their conversation was interrupted by the sound of explosions outside.

"Now what?" said Jill.

Sam said it was the start of the fireworks display that had been scheduled for the night.

Pat reached for his crutches and handed Sam his. "Let's go out and watch it!"

The three then left the hospital to go out and watch the celebration display. Fireworks exploded over the cityscape. Pat, Sam, and Jill watched from the edge of the swampy river.

Jill looked at the flotsam floating in the river. "Never again." Sam asked what she meant.

"I never want to see this river ever again."

Pat nodded. "Ditto that for me too. Never forever do I want to see this place again."

Sam took Jill's hand. "Well, within two days, we'll all be on our separate ways."

Jill looked into Sam's eyes. She could see them well up. "Yes, but our time here will never separate us."

Around this same time back in Mendota, Robert and Sara were walking through what remained of the site of the Dakota concentration camp. An area outside of what was the gate to the camp was turned into a burial ground. Sara noticed some White women kicking up dirt in the area, and she walked over to them. One of the young women who couldn't have been more than twenty was very excited as she reached down to pick something up. She held a human bone in the air and squealed with delight.

Sara ran over. "What is that? Why are you so happy?"

The woman waved the bone in front of Sara's face. "It's the leg bone of a savage child, I think."

This angered Sara. "Are you crazy? Put that back!" "No! I'm keeping it as a souvenir."

Sara screamed at her, "Why? That's a dead child! An innocent child. You should be ashamed!"

The woman did not back down. "You mean a dead red savage heathen."

Robert noticed the commotion and rushed to Sara's side. "What's going on here?"

The woman turned and snapped at Robert, "None of your business, you godless demon."

Sara shot back at her, "You should watch your mouth."

The woman reacted with "You should watch who you spend your time with."

"He's my friend, and he's more of Christian than you'll ever be."

The young woman countered with "Christians don't rape and slaughter women and children."

"They don't rob graves either."

The woman shook the bone in the faces of Sara and Robert. "Do your parents know you play with the children of Satan?"

"My mother is a decent woman and does not approve of people like you, and my father died fighting for the rights of all free people, including the natives of this land."

"You mean your father died to protect the rights of all free White people."

Robert took Sara by her hand and started to lead her away. "And what about you? You spawn from hell. Have your parents ordered you to sully this young White girl for revenge?"

Robert pulled Sara from the scene as she turned to confront the woman one more time.

"You should be ashamed of yourself. Put that child's bone back and leave these people to rest. You've killed enough. There's no need for any more."

"Quite the little know-it-all, aren't you? You won't feel so smart when your savage boyfriend is ripping you apart."

Robert and Sara headed off in the direction of the ferry landing.

The woman dropped the bone back into the dirt, then huffed off with her friends, turning back to give Sara one last shot. "You can mark my words. Generals Sibley and Sully will never let these monsters rise again."

Robert and Sara paused to step back. They reburied the bone and moved on. They walked back toward the ferry dock. Old Bob Thunder, the ferry boat "puller," was waiting for them. They boarded the boat and headed back across the river to the Mendota landing.

That evening, as Sara and her mother lay in the bed that Louise and Dan used to share, it became apparent to Louise that something was troubling her daughter. She asked Sara what was wrong.

Sara asked her mother, "Do you think I can trust Robert?" Louise asked in what way did she mean that.

"An older girl today said that he would sully me and called him a devil among other unkind things."

"What did you and Robert do to make her say such things?" "Nothing! I swear it! She and her friends were trying to rob the grave of an Indian child, and I stopped her… Then she got angry."

Louise thought for a moment. "I think you are old enough to know what is right from wrong and not to pay attention to people that say such things."

"Sure, but that doesn't answer my question."

Louise continued, "I think Robert is a fine young man. He has been very helpful around here with your father and brothers gone, and his mother is quite sweet as well, and since they have both taken the faith, I think you can trust his word."

"I agree, and I don't fear him in any way. He's kind and funny."

Louise answered that those were both good qualities to find in a man.

Then Sara asked, "When do you think the boys will be home?" Louise pondered the question for a moment. "I don't know. But

I think John will make it home before William."

Sara smiled as she snuggled close to her mother. "I'm so glad they came through it okay."

Louise held on to her daughter. "Me too! It seems like it has been forever."

Sara kissed her mother good night. "I never want to see that kind of forever again in my life."

Louise stroked her daughter's hair. "We can only pray."

Situated nearest the steamboat landing at the foot of Seventh Street SW was the lines of the Washington and Alexandria Railroad. At this junction, Armory Hospital was less than a quarter mile. The hospital was spilling out the last of its patients in early May of 1865. Pat, Jill, and Sam, who were now also being released, were waiting together at the train station.

Sam turned to his two cohorts. "I hear the entire population had been turning out to see the Lincoln funeral train at each stop on his way home to Illinois."

Jill sighed. "So the papers say."

Pat hung his head. "He was a great man. Dreadful how it ended for him."

Sam nodded. "It's particularly sad he won't be here to review the grand army as it parades through DC next week."

"That would be something to see, wouldn't it?"

Jill looked at both. "We can extend our stay at the hospital if you want and leave after the official end of it all."

"It would be nice to see the boys from the old regiment one last time," said Sam.

Pat agreed.

Sam thought for a moment. "And maybe hitch a ride home with them instead of going on our own?"

Pat said it was a thought that had crossed his mind.

Then Jill said, "Well, you boys do what you like, but I'm catching my train today. And here she is!"

Jill's train had pulled into the station. Sam and Pat walked her to the platform edge to help her board.

Sam leaned in to kiss her hand. "I think you are right. In some ways, going it alone gives us time to settle our minds."

Pat shook Jill's hand, thanked her for all her help, and then said, "Agreed. Home it is. Today!"

Teary-eyed Jill said her goodbyes. "Don't forget what we did here."

Sam told her it would be impossible to forget her.

Pat added, "We all know how to write, so let's make the most of it."

Sam replied, "You'll both be getting mail from me as soon as I'm settled. I expect the same from you two."

They all took each other's hands and shook on their promise. A crowd of people had now gathered as these two crippled Union soldiers were saying farewell to a Colored woman. Pat and Sam ignored the snide remarks. Pat took Jill's hand and lightly kissed it.

Sam then stepped up to hug her and kiss her cheek. "I know it's not proper to say it, but you'll be in my heart forever."

Pat looked away and simply said, "Never again, huh?"

Jill boarded the train. The men waved as it pulled away from the station. They both choked back their emotions.

Pat slapped Sam on the back, "Well, laddie, at least we ride together as far as New York!"

Sam forced a smile. "Let's hope they have plenty of beer on that train."

With Sam on his cane and Pat on his crutches, they hobbled together to the nearest bench and took a seat to wait for their train.

Pat tried to make light of the situation. "Let's hope I can change your mind to get off with me before we make your transfer."

General Sibley had returned early to Fort Snelling and his Mendota home in late 1864. His part in the "relocation and pacification" of the Dakota was complete. During the winter of 1864, Wakanozanzan (Medicine Bottle) and Shakopee III were illegally kidnapped by British soldiers in Canada and brought to Fort Snelling in Minnesota. Wakanozanzan was charged with killing Philander Prescott, a civilian who was a friend of the Dakota for many years along with many White men, women, and children whose names were unknown in Brown, Renville, and other counties in the state of Minnesota. Sibley and his wife, Jane, discussed the case of the two Natives.

Jane was very direct with her husband. "How long do you suppose this trial will last?"

Sibley knew she would be worried about his continued time away from her. "I suspect the better part of a year."

"Do you think you'll be called back to continue in the Indian war?"

He lit one of his cigars and sat down. "Not very likely. With the war now complete, there will be many more regular army men looking for permanent promotions and duty in the Prairie wars."

Jane asked about the reconstruction of the nation.

"With Lincoln now dead, what do you think the prospects for his reconstruction will become?"

"It's hard to say. President Johnson was not much of a vice president in my opinion and is not familiar with Indian laws and treaties. From what I hear about him, he favors the complete extinction of the race. I'm sure he'll appoint generals who feel the same way." Jane asked if the new president would have any influence in the upcoming trial.

"Whatever our court here decides, I'm confident he will not be as just as Lincoln was in his decision to pardon those where there was insignificant proof of murder and ravagement," replied Sibley.

Jane now turned her attention to the Minnesota regiments. "When do you expect all of the Minnesota regiments back and mustered out?"

"Before any of our state boys return, they must first participate in the Grand Review."

Jane asked about the Grand Review, not knowing exactly what it meant.

"All US troops will march through Washington, DC, in a Grand Review of the Armies before the president and the generals who commanded them."

Jane asked when this would happen.

Sibley answered, "Grant's army on May 23 and Sherman's on the twenty-fourth."

Jane then asked about the prisoners who had been released. "Are you concerned about William Simmons?"

"Of course, I am. After all, you did break promises to his mother, which destroyed our friendship and possibly his life."

Sibley told Jane to stop worrying and that all the prisoners were now on their way home.

Jane responded, "I read that many have died after release."

Sibley said that, yes, it was true, but it was an unfortunate part of the war and she should forget about it.

"I just pray that boy makes it home alive and in good health." "Well, as far as we know, he's okay, and his brother is well with the Second Regiment," answered Sibley.

Jane wanted to know where the Second Regiment was at this moment.

"With the Fourteenth Corps somewhere in North Carolina."

Jane now turned her concern to Louise. "Has Louise been given this information about the Grand Review and the dates of the Second Regiment's mustering out?"

"Yes, couriers from the fort have visited with all the family members."

"Maybe I should pay her a visit?"

Sibley put out his cigar and replied, "I think that is a good idea. It may be time to start putting this unpleasantness behind us."

Jane said that she wanted him to come with her. She ordered him to go with her to see Louise. Sibley could not understand why.

Jane explained, "As I said before, this does, in many ways, fall on you."

Sibley turned away in shame and headed for the upstairs bedroom. "I don't know if I can face her."

Jane lashed out at him. "You can face the horrors of what you did to those Dakota you had locked up in that camp, but you can't face one mother of a boy you sent to his possible death and torture? What kind of a man are you?"

Sibley asked what she meant by using the word *torture*. "Henry! Come on! Even I know how those prisoners were treated. It's in all the papers. Those who escaped or were lucky enough to be exchanged have been giving reports for over a year."

Sibley gave up the argument, "Okay, I'll go with you to see Louise."

"When?" she asked.

He said whenever she wanted and to set a time and day. "I think you should be the one to set the time."

"Why me?" he asked.

"It's been over a year since you talked to her. You can't avoid this."

"Yes, I suppose you are right. I'll send a courier." "No!" She ordered, "You'll go alone."

The next day, Henry did go alone. He knocked on the door of the Simmons cabin. Sara answered it. She called out to her mother, who was sitting in the cabin. Louise asked who it was that had come to see them. Sara said it was Mr. Sibley.

Louise answered harshly so that she was sure Henry could hear her, "Turn him away please."

Sibley pushed past Sara and entered. "Louise, please. We need to speak. I have news, and I wish to apologize."

Louise would not face him. "No need. I got the standard message from your courier."

"But that's not everything."

"What else could there be? William has been released, and the Second is marching through the Carolinas on their way to DC. What else is there to know?"

Sibley pleaded, "It's about Jane." Louise relaxed. "What about her?"

"She wants us all to meet and talk things out." Louise asked what for.

"We are still neighbors, and we wish to remain cordial ones," replied Sibley.

Sara butted in, "Don't you have more Indians to kill?" Louise snapped at her daughter, "Sara! Not now!"

Sibley was taken aback but moved cautiously to take a seat next to Louise. He spoke quietly, "It's finished now. All the killing is done." Sara spoke again, "What about Medicine Bottle and Shakopee?"

Sibley politely answered Sara, "They'll get a fair trial."

Louise shook her head and whispered more to herself, "The killing never stops."

Sibley leaned in closer to her. "It has now. I'm not returning to the Dakotas. I'm staying here to help finally bring peace between us and the Natives."

Louise moved away from him. "I don't believe anything you say anymore."

Sibley tried again, "Please, give Jane and me one more chance. She misses you and Sara."

Louise was near tears. "I miss her friendship too. You can relay to her that I will meet with her."

Sibley prepared to leave. "Thank you. For her sake."

He headed for the door as Louise answered, "But only on her terms and only with her."

Sara held the door open for him as he stepped out. "Fair enough. I'll relay your wishes to her."

Louise, overcome with grief, began to weep as Sara closed the door on Sibley.

It was only a matter of days before Jane called on Louise. Louise invited her most cordially.

Jane was the first to speak, "I hope this does not have to be awkward for us."

Louise hesitated a moment. "I feel the same, but..." Jane looked puzzled.

Louise continued, "I expected more from Henry." "How do you mean?" asked Jane.

"I was hoping for a proper apology."

Jane was feeling anger rise in her. "He never apologized to you?" "Not in any formal way, just a simple 'I'm sorry.' Sorry for what, I don't exactly know."

Jane immediately understood. "Then please accept my apology." Louise told her to continue.

"Louise, I am so sorry for the loss of your husband, the suffering your boys have been through, and, most importantly, the loss of our friendship because of the misguided deeds of my husband and myself. Please accept my sincere apology so that we may put these terrible past years behind us."

"Thank you. I do accept your apology, but please be patient with my grief. I'm afraid I can't fully be at peace until both of my boys are safely home."

Jane nodded and began to speak before Louise cut her off.

"No, don't say any more. How about some conversation away from the war news?"

Jane agreed and changed the subject, "Okay. May I ask how Sara is doing?"

"She's fretting awful lately about her brothers. She has a terrible fear that things are not well with them."

Jane tried to ease her fears, "But reports from the fort say that—"

Louise was becoming impatient. "I know what they say, but still she is as restive as a wild horse."

Jane started again, "Rumor has it that she is being courted by a savage."

Louise was set off guard. "I'm afraid we don't use that word around here anymore. Robert has proven himself to be a very civil and decent human being."

Jane pushed the matter. "You don't fear for her well-being?"

Louise answered pensively, "Of course, I do, but not from him or any of the civilized Natives."

Jane wasn't having any of it. "I don't know if I could ever feel that way after the great uprising of '62."

Louise answered, "Sara and Robert have taught me a lot. She spent most of her time last summer helping the missionaries at the concentration camp before it was closed while all the remaining Dakota were being moved out to the territories."

Jane felt a slight amount of shame but didn't show it. "I'm afraid I never got a close look at that place. Henry wouldn't allow it."

Louise answered somewhat sarcastically, "No place for civilized White women, I suppose?"

"Yes, which surprised me, given all his years as a friend of the Natives. I would have thought he would like me to have seen the result of his work."

Louise answered with a dig, "And a father of a bastard Indian daughter as well."

"Yes, but poor Helen never took to White ways in the way he hoped, and I suspect he was very disappointed in her, especially after she married a Native."

"It's a shame for sure, her dying soon after marrying that Chippewa man," replied Louise.

Jane only nodded, and then suddenly Sara burst through the door. Jane greeted her, "Hello, Sara."

Sara said hello in return, and Louise asked her where she had been.

"Robert and I have been down to the shallows to collect some smoke weed and catfish for his mother."

Jane had never heard of smoke weed and asked about it. Louise answered for her daughter, "His mother calls it kinni-kinnic, but it's just some weeds that they use as a medicine for many things."

Jane asked if she had tried it for anything. Louise said she had used it for her headaches and sleepless nights. Jane asked if it worked. "Yes, quite well actually, but it also makes me very hungry." Louise could see that the tension between the women had now eased. "Well, that's not good, especially with the lack of food over these past years."

Sara interjected, "Robert's mother always has fry bread waiting when she smokes it. And she even taught me how to make it."

Jane seemed shocked and asked Louise if this was all true. "Yes, and I'd have to say Sara has learned quite a lot about survival on the prairie since her friendship with Robert."

Jane could feel their friendship starting to become reestablished. "That's great! Skills like those will come in handy one day."

Louise then asked if Sara had heard any news from the fort that day.

"Yes, the Fourteenth Corps is on the way to Richmond and then DC, and without opposition, that should be a fine march."

Jane then turned to Sara. "Sara, I hear you've been nervous over your brothers lately."

"Yes, more so than ever."

Jane spoke in a comforting tone, "I shouldn't be too concerned. The war is over now, and it's just a matter of time for all to be rejoined with families again." Jane could see how upset Sara was and asked what the real trouble was.

Sara wrung her hands. "I heard that many released prisoners are dying on the road after their release."

Jane then tried to ease her fear, "William has gone through so much. I think he may have only gotten stronger from his confinement."

"Really? Do you think so?"

"He was always the strongest one of you all." Louise answered for them both, "That's true."

After a long siege, Grant captured Petersburg and Richmond in early April 1865. As the fall of Petersburg became imminent, on Evacuation Sunday (April 2), President Davis, his cabinet, and the Confederate defenders abandoned Richmond and fled south on the last open railroad line, the Richmond and Danville.

The retreating Confederate soldiers were under orders to set fire to bridges, the armory, and warehouses with supplies as they left. The fire in the largely abandoned city spread out of control, and large parts of Richmond were destroyed, reaching the very edge of Capitol Square mostly unchecked. The conflagration was not completely extinguished until the mayor and other civilians went to the Union lines east of Richmond.

The Fourteenth Corps crossed the long bridge over into Richmond on the first of May 1865. The Second Minnesota Regiment, along with the other regiments of their division, was encamped on the outskirts of the city. No passes were issued, and if the men wished, they were given free rein to roam the city at various times but were required to be back in their camps before midnight.

John and Vandyke wandered about together taking in the sights of the city, which had now been reduced to destruction. They visited what was left of the burned armory. Standing on the bluffs above the river, they looked down into what was once Belle Isle Prison.

Vandyke knew John had his brother, William, in mind as he spoke to him. "So this is where the famous prison was?"

John looked over what was nothing but a clean riverbank. "It looks pretty clean now."

Vandyke nodded knowingly. "Sometimes all a place needs is a good fire to return it to normal."

John laughed. "I can only imagine what William went through here."

Vandyke nodded. "His letters weren't very explicit. We never actually got one from him, did we? I mean from what your mother wrote of his letters to her."

John had nothing more to add.

Vandyke continued, "Andersonville was much worse from what we've learned."

John shrugged. "Well, it's over now."

"I'll believe it when we get our discharge papers," said Vandyke.

John said he had seen enough there and said they should move on.

Vandyke agreed, "Yeah, let's try to find that tobacco factory they held them in before shipping them off to Andersonville."

John hesitated to move. "Sure, but first I want to go into that camp and rummage around."

Vandyke asked why he wanted to do that. "A souvenir to bring back to William."

Vandyke asked, "You don't think he has any?"

"It was not like him to pick up things along the way. You know he liked to travel light."

"Yeah, besides, I think we have enough souvenirs packed inside our brains."

John nodded in agreement. "That's for sure. Maybe after we get home, the dreams will stop."

"Let's hope so," replied Vandyke.

The boys walked down into the remains of the Belle Isle camp. John kicked around in the ash and dirt. He kicked up a twisted and bent spoon and put it in his haversack.

Vandyke was becoming impatient. "Can we go now? I hear there are ladies in town who are selling sweet cakes on the new black market."

"Sure. Let's get us some before they're all gone."

The street where the old tobacco factory (Pemberton Prison) stood was destroyed. Passive Confederate soldiers roamed about looking like so many lost souls. A black market of stolen US food supplies had been set up and was now being controlled by the women of Richmond. John and Vandyke looked over the scene. Stopping at one table where apple pies were being sold, they waited in line to get one for themselves.

Vandyke pointed to the goods laid out before them. "Can you believe this? One pie for five US greenbacks." Vandyke noticed John was anxious to get his hands on one of the pies.

John rummaged in his haversack for some coins. "Back home, that would be a penny."

Vandyke asked him if he had any cash.

John pulled out a handful of bills. "Only these worthless Confederate notes."

The woman tending the stand overheard him and reproached him, "We don't take Confederate bills! Nobody does! So move on, blue belly."

A Confederate soldier standing in line spoke up, "Show some respect, miss. They beat us fair." The soldier turned to face John and Vandyke. "Where you boys from?"

John told him they were both from Minnesota.

The rebel soldier was taken aback. "Did I see you boys at Gettysburg? I was with the Twenty-Eighth Virginia. You took our flag."

Vandyke corrected him, "That would have been the First Regiment, Second Corps. We are with the Second Regiment, Fourteenth Corps. Sherman's army."

"So you're bummers, huh?"

Vandyke continued, "Yup, Uncle Billy's bummers. That's what they say, but—"

John spoke, "We didn't take part in any of the burning and looting."

The rebel soldier scoffed. "I can't say I would have been so kind if the sides had been reversed."

They reached the head of the line.

The rebel soldier offered to pay. "Let me get that pie for you boys. The ingredients belong to the benevolent North anyway."

The rebel soldier paid for the pie in US cash. Vandyke asked him where he had gotten the US greenbacks.

"I sold my rifle to a boy from New York who wanted a souvenir."

John looked a bit bewildered. "Won't you need your rifle for hunting and protection when you get back home?"

"Why would I want to kill game with a rifle designed to kill men? No, I have good proper game rifles at home."

John nodded in agreement.

Vandyke was still about the money. "Those New England Yankees always seem to get their pay on time. We're three weeks overdue."

"I figured as much when I saw you pull out that wad of Confederate notes. We didn't get any pay for the past year."

Vandyke added, "Got to hand it to you boys. You sure are some tough nuts to hang on with so little."

The rebel answered in a Southern accent that made his words nearly impossible to understand to John and Vandyke, "They said it was our state's rats we were fighting for. Whatever that means, I'll never know."

John thanked him for his kindness.

The rebel soldier shook his hand. "Let's hope we can meet again one day under better terms."

Vandyke then took his hand. "I'll never or forever see you as an enemy again, my friend."

The three men split up and went their separate ways.

As they walked farther into the city, John asked, "Have you seen enough?"

Vandyke looked exhausted. "I think so. I want to get back to camp and get a long sleep."

John added, "Moffett says we need to make a sixteen-mile march every day if we are to make it to Washington in time for the big review."

Vandyke asked when that was.

John answered, "May 23 for the Army of the Potomac. The twenty-fourth for us."

"Sixteen miles a day on good roads with nobody shooting at us?"

John replied, "Nothing to it. Just wish William was here to be part of it."

Vandyke reassured him, "I'm sure he is sitting comfortably on some boat headed north."

"I sure hope so," said John as they continued in silence back to their camp.

Private William Simmons of the Second Minnesota Volunteer Infantry remained at Camp Fisk, outside Vicksburg, Mississippi. He and others from Andersonville were technically still prisoners as they awaited their exchange after the end of the war. A unit of US Colored Troops had recently served as part of the prison guard. He and Otis prepared quarters for themselves. Al had been put into a temporary tent hospital run by US Army surgeons. It had been raining for days, and with the northern snow melting, the Mississippi River had over-run her banks.

Otis looked about the camp and saw what remained of the once-grand army of the republic. "Well, this is quite a change from Andersonville."

William sighed with relief. "I'm almost starting to feel alive again. Fresh water and plenty of it. New shelter halves and blankets. Who would have ever thought a couple of pieces of cloth could bring such comfort?"

Otis added, "And food enough to eat!"

William pulled a hardtack biscuit from his haversack. "Yes, but they won't let us eat all we want."

Otis told him to put it back. "You've seen what happens when you stuff yourself after starving for so long."

"Yeah, all those poor boys who died while finally eating and those who died on the march to this place. What a shame. I thought we'd lose Al on that march here."

Otis looked toward the hospital tent. "From the looks of him, we still might."

William changed the subject, "They're issuing us new clothes tonight. And I'm going to write a letter to Mary once we get settled in."

"You should tell her to meet you at the Louisville landing." "Do you think we'll have time?"

"Sure, it's where we change boats. I get off there, and you head northwest by another boat. There will be plenty of time. You know how slow these people are."

William had other things on his mind. "The Sanitary Commission men are out today and giving out towels, combs, and soap."

Otis noticed but had other news. "I saw that. I also heard there was a riot here a couple of weeks ago."

"What kind of riot?"

Otis explained, "The White prisoners would not take orders from the Negro guards, and shooting took place. One darky and his horse were killed."

William asked if that was all that happened.

"No, the Coloreds were removed in the night and replaced with the White guards we have now."

William told Otis that he had heard about the Black guards being in the camp and was surprised to see there weren't any around when they arrived. Otis wanted to know what the date was. William told him it was April 18, the day that Lincoln would be lying in state. Otis commented, "Surely his death is a sad day for the nation.

He would have done well to the South. I'm not sure about his replacement."

William did not like Johnson. "Yes, I think Johnson will seek revenge."

Otis then said, "He's a true Southern man. He'll take it all out on the darkies."

As pardoned prisoners walked toward the boat landing, the conversation turned to release dates.

"The Missouri men are being paroled today."

Otis followed up on William's comment, "Illinois boys went yesterday. I heard the rest of us will be crammed in whatever boats they can find. I'm sure they'll be overloaded. Even so, it can't be as bad as anything in the camps."

"I just hope we can find a spot to lie down... I don't have the strength to stand for another entire journey," replied William.

"Don't worry. I'll make a spot for us even if I have to throw others overboard."

William laughed. "If you do, make sure they are some of those raiders we had to contend with."

"Some of those boats are so overloaded the decks are collapsing and beam supports are being put in to hold the capacity of men," commented Otis.

William asked when he thought their turn would come. Otis told him he had heard they were scheduled to go out on the twenty-fifth of April.

William made a mental note, then remembered Al's condition. "We better see to Al and make sure he's capable. I think we should stay together."

Otis agreed. "Why not? We haven't been separated yet, but he'll have to make the final leg with you."

A couple of days later, Otis and William stood at the edge of the Camp Fisk boat dockage. Looking out over the vast, swollen banks of the Mississippi River, they watched released prisoners boarding steamers that would take them home. William mentioned to Otis that they only had four more days to wait. Otis had been keeping track too.

William pointed to the boats. "What are they waiting on? Look out there. Some of those boats seem half empty."

"I guess there's a huge steamer coming back up from New Orleans that has made a deal to take the balance of the rest of us in one trip."

William asked why New Orleans.

"Yeah, that's the drop-off point for Confederate prisoners that have been released. They go down the river and then back upriver."

"The balance of us, huh? That's a whole lot of people on one boat. It better be a big one."

Otis grinned as if he was responsible for finding the finest steamer of all. "The biggest and the best, I'm told."

William now turned his thoughts to Al again. "You think Al will last four more days?"

"He looked better this morning, and one of the orderlies said, dead or alive, everyone was to be out of the camp by the twenty-fifth."

"I guess we'll be carrying him aboard ourselves" was William's reply.

"I figured as much. Anyway, on the twenty-fourth, we have to line up at the Sanitary Commission tent and fill our haversacks with enough food to get us home."

William looked surprised. "Two weeks of grub in one bag?" Otis commented that they had better find some extra bags.

William said he had nothing left to trade.

"I know where we can get some for free." William asked where.

"The hospital tent has plenty lying around that they issued to those who died off."

William knew this would be an easy heist. "Fair enough. They won't be using them anyhow."

On the twenty-first of April, the riverboat steamer *Sultana* was unloading Confederate prisoners and other supplies in New Orleans. While the men and dock workers ran down the gangplank to unload, the captain of the boat, a young man named James Mason, held a conversation with his chief engineer Nathan.

"Nate, we need this boat in Vicksburg in three days. Can you do that?"

"If we increase pressure to the maximum, we can keep up our speed, yes. But remember, we will be pushing against a flood current and one of the boilers I have concerns about."

Mason scoffed at his comment. "This boat is practically new. She's barely three years old."

Nathan expressed his concern again, "Yes, but the boilers have to be recertified every year."

Mason asked if that had been done.

"No. As I told you before, your being behind on payments has forced us to overwork this steamer, and all maintenance has been put off."

Mason scoffed again. "Don't worry about it. I've made a deal with the chief quartermaster at Camp Fisk in Vicksburg that will solve all of our financial problems."

Nathan asked what kind of a deal he had made.

"It's not your problem. Let me take care of it. Your problem is to keep up as much steam as possible. I need to be in Vicksburg on time. There's a race to get those last prisoners out of there."

Nathan was confused by what kind of race he was talking about. "A race we need to win at all costs. Now tell me what we are hauling upstream from here."

Nathan answered, "Seventy deck passengers, a small number of livestock, and our crew of eighty-five."

"That's a full load right there. Best we take on more coal and any lumber we might need to reinforce the decks."

Nathan could not imagine why they would need to reinforce the decks and was having real concerns about the safety of the boat. He wanted to know why.

Mason answered abruptly, "You'll see soon enough. Now get back to your job and see me when you have steam up and ready to cast off."

Nathan saluted and went back below decks to tend to his machines.

SULTANA

*The wreck of the Sultana was discovered in 1982,
thirty-two feet belowground in a soybean field in
Arkansas. The river had changed course so much
over time that it was two miles from the river when
it was found.*

The *Sultana* was a Mississippi River side-wheel steamboat. Constructed
of wood in 1863 by the John Litherbury Boatyard in Cincinnati, she
was intended for the lower Mississippi cotton trade. The steamer
registered 1,719 tons and normally carried a crew of eighty-five.
For two years, she ran a regular route between Saint Louis and New
Orleans and was frequently commissioned to carry troops. Under the
command of Captain James Cass Mason of Saint Louis, the *Sultana*
left Saint Louis on April 13, 1865, bound for New Orleans, Louisiana.
On the morning of April 15, she was tied up at Cairo, Illinois, when
word reached the city that President Abraham Lincoln had been shot
at Ford's Theater. Rumors of the assassination had spread from there,
but no official word had been spread downriver.

Immediately Captain Mason grabbed an armload of Cairo
newspapers and headed south to spread the news, knowing that
telegraphic communication with the South had been almost totally cut
off because of the war. With an armload of papers in hand, Mason was
greeted on deck by his chief engineer Nathan, a man of about thirty.
As Mason came aboard, he was confronted by his engineer.

He could see the captain had newspapers, but he asked anyway,
"What do you have there, Captain?"

Mason pushed him aside. "We're heading south to spread the news."

"I think everyone knows by now that the war is over," said Nathan.

Mason paused. "Sure, they do, but with telegraph lines out, the word of Lincoln's assassination hasn't reached everyone. All the lines from Vicksburg to New Orleans have been destroyed."

"So this is it? We are making a news run?" asked Nathan. "That's not all. The first stop is Vicksburg."

Nathan asked what for.

"I have a meeting with the chief quartermaster there." Nathan asked if he meant the quartermaster Hatch.

"Yes. We've dealt with him before when we ran supplies to the Union Army and troops down the river, and now—"

Nathan finished for him, "And now they want to bring those same troops back home?"

Mason continued, "Not quite. Released prisoners. They've set up a parole camp there, and—"

"Let me guess. There's money to be made." "Yes, and plenty of it," finished Mason.

Nathan then asked if there was enough to pay off the debts Mason owed on the boat to regain his ownership.

"Yes, and much more," replied Mason. Nathan asked what they were paying per head.

"Five dollars per enlisted man and eight dollars per officer" was the answer.

Nathan seemed confused.

"You know our capacity is only 376 passengers. That hardly seems enough to make a profit with."

Mason told him to leave the worrying to him and then handed Nathan the newspapers. "Stow these papers for me. I'm going to run back into town and get some more. Once you're done with that, get back to your duties and be ready to cast off when I get back."

Nathan obeyed and then headed into the pilothouse with the papers as Mason ran down the gangway to shore.

Within the hour, Mason returned and the *Sultana* was ready to depart. With Captain Mason standing nearby, Nathan took the helm of the *Sultana*. Mason gazed out the forward window of the pilot-house as the steamboat left its dock and headed out into the swollen Mississippi River.

Mason gave orders to his helmsman, "Easy does it, Nathan. Since I sold out my controlling interest in this boat, I intend on profiting from it and buy her back. We need to keep her tip-top."

"Yes, sir, Captain. I would say it's about time you get out from under your debt and take full ownership."

"Indeed. Now tell me what the inspection report said." Nathan then asked which report he was referring to.

Mason answered, "The government inspector's report from our stop in Saint Louis."

Nathan asked if he meant the one from April 12. Mason answered a very definite yes.

Nathan gave his impression of the report, "If I remember correctly, it briefly said the *Sultana* 'may be employed as a steamer upon the waters specified.'"

Mason asked for the exact meaning of that.

"That the boat is safe to use on all river ways. They found nothing of concern, but…"

"But what?" asked Mason.

Nathan said that he had crew members with concerns. Mason wanted to know who specifically.

"The fireman Jackson."

Mason scoffed. "The niggra coal shoveler?" "Yes, that's him. And others too."

Mason asked what the issue was.

Nathan told him, "Those boiler repairs we made on previous trips to Natchez and at Vicksburg. They say the work is shoddy."

Mason scoffed again. "What would anyone in the Black gang know about the mechanics of this boat?"

Nathan responded, "I trust those men. Maybe they can't read, but they have a sixth sense about those machines."

Mason was now becoming angry. "Are you going to trust the safety of this boat to ignorant apes or the government inspectors?" As the *Sultana* headed into the open waters of the river, Mason's anger exploded. "You get those men off this boat as soon as we reach New Orleans! Replace them with a new crew. I'll have no voodoo monkeys spooking everyone on this boat."

Nathan was shocked by his outburst. "Yes, Captain, but…" "Now what?"

Nathan sheepishly replied, "Maybe we should do a refit once we get to New Orleans."

Mason dressed him down again, "We won't have time for that! Besides, the force of this current downstream, we can glide right into the city without any trouble at all."

"That's true, sir. Perhaps I should shut down the boilers and let us coast down?" said Nathan.

"What's the point of that?"

"We could save on coal and reduce pressure on the boilers."

Mason began to calm but still lashed out. "No! I want steam up in case we need it in an emergency, but you can reduce it if you feel better about it."

"Yes, sir, I think I will."

Mason ended the debate, "So be it. Can we now continue this journey without any more worries? Make headway to Vicksburg."

"Yes, sir. But why Vicksburg?"

"I told you! I have business there with Colonel Hatch. I need to finalize our manifest of prisoners to take on board. All ahead one-third."

Nathan rang the engine room to take the boat to one-third speed, and the *Sultana* churned along leisurely in the wide expanse of the Mississippi River.

The next morning, the *Sultana* arrived without incident at Vicksburg. Mason met with the young and handsome colonel Hatch in his temporary tent office set up near the Vicksburg-Camp Fisk landing.

Hatch greeted Mason and got straight to business, "Welcome to you, Captain Mason. General Smith told me you two had spoken and had come upon an agreement."

Mason shook his hand and replied, "Yes, that's true. He promised me a full load of soldiers I could take north on my return upriver."

Hatch asked how many he could legally carry.

"Legally I can take 376, but that would hardly cover my fuel costs."

Hatch then asked if it were possible for him to take 1,300. "I'm sure we can squeeze that many on board, but it certainly won't be comfortable."

Hatch snickered. "These boys are used to being uncomfortable." Mason then asked if Hatch could guarantee the price.

"Yes, whatever the general and you agreed on will be paid, plus my percentage of course."

Mason was a bit confused. "Your percentage?"

Hatch winked knowingly. "Think of it as a handling fee." Mason asked how much his percentage was.

"Ten percent. I'll take it off the top and off the books before you get your end. Nobody will ever know."

Mason asked if that was legal.

Hatch took Mason's hand. "I'm sure you want to get your boat back in your own hands as soon as possible."

Mason nodded and said that indeed he did want his boat back as soon as possible.

Hatch responded, "Maybe I can sweeten the pot a bit then."
"How's that?"

"Find more room on your decks. I need this camp cleared out as soon as possible. In the next week or so, the last boats will be taking as many men as they can handle."

Mason did not respond.

"You don't want to miss out on this opportunity. The last boats out will get the bulk of the men and the bulk of the profits."

Mason finally spoke, "I have to complete my run to New Orleans but should be back by the twenty-third or twenty-fourth, if that's okay."

Hatch nodded in agreement. "No later than the twenty-fourth. I want the last boat out no later than the twenty-fiftth."

Mason then handed Hatch a bundle of newspapers. "Before I leave, I have to give you these."

Hatch took them. "What's this?"

"With the telegraph lines down, I figured you had not got the latest news on Lincoln."

Hatch took a quick look at the headline and read that Lincoln had been assassinated. "Yes, so it's true then? This is shocking news!" "Yes, terrible news for all the darky lovers. You may want to post some of those prints for all to read."

Hatch nodded. "Yes, I will, and thank you." The men shook hands.

"Well then, I'll be on my way and hope to see you in a few days."

Hatch held open the tent flap for him. "Have a safe trip and try to hurry back. You don't want to miss your chance."

Mason left for his boat. "Thank you. I'll be looking forward to the completion of this task and an end to this awful war."

Back aboard the *Sultana*, Chief Engineer Nathan and the fireman Jackson looked over the boilers that had been repaired on the earlier trips.

Jackson was overly concerned. "Mr. Nathan, I have a bad feeling about this trip upriver and these boilers."

"I know. I know. You think the patches won't hold."

"Not with all the steam we'll need to push against that current.

Lordy, Mr. Nathan, you know how this river is in the spring." Nathan told him there was no need for him to worry. "Why? Are we staying on here for proper repairs?"

Nathan was not unkind in his answer but made it final. "No! You boy, on Captain's wish, are being let off here." "But why, Mr. Nathan?"

"The captain thinks you are a Jonas and will only bring bad luck."

Jackson was not having it. "I ain't no Jonas. Your bad luck is right here in these two temporary patches. They were hissing and singing to us all the way downriver. You've got to understand."

Nathan tried to go easy on him. "I do understand, but I'm not the captain nor the owner of this boat."

"He ain't the owner either."

"You're right, but he expects to be and the only way for him to do that is to fill this boat with those prisoners and get them upriver." Jackson pleaded, "But I don't want to leave. I got no home here."

"I'm sorry, but those are the orders. I suggest now you pack your bag and leave before he comes down here."

Jackson then asked who would replace him.

"The captain is already ashore and looking for a new man."

Jackson left the engine room in a huff. Nathan took the ladder topside.

The *Sultana* had left New Orleans and was headed upriver. In the meantime, a change of command had been made at Camp Fisk. Confederate authorities had finally agreed to parole the prisoners waiting at Camp Fisk. General Dana (former colonel of the First Minnesota) ordered that muster rolls listing the names of the men be prepared as quickly as possible so that the soldiers could be immediately transported by train to Vicksburg to board steamers tied up at the docks.

The nominal officer in command of the prisoner exchange was Captain George Augustus Williams. A graduate of the United States Military Academy at West Point, Williams was a veteran of more than thirteen years of service in the regular army but had never risen above the rank of captain. While serving as the provost marshal at Memphis, Tennessee, in 1864, he had been dismissed from service because of "excessive cruelty to prisoners and gross neglect of duty." He was saved from disgrace by the intervention of the Union general Ulysses S. Grant, whose written testimonial helped persuade the army to reverse his dismissal.

When military business took Captain Williams away from Vicksburg in mid-April, Captain Frederic Speed, a fine officer in his midthirties and assistant adjutant general for the Department of the Mississippi, volunteered to be his interim replacement. Since Williams was still absent when the Union troops were paroled, Speed began to assemble the rolls and arrange transportation for the war-weary soldiers. The first contingent of 1,300 anxious troops was shipped upriver on the *Henry Ames*, followed soon after by 700 soldiers aboard the *Olive Branch*.

Speed discussed this with Hatch, "Colonel Hatch, now that I am in command, I hope you do not object to me releasing these troops."

"I only object that you are not following proper procedures," replied Hatch.

Speed wanted to know exactly what he meant by the insult.

Hatch told him, "Before men can board, proper rolls must be recorded."

Speed had another idea to expedite the movement of the prisoners. "I don't see why we can't just have them board and finish the rolls once they are on their way."

Hatch told him that this made no sense.

Speed was wise to Hatch's scheme. "Are you afraid all prisoners will be gone before the *Sultana* arrives so you can collect your kickback?"

Hatch was taken aback. "What do you know about me and the *Sultana*?"

Speed told him he had heard rumors.

Hatch made his argument, "Well, I think you should stop the boarding until Captain Williams arrives, and then he can make the proper decision as to how this is to be accomplished. We had direct and thorough orders from Lincoln's office."

"And he's dead now, so?"

Hatch shot back, "I outrank you, and I tell you we will wait for Captain Williams."

Speed stood down for the time being. "Okay, but I think he'll agree with me that we must get these men out of here without any more delays."

Hatch agreed.

Speed continued, "But I'm ordering the *Olive Branch* and *Henry Ames* to cast off with their loads now. You can have the rest for the *Sultana*."

Hatch said this was fine and expected the *Sultana* within forty-eight hours.

Back aboard the *Sultana*, as the boat headed upstream, the fire-man Jackson's concerns proved justified when steam was discovered escaping from a crack in one of her four boilers. Thus, the *Sultana* reached a point about ten miles south of Vicksburg, forcing her to continue up the Mississippi at a greatly reduced speed. Fearing that the crack posed a significant threat to the safety of the steamboat, her chief engineer Nathan declared that he would not proceed beyond Vicksburg until necessary repairs were made. Nathan inspected the crack and headed topside to see Captain Mason. He reported to Mason that he reduced speed for fear the boilers blow up. Nathan entered the pilothouse to see Mason at the wheel.

"What is it, Nathan? Why are we slowing down?"

"Sir, I had the men back off on the pressure. I think fireman Jackson was right."

Mason protested, "What do you mean he was right?"

Nathan explained, "One of the boilers has a crack in that most recent repair. Steam was escaping."

Mason scoffed at the idea.

Nathan continued, "If we keep up the pace you want, I'm afraid one of the boilers might blow."

Mason was becoming angry. "Chief, we have a schedule to make. We have only about ten more miles to go."

Nathan pleaded, "Ten miles is nothing. Even at half speed, you'll make your deadline. Please don't risk the boat and your payday."

Mason gave in with a stipulation, "All right, but we had better pull in before dark, or that bonus I promised you will be in my pocket and not yours."

"Fair enough. I'm sure we'll make it at half speed." Mason agreed, "Okay, but no slower than that."

Nathan left the pilothouse and returned to his station below decks.

The *Sultana* finally docked at Vicksburg early on the evening of April 23. Arriving so soon after the departure of the *Olive Branch,* the *Sultana* almost did not get any prisoners to carry north. Captain Speed, aware that the rolls of only three hundred of the remaining soldiers had been prepared, reported to General Dana that no prisoners would be shipped on the *Sultana;* he could not, he said, complete the remaining paperwork before the steamer's scheduled departure on the following day. Furious when he learned that his steamer was to get none of the prisoners promised him, Mason went immediately into Vicksburg and met with Colonel Hatch, General Smith, and Captain Speed.

Captain Speed was stern with him. "Captain Mason, I refuse to board any of the prisoners until all the muster rolls have been completed."

"You mean to tell me I will have no prisoners for tomorrow's journey?"

Captain Williams intervened in defense of Mason, "Captain Speed, there is no need for the muster rolls now. Priority is to get these men out of here and back to their homes."

Speed asked what he suggested he do.

Williams answered, "The men can merely be checked off as they go aboard and the rolls completed after the departure of the boat."

Speed thought for a moment. "Very well, but will General Dana approve?"

"I will go directly to Dana now and inform him that all the prisoners remaining at the parole camp and in the hospital at Vicksburg shall be shipped as planned on the *Sultana.*"

Mason now seemed relieved. "Thank you, Captain Williams.

That is a relief to me as time is now very critical for us." Williams wanted to know what he meant by that. "We have a leaky boiler that needs immediate repair." Williams asked how long it would take.

"My chief engineer says one week for a proper job." Williams told him he did not have time for that.

Mason defended himself, "I realize that, so I've contracted a local man, a boilermaker, R. G. Taylor. Do you know him?"

"Yes, he does some work on the boats here. He's very good."

Mason was pleased, knowing he would get his cargo. "He assured me he can do a temporary patch that will hold until we reach Saint Louis, where the permanent repair can be done."

Williams wanted to know how soon he could finish.

Mason answered, "He's already started and says we can be on our way tomorrow as planned."

"Is he certain of the safety?" asked Williams.

"He argued that it was not wise to put a temporary patch, but I won out," said Mason.

The next morning, Williams and Speed traveled the four miles to Camp Fisk. The two officers agreed that Speed would remain at the parole camp to supervise the loading of the men onto the trains while Williams would ride on the first train back to Vicksburg, where he would keep count as they boarded the *Sultana*. The tired but excited former prisoners, grouped according to their native states, quickly climbed onto the first train.

The confidence that Williams and Speed had in the ability of the *Sultana* to carry all the remaining prisoners was not shared by a less experienced younger officer, Captain William F. Kerns, the quartermaster in charge of river transportation. Kerns met with Williams in his office at camp Fisk.

"Captain Williams, I do not trust the capability of the *Sultana* to carry such a load of prisoners, especially if she is now in for repairs."

Williams asked what he suggested he do.

Kerns was anxious to fill other boats. "The *Lady Gay* is a new boat much larger than the *Sultana* and would be a better choice in my opinion."

Williams knew that cash had already changed hands regarding the *Sultana*. "Maybe, but we have already paid Mason to do the job."

Kerns stood his ground. "Well, I still protest. The *Lady Gay* is a much stronger vessel. I still believe all the prisoners should travel with her."

Williams did not outrank Kerns, but he had been in service longer and insisted, "The *Sultana* will take them, and that's final."

Kerns had to respect him and suspected there was money involved. He knew of Hatch's reputation. "Okay, but a temporarily patched boiler could prove fatal or, in the least, slow their progress and offset the schedule."

Kerns could not win the argument. The *Lady Gay*, therefore, headed north from Vicksburg without a single paroled prisoner on board. A few minutes after the departure of the *Lady Gay*, Captain Williams and the first trainload of former prisoners—an estimated 570—pulled into Vicksburg. These men joined 398 soldiers already on board the *Sultana*, who probably came from the military hospital. Thus, the *Sultana* then exceeded her carrying capacity by more than 600. Among this first contingent was William Simmons. He noted in his diary that the "*Sultana* [was] a large but not a very fine boat." As the day wore on, two more trainloads of men boarded the *Sultana*. Captain Williams, whose responsibility was to count the soldiers as they went aboard the steamer, was not at the dock when the second group of men walked across the *Sultana*'s gangplank.

Consequently, four hundred soldiers were not added to his tally.

After this second load of soldiers boarded the *Sultana*, Captain Kerns warned Colonel Hatch that too many prisoners were being placed on the one steamer, "Hatch, I believe we have too many prisoners on this one boat. I think we should separate some of these men and put them on the *Pauline Carroll*, which has just recently arrived." Hatch, fearing he'd lose his percentage of government money, protested, "No! I promised Mason he'd get a full load."

Kerns was about to lose his temper. "He has a full load now!"

Hatch was now angered. "We'll see about that. I'm sending a telegraph now to Captain Speed at Camp Fisk and will ask for his approval."

The telegraph was immediately sent from his office.

Kerns continued his case, "Speed did not oversee the boarding of the second group that got off the train. I don't think he realizes that the *Sultana* is severely overloaded already."

Hatch ignored him. "The *Sultana* is a fine boat and can handle more men than you think."

Speed's answer came in on the telegraph. Hatch took it and looked it over.

Kerns asked what Speed said.

Hatch grinned and replied, "He is quite certain there are no more than 1,400 men on the *Sultana*, and he adds, 'No, they can all go on the one boat.'"

Kerns now knew there was a shady deal that had been made. "Was that the deal you made with Mason?"

"Yes, that's what we paid for, and that's what he will take. Now, with Captain's Speed blessing, I will not divide those men onto another boat."

Kerns responded unkindly, "You must be making a killing on this. I hope you can sleep well if things go wrong."

The final load of prisoners was marched aboard the boat. Included in this lot were Otis, Al, and William. Al was too sick to walk on his own and was carried aboard by two other prisoners. As they moved aboard, other prisoners were being removed by way of another gangplank. Otis pushed his way through the crowd of men looking for a spot to settle himself and the other two.

Otis turned to William. "Keep an eye on Al. I'm going to find us a place to lie down in this mess."

William, looking at the situation, only shook his head in defeat. Meanwhile, Dr. George S. Kemble, the medical director of the Department of the Mississippi who visited the *Sultana* after the second trainload of men had boarded, shared Kerns's view. Concluding that the steamboat was too crowded for the comfort and safety of the sick men, Kemble sought and received permission from General Dana to remove 23 men who were confined to cots from the *Sultana*.

He also redirected a column of 278 soldiers who came from the hospital.

While William watched the men offloading, Otis finally returned with news. "I've found a great spot, but we need to hurry. Help me carry Al."

William asked where to.

Otis pointed to the smokestacks which rose high above the pilothouse. "Up there on top of the pilothouse next to the bell, the hurricane deck, I think it's called. Next to those two smokestacks, there's open space where we can bed down."

William thought that seemed perfect for the time being.

The men made their way through the crowds and climbed the ladder to the roof of the hurricane deck. They found a spot that nobody had taken and spread out their blankets.

William was puzzled that they had found an open space. "Odd that there is nobody up here. It seems perfect."

Al managed to whisper out a response, "Think about it. These smokestacks are going to be red hot a few minutes after we push off. Cool breeze or fair weather, it won't matter. We'll roast up here."

Otis asked if he should look elsewhere.

"No, this is fine. I don't want to be moved again."

William looked at his friends. "Okay, I've got full canteens for us. I guess we'll just sweat it out."

Otis was pleased. "This is still a luxury no matter how we look at it, considering the past year."

While the exact number of people loaded onto the *Sultana* on April 24 remains unknown, there can be no question that the steamer was grossly overcrowded. The human load was so great that it was necessary for the crew to install extra supports for the upper decks, for fear that the sagging floors might collapse.

Captain Speed was shocked when informed by George Williams that he had counted 1,996 men boarding the ship, several hundred more than his estimate. What Speed did not realize was that Williams's figure only included the prisoners from the first and third trains since the soldiers from the second train boarded the *Sultana* without being counted. In reality, the steamboat carried as many as 2,100 soldiers, approximately 100 civilian passengers, and 85 crewmen for a possible total of more than 2,300 people, more than six times the vessel's legal limit.

Below decks, in the engine room, Chief Engineer Nathan inspected the temporary patch as he was followed around the engine room by William J. Gambrell, the first clerk and part owner of the *Sultana*.

"How do you feel about this, Nathan?"

"This is not a proper fix. I wish we would have waited and done the job right."

Gambrell nodded. "I have to agree. I've got a bad feeling about this." Nathan looked on the positive side. "Maybe at half or one-third speed we'll make it, but you know Captain Mason will push it."

Gambrell was not so positive. "If we arrived safely at Cairo, it will be the greatest trip ever made on the Western waters. There are more people on board than have ever been carried on one boat on the Mississippi River."

Nathan looked away. "I think that is the captain's intent." Gambrell asked why.

Nathan told him, "To make a name for himself as well as enough cash to buy this boat back so he can be the sole owner."

Gambrell laughed. "Luck better be on his side."

Nathan changed the subject back to the load, "Do we have an accurate count of numbers of souls on board, not counting the regular crew and passengers?"

Gambrell answered, "The army didn't do a complete count, but I have, and we are close to six times over the limit."

This sunk into Nathan's fears. "Not only do we have to worry about boilers holding up, but any shift of bodies on board could capsize this thing. What's your estimate?"

"I'm certain we have over 2,300 on board," answered Gambrell.

Nathan slammed his fist into one of the boilers. "Complete insanity! I should have gotten off at New Orleans."

Gambrell turned to leave. "I'm heading topside and seeing to the castoff."

Nathan turned back to his crew.

At 9:00 p.m. on April 24, the *Sultana* slowly backed away from the wharf at Vicksburg and headed north on the flood-swollen Mississippi River. The enormous weight of the passengers and cargo on the decks of the steamer worried her crew. Gambrel met Major Fidler, an older officer on deck.

Gambrell took a spot next to the rail with Fidler. "Well, Major, we are underway."

Fidler seemed a little nervous. "Don't you mean overweight? Yes, and just barely on time. You look as concerned as I feel, Gambrel."

"Yes, I am, as are most of the crew."

Fidler asked why that was.

Gambrel answered, "We are way overloaded, and I fear any sudden movement by the prisoners could cause the decks to collapse. Also too many men crowding to one side of the deck could result in this boat capsizing."

Fidler shared his concern about the overly excited men. "As excited as these men are to get home, we may have a problem with that."

Gambrell agreed.

And so the *Sultana* churned upstream on her first leg of the journey north. She stopped briefly that night at Memphis to take on coal. The next day, the horrifying scenario of the *Sultana* capsizing almost played out when she docked briefly at Helena, Arkansas. Word quickly spread among the passengers that a photographer was setting up his camera on the west bank of the river. The excited soldiers, including Otis, hoping to be caught on film, quickly moved to the port side of the boat, causing the *Sultana* to list dangerously. William was disturbed to see Otis run off to join the others at the rail. He anxiously asked Otis where he was going.

Otis told him, "There's a photographer on the riverbank setting up to take our photo. I want to be in it."

William reached out to hold him back. "In it or not, nobody would ever recognize you. Stay here with us."

But Otis was caught up in the excitement and made his way down the ladder and pushed himself to the rail along with hundreds of other men. The boat listed dramatically. Al and William were knocked off-balance and slid along the roof of the hurricane deck before they could regain their position.

Fidler called out to the soldiers, "Men! Get back to your positions! She's about to roll over."

The men, now realizing the full danger they were in, rushed back to their spots; and the *Sultana* regained her balance. The resulting photograph, however, is the last picture taken of the steamer, as well as of many of those on board. For weeks later, it would run in all the national newspapers.

On the morning of April 26, William jotted down in his diary that the weather was fine and the boat was making its way upstream quite well and he was feeling great. Otis had prepared breakfast for the boys and was heating a pot of coffee next to the smokestack. Al was not feeling so good, but he had seemed to improve somewhat. He was at least more cheerful than in the past and was once again able to stand and walk. William helped him to his feet and walked with him to the railing of the hurricane deck so they could both look out over the river.

"Can you imagine it, Al?"

Al seemed puzzled by the remark and asked what he meant. "Ten days or less and you will be in your bed in Saint Peter."

Otis joined the two. "Finally a decent place for you to convalesce."

William added, "I had my doubts about you making it."

Otis continued, "Yes, especially after that bizarre escape attempt of yours at Andersonville."

Al smiled. "I have both of you to thank for everything." "As we have to thank you," said William.

Al asked what for.

Otis summed it up, "Keeping us alive at Belle Isle for one thing." The *Sultana* began to slow.

Al changed the subject, "Why are we slowing?" Otis and William looked out toward land.

Otis said to no one in particular, "It appears we are pulling up to some barges."

The chief engineer Nathan had reached the hurricane deck and overheard the boys. "We are scheduled to take on a thousand bushels of coal at Hopefield, Arkansas."

Al asked him, "Didn't we just take on a load yesterday?"

"No, that was a special cargo load of sugar, but we will stop for more coal at Cairo."

The boat shifted.

Otis reached for the rail. "This boat sure seems unsteady." "Unsteady she is. She's way overloaded. And we are burning far too much coal," said Nathan.

William asked why that was the case.

"I have orders to keep up full steam. The captain wants to stay on schedule."

Otis asked if it was possible to push the boat that hard all the way to Cairo.

"Well, the captain is sure trying to. But he's as worried as me."

William now became worried as well. "What is he worried about?"

"You all noticed her list when we pulled in yesterday?"

"Yes, but nobody is foolish enough to be running from side to side again."

"It's not just that," replied Nathan. William asked what else.

"We have to do a permanent repair to one of our boilers, which we should have done in Vicksburg."

Otis now became concerned. "So why wasn't it done?" Nathan replied it was all simply about money and politics. "What has the captain said? Is he afeard?"

Nathan looked at Otis, sensing his worry. "In passing, he said to me that he would give all the interest he had in the boat if it was safely landed in Cairo."

William said that did not bode well with them.

"You're right, but Cairo is where we unload most of you people, and after that, it should be an easy trip with no worries."

374

Otis now relaxed a bit. "That's where I get off. When do we reach Cairo?"

Nathan responded with a common river boatman's quote, "Tomorrow evening, God willing, and the river don't rise."

Al asked, "Can it rise any more?"

"No, I believe she has reached flood stage and is on the decrease. Don't you boys fret. I'll get you to Cairo for sure."

William now turned to Al. "Al, maybe we should get off with Otis and book a separate passage on to Saint Paul. I can visit Mary, and you can spend a couple of days in her hospital."

Al nodded in agreement and then went back to his bedding on deck.

Sultana spent two days traveling upriver, fighting against one of the worst spring floods in the river's history. At some places, the river overflowed the banks and spread out three miles wide. Trees along the riverbank were almost completely covered until only the very tops of the trees were visible above the swirling, powerful water. To overcome the raging river and make time, Mason had the boilermen increase the pressure of the boilers.

Above decks, the cargo of released prisoners made themselves as comfortable as possible. They were unaware of any problems below decks. They knew there had been a delay in their boarding but did not know it was because of a faulty boiler.

By 2:00 a.m. on April 27, the top-heavy *Sultana* had reached a point seven miles north of Memphis, where the river was nearly four miles wide. Most of the passengers slept on the crowded decks as stokers shoveled coal to feed the four massive boilers that were located on the main deck between the waterwheels. Rising above the boilers were the upper decks constructed of light, flimsy wood that was coated with highly combustible paints.

Suddenly three of the huge boilers exploded with a volcanic fury that a witness on the shore described as the thundering noise of a hundred earthquakes. The blast tore instantly through the decks directly above the boilers, flinging live coals and splintered timber into the night sky like fireworks. Scalding water and clouds of steam covered the prisoners who lay sleeping near the boilers. Hundreds were killed in the first moments of the tragedy. The upper decks of the *Sultana*, already sagging under the weight of her passengers, collapsed when the blast ripped through the steamer's superstructure. Many unfortunate souls, trapped in the resulting wreckage, could only wait for certain death as the fire quickly spread throughout the hull. Within twenty minutes of the explosion, the entire superstructure of the *Sultana* was in flames.

The first explosion tore straight up through the decks at a forty-five-degree angle, destroying everything in its path. The decks began to collapse immediately. The hurricane deck fell into the pilot-house and was immediately crushed by one of the falling smoke-stacks. Captain Mason was killed under the weight of the smokestack debris and fire that ensued.

The luckiest of the passengers were those who were thrown overboard by the force of the explosion. This included William and Al. Otis, unfortunately, fell through the collapsing deck and was also crushed by falling debris. As fate would have it, he was never seen again and presumed drowned along with hundreds of other unfortunates. The shock was so sudden that neither Al nor William had time to do or say anything. The force of the explosion threw them hundreds of feet into the air. Al landed feetfirst in the cold river. He went down many feet underwater and came up gasping for air in shock.

William splashed down near Al, but the force of the landing knocked him unconscious. Even though he regained consciousness within moments, he was sucked under by the strong current and was pulled downstream. He came up for air many times yelling and gasping for help, but in the confusion with hundreds of other prisoners in the same condition, help did not come. William had never been a strong swimmer, and even though he had grown up on the banks of the Mississippi, it would now consume him. His last thoughts were of his mother, sister, and home in Mendota, which he would never see again. Any person below decks was trapped and waited to be burned alive or drowned.

From the shore, witnesses said the explosion on the Sultana was volcanic. The boilers were located on the middle deck between the paddle wheels and under the wheelhouse. The first boiler exploded and then two more in immediate succession.

Soldiers from Kentucky and Tennessee were among the first to die because they'd been packed in next to the boilers.

One witness said, "It was like a tremendous bomb going off in the middle of where these men were. The shrapnel, the steam, and the boiling water killed hundreds."

The burning wreckage began to drift slowly downriver as those on board fought to survive. With only seventy-six life preservers and two small lifeboats available, most of those who survived the blast jumped for their lives into the river. In the hours before dawn, hundreds of soldiers and civilians struggled in the river as they awaited rescue. But help did not come until 3:00 a.m., an hour after the explosion. The *Bostonia II*, plowing downriver, came upon the *Sultana* engulfed in flames and immediately began to haul the survivors from the water around the wreckage.

Without a pilot to steer the boat, *Sultana* became a drifting, floating hulk. The twin smokestacks toppled over, the left-hand one back into the blasted hole and the right-hand one forward onto the crowded forward section of the upper deck. The forward part of the upper decks collapsed into the exposed furnace boxes, shoving kindling into the open fireboxes which soon caught fire and turned the remaining superstructure into an inferno. Like William, Al was blown off the boat and landed in the river. But unlike William, he landed within reach of a timber that a small group of men was clinging to. One soldier reached out to him and pulled him close enough so that Al could also get a handhold onto the timber.

Survivors of the explosion panicked and raced for the safety of the water but, in their weakened condition, soon ran out of strength and began to cling to each other. Whole groups went down together. While this fight for survival was taking place, the southbound steamer *Bostonia II*, built in 1860 but coming downriver on her maiden voyage after being refurbished, arrived at about 3:00 a.m., an hour after the explosion, and arrived at the site of the burning wreck to rescue scores of survivors. Al and the fellows he was with were passed up by this boat, but luckily they were rescued by some former Confederate soldiers who had seen the explosion from their point across the river on the Arkansas side. These former enemies who would have, just weeks before, been happy to kill all of these "Yankees" now became angels of mercy. Having grown up on the river, these rescuers knew all too well the dangers of the Mighty Miss. At the same time, dozens of people began to float past the Memphis waterfront, calling for help until they were noticed by the crews of docked steamboats and US warships, which immediately set about rescuing the half-drowned victims.

Eventually the hulk of *Sultana* drifted about six miles to the west bank of the river and sank at around 9:00 a.m. near Mound City, Arkansas, about seven hours after the explosion.

Other vessels joined the rescue, including the steamers *Silver Spray, Jenny Lind,* and *Pocahontas*; the navy ironclad USS *Essex*; and the side-wheel gunboat USS *Tyler*.

Passengers who survived the initial explosion had to risk their lives in the icy spring runoff of the Mississippi or burn with the boat. Many died of drowning or hypothermia. Some survivors were plucked from the tops of semisubmerged trees along the Arkansas shore. Bodies of victims continued to be found downriver for months, some as far as Vicksburg. Many bodies were never recovered.

In Memphis, sailors stood on the decks of United States Navy gunboats, watching the red glow from the dying steamer that lit the northern horizon; yet no rescue effort was launched until approximately 3:20 a.m., by which time cries could be heard from out across the river. As cutters from the gunboats began sweeping the river in front of Memphis for survivors, their crews were directed in the darkness by the victims' screams for help. A sailor aboard the USS *Tyler* wrote in the ship's log, "Of all the sounds and noises I ever heard, that was the most sorrowful, some cursing, calling for help, and shrieking. I will never forget those awful sounds."

About 760 survivors were transported to hospitals in Memphis. Fortunately, since Memphis had been captured by Federal forces in 1862 and turned into a supply and recuperation city, there were numerous hospitals in the city with the latest medical equipment and trained personnel. Of the roughly 760 people taken to Memphis hospitals, there were only 31 deaths between April 28 and June 28.

When the sun rose in the eastern sky, more than 1,700 were dead or dying. Among the fatalities were Captain Mason, William Gambrel, Major Fidler, Corporal Otis Nelson, and Private William Simmons.

As bodies drifted down the river, what was left of the *Sultana* drifted to the eastern side of the river and came to rest on the Arkansas side, which had been under Confederate control just a few weeks previous. Rescue would now come from former enemies. John Fogleman had been a riverboat raider during the war and had fought for the Confederacy. Now he and his sons watched the grand old steamer burn. The Foglemans had no boats of their own, so John Fogleman rallied his sons to quickly lash together some logs to make a raft.

A newspaper account of the time recorded what John Fogleman witnessed and how he reacted:

> "The wind blew the fire to the rear, burned that out," Frank Fogleman says. "The paddle wheel fell off one side, caused the boat to turn side-ways. The other paddle wheel fell off. Eventually the Sultana turned so that the wind was pushing the flames toward the bow, where twenty-five soldiers remained. We were able to put together some logs to make a raft and go out and take people off the boat as it drifted back this way," Fogleman says. "To save time, they would set the people off in treetops and go back to the boat to take more off."

All twenty-five soldiers were rescued, and the Fogleman home became a refuge for these *Sultana* survivors. Another newspaper report was of ex-Confederate Franklin Hardin Barton:

> "He served in the Twenty-Third Arkansas Cavalry, and he was tasked with, among other things, raiding ships going up and down the river," Frank Barton says. "A few weeks earlier, he might have been attacking the *Sultana* if it had come in."

Instead newspaper accounts say Franklin Barton saved several Union soldiers.

More than 500 of those who made it to shore were placed in hospitals; the Soldiers' Home at Memphis took another 241. Many of these injured did not live to enjoy the freedom they had so recently won. Sergeant William Fies of the Sixty-Fourth Ohio Infantry, in describing the grim sights in one of the hospital wards, wrote that he

> was placed in a ward with quite a number who were severely scalded, or otherwise badly injured, and such misery and intense suffering as I witnessed while there is beyond my power to describe. The agonizing cries and groans of the burned and scalded were heartrending and almost unendurable, but in most cases, the suffering was of short duration as most of them were relieved by death in a few hours.

Young sergeant Fies witnessed Al being brought into the hospital just after sunrise on the twenty-seventh of April. He had been burned on his hands and legs and was covered in mud. Fies had not suffered much in injuries and henceforth volunteered to help with the wounded. He approached Al and asked him how he was doing. Al was grateful that someone was now paying some attention to him and responded that he was doing okay considering what had happened. Fies felt pity for this young man, who, he could tell, had suffered far more than just the survival of the *Sultana* disaster.

"Yes, compared to most of the lot here, you look fairly well. Your burns don't look too bad."

Al could not see how badly he was hurt and simply replied as if asking, "No?"

Fies looked him over. "I'm not a doctor, but I've seen worse, and they should heal up just fine."

Al began to cough uncontrollably.

Fies asked if he could fetch him some fresh water. "Yes, thank you. I think I swallowed some river mud." Then Fies asked where he was from.

Al told him he was from the Minnesota River valley.

Fies grinned knowingly. "Then a little muddy river water won't hurt you."

This made Al feel welcome. He then asked where Fies was from.

He answered, "Ohio River valley myself. That was quite some explosion, huh?"

Al thought for a moment. "I don't remember that part. I was asleep on top of the hurricane deck. Next thing I know, I'm flapping around in cold water, then being pulled up onto a timber with some other lucky souls."

Fies told of his recollection, "I was sleeping on the bow near the railing, just enjoying the cool river breeze. The explosion shook me to my bones. I got up and saw the fire."

Al asked what happened next.

"The boat was still afloat and was headed for shore, and I thought my best bet was to wait for the fire to burn out, then just step off on to the shore."

Al asked if that is indeed what he had done.

"Not quite. The fire kept getting closer, so I jumped with everyone else who hadn't yet and made a mad swim to the shore. Caught a tree and hung on until a cook on the *Tyler* plucked me out."

Al asked if he was badly hurt.

"Not so one would notice. Just exhausted, hungry, and cold mostly. Still trying to recover from Andersonville."

Al said he was all too familiar with that.

Fies nodded knowingly, then asked again if there was anything special he could do for him.

"Can you look around to see if my partners made it in here?"
"Sure. What are their names?"

"Corporal Otis Nelson from Indiana and Private William Simmons from Minnesota."

"Sure. I'll make the rounds and see what I can find out. It may take a while, but I'll get back to you."

Al thanked him for his kindness as Fies left to start questioning patients and staff.

On May 19, 1865, less than a month after the disaster, Brigadier General William Hoffman, commissary general of prisoners who investigated the disaster, reported an overall loss of soldiers, passengers, and crew of 1,238. In February 1867, the Bureau of Military Justice placed the death toll at 1,100.

Three weeks later, a couple of brothers were paddling along the coast of the river just north of Memphis in a small boat. They were the Hayes brothers—former Confederate raiders Eric, who was twenty-four, and Larry, twenty-two.

Eric noticed wreckage from the *Sultana* washed up on the shore and tugged at his younger brother who was fishing. "Do you think that stuff is from the *Sultana?*"

All kinds of debris had been washing up on the riverbanks since the accident, and these boys were always on the lookout for anything of value.

Larry put down his fishing pole and turned to see what his brother was pointing at. "Let's go take a look. It probably is."

Eric pulled at the oars to turn the boat around and head back upstream. "You know, it's a shame. We managed to avoid much of that war for all four years, and then at the end, we find ourselves face-to-face with the gruesome results of it."

Larry winced at the possibility of finding a corpse. "I hope we don't come upon any more bodies today."

Eric nodded. "Yankees or not, I still feel sorry for those boys."

Larry responded, "Can you imagine Ma waiting on one of us to come home and never finding out what became of us?"

"Like those last three boys we came across. No identification. Nothing."

"Yep, just an unmarked grave in Memphis."

Eric said one good thing had come out of the disaster, though. Larry asked what that could be.

"The catfish sure have been plump this spring."

Larry gagged. "Don't make my stomach turn thinking of it." "Not any worse than those rats we lived off in the caves outside of Vicksburg."

Larry said that was different because, at that time, they were actually starving.

The two men paddled their boat up to the wreckage and pulled their boat ashore. They got out and inspected the wreckage.

Eric moved a few large timbers. "Nothing here of any value. Just burned up timbers."

Larry looked upstream. "Yeah, I'm going to go check upstream a bit and see what got stuck in the treetops and bushes."

"Don't push your luck. Let's get some catfish and go home."

Larry moved upstream on his own. "No, just one look. We might get lucky."

Eric asked in what way could they get lucky.

"Like the Unger brothers who found that chest full of silverware."

Eric shrugged it off and got back in the boat, ready to shove off. "With our kind of luck, we'll find a corpse with a chest full of maggots."

Larry moved on alone. "Well, I'm going. Call out if you catch anything."

Eric yelled back, "Call out if you find anything of worth!"

Eric pulled the boat back into the river and continued to fish. Larry waded upstream and disappeared into the trees and underbrush of the swollen river's edge. Within moments, he spotted something white in the distance hung up in a treetop. His heart sank as he realized it may be a person.

He yelled out to his brother, "*Eric!* Come back!"

Eric swung the boat around and rowed back. He pulled the boat ashore and then waded off to catch up with his brother. "What is it?"

Larry pointed. "Over there, in that treetop. See that white thing?"

"Yeah. What do you suppose?" "Don't know. Another one maybe?"

Eric, afraid they had found another body, wanted to turn back. "I hope not."

The brothers crept up on the object and saw a backlit silhouette of a body.

Eric gasped. "Sure enough, another one."

Larry moved out ahead of his brother, breaking a limb from a tree to use as a poke stick. "That makes four this month."

Eric sighed. "Well, let's get him out of there."

Larry hesitated. "Maybe we should just report it and let those soldiers in the camp take care of it."

Eric now saw an opportunity. "Are you kidding? It's five dollars per head."

Larry now wanted no part of this gruesome affair. "Somebody may have already taken the head and collected."

"In that case, we'll report it and leave him be," replied Eric.

The brothers reached the body and gingerly poked at it with their sticks. The body was partially decomposed. Birds and river rats had devoured much of the face and exposed skin.

Eric covered his face with his shirt sleeve. "This one smells worse than the others."

Larry told him to not think about it, and then Larry pulled a plug of tobacco out of his pocket and broke off some small pieces. "Here, shove these up your nose and let's check this boy's pockets to see if he has any greenbacks on him."

Eric took the tobacco. "Thanks. Well, he still has his head, so we've already made ourselves five."

The two men yanked the body from the tree and dragged it up onto the dryer ground. They rummaged through its pockets. Larry pulled a rubberized pouch from the tunic pocket. Eric asked his brother what he had found.

"I don't know. Looks like some kind of book or maybe a wallet?" Eric told him to hurry and open it up.

Larry opened the pouch and pulled out a journal. He opened it and began to haltingly read the inside cover page, "William Simmons, Second Minnesota Volunteer Infantry."

Eric was overjoyed. "*Yahoo*! That's two dollars more for one they can ID."

Larry looked at his brother with disgust. "Sad, isn't it?" Eric asked what he meant by that.

"He's one of us."

Eric said, "We ain't no Yankees."

Larry was becoming overcome with grief. "Neither is he. He's just a dead river boy. He probably grew up on this same river just like us and had to come all this way just to die in it."

Eric sobered. "Yeah, I never thought of it like that. Well, let's load him up and go collect our reward."

They loaded William's body onto their boat and rowed off with him.

The brothers delivered William's body to the Camp Fisk hospital. An orderly at the hospital greeted them. "What have we got here?" he asked.

Larry answered, "We found him in a treetop about a mile downriver."

Eric added to the finding, "He's got identification too."

The orderly directed the boys to an empty cot. "Wait here. I'll get the quartermaster. Just lay him on that cot over there."

The brothers laid out William as the orderly left to get the quartermaster.

The quartermaster returned to Larry and Eric and, seeing Eric holding the journal, asked him, "You say he has identification?"

"Yes, here it is." Eric handed over the journal.

The quartermaster read the cover page, then handed Eric a chit. "Okay, take this outside to graves registration, and you can collect your reward. Do you know where it is?"

Larry told him that, yes, they knew where it was as they had already delivered three other bodies in the past month. The brothers thanked the quartermaster and were about to leave when the quartermaster stopped them.

"Hold up. Take the boy with you and give him and this book to the officer out there."

The brothers lifted William's body and took him outside.

The Homecoming

War is over…if you want it.

—John Lennon

In late May of 1865, on as beautiful a spring day as there ever was in the Upper Mississippi River valley, General Sibley was handed a dispatch. He opened it, read for a moment its contents, then summoned his adjutant officer, Lieutenant Olsen.

Olsen entered his office. He could see that Sibley was distressed. "General, is there something I can do for you?"

Sibley eyed the young officer, then pushed back from his desk. "Normally yes, but this matter I must tend to myself. Please just oversee things here while I'm gone."

Olsen asked when he would return.

"Within the hour, I hope. I just have to deliver some news across the river in Mendota."

Olsen saluted and took command of the office as Sibley picked up his dispatch and left his office.

Sibley took the quarter-mile walk out of the front gate of the fort and followed the winding road down to the riverbank ferry landing. He hopped aboard the ferry and leaned against the rail as old Bob Thunder pushed off the ferry raft. Within a couple of minutes, they reached the Mendota side of the river. Sibley handed his fare to old Bob Thunder as he stepped off the ferry and headed up the path that led to the village of Mendota. He walked on past the Simmons cabin, pausing for a moment to look at the axe still stuck in the tree stump, then continued to his own home.

Jane greeted Henry as he entered the house. She noticed his disposition. "Henry! What's wrong?"

Henry handed her the dispatch to read for herself. She broke down and sobbed.

Henry fell into his most comfortable chair. "I just can't… I can't…"

Jane was taken aback. "You haven't told her?" "No. I came straight here."

Jane took him by his arm and pulled. "I'll go with you. Come on."

Henry pulled back. "No, I have to do this alone. It's my fault." Jane asked if he was sure.

"Yes, but follow up in an hour, will you? I'll give her the news, then I must get back to my duties."

Jane said that she would, of course, do that. Henry Sibley then took the lonely walk back down the hill to the Simmons cabin, not at all sure of how he would present the news of her son's death.

Louise opened the door for Sibley. He entered, and Louise invited him to sit. She could tell he was visibly upset.

"What is it, Henry? Do you have news?"

Sara then entered the room. "It better be good news," she said.

Henry dropped the dispatch telegram onto the table. "I just can't."

Louise picked up the telegram and scanned it. She then dropped to her knees, weeping hysterically.

Sara ran to her side and picked up the dispatch and scanned it as well. "The *Sultana*? No! It can't be true."

Sibley could barely speak. "I'm so sorry. He's been identified, and his body is being sent here to the fort. I have no words."

Sara was ready to blame him. "This is all your fault!" Sibley then headed for the door. "Jane will be here shortly."

Sibley left their home as Sara and Louise held each other in their grief.

At 9:00 a.m. on the bright sunny morning of May 23, 1865, a signal gun fired a single shot; and Major General George Gordon Meade, the victor of Gettysburg, led the estimated eighty thousand men of the Army of the Potomac down the streets of Washington from Capitol Hill along Pennsylvania Avenue, past crowds that numbered into the thousands. The infantry marched with twelve men abreast across the road, followed by the divisional and corps artillery, then an array of cavalry regiments that stretched for another seven miles.

The mood was one of gaiety and celebration, and the crowds and soldiers frequently engaged in singing patriotic songs as the procession of victorious soldiers snaked its way toward the reviewing stand in front of the White House, where President Johnson, Commanding General Ulysses S. Grant, senior military leaders, the cabinet, and leading government officials awaited. At the head of his troops, Meade dismounted when he arrived at the reviewing stand and joined the dignitaries to salute his men, who passed for over six hours.

On the following day at 10:00 a.m., Sherman led the sixty-five thousand men of the Army of Tennessee and the Army of Georgia with an uncharacteristic semblance of military precision past the admiring celebrities, most of whom had never seen him before. For six hours under bright sunshine, the men who had marched through Georgia and those who had defeated John Bell Hood's army in Tennessee now paraded in front of joyous throngs lining the sidewalks. People peered from windows and rooftops for their first glimpse of this western army. Unlike Meade's army, which had more military precision, Sherman's Georgia force was trailed by a vast crowd of people who had accompanied the army up from Savannah—freed Blacks, laborers, adventurers, and scavengers. At the very end was a vast herd of cattle and other livestock that had been taken from Carolina farms.

Among the troops that made up Sherman's army was the Second Minnesota Regiment. When it was discharged in 1864, the men who reenlisted were reformed into their regiment and filled up with new recruits. No longer of the proper regimental size, it finished the war as a smaller but still proud unit. In the regiment marched John, Vandyke, and their sergeant major Moffett. All survivors of the war were now on the very beginning stages of the long road home. These three were what was left of the band and musicians. They marched three abreast at the head of their regiment.

As they approached the reviewing stand, the unit was given the order to march at right shoulder shift, meaning their rifles and bayonets, which had now been polished to a high luster, were placed in the position of attention. All eyes turned right on command. Their tattered battle flags were brought to present colors. After they passed the inspection of the reviewing stand, they were given the order of route step, which was a marching position of at ease. They could now walk on out of step at a leisurely pace and talk quietly if they wished. General Sherman was standing proud and erect on the reviewing stand. His men had marched farther and harder than all of the other Union Army corps. As they passed, he saluted each unit; and when the Second and Fourth Minnesota Regiments came into view, he noticed some men had not received new uniforms as they marched in worn-out boots and some with pants so worn and torn that their skin was exposed.

Chocking back his pride, he muttered to President Johnson, "Splendid legs."

In the ranks, they heard none of this.

But Vandyke was the first to speak, "Oh, how I wish William could see this."

John beamed with hope and pride. "We can tell him all about it."

Moffett was as well so very proud of his boys. "Not to worry, boys. He's on his way home now, and I'm sure he'll get there before us."

John asked how he was so sure about that.

"The war might be over, but the logistics in discharging all of us will take months, I suspect. If we get our orders before the end of June, I'll be shocked."

Vandyke was not at all pleased with this. "The hell you say!" John was more accepting of their situation. "I guess we can handle another six weeks or so."

At the very time these words were being spoken, Jane Sibley had come down the hill to visit with Louise and Sara. The three sat silently as Louise and Sara were still overcome with grief. Sara prepared coffee for the two women. Jane had brought a platter with a fine rhubarb pie.

Sara held out a cup and saucer to Jane. "Coffee for you, Mrs. Sibley?"

Jane thanked her and let her pour the coffee. The three picked at the pie and sipped their coffee in a long, drawn-out silence until Louise finally spoke.

"It's all my fault."

Jane told Louise she must not think like that.

Louise protested, "But I went against my natural instincts as a mother."

Sara tried to console her, "Momma, you couldn't help it. Those boys pestered you something terrible, remember?"

Louise held her daughter's hand. "Yes, I know, but I should have been more firm."

Jane offered more words that made no difference, "Henry and I are to blame as well, and he feels it most dreadfully. All these losses have taken a toll on him."

Louise mumbled to herself, "How will I ever carry on?"

Sara squeezed her mother's hand. "Ma, you still have me and John."

Louise was now thinking of her only surviving son. "John? I don't know. I fear for him terribly as you did for William."

Sara tried again to offer some reasoning, "Yes, but he's not in a prison, and we just got a letter from him last week. He'll be home soon."

"I'll believe it when I see him here in our home," said Louise.

Jane offered some more words of encouragement, "They are to be mustered out within six weeks."

"But, Jane, he wrote that some units are being sent back into rebellious states to police and protect."

"All Minnesota boys are coming home. Henry said none are being held back, especially units that were reformed after their service was up in '64, which the Second is one of."

Louise, looking for hope, asked if she was sure of this.

"Yes, I promise."

"This better not be another one of Henry's deceptions," Louise added.

Jane calmed her. "There is an official posting from the governor at the fort. I've seen it. John is coming home safe and fit."

Sara replied now sarcastically, "As is William. Fit in a box." Louise reprimanded her, "Sara? Really?"

Jane was looking for something positive to add. "At least he was identified and found."

"That's some consolation, I suppose," replied Louise.

Sara now added, "He'll lie next to Daddy. That's better than all those poor souls who were never found."

Louise broke down again, "He shouldn't have died that way."

Sara, being her usual bitter self, replied, "Neither should all those Dakota that was kept in that camp at the fort."

Sara was not prepared for Jane's remark of support. "That's so true, Sara."

Sara snapped back at her, "Why didn't your husband stop that?"

Jane tried to reason with her, "It was not in his hands. That was a federal law decision made by the president and Congress."

Sara kept at it, trying to get a rise out of Jane, "So what are his next orders?"

"He's been ordered to oversee the trial of Medicine Bottle and Shakopee III," Jane said.

Sara corrected her, "You mean Little Six?" "Yes, that's right."

Sara was looking for a debate, it appeared. "Do you know they were illegally captured and drugged by Canadians and returned for a thousand-dollar bounty?"

"I do not know the details of their capture, just that they are to be tried for murder like the others were for the '62 uprisings."

Louise now joined in on the discussion though her mind was still on her grief, "Do you think they can get a fair trial with Johnson in office as president? I hear he is weak on the law and generally out for revenge."

Jane summed it up, "I don't rightly know. Henry agrees that it will be tough. There are not many good witnesses that favor their defense."

The women finished their pie and coffee. Sara cleared the table as Jane prepared to leave.

"I know I've been of no solace to you two, but please forgive me. I'll leave you now to your grief."

Louise saw her out. "Stop by again at any time." Jane nodded and left. "Of course, if I'm no bother."

When the war was over, the city of Cairo, Illinois, became a staging area for many of the freed slaves arriving from the South. Many of these people also returned to the South or moved elsewhere but more than three thousand decided to remain in Cairo. The decidedly Southern influence of most of the White residents and the large influx of African Americans would spawn racial tension that would last for well over a century. During the next two decades, Cairo's African Americans banded together to form a new society complete with their institutions and culture, especially as they found themselves facing prejudice and hatred from White citizens.

Black women, who were overwhelmingly employed in household service, also struggled for workplace justice by contesting their White employer's exploitative demands. Initially the Black population supported the Republican Party until they perceived that White Republicans resisted Black demands for equal education, government jobs, and more Black legislators. The White citizens retaliated by using the law, customs, and sometimes violence to reassert their White supremacy.

When Jill arrived back home in late April of 1865, what she saw was all too familiar to her. The spring floods had nearly washed over the fifteen-foot high levee that was built to protect the city, and as usual, the streets and low-lying areas of town had turned into mosquito-infested mudholes.

Cairo had become the hub for transporting soldiers and goods into the western regions of the nation. It was becoming a boomtown. Jobs as laborers and servants were plentiful for African Americans. Jill could have taken work in any White household as a maid or cook, but with the US Navy and Army still occupying the city, there was a full military hospital that still needed qualified people.

Jill reported to the hospital soon after she got settled in at her mother's home. Given her experience at the Armory Hospital, she was welcome to the doctors and orderlies still working there. She was hired immediately to work aboard the USS *Red Rover*, a steamboat that had been converted into a Union hospital.

One of the first things she did after she got settled into her new position as a nursing assistant was to pen a letter to Sam Bloomer, who was now back home in Stillwater, Minnesota.

Sam arrived home in late April as well. Within days, he was back to work on repairing his home and putting in his vegetable garden. Oscar Cornman had been a very close friend of Sam before the war. They enlisted together and were both wounded at the Battle of Antietam. Oscar died, and Sam watched his body bloat over the next day as it lay near the cornfield fence where they had fought. Oscar had a sister, Sally, whom Sam had a romantic interest in before the war; and Sam had been the one to write to her about her brother's death. After Sam was wounded and left for Washington, his interest in Oscar's twenty-four-year-old sister waned. But she would be the first to greet him when he returned to Stillwater. Sam invited her into his home. The meeting was cordial and nothing more.

"Sam, I have some news you may be interested in." Sam asked what kind of news it was that might be.

Sally informed him, "I'm sure you know the First Minnesota is soon to return to Fort Snelling for mustering out."

He told her he assumed as much but did not know of any details.

Sally nervously asked him, "I thought maybe we could go together to welcome them home."

Sam said he was unsure, and Sally asked how that could be. "It's been nearly three years. I doubt anyone would recognize me. I've changed a lot."

Sally countered his argument, "We've all changed. You have to go. You were their color sergeant, and…"

"And what?" asked Sam.

"We must do it for Oscar at the least."

Sam hesitated for a moment, then spoke, "In that case, I can't refuse."

Sally was now relieved. "Great! I'll make arrangements. We can take my buggy and make a weekend out of it."

"Okay, but this is for Oscar, not me."

Sally was pleased enough, then excused herself and saw herself out.

On the day after the review, the Fourteenth Corps, including the Second Minnesota, left the bivouac at Alexandria and moved about ten miles to find a fresher and cleaner camping ground, about three miles north of Washington. Here the officers and men were freely allowed to visit the city. John and Vandyke made their way to the Armory Hospital. The weather was pleasant, and they had plenty of rations with them. New uniforms had been issued while they were in camp at Alexandria. They looked sharp and contented as they headed to the old Armory Hospital, which was now a part of the new DC mall.

Vandyke asked John, "Why do you want to visit the Amory Square Hospital?"

John thought it should have been obvious but answered anyway, knowing Vandyke would pester him until he got a response, "It's where my father spent his last days. I want to see the remains of the place before they shut it down."

Vandyke pulled a raw potato from his haversack and bit into it. "Are they still treating soldiers there?"

"Of course. Sick and wounded were being brought even after all of the surrenders."

Vandyke then asked if he thought anyone there would still remember his father.

"I doubt it, but I'll ask anyway."

As the boys walked toward the mall, they passed many other Union troops who were also taking in the sights of Washington, DC. "That was quite a parade the other day," commented Vandyke.

John nodded. "Six and a half hours and over twenty miles. Just like another day on the march through Georgia."

Vandyke thought that over for a moment. "I wonder how far we have walked over the past four years. William was so good at keeping a record of miles."

John had an answer. "The colonel gave an official record of 5,153 miles for '62, '63, and '64, adding to that the miles William kept for '61, and am still working on '65."

Vandyke asked if he had an estimate.

"As of the end of May, I estimate 7,300 miles."

"And we still have a ways to go before we hit old Fort Snelling," added Vandyke.

John continued with his mental tally, "Even with the train and boat rides, I figure we'll make another couple hundred at least. You know, we are going to have to walk a lot between stations, and probably they'll drop us in Saint Paul and make us walk the final miles to the fort."

Vandyke said he would not complain about any of those added miles. John agreed, and they were now close to the Armory Hospital. They were there within a minute.

John and Vandyke wandered through the hospital, which had, by now, been partially emptied of patients; but there were still more than half the beds full. They came upon a lone doctor.

John stopped him and made his inquiry. "Doctor, my father died in this hospital in December of '62. Is there anyone here who might know something about his demise?"

The doctor asked for the name and regiment. John gave him the details.

The doctor replied, "We had a VRC officer here from the First that might know something."

John asked if he could speak with him, and the doctor informed him that Sam had already been discharged and was probably back home in Minnesota. The doctor then asked what he'd like to know.

John answered, "I'd like to know if he suffered much or if he had a peaceful end."

The doctor asked if he died from wounds or sickness. John told him he thought it was dysentery.

The doctor gave him a satisfactory answer, "This hospital was and still is notorious for taking in the most severe cases. Every soldier here suffers in their way, but we see to it that they are eased on into their passing with as little pain and misery as possible."

Vandyke had wandered off to talk to some of the patients. The doctor told John he was sorry that he could not be of any more help, then excused himself. John thanked him and told him that his words meant a lot to him. The doctor continued with his rounds, and John took Vandyke by his arm to lead him out of the hospital.

John and Vandyke exited the hospital and stood outside to take in the filth of the river.

John turned to Vandyke. "Unbelievable, the filth in this city." Vandyke turned away from the stench that arose from the river.

"Sure is putrid. Hey! I've got a couple of new greenbacks. How about we find a nice restaurant and get us a decent meal?"

John was very much in agreement with that. "I can't think of a better way to reward ourselves on our 7,300-mile walk."

They sauntered off arm in arm and headed back into the city proper.

Even with the war over, the mood back at Fort Snelling was not as celebratory. All the cheering and excitement had ended weeks ago. Now was time for thought and recollection. Soldiers who had been released early were beginning to trickle in. Also the dead who could be identified from various graves across the many battlefields were being sent home.

Louise, Sara, and Jane Sibley were waiting at the Saint Paul levee steamboat landing for the delivery of William's casket. The casket was loaded onto an ox cart and driven along the road leading to Fort Snelling. At the fort, William, of course, was but one of many. On the day he arrived that late May, his casket was met by Henry Sibley and a squad of soldiers. They escorted the casket and followed the ox cart that carried him out of the fort gate.

William was to be laid to rest next to his father. The casket was carried to the open grave. As they moved it into position, the honor guard swung it around, and the corner of the casket hit the axe handle that had been stuck in the tree stump for the past four years.

Sara, standing next to her mother, gasped. "Oh, Mama! They need to be more careful."

Louise told her to hush.

The soldiers went through the motions of burying their comrade. Sara refused to watch. She kept her focus on the axe in the tree stump. After the ceremony had ended, Sara, Louise, and Jane headed into the cabin. Henry marched off with his soldiers and returned to the fort.

The three women reminisced alone. There was not much of a reception set up for William's funeral. They sat in silence for a while until Sara heard some talking outside. She then went to the door and opened it to see who was out there. Robert and his mother had come. Sara showed them in. First to Dance had brought food. She held it out to Louise.

Louise acknowledged her graciously and told her, "Please, just set it on the table, Dance."

Sara asked Robert what they had brought.

"Just some sweet fry bread, but my mother wants to have a peace smoke with your mother."

Sara was a little bit put off. "A peace smoke? What exactly does that mean?"

Robert nudged her a bit. "You know, the weed?" Sara asked why.

"To calm her heart and help her rest." Sara asked if it worked for that.

"Sure. During the uprising, she smoked it every night so she could sleep."

Sara thought this was good. "Well, that would be a big help. She hasn't slept for days. Would she mind if I had some too?"

"I think we will all share, even Mrs. Sibley, if she wants," said Robert.

First to Dance had been listening. She smiled and packed her pipe with the combination of weeds. Jane nodded to her and gestured to say she would like to try some too. First to Dance lit the pipe, took a long draw off it, held her breath, and gestured to Jane to do the same. She then passed the pipe to Jane, who cautiously took a draw and then nearly collapsed from coughing. Everyone laughed, and the pipe was passed around to all.

After Jane caught her breath, she commented, "Wow! That's some strong medicine. I'm feeling a little dizzy."

Robert told her they had plenty and that she should try some more. Sara was lost in thought, and Louise noticed.

"What's wrong, Sara?"

"I wish we could have had one last look at William."

Louise tried to reassure her, "You remember what that Vicksburg surgeon wrote, that the river rats had eaten away most of his face?"

Sara shook it off. "Yeah, but even so."

Louise was firm. "We don't need any more nightmares from you."

Robert added, "Maybe it's best to remember him as he was before he left."

Jane then added, "Robert is right. Let's remember William as the wild, fearless boy he was."

First to Dance spoke in her native language.

Robert translated, "My mother says that his spirit will live on with all the other great warriors."

First to Dance passed the pipe one more time. Soon the group was falling asleep. Sara was about to nod off when suddenly she woke and jumped from her seat, startling her mother.

"What's wrong now?"

"Nothing. I'm just now suddenly very hungry." Robert and his mother laughed.

Robert had to translate again, "That's why we brought the sweet fry bread. That's part two of the medicine."

They all gobbled up the fry bread, and then all drifted off to sleep.

The next morning, Jane, Sara, and Louise woke to find themselves alone in the cabin. Louise noticed that First to Dance and her son had gone.

She shook Sara awake. "Where did they go?"

Sara had woken earlier to see them leave. "They wandered off before the sun came up."

Jane was the last to wake up. Taking a long stretch and yawn, she remarked, "What a restful night."

Louise agreed with her that finally she, too, had a good rest. Sara pointed to the table at a bundle left by First to Dance.

"Mama, look! She left us some kinnikinnick."

Louise rose to inspect the bundle. "Well, that was very thoughtful of her, Sara. Do you know where to find this stuff and how to prepare it?"

Sara had learned all about it from Robert and his mother. "Yes. The riverbank is full of it, and after you cut it, there are other bushes and barks you can combine it with to make different kinds of smoke for various occasions, odors, and remedies."

"Please show me. I think I like this medicine," Louise said as she sniffed the bundle of herbs.

Jane took a sniff as well. "It sure was helpful, and when you two decide to go on a scouting outing to get some more, take me with you please."

Louise said she promised to do just that. Jane then said she should head home as Henry may be worried about her even though he knew she was spending the night at the Simmons home.

Sara asked, "Wouldn't he be at the fort by now?"

Jane answered that he would but she dare not bother him at his office.

Louise commented, "I thought officers' wives were allowed anytime."

"They are, but he's just started preparing the trial for Medicine Bottle and Little Shakopee," Jane informed her.

Louise then asked when the trial was to begin.

Jane told her, "Late summer or early fall, but Henry thinks they won't get a verdict until October or November." Jane thanked her hosts and then exited the cabin.

On the sixth of June, the Third Division of Fourteenth Army Corps was reorganized. Colonel J. W. Bishop, formerly of Second Minnesota, was formally assigned to command the First Brigade, now consisting of the 2nd Minnesota, 18th Kentucky, 31st Ohio, 101st Indiana, and 23rd Missouri Regiments. On the ninth, he assumed command of the division, General Baird having taken leave of absence. On the thirteenth of June, his commission as brigadier general by brevet, dated April 9, 1865, was received and was duly announced to the regiment. On the evening of June 13, the officers and men of the regiment came to the division headquarters en masse to present their congratulations.

As the men of the regiment watched the ceremony of the installment of their general, Vandyke turned to John. "Well, this is fitting."

John asked what he meant by that.

"Bishop was a good colonel for us, and he deserves this." Moffett, standing next to his boys, added, "He certainly does, and we should all be proud of what he accomplished, especially at the ridge."

"That's a day we'll never forget," added Vandyke.

Moffett turned to John. "By the way, John, I forgot to give you this." Moffet then reached into his haversack and pulled out some mail. "Here's some mail from home. I hope it's good news."

They headed off in separate directions. John opened his letter and sat down to read. Vandyke noticed immediately that the news John had received was not good. John was at a loss for words. He began to weep.

"No...no...it can't be," he said through his tears.

Vandyke knew it had to be about William. John dropped the letter at his side. Vandyke picked it up and read it.

In a voice loud enough for many to hear, he moaned, "The *Sultana*? This has to be a mistake!"

Moffett overheard the word *Sultana* and came running over. Vandyke handed him the letter.

He, too, scanned it. "Unbelievable. And here I was expecting him to be the first to greet us back at Snelling."

John, trying to cover his grief, whispered, "He will. Mom buried him next to Dad."

Vandyke leaned in to hug his friend. "I can't think of anything worse."

Moffett regained his military bearing. "This may not be the right time for this announcement, but I do have some good news."

Vandyke asked what could be good now. "We have our orders," replied Moffett. John quietly asked, "What orders?"

Hoping this would cheer up his boys, Moffett told them, "Tomorrow we leave for home."

Vandyke asked for details.

Moffett answered, "By rail to Parkersburg, on the Ohio River, and thence by steamers to Louisville, Kentucky."

John finally gained some composure. "Louisville? I wonder if she knows."

Vandyke asked who even though he did know.

John answered as best he could, "His sweetheart, Mary." Moffett, thinking he could cheer them up some more, added,

"I'm sure we'll have some free time in Louisville if you want to pay a visit. I'll see to it that you are relieved of any duty while we are there." John thanked him and told him that would be a great relief.

Moffett suggested that they should return to camp and start preparing to move out on the next day. Moffett led the way as they walked off toward their campsite.

On the afternoon of June 14, the regiment loaded up onto the train. The troops traveled in open coal cars, which, at the time, were the only cars to be had for them. They would have been comfortable enough in fine weather; but it rained all the first night on the road, drenching the men, and with the coal dust, making their beds decidedly dirty and uncomfortable.

Vandyke, Moffett, and John spread their army blankets over the coal, covered themselves with their rubberized shelter halves, and tried to rest. The rain pelted them and made their lives on the first leg of their journey home as miserable as any time they had in the past four years of service.

As the train rumbled along, Moffet asked John and Vandyke if they were comfortable enough.

"As comfortable as we've ever been," said Vandyke.

John's mind was elsewhere, and he asked when the division headquarters was to leave DC. Moffett told him they would be leaving the night of the fifteenth.

Vandyke rolled up in his rubber blanket and scoffed. "I bet they're not traveling in open coal cars."

John simply pointed out the obvious. "Rank does have its privileges."

"I'll remember that for the next war," cracked Vandyke. "What about that, Sergeant Major?" asked John. "What about what?" asked Moffett in return.

"The troops being sent to Texas and other Southern states." "Yes, there has been talking of Confederate forces holding out in some parts and willing to start a guerrilla war," said Moffett.

Vandyke asked what a gorilla war was.

Moffet smiled at the young man's ignorance. "It sounds the same but is spelled differently."

John tried to clarify, "You know, like Mosby's raiders. Hit-and-run stuff."

Vandyke nodded and turned to his sergeant. "Sure, but do you think we'll be sent out for that, Sergeant Major?"

"Not from what I've heard. I think this is it for us."

John was now thinking of home once again. "I'll just be glad to get off this car and get into a decent bed for once."

"And some decent food," added Vandyke.

"Division is to have food waiting for us in Cumberland," said Moffett as if he were the one who ordered it.

John then inquired if the division was getting in ahead of them.

Vandyke answered in his usual sarcastic tone, "What do you think? I bet they are traveling first class too."

Moffett told the boys to settle down and get some rest. They soon fell off to sleep, covered in wet black coal mud.

Division headquarters left Washington by a passenger train in the evening of the fifteenth and, passing the troops on the road, arrived at Cumberland in time the next morning to have hot coffee supplied to all the troop trains as they came along, which was gratefully appreciated by the tired and hungry men. Men of the Second Minnesota—wet, cold, and covered in black coal mud—lined up to get their fill.

Vandyke noticed another regiment being pulled out of line and put on another train. "Who are those guys? Where are they going?" Moffett took him aside. "Don't worry about it. They're probably headed to Texas or Missouri for police duty." Moffett then pointed to another train that was being hitched to a new locomotive. "That's our train."

Vandyke brightened as he saw the new cars. "Are those real passenger cars?"

Moffett patted him on his shoulder. "That's right, my boy. Coach comfort to Parkersburg. We'll be there on Sunday. Monday we'll be on steamers headed down the Ohio River to Louisville."

Vandyke lifted his cap to the sky and yelled, "Hurrah for that!" John then asked what was to happen after they reached Louisville.

"I suspect we'll encamp there and wait for our final orders," answered Moffett matter-of-factly.

Vandyke hurrahed again. Moffett asked Vandyke if he wished to be released from the regiment at Cincinnati, seeing as he was originally from Ohio. Vandyke said he had no interest in going back to his home or home state. He considered himself a Minnesota man now and hoped he would be welcome to settle there. John and Moffet both encouraged him to do so.

Sunday the eighteenth, the regiment embarked on a fleet of steamers for the trip down the Ohio River. They had a most delightful voyage, passing Cincinnati at 6:00 p.m. on Monday and arriving at Louisville Tuesday morning, the twentieth, and marching out on the Bardstown pike, encamped about four miles south of the city of Louisville.

Moffett addressed his boys as they got ready to make camp, "Well, I think you noticed that some boats stopped at Cincinnati."

Vandyke asked him why that was of any importance.

"It's worth noting because those are the last of the troops that are being sent south, and they find themselves in service indefinitely."

Vandyke muttered, "Poor slobs."

John laughed and agreed with him, "Yeah, that's one way to look at it."

Moffett continued, "So it's guaranteed we'll be mustering out. But—"

John waited for the worst. "There's always a but."

"As I was saying, but we may be here for a few weeks or longer. You'll be given daily passes. Enjoy Louisville." Moffett then turned and departed for the officer's tent.

Vandyke seemed finally at ease. He shook John's hand heartily. "That's great, John. You can now spend more time with Mary."

John seemed troubled at the reality of his situation. "Yeah, we'll see."

John and Vandyke were the first in line the following day to accept passes from their sergeant major. In camp, many locals had shown up to greet the troops and offer them rides into town. John and Vandyke were offered a ride in a flatbed wagon. Upon asking what the fare would be for a ride to the hospital, the owner of the wagon declared that the ride was free. They accepted the hospitality of the older gentleman and had a pleasant though bumpy ride direct to the front gate of the hospital. Upon disembarking from the wagon, John asked if Vandyke would like to tag along with him to see Mary. Vandyke declined. Even though he would have liked to see her, he feigned that he would like to walk the town and perhaps explore on his own.

John entered the hospital, and it only took asking a couple of questions before he was directed to where he could find Mary. He found her in one of the wards caring for sick and disabled Union soldiers who were in the final days of their rehabilitation and preparation for discharge. John introduced himself, and Mary told him to wait a few minutes for her to meet him outside on the veranda.

John found his way back outside and took a seat on a bench next to a one-armed soldier. They made a brief introduction, but as warriors do who had seen what they had seen, they had no reason to converse. They sat in silence until Mary arrived with a tray of coffee and biscuits. John explained in detail all he knew of William's death and suffering in the prisons. Mary, of course, did not take it well; but after she composed herself, she thanked John and told him she was glad she had received the news from him instead of having to wait for endless months or years to ever know what had finally become of her first love.

John searched for some comforting words, but came up short with only "I know William was very fond of you."

Mary wiped her eyes and said in response, "I should have expected the worst. His letters from the beginning were never very encouraging."

John then said something he regretted as an insensitive remark, "I think you got more correspondence from him than I did."

Mary asked if that was true.

"I only got one letter from him after his transfer to Andersonville. My mother had to forward all his news to me, which was never very good."

Mary broke down again with emotion. "I feel so sorry for her. I knew about your father and now this. It must be terrible for her."

John hung his head. "I can't imagine. I'm afraid she'll blame herself for all of this."

Mary simply wept. "She didn't start the war."

John was feeling an urge to leave. "True, but she will think she could have fought harder to keep us home."

Mary sensed that John was uncomfortable, so she reached for his hand. "Maybe, but do you know how many boys I've had to listen to who ran off to leave their mothers and family and then, after ending up here, regretting it?"

John just shook his head and quietly said, "I suppose quite a few."

Mary squeezed his hand harder. "Indeed. This war has been an endless line of misery."

John pulled away, feeling a bit ashamed that he was infringing on his brother's lover's feelings. "The *Sultana*? Can you believe that?"

Mary rested her hand back in her lap. "I had no idea he was even on that boat."

John was angered now. "All because of greed, those men and boys died."

Mary now lost her composure and fell into John's arms, weeping.

John was not sure how to react. He could only get out her name. "Mary?"

"Yes?"

John now felt comfortable enough to ask the question that had been on his mind. "Would you mind if I were to visit you while we are in Louisville?"

Mary sat straight up. "No, I think I would like that very much." "Perhaps you could show me something about the city? I believe we will be in camp here for a few more weeks."

Mary smiled and wiped away the remaining tears. "Yes, I'd love that. My duties have slowed to almost nothing. I can make time just about any day as long as I clear it with the doctors."

John was relieved. He felt he had finally settled his final duty of the war. "Great! How about the day after tomorrow, around noon?"

Mary agreed to the date. She shook his hand as John got up to leave.

While the Second Minnesota Regiment was still waiting for its orders to head home, Al had found his way to the Simmons homestead. He noticed the graves of Dan and William, paused a moment to read the markers, then headed to the door. Sara answered and let him in. Louise greeted him. Al was finally in good health and a new uniform. He had been promoted to corporal and wore the two stripes to indicate it. Sara and Louise took in his full appearance.

"Hello, I'm Albert Masterman."

"What can I do for you, Corporal?" asked Louise.

"Huh? Oh, yes, I'm not used to the rank. I was just promoted the other day. Why? I have no idea. A lot of us getting out have been promoted."

Louise smiled and showed him to a chair. "Yes, well, you should be proud. Now what is it I can do for you? Do you have a message from the fort?"

"No, I had just come to pay my respects to your son and husband."

Louise was momentarily taken aback. "Did you know them both?"

"No, only William. We were in Belle Isle and Andersonville together. But he spoke of your husband often, so I feel I know him as well."

Sara now asked of Al, "Were you with William aboard the *Sultana*?"

"Yes…yes, I was, and I owe my life to him."

Sara pressed for more, "Did he save you from the sinking?" "No, but he saved me many times in those awful prisons. He kept me healthy and kept my spirits up when I was on the verge of giving up."

Al was painfully aware that Sara was still grieving when she asked of him, "How is it you came back and he didn't?"

Louise found this to be impolite of her daughter and called her out, "Sara!"

"But, Ma, we need to know the details!"

Louise now calmly asked of Al, "Were you with him at the end?" "In a way, yes. We were sleeping on top of the hurricane deck when the boilers blew."

Sara asked what happened after the explosion.

"He and I were blown sky-high. Our best friend Otis disappeared into the falling deck. I mean like we flew higher than the treetops. I never found out what exactly happened to Otis, and the last I saw of William, he was trying to swim to shore as was I."

Sara wept. "And he never made it…but you did."

"I saw him go under, and I just got lucky is all I can say about it."

Sara did not find this comforting. "Lucky? Why should you be the lucky one?"

"The moment I felt myself slipping under for the last time, a hand reached out and pulled me onto a small boat."

"A small boat?" asked Sara.

"Yes, some of us were rescued by former Confederate soldiers who saw the explosion and fires and came out to form rescue parties."

Louise was now weeping. "I just can't believe he went through all that just to die on his way home."

"It certainly is the worst scenario… I know," replied Al.

Louise now reached out to Al as she saw the tears in his eyes. "Just tell me honestly if you think he suffered."

Al put his arms around Louise and hugged her as if she were his mother. "We all suffered horribly in those camps, but his end in the river, I believe, was quick and peaceful."

Louise then asked how did he know how to find them.

Al answered, "When I was pulled out of the river, I was put in the same hospital that all the recovered soldiers were. After I was well enough, I asked around for William. I was told that he had passed on and was about to be shipped home."

Sara asked if that was all there was to his story.

"No, actually my purpose for coming here was to give you this." Al then handed over William's journal to Louise.

"Why was this not sent back with his body?"

Al explained, "I demanded that I be given it by his request if he were to pass on at any time. It was a promise we made in Andersonville, and I intended to keep it."

Louise held the journal close to her breast. "I'm glad you did. Thank you so much. This is very dear to my heart as you can imagine."

"No…no… I should thank you for raising such a fine man."

Louise then handed the journal off to Sara, who held it to her heart for a moment.

Al set off to leave. Sara showed him out. They walked out to the gravesite together and stopped at the axe that was stuck in the stump. Sara stepped up to try and remove it as she always did when passing it. The axe wiggled a bit but did not come out. Al asked if he could give it a try.

"It's been in there since Dad left. Nobody can budge it. But William's casket knocked it a little bit loose, I think." said Sara.

Al gripped the handle and began to rock the axe back and forth. The ax-head screeched in the wood. Sara forced her way in and gripped the handle as well. They both yanked and pulled with all their strength. The axe suddenly popped out, tossing both on the ground. They came up laughing.

Sara brushed off her dress. "Wow! I thought that thing was in there forever."

Al teased her, "You know what this means?" Sara asked what it meant.

"A lumberman told me anyone who can pull a stuck axe out of an old stump is in for good luck."

Sara sighed. "I always waited for William to come home because I believed he was the only one who could do it."

Al took her hand and looked her in her eyes. "I believe his back was in on it today."

Al then told Sara he would stay in contact with her. He dusted himself off and headed for the river ferry landing. Sara brought the axe to the cabin and leaned it against the exterior wall, then went back inside to join her mother.

In Louisville, John had been visiting Mary as often as he could. He would have spent every day with her if her schedule allowed it. Occasionally they were chaperoned on their walks about town by either Mary's mother or aunt or Dr. Smith. Usually they walked alone. Mary would tell John of the history of Louisville, and John would tell her tales of life along the Minnesota and Mississippi Rivers. On the morning of July 7, the couple took a final walk along the boardwalk that paralleled the river. It was clear they had now found affection for one another, and an unwanted separation was on their minds.

Mary asked if he had any word on the date of his discharge. "We have our final inspection in three days, July 10."

She then asked when he was to leave.

"The next morning, in ten days or less, we should all be getting paid out and on our way home."

"And home is just across the river from the fort, right?" asked Mary. John nodded.

"I remember everything you and William told me about your home. It sounds lovely. I truly would like to see it one day."

John was feeling nervous and at a loss for words. "I wish you would."

Mary, as well, was unsure of what to say but blurted out, "William invited me."

John responded quickly, "That invitation still stands. I could send for you after I get resettled."

Mary thought this would be improper and told him so. John questioned why it would be.

"Well, I did make promises to William."

John stopped Mary, and they stood by a railing that separated them from the river.

"Yes, well, things have changed, and if it's all the same to you, I don't think he would mind if I was to court you."

Mary had wanted to plead with John to stay in Louisville after his discharge but instead just said, "I always have wanted to see the Wild West."

John responded, "You'd have nothing to fear. William and I will always be by your side."

John then took her hand, and they proceeded on their stroll.

On the tenth of July, the rolls for the Second Minnesota were ready; and the final inspection, muster, and parade were made. Orders relieving all detached-duty men had been received, and the camp and garrison equipage were turned over to the quartermaster. The corps commander issued his farewell orders, directing the regiment to proceed to Fort Snelling, Minnesota, for final discharge and accompanied them with a complimentary letter.

The next morning, July 11, they marched out of their camp, leaving the tents all standing for the next division coming in. The march was resumed to Louisville. There they crossed the Ohio River and, at ten o'clock, left Jeffersonville by train for Chicago, where they arrived at 6:00 p.m. On the twelfth, the regiment was quartered in Soldiers Rest.

Early on the thirteenth, they marched through the city and took the train for La Crosse by way of Watertown, Wisconsin. Reaching La Crosse at 2:00 a.m. on the fourteenth, they then went immediately on board the steamer *McLellan* for Saint Paul. At Winona, at eight o'clock, a crowd of people was at the levee to meet them; and the captain kindly consented to hold the boat there long enough to permit them to go ashore for a parade march. Winona had hospitably entertained on them once again.

The next morning, the fifteenth, they landed at the lower levee at Saint Paul. The city seemed to be having a general holiday, and crowds of people were on the bank to welcome them with bands of music and salvos of artillery and a parade of the fire department and other organizations. The grand procession marched in column of platoons up Third Street to Wabasha and by that street to the capitol, where they were received by the mayor of the city and governor of the state. They then were invited to a bountiful collation, which the ladies had spread for them in the capitol building and which they personally served to the hungry soldiers with gracious words and kind attention. All this over, their march was resumed to the upper levee, where they embarked for Fort Snelling. They reached the fort by 4:00 p.m.

At about 6:00 p.m., they were encamped on the parade ground at the historic post, where, four years before, they had been mustered into the service. Here they were obliged to wait several days for their final payment. The camp was enlivened by visiting friends during the day and throngs of people coming out from Saint Paul and Minneapolis in the evening to attend their dress parades. At the close of the last parade, Wednesday, July 19, a brief farewell address was made to the regiment by the colonel. The next day, the twentieth, the final payment was made; and the men received their individual discharges. The Second Regiment of Minnesota Veteran Volunteer Infantry ceased to exist.

As John received his final payment and an outgoing promotion to sergeant, his mother and sister were anxiously waiting for him to exit the main gate of the fort. John received his stripes and final discharge papers, then ran to the gate to greet his family in open arms. Louise could not hold back her tears. She embraced him like never before. "Finally! It's over, and you are back where you belong."

John, choking up, spoke quietly into her ear, "I realize now we should have listened to you."

Sara tugged at his tunic. "I warned you."

John hugged his sister. "We should have listened to you and Dad too."

Louise gathered up her children and pushed them toward the gate. "Enough of this. Let's get on home."

They followed the road from the main gate down to the ferry landing and made their way home.

The men dispersed to their homes with a loyal pride in the record made by their regiment, with a warm and steadfast friendship for each other as comrades, and with the satisfaction that comes only from duty well performed.

End of Book 1

ACKNOWLEDGMENTS

While it is impossible to acknowledge all the people who, over the years, have given their time and expertise to this book, many deserve special mention here.

My editor, Dr. Renata Jackson, though having little knowledge of the history surrounding this story, recognized the historical and entertainment value of this book and encouraged me to complete it. Over weeks and months, she not only gave this manuscript line-by-line scrutiny but greatly improved it with her brilliant perceptions. This she did for me despite her intense administrative and teaching responsibilities as a filmmaking critical studies professor at the University of North Carolina School of the Arts.

The National Archives and Library of Congress in Washington, DC, was tremendously supportive in opening its archives as I researched the American Civil War and provided me with articles, photographs, and access to veterans' files.

Flesh was given to the text by the many National Park Service employees and guides who gave their time to explain in detail the actions which took place on all the various battlefields and locations that appear in the story. They were quite animated in their presentations (to the point of mouth foaming), which, at times, made it difficult to digest so much of their knowledge; but nonetheless, they brought realism to this story. Quite often, they opened records to me that are generally closed to the public.

The Minnesota Historical Society in Saint Paul, as well as the Historical Center at Fort Snelling, was of course the driving force behind this book.

I would also like to acknowledge the Museum of the Confederacy in Richmond, Virginia, for allowing me to search their archives and point me to locations that appear in the book so I could paint a mental picture of the time and places that are featured in the book.

Thanks to the many individual reenactors from the various Civil War reenacting regiments that I was either a member of or spent time learning the evolution of the Civil War soldiers from—in particular, the First Minnesota Volunteer Regiment Company A of Saint Paul, Minnesota; First Minnesota Company D, the Lincoln Guards, of Maryland; Forty-Seventh New York Volunteers of Charleston, South Carolina; Fifty-Fifth Massachusetts of Charleston, South Carolina; Fifty-Fourth Massachusetts Company B of Savage, Maryland; the Fifty-Third Pennsylvania of South Central, Pennsylvania; and the Twenty-Sixth North Carolina Regiment of Central North Carolina.

Finally I want to thank family and friends whose personalities I used to create the characters and for struggling through the reading of the first drafts and encouraged me to continue. Their love, wisdom, and encouragement gave me the strength to finish this book.

ABOUT THE AUTHOR

Dane Pizzuti Krogman holds a BFA and MFA from the University of Minnesota, where he specialized in Asian art history with a concentration in textile and surface design. He has taught at Cal Poly Pomona, the College of Charleston, Virginia Commonwealth University, and the University of North Carolina School of the Arts. He has also worked as a freelance designer, a pictorial artist, an owner of a scenic design company, and a spec writer for feature film scripts. His graphic novel, *Skeleton Boy*, won the grand prize for best graphic story in the 2003 Hiroshima Peace Memorial Contest. The book is now part of the Hiroshima Peace Memorial Library. He has been a US Civil War and Indian Wars scholar for most of his life.